Nietzsche and Morality

Nietzsche and Morality

EDITED BY

Brian Leiter and Neil Sinhababu

CLARENDON PRESS · OXFORD

OXFORD

UNIVERSITY PRESS

Great Clarendon Street, Oxford ox2 6DP

Oxford University Press is a department of the University of Oxford.
It furthers the University's objective of excellence in research, scholarship,
and education by publishing worldwide in

Oxford New York

Auckland Cape Town Dar es Salaam Hong Kong Karachi
Kuala Lumpur Madrid Melbourne Mexico City Nairobi
New Delhi Shanghai Taipei Toronto

With offices in

Argentina Austria Brazil Chile Czech Republic France Greece
Guatemala Hungary Italy Japan Poland Portugal Singapore
South Korea Switzerland Thailand Turkey Ukraine Vietnam

Oxford is a registered trade mark of Oxford University Press
in the UK and in certain other countries

Published in the United States
by Oxford University Press Inc., New York

British Library Cataloguing in Publication Data

Data available

Library of Congress Cataloging in Publication Data

Data available

Typeset by Laserwords Private Limited, Chennai, India
Printed in Great Britain
on acid-free paper by
Biddles Ltd, King's Lynn, Norfolk

ISBN 978−0−19−928593−8

CONTENTS

NOTES ON CONTRIBUTORS

Simon Blackburn is Professor of Philosophy at Cambridge University.

Maudemarie Clark is George C. Carleton, Jr. Professor of Philosophy at Colgate University.

David Dudrick is Assistant Professor of Philosophy at Colgate University.

Thomas Hurka is Chancellor Henry N. R. Jackman Distinguished Professor of Philosophy at the University of Toronto.

Nadeem Hussain is Assistant Professor of Philosophy at Stanford University.

Christopher Janaway is Professor of Philosophy at the University of Southampton.

Joshua Knobe is Assistant Professor of Philosophy at the University of North Carolina at Chapel Hill.

Brian Leiter holds the Hines H. Baker and Thelma Kelley Baker Chair in Law and Philosophy at the University of Texas at Austin.

Peter Poellner is Senior Lecturer in Philosophy at the University of Warwick.

Bernard Reginster is Associate Professor of Philosophy at Brown University.

Mathias Risse is Associate Professor of Public Affairs at Harvard University.

Neil Sinhababu is a Charlotte W. Newcombe Fellow and a PhD candidate in philosophy at the University of Texas at Austin.

R. Jay Wallace is Professor of Philosophy at the University of California at Berkeley.

Introduction

Brian Leiter and Neil Sinhababu

Moral philosophy has long situated its problems, positions, and arguments with respect to the views of the important historical figures in the field. Aristotle, Kant, Hume, and Mill, among others, have loomed large in ethics over the last century, so much so that those contemporaries influenced by them often self-identify as Kantians or Humeans, or as working out 'Aristotelian' or 'Millian' views as a way of defending answers to contemporary questions in moral philosophy.

Yet the historical orientation of moral philosophers has, to date, largely neglected one figure who ought to command at least equal attention, namely, Nietzsche. The reasons for his neglect in Anglophone philosophy are, to be sure, understandable. The general timidity and conservatism of English-speaking moral philosophy—its inclination to *elucidate* and *defend* morality; its commitment, more often than not, to the moral status quo and to common-sense (certain utilitarians honorably excepted!); its lack of interest, until relatively recently, in psychological questions—made it generally inhospitable for a critic as radical and as naturalistically inclined as Nietzsche. Until recently, moreover, few English-speaking philosophers (Philippa Foot and the late Bernard Williams are notable exceptions) even tried to defend watered-down versions of the radical views of morality and its value that we associate with Nietzsche. Making matters worse, most scholarly writing on Nietzsche has not been done by scholars conversant with serious philosophy, meaning that philosophically minded value theorists were unlikely to find reading the secondary literature on Nietzsche very rewarding.

The last twenty years have marked a dramatic change in this state of affairs. Increasingly, talented moral philosophers—Simon Blackburn, Thomas Hurka, Nadeem Hussain, Joshua Knobe, Mathias Risse, and R. Jay Wallace are representatives in this volume—have begun to think seriously about Nietzschean ideas.[1] At the same time, scholars interested in Nietzsche have produced a body of work of considerable philosophical sophistication that now rivals what we have come to expect from philosophically informed work on figures like Aristotle and Kant.[2] This volume capitalizes on both developments by presenting a collection of new essays that should interest moral philosophers *and* Nietzsche scholars, as well as those historians of philosophy who may still worry that work on Nietzsche is too often done in the obscurantist style of Jacques Derrida or the philosophically superficial style of Walter Kaufmann. The essays collected here both try to advance philosophical understanding of Nietzsche's ethical views—his normative and metaethics, his moral psychology, his views on free will and the nature of the self—and to make Nietzsche a live participant in contemporary debates in ethics and cognate fields. Thus, the volume should appeal not only to audiences with an historical interest in understanding the positions that Nietzsche adopted, but also those primarily interested in debates in moral philosophy. We hope this collection will mark Nietzsche's arrival as a co-equal figure in moral philosophy with the other historical greats.

We have organized Nietzsche's contributions to ethics into two broad areas, reflecting both his philosophical interests and ours. In Part I, contributors look at Nietzsche's 'positive' ethical views (the criteria by which he evaluates and commends persons and cultures), as well as the moral psychology by which he tries to undermine competing systems of ethical evaluation. In Part II, contributors consider Nietzsche's views about the metaphysics and epistemology of value (and, to a more limited extent, the semantics), topics of enormous interest to philosophers over the past thirty years, and ones which have, only recently, attracted attention from Nietzsche scholars.

Part I begins with 'Nietzsche: Perfectionist', in which Thomas Hurka, the leading proponent of perfectionism today, argues that 'perfectionism'—the view that the good is constituted by the achievement of excellence—best captures Nietzsche's positive ethical views. Hurka reads Nietzsche as being what he calls a maximax agent-neutral consequentialist. According to this striking view, agents should act so that the person who is the most excellent will achieve the greatest excellence possible. Hurka reads Nietzsche as finding the excellence of an agent in two properties of that agent's goals. First, there is the *extent* of each goal, in terms of the amount of time and number

---

[1] For an overview, see, e.g., Brian Leiter, 'Nietzsche and the Morality Critics', *Ethics* 107 (1997): 250–85.

[2] See, e.g., Maudemarie Clark, *Nietzsche on Truth and Philosophy* (Cambridge: Cambridge University Press, 1990); Peter Poellner, *Nietzsche and Metaphysics* (Oxford: Oxford University Press, 1995); John Richardson, *Nietzsche's System* (Oxford: Oxford University Press, 1996); Brian Leiter, *Nietzsche on Morality* (London: Routledge, 2002); Bernard Reginster, *The Affirmation of Life: Nietzsche on Overcoming Nihilism* (Cambridge, Mass.: Harvard University Press, 2006), as well as many of the essays collected in J. Richardson and B. Leiter (eds.), *Nietzsche* (Oxford: Oxford University Press, 2001).

of persons and objects that it involves. Second, there is the degree to which the agent's goals are *unified* with each other. The resulting notion of excellence is strictly formal, which, Hurka argues, is a particularly natural development of a perfectionist view.

Bernard Reginster's 'The Will to Power and the Ethics of Creativity' takes the will to power as central to Nietzsche's positive ethics, but understands it quite differently than one reading of Nietzsche's perfectionism which Hurka rejects. Reginster treats the will to power as a higher-order desire to overcome resistance to the satisfaction of one's other desires. Reginster argues that since creativity involves the overcoming of resistance, and since the will to power is a desire to overcome resistance to the satisfaction of one's desires, it is easy to see why an agent with a strong will to power would be drawn to this sort of creative activity. With this understanding of the will to power and creativity in hand, Reginster sketches out an 'ethics of creativity' that forms a distinctive part of Nietzsche's normative thought, and which permits us to understand many of Nietzsche's puzzling views and statements—for example, his attraction to agonistic conflict and his appreciation for impermanence and an indefinite 'becoming'.

The remaining essays in Part I turn from Nietzsche's positive ethics to his critique of other moral views through the development of a distinctive moral psychology. In 'Nietzschean "Animal Psychology" versus Kantian Ethics', Mathias Risse uses Nietzsche's naturalistic moral psychology to raise objections to Kantian views like those of Christine Korsgaard. Risse argues, in particular, against the claim that third-person accounts of moral psychology have no bearing on a morality which purportedly guides us from the first-person perspective. Nietzsche, for example, explains deliberation and action entirely in terms of a system of desires, without any separate will or agent. If a Nietzschean account is correct, then the Kantian view that deliberation proceeds from a standpoint detached from all desires could not be maintained. Indeed, Risse argues, if deliberation and action are to be explained entirely in terms of a system of desires, there will be no agent outside the system of desires for whom desire-driven action is not heteronomous. Risse concludes by sketching an alternative, Nietzschean conception of the unity of agency.

Joshua Knobe and Brian Leiter argue that if competing views in moral psychology ought to be answerable to the best empirical evidence about what human moral psychology is *really* like, then the broad outlines of a Nietzschean view—crudely, that individuals are born with a certain psycho-physical package of traits, which play a powerful (but not exclusive) role in determining behavior—are far more plausible than the (to date) more popular Aristotelian and Kantian paradigms, which assign far more importance than the evidence warrants to upbringing and conscious choice. Knobe and Leiter review a variety of kinds of evidence from empirical psychology and behavioral genetics that suggest that Nietzsche was far closer to the *reality* of moral psychology than either Aristotle or Kant.

In the final two essays in Part I, Jay Wallace and Christopher Janaway offer interpretations, respectively, of the first two essays of Nietzsche's most famous treatise in ethics and moral psychology, *On the Genealogy of Morality*. In '*Ressentiment*, Value, and Self-Vindication: Making Sense of Nietzsche's Slave Revolt', R. Jay Wallace defends what he calls an 'expressive interpretation' of the first essay of the *Genealogy of Morality*, contrasting it with the strategic interpretation of the rise of slave morality, according to which the oppressed invent 'slave morality' as part of a conscious strategy for revenge against the masters. How, Wallace asks, would the oppressed come truly to accept a system of values which they invented purely for strategic purposes? On his preferred, alternative reading, slave morality arises as an expression of the negative emotional orientation that slaves have towards the powerful. Although this does not entirely fit the text, Wallace argues this makes the best moral psychological sense of the state of mind of the slaves as Nietzsche portrays them, once we appreciate the central role that the need for self-vindication plays in human lives.

According to Christopher Janaway's 'Guilt, Bad Conscience, and Self-Punishment in Nietzsche's *Genealogy*', the central thought of the second essay is that 'having a bad conscience or feeling guilty is a way in which we satisfy a fundamental need to inflict cruelty'. Humans have an instinctive drive to inflict suffering, according to Nietzsche, and when they are unable to discharge this instinctive drive towards cruelty on another person, they inflict suffering on themselves. Guilt, on Janaway's reading, is the form that cruelty takes when it is both internalized and regarded as legitimate. Christian morality, in turn, has developed the feeling of guilt farther than any other system: by condemning the instincts towards aggression and physical gratification that all humans have, Christianity finds ways to make people feel that they are legitimate objects of severe punishment, thus offering a way of satisfying the same desire for cruelty that it condemns.

In Part II, contributors turn to Nietzsche's metaethical views, that is, to his views about the metaphysics, epistemology, and, sometimes, semantics of value. The section starts with Nadeem Hussain's provocative 'Honest Illusion: Valuing for Nietzsche's Free Spirits', which defends the view that Nietzsche is a 'fictionalist' about value. A central task of the 'free spirits' to whom Nietzsche addresses his philosophy is the creation and revaluation of values, yet, Nietzsche claims, these free spirits must conceive of reality *as it is*. Since Nietzsche appears to claim that nothing actually has value in itself, how, then, can the free spirits successfully engage in valuing and creating values if they correctly perceive that nothing is valuable in itself? According to Hussain, we should understand Nietzsche as recommending a practice of regarding certain things as valuable in themselves, even while knowing that they are not really valuable. This is the same kind of thing we do in appreciating fictional works—while knowing that fictional events are not real, we regard them as real. Free spirits, then, will engage in a fictionalist simulacrum of valuing.

In 'Nietzsche and Moral Objectivity: The Development of Nietzsche's Metaethics', Maudmarie Clark and David Dudrick argue that in his early work *Human, All Too Human*, Nietzsche took the view that a naturalistic picture of the world would not include values, with the consequence that all moral judgments would, necessarily, be false (all such judgments would predicate properties that nothing in the world actually possessed). In treating all moral claims as false, Nietzsche would have had to assume a cognitivist semantics for evaluative discourse, which, combined with his anti-realism about value (there are no metaphysically objective facts about value), would make him an error theorist.[3] But, according to Clark and Dudrick, his view changed by the time of *The Gay Science*. In this later work, Nietzsche leaves room for human beings to give value to an otherwise value-free world, in virtue of their dispositions to regard things as valuable in some way. Clark and Dudrick argue that relevant portions of *The Gay Science* are most naturally interpreted as expressing a kind of non-cognitivism about value judgments. While it remains true, on this view, that the scientific picture of the world has no place for value, Nietzsche now argues that perspectives embodying human interests perceiving value are not to be rejected. Nietzsche's view in *The Gay Science*, Clark and Dudrick argue, is that value claims can be objective even if they come from a perspective constituted by desires. What is important for objectivity is the capacity to step back from one's personal desires and appraise things from different perspectives—often, those embodying a common point of view. Nietzsche's claim to objectivity arises precisely from his ability to make these kinds of appraisals.

In 'Affect, Value, and Objectivity', Peter Poellner observes that Nietzsche often likens affective experiences to perceptions of value: we perceive value as having some kind of objective existence in the objects of our affective states. Poellner calls this the phenomenal objectivity of value, and argues that Nietzsche sees values as essentially dependent on affective states, which thus do not discover a realm of values existing apart from them. He defends this view as a plausible account of the metaphysical status of value. Values, then, lack a particular sort of metaphysical objectivity, leading to conflicts between the way that philosophically reflective agents will know values to be, and how they will perceive them. Poellner presents Nietzsche as arguing that this conflict should be resolved in favor of the phenomenal objectivity of values, and that failure to be guided by values because they lack metaphysical objectivity bespeaks a dangerous commitment to ascetic ideals and the 'will to truth'.

In 'Vengeful Thinking and Moral Epistemology', Neil Sinhababu argues that on Nietzsche's account in the First Essay in the *Genealogy*, the slaves' wish for revenge against their masters generates their moral beliefs through a process of wishful

---

[3] Brian Leiter expresses doubts about whether any semantic view can be ascribed to Nietzsche in 'Nietzsche's Metaethics: Against the Privilege Readings', *European Journal of Philosophy* 8 (2000): 277–97. Hussain responds to these worries in the 'Historical Postscript' to his contribution to this volume.

thinking. This revenge fantasy involves the nobles being judged and punished by a just God who detects an objective property of moral badness in them. Wishful thinking—or in this case, 'vengeful thinking'—thus leads them to believe that God, an afterlife of reward and punishment, and objective moral properties exist. This mode of 'vengeful thinking' underwrites, in turn, two kinds of arguments against non-reductive naturalistic moral realism. According to the Explanatory Argument, we are not justified in believing hypotheses that are not part of the best explanation of our observations. On Sinhababu's interpretation, Nietzsche explains the origins of moral belief with reference to vengeful thinking, which requires no actual moral properties. According to the Unreliability Argument, we are not justified in believing that p if we know that an unreliable historical process of belief-formation has caused our acceptance of p. Vengeful thinking is, however, a paradigmatically unreliable historical process. Thus, coming to know that the Nietzschean account is true would eliminate our justification for belief in moral properties. Depending on how the histories go, the Unreliability Argument can give us reason to reject irreducible moral properties while leaving irreducible properties in other domains unharmed.

In 'Perspectives, Fictions, Errors, Play', Simon Blackburn distinguishes between regarding two views as 'perspectival' and regarding them as involving error—if the difference is only a matter of perspective, no view need be in error. He then criticizes the cognitivist semantics for moral terms that makes error theory possible by requiring metaphysical underpinnings for value claims. Blackburn argues that since the errors involved in false moral claims are moral errors and not metaphysical errors, moral claims do not require the metaphysical foundations that error theorists say they lack. Against the fictionalist reading of Nietzsche, Blackburn argues that such a view would make it hard to generate the practical consequences that Nietzsche wants, like the rejection of Christian morality in favor of some other value system. In order for fictionalism to change our behavior, some contrast between the fictional and the real is required, and a 'global' fictionalism about value does not allow for any real values. Blackburn finally addresses the concept of 'play', which has seemed more attractive to some of Nietzsche's interpreters than to Nietzsche himself. Offering the example of Harold Skimpole from Dickens' *Bleak House*, Blackburn argues that a recommendation to take values as unseriously, and as a mere matter of play, leads to a very unappealing ethical view.

We hope this collection of new essays by leading moral philosophers and Nietzsche scholars will establish Nietzsche's rightful place as one of the most creative and insightful figures in the history of moral theory, and will stimulate other moral philosophers to engage with his ideas and arguments.

Part I

Normative Ethics and Moral Psychology

1

Nietzsche: Perfectionist

Thomas Hurka

Nietzsche is often regarded as a paradigmatically anti-theoretical philosopher. Bernard Williams has said that Nietzsche is so far from being a theorist that his text 'is booby-trapped not only against recovering theory from it, but, in many cases, against any systematic exegesis that assimilates it to theory.'[1] Many would apply this view especially to Nietzsche's moral philosophy. They would say that even when he is making positive normative claims, as against just criticizing existing morality, his claims have neither the content nor the organization characteristic of moral theory.

To me this common view is the opposite of illuminating. I take it as uncontroversial that Nietzsche's positive moral views fall under the general heading of what today is called perfectionism. They are centred on a conception of the good, which they commend actions for instantiating or promoting, but this conception does not equate the good with anything like pleasure or the satisfaction of desires; instead, it locates the good in objective human excellences that for Nietzsche centre on the concepts of power and strength. Like other moral views, perfectionism can be developed as a systematic theory, and when it is, a series of questions arise about its structure and content. If one reads Nietzsche with these questions in mind, it is striking how often, without formulating them explicitly, he suggests answers to them. And when one combines those answers, the result is a perfectionist theory of a distinctive Nietzschean stripe. Perfectionism has been embraced by, among others, Plato, Aristotle, Aquinas, Leibniz, Hegel, Marx, Bradley, Brentano, Rashdall, and Moore. In my view Nietzsche is

---

[1] Bernard Williams, 'Nietzsche's Minimalist Moral Psychology', in his *Making Sense of Humanity and Other Philosophical Papers 1982–1993* (Cambridge: Cambridge University Press, 1995), 65–76; quotation on pp. 65–6.

the most theoretical of the perfectionists before, say, Brentano, that is, the most likely to recognize and answer theoretical questions. His answers also have a characteristic merit. A standing temptation for moral philosophers, and indeed for philosophers generally, is to avoid difficult theoretical questions by making optimistic factual claims about the world that make competing answers to them compatible. It is characteristic of Nietzsche to reject such optimistic claims and insist that the questions be faced directly. He does this, for example, when he denies that the beliefs most useful to us are most likely to be true, and also at many points in his presentation of perfectionism. The result is a version of that view that brings out especially sharply its distinctive features and its distinctive dangers.

In this essay I will consider three aspects of Nietzsche's perfectionism: his most fundamental account of human perfection, the moral structure within which he embeds that account, and the more specific human states he takes to instantiate perfection.

1. The Will to Power and Human Nature

It is useful to distinguish between broad and narrow senses of the term 'perfectionism.'[2] In a broad sense perfectionism is any moral view centred on a conception of the good that values human excellences regardless of how much a person enjoys or wants them. As so understood, perfectionism can affirm many different values: knowledge, the achievement of difficult goals, moral virtue, the creation or appreciation of art, deep personal relations, and more. In a narrower sense, perfectionism is a version of this view that grounds its substantive values in a more abstract ideal of realizing human nature. Its central claim is that the human good consists in developing whatever properties are fundamental to human nature, and if it affirms specific goods such as knowledge and achievement it is for embodying these properties.

What I take to be uncontroversial is that Nietzsche is a perfectionist in the broad sense, but it is often held that he is also a narrow perfectionist. On this reading he holds that it is fundamental to human nature to exercise a will to power and that the best individuals are therefore those who are most powerful. Many texts supporting this reading come from *The Will to Power*, but others are in texts Nietzsche published, such as *Thus Spake Zarathustra* and *Beyond Good and Evil*. Whether he accepts narrow perfectionism does not affect the rest of his view, which even without it can have the same structure and substantive values. But it is fruitful to ask how, if he does accept narrow perfectionism, he addresses the various issues it raises.

---

[2] See Thomas Hurka, *Perfectionism* (New York: Oxford University Press, 1993).

The first thing a narrow perfectionism must do is specify its concept of human nature, or explain which type of properties it takes to be fundamental to our species. Here different views have been taken, for example, that the relevant properties are those distinctive of humans, or essential to humans, or essential to and distinctive of humans. Since many distinctive human properties are morally trivial, such as making fires,[3] perfectionists who talk of distinctive properties are best read as valuing only the subset of them that are also essential to humans, or that constitute humans' specific difference. But even with this restriction distinctive properties seem of no interest to Nietzsche. He does not care what distinguishes humans from other species, but says the will to power is fundamental to us because it is fundamental to all living things, and even to all things period. And by 'fundamental' he often means essential, speaking of 'a world whose essence is will to power' and of the will to power itself as 'the innermost essence of being' (BGE: 186; WP: 693).[4] So if Nietzsche is a narrow perfectionist, he equates human nature with those properties—or the one property—that is essential to humans and also to everything that exists. Different beings instantiate this property to different degrees: a human's will to power is stronger than a snail's, which is stronger than a rock's. But essential to them all is the same fundamental property. In its structure, therefore, Nietzsche's narrow perfectionism is similar to Hegel's, where there is likewise a common essence for all things, that of instantiating Absolute Spirit, which different beings do with different degrees of adequacy and value.

Narrow perfectionism is commonly associated with metaethical naturalism. On this interpretation the theory starts from purely factual claims about human nature, derived, say, from biology, and then takes them to entail conclusions about value directly. To philosophers such as Alasdair MacIntyre and Bernard Williams this is the main interest of perfectionism: that it offers to provide foundations from outside morality for our moral beliefs.[5] But in my view naturalist formulations of perfectionism are open to the standard objections raised by Sidgwick, Moore, and others against naturalism generally and should be rejected on that basis. In setting them aside, however, we should not move to an opposite interpretation proposed by some contemporary philosophers. They say that perfectionism does not derive values from facts because its claims about human nature are themselves evaluative, identifying as essential to humans those properties we already think most worth developing.[6] The

---

[3] Bernard Williams, *Morality: An Introduction to Ethics* (New York: Harper & Row, 1972), 64.

[4] See also BGE: 259; GM II, 12; WP: 55.

[5] Alasdair MacIntyre, *After Virtue* (London: Duckworth, 1981), chs. 5, 7; Bernard Williams, *Ethics and the Limits of Philosophy* (Cambridge, MA: Harvard University Press, 1985), ch. 3.

[6] Jennifer Whiting, 'Aristotle's Function Argument: A Defense', *Ancient Philosophy* 8 (1988), 35, 38–9; Martha C. Nussbaum, 'Aristotle on Human Nature and the Foundations of Ethics', in J. E. J. Altham and Ross Harrison (eds.), *World, Mind, and Ethics: Essays on the Ethical Philosophy of Bernard Williams* (Cambridge: Cambridge University Press, 1995), 93–5, 100–2.

trouble with this proposal is that it makes the narrow theory vacuous, reducing its claim that it is good to develop the properties essential to humans to the tautology that it is good to develop the properties it is good to develop. And there is an alternative interpretation intermediate between this and the naturalist one. It treats the general principle that the human good consists in developing the properties essential to humans as substantive or non-analytic, while any claim that specific properties are essential is factual. By itself the latter claim has no evaluative implications; those follow only given the substantive moral principle. But the principle needs the factual claims if it is to have content. On this reading a defence of narrow perfectionism must take a coherentist form. It must show that the general perfectionist principle is intuitively appealing in itself, as many philosophers have found it to be, and also that given which properties are in fact essential to humans, the principle has attractive implications about which specific states of them are good. Because these two tests are independent, the view's passing both would count significantly in its favour. But they are independent because, while the general perfectionist principle is evaluative, the claims about human nature that give it content are not.

It is unclear whether Nietzsche accepts a naturalist version of narrow perfectionism or this alternative one. When he says, 'There is nothing in life that has value, except the degree of power—assuming that life itself is the will to power'(WP: 55), does he take his evaluative conclusion to follow directly from his premise about life or only given an additional substantive principle? I do not see that Nietzsche's texts clearly support one answer over the other or, more generally, support any clear metaethical position. But I will assume that he at least takes his claim about human nature to be factual, as both these interpretations do. And there is further support for this assumption in the way Nietzsche defends that claim.

If it is to avoid vacuity, narrow perfectionism must not only assign non-evaluative meaning to claims about human nature, but also have a way of establishing those claims that does not depend on moral beliefs. Here many perfectionists use a method that fits recent writing about essential properties. Hilary Putnam and others have argued that we identify a kind's essential properties by seeing which properties play a central role in the explanation of its other properties, so that, for example, the atomic structure of gold is essential to gold because it explains gold's colour, weight, and so on.[7] Similarly, many perfectionists argue that certain properties are essential to humans because they are central to the explanation of human behaviour. In many cases the explanations they cite are teleological. They say that all human behaviour is directed to a single goal, namely developing certain properties, and that these properties are essential to humans because they constitute this goal. Hence the

---

[7] Hilary Putnam, 'Is Semantics Possible?' and 'The Meaning of "Meaning" ', in his *Mind, Language, and Reality: Philosophical Papers Volume 2* (Cambridge: Cambridge University Press, 1975).

common association between narrow perfectionism and a 'teleological conception of human nature.' Now, Nietzsche certainly accepts this general explanatory method of identifying essential properties. In *Beyond Good and Evil* he writes,

Suppose, finally, we succeeded in explaining our entire instinctive life as the development and ramification of *one* basic form of the will—namely of the will to power, as *my* proposition has it . . . then one would have gained the right to determine all efficient force univocally as—*will to power*. The world viewed from inside, the world defined and determined according to its 'intelligible character'—it would be 'will to power' and nothing else.   (BGE: 36)

The explanations he appeals to also look teleological. They cite not only will, but will to a certain goal, namely will *to* power and even to the maximum of power. *The Will to Power* says that all intentional actions derive from 'the intention to increase power' (WP: 663);[8] *The Genealogy of Morals* concurs:

Every animal . . . instinctively strives for an optimum of favourable conditions under which it can expend all its strength and achieve its maximal feeling of power; every animal abhors, just as instinctively, . . . every kind of intrusion or hindrance that obstructs or could obstruct this path to the optimum (I am *not* speaking of its path to happiness, but its path to power, to action, to the most powerful activity).   (GM III: 7)

But teleological explanations are not the only ones that can underwrite a claim about essence; gold's atomic structure is essential to it even though gold has no tendency to realize that structure to higher degrees. And Nietzsche's appeal to teleological explanations creates difficulties that he of all philosophers should avoid.

Teleological perfectionisms are committed to some version of the claim that humans tend naturally to develop their natures to the highest degree. One version of this claim, associated with Hegel and Marx, says that whatever happens in individual lives, the general direction of human history is toward the fuller development of humans' essential properties. Other versions say that individuals tend naturally to develop their essence, often because that is what they most fundamentally desire, either as such or under some co-extensive description, with everything else desired as a means to this single goal. A related claim is that developing one's essence is most pleasant, perhaps because pleasure just is the perception of an increase in one's perfection; given most humans' desire for pleasure, this again implies at least some tendency to perfection. Now, these various claims are in two ways optimistic. First, they assert that the world is arranged so that the natural tendency is for good to be achieved; if humans are free from obstacles, they will naturally lead the best lives they can. Second, the claims imply that there is no conflict between perfection and other candidate goods. If humans want above all to develop their essence, then the most

---

[8] See also WP: 675, 688.

perfect life is also the one that most satisfies their desires; if perfectionist activities are most pleasant, then the life with the most such activities also contains the most pleasure. There can still be a philosophical question about why this life is best: because it realizes the human essence or because it satisfies desires or is pleasant. And many perfectionists have thought this question vitally important. But at the practical level the tendency claims imply, optimistically, that there is no conflict between perfection and non-perfectionist goods such as pleasure and desire-satisfaction. In the realm of value, one can have it all.

Nietzsche is distinctive among perfectionists in rejecting, often vigorously, these optimistic factual claims. Whereas some might think the tendency of Darwinian evolution is to produce ever higher life-forms, Nietzsche thinks natural selection works systematically against the highest values and frustrates their achievement;[9] he likewise denies that there has been progress in human history.[10] More generally, he holds that the greater a person's potential for perfection the less likely he is to achieve it: by 'the law of absurdity in the whole economy of mankind,' the conditions for the success of the well-constituted are more complicated and therefore less often supplied (BGE: 62).[11] Nietzsche famously denies that the most perfect life is most pleasant; far from these two values always going together, suffering, and even great suffering, is needed for real achievement.[12] He also sometimes denies the claims about desire. This is implicit in his remarks that powerful individuals need self-discipline and hardness toward themselves, presumably to control impulses that would lead them away from perfection; in his accounts of resentment and the slave-revolt in morality, which involve individuals' choosing lesser forms of will and therefore less value for themselves as well as others; and in his definition of decadence as a state in which 'the will to power is lacking' and an individual 'prefers what is disadvantageous to itself' (A: 6).[13] This important strand in Nietzsche's thought implies that obstacles to perfectionist achievement can arise not only outside a person, in unfavourable external circumstances, but also inside, in his own anti-perfectionist tendencies or 'inner hopelessness' (BGE: 269). But how is this view compatible with his apparent use of teleological explanations to identify the human essence, and especially with his claim that all human actions aim at an 'optimum' of power? Does the latter not imply an exceptionless tendency to power? The difficulty here surfaces very clearly in John Richardson's book *Nietzsche's System*. Richardson defends a narrow perfectionist reading of Nietzsche like the one I am exploring, on which the will to power is the supreme good because it is essential to all beings, and is essential to them because power is the goal of all their action. Richardson also says there are higher and lower

---

[9] GM I: 17; TI IX: 14; WP: 243, 401, 647, 684, 685.   [10] A: 4; WP: 90, 339.

[11] See also BGE: 269; and WP: 252, 684, 685, 864.

[12] GS Pref: 3; BGE: 225, 270; WP: 382, 910, 957, 1030.   [13] See also EH 1: 1–2; TI IX: 35.

forms of power, which he calls 'active' and 'reactive', and allows that Nietzsche thinks humans sometimes prefer the lower forms, for example, prefer resenting others to developing their own capacities. But how is this last claim consistent with the strong teleology Richardson attributes to Nietzsche? How can people always seek the greatest power yet sometimes prefer lesser power?[14] His attempts to resolve this difficulty are not persuasive. He says, first, that the reactive forms of will are logically dependent on the active forms,[15] but this does nothing to explain how the reactive can ever be preferred. He then says that Nietzsche's claim about essence is 'ineliminably, a claim of the valuative priority of the active,' because we 'find the essences of things when we find the highest and best they can become.'[16] But this proposal reduces Nietzsche's narrow perfectionism to the vacuity mentioned above: that we should develop the properties we should develop. It also does nothing to resolve the difficulty, so long as Nietzsche still holds that all activity aims at a maximum of power. And in my view the difficulty is simply unresolvable. Nietzsche's recognition that people sometimes and even often prefer lower to higher exercises of power, and do so for internal rather than external reasons, is flatly inconsistent with the teleology that seems to underlie his power-ontology.

I think Nietzsche's best move here is to abandon his strong teleology. This would allow him to extend his denial of the optimistic tendency claims, so in no realm does the good tend naturally to prevail, and also to insist more strongly on the practical importance of perfectionist judgements, or on how accepting them can change the way we act. If the will to power always goes along with other goods, it makes no practical difference whether we embrace it or them as our fundamental goal. If the two can diverge, however, the choice between them is vital, and we will live less well if we make it wrongly. Nietzsche's teleology is also not needed for his narrow perfectionism. As I have said, the explanations that show properties to be essential to a kind need not be teleological; they are not so for gold, and need not be for humans. Nietzsche could say that humans essentially exercise a will to power because in all their actions they try to transform the world in light of a goal they have formed, and that some of their actions exercise more power than others. They do so, for example, when achieving their goal involves transforming more of the world; thus, a person who successfully redirects all human activity for centuries to come exercises more power than if he merely tied his shoelace. Actions also manifest more power when their goal is more intricately structured, so achieving it involves bringing about more

[14] People could prefer lesser power if they falsely believed it was greater, but where could the false belief come from? In Nietzsche's picture it would have to result from self-deception, but how could a desire for the greatest power lead people to form beliefs that cause them to achieve less power?

[15] John Richardson, *Nietzsche's System* (New York: Oxford University Press, 1996), 43.

[16] Ibid. 43–4.

complex relations among its parts. But Nietzsche need not say that people always seek power, and even less a maximum of power, under that description or as such. Whenever they exercise their will they do so by pursuing some particular goal, and he can allow that their primary commitment is to that goal and not to the more abstract idea of power. More specifically, he can allow that their attachment to a particular goal can make them prefer it to other goals whose achievement would involve higher forms of power, and in particular allow that they can prefer reactive to active forms of will. Whenever they act they exercise power, but they do so by pursuing particular goals that may distract them from greater power.

I have argued that Nietzsche should abandon his strong teleology because it conflicts with one of his most valuable contributions, his vigorous denial of optimistic claims about natural tendencies. But his teleology also conflicts with the structure of his perfectionist view, and I now turn to that topic. Nietzsche may combine this structure with a narrow perfectionist identification of the human good, but he could also affirm it given a merely broad perfectionism, one that does not ground its values in human nature. Having spent the first part of this essay examining the possibility that Nietzsche is a narrow perfectionist, I now consider questions about the structure of his view that are independent of that issue.

2. Moral Structure

I have described perfectionism as 'centred on' a conception of the good, and it is time to explain what this means. Perfectionism as currently understood is a version of consequentialism, which means it evaluates acts by the total amount of good they produce. More specifically, it is a version of maximizing consequentialism, which says the right act is always the one that will result in the most good possible. A maximizing structure is not essential to consequentialism, which can equally well make the satisficing claim that acts are right so long as they produce outcomes that are 'good enough.'[17] But while satisficing may be plausible for hedonic values such as pleasure, it is not so for perfectionist values. As the terms 'excellence' and 'perfection' suggest, these values call intuitively for a maximizing approach. (The motto of the Olympics is not 'Reasonably fast, reasonably high, reasonably strong'; the longtime recruiting slogan of the US Armed Forces was not 'Be at least two thirds of all that you can be.') And there is another point where perfectionism differs from hedonistic consequentialism. The latter evaluates acts by their consequences in the everyday

---

[17] Michael Slote, *Common-Sense Morality and Consequentialism* (London: Routledge & Kegan Paul, 1985), ch. 3.

sense of that term, that is, by states of affairs that follow after an act and are separate from it. Perfectionism does this some of the time; it can say that an act, say, of educating oneself, is right because of the goods it will lead to. But perfectionism also often commends acts for embodying excellence themselves. If it values moral virtue or the achievement of difficult goals, it can say an act is right because it instantiates these goods and so contributes to good outcomes not causally but as a constituent. This is in fact an important feature of perfectionist consequentialism: to evaluate acts largely by their own intrinsic nature.

Nietzsche's moral view certainly seems consequentialist in this sense. He does not accept any of the prohibitions that distinguish deontological moral views from consequentialist ones and can make an act wrong even when its outcome is best. His discussion of promising, for example, is not interested in any duty to keep promises at the expense of good outcomes, but only in the values and especially forms of will the practice of promising embodies. He sometimes judges acts by their consequences in the everyday sense; if he commends suffering, for example, it is not for its intrinsic properties but for the perfection it makes possible in the future. But he also often judges acts by the perfection and especially the strength of will they embody themselves, so their contribution to good outcomes is through their own nature. He also makes maximizing claims. Just as his teleology emphasizes that humans want not just some power but the greatest power attainable,[18] so his ethics enjoins the continued pursuit of ever greater goods. He likewise accepts the consequentialist demand to measure values, speaking of a person's 'quantum' of power[19] and suggesting that the 'attempt should be made to see whether a scientific order of values could be constructed simply on a numerical and mensural scale of force' (WP: 710). He never actually constructs this scale, but as we will see, identifies several features that count for or against a person's degree of power and that can in principle be measured. Contemporary moral anti-theorists are especially skeptical of the attempt to measure values; Nietzsche does not share that skepticism.

If Nietzsche's moral view is consequentialist, it faces two more questions: Whose good is each person to aim at, just his own or that of all people? And how are particular goods aggregated across the times in a person's life and, if this is relevant, across the persons in a society? I begin with the last question, about social aggregation, because it is the key to the structure of Nietzsche's perfectionism.

Nietzsche is famously antiegalitarian, favouring an aristocratic society and a strict 'order of rank' among individuals. And his antiegalitarianism rests on a distinctive view about social aggregation, whereby the value in a society depends not on the total

---

[18] See especially his vigorous rejection of the view that humans want only self-preservation, or only the minimal realization of their essential properties needed to stay alive (GS: 349; BGE: 13; WP: 650, 651).

[19] WP: 382, 674, 689, 855; WP: 480 and 485 speak similarly of the 'measure' or 'degree' of power.

or average perfection of all its members but on the excellence of its few most perfect members. This view is expressed repeatedly in Nietzsche's writings, from the earliest to the latest. A famous passage in *Schopenhauer as Educator* says, ' "Mankind must work continually at the production of individual great men—that and nothing else is its task." . . . how can your life, the individual life, receive the highest value, the deepest significance? . . . only by your living for the good of the rarest and most valuable exemplars' (U III: 6).[20] *Beyond Good and Evil* says a healthy aristocracy sees itself not as a function of the general population but as 'their *meaning* and highest justification,' and therefore 'accepts with good conscience the sacrifice of untold human beings who, *for its sake*, must be reduced and lowered to incomplete human beings, to slaves, to instruments' (BGE: 258).[21] *The Genealogy of Morals* adds, 'The well-being of the majority and the well-being of the few are opposite viewpoints of value: to consider the former *a priori* of higher value may be left to the naivete of English biologists' (GM I: 17).[22] And *The Will to Power* frequently echoes these claims, saying, for example, '*Basic error*: to place the goal in the herd and not in single individuals! The herd is a means, no more!' (WP: 766).[23] Since this view is the opposite of John Rawls's famous maximin principle, it can be called a 'maximax' view. Whereas Rawls wants society to maximize the well-being of its worst-off individuals, Nietzsche wants it to concentrate on the best, since only their perfection has value. Reflection on Rawls may suggest a 'lexical maximax' principle, according to which society should first maximize the excellence of its best individuals, then when nothing more can be done for them, the next-best individuals, and so on.[24] But this lexical principle seems less true to Nietzsche's view than simple maximax: he seems to find no value whatever in the achievements of lesser humans, so once the best have developed as far as they can it is a matter of indifference what other individuals do.

A maximax view is extremely radical, since it favours unequal distributions of resources and opportunities given almost any assumptions about the world. Even if people's talents are exactly equal, society will do best if it arbitrarily selects a few individuals and devotes all its energies to them, since then the greatest perfection will be as great as possible. Perhaps because the principle is so radical, some commentators try to deny its role in Nietzsche's thought. Walter Kaufmann says Nietzsche's interest in the best individuals derives from his belief that most lives have zero value, and 'no addition of such zeroes can ever lead to any value.'[25] But though this interpretation is supported by one text (WP: 53), it does not fit the general tenor of Nietzsche's thought.

---

[20] See also U II: 9.   [21] See also BGE: 126, 199, 257, 260, 265; and GS: 23.

[22] See also GM III: 14.   [23] See also WP: 246, 252, 373, 660, 681, 877, 881, 987, 997.

[24] For Rawls's lexical principle, see John Rawls, *A Theory of Justice* (Cambridge: MA: Harvard University Press, 1971), 83.

[25] Walter Kaufmann, *Nietzsche: Philosopher, Psychologist, Antichrist*, 4th edn. (Princeton, NJ: Princeton University Press, 1974), 150.

Recall *Beyond Good and Evil*'s claim that lesser individuals must be 'reduced and lowered to incomplete human beings,' that is, denied some perfection they could achieve (BGE: 258). James Conant has recently attempted a more thoroughgoing denial of Nietzsche's antiegalitarianism, claiming that his interest in outstanding individuals does not imply that only their achievements matter but instead reflects their capacity to serve as models who can inspire everyone to lead better lives.[26] But Conant does not consider the full range of Nietzsche's maximax texts, discussing only *Schopenhauer as Educator* and especially the passage from it quoted above. And even his treatment of this passage is highly selective. First, he ends the passage in mid-sentence, not acknowledging that, after directing us to live for the good of the most valuable exemplars, Nietzsche adds, 'and not for the good of the majority, that is to say those who, taken individually, are the least valuable [*wertlosesten*] exemplars' (U III: 6). This is hardly the remark of an egalitarian. Second, Conant does not acknowledge that the first and last two sentences of the passage are separated by about a page of text that makes further strongly antiegalitarian claims, for example, that the 'only concern' of a biological species is 'the individual higher exemplar' and not 'the mass of its exemplars and their well-being' (U III: 6). In fact, this intervening text utterly demolishes Conant's main interpretative argument. He claims that the antiegalitarian reading of *Schopenhauer as Educator* rests on a mistranslation of Nietzsche's '*Exemplar*' as 'specimen.' Whereas this term has misleading biological connotations, Conant says, Nietzsche's use of *Exemplar* is continuous with Kant's in *The Critique of Judgement* and that of the German Romantics, for whom an exemplar is a creative genius we all can emulate. But the intervening text Conant omits is precisely about biology, suggesting that we apply to humans a lesson that can be learned from 'any species of the animal and plant world.' So the biological analogies are made by Nietzsche himself! The intervening text also uses the word *Exemplar* three times to refer to members of animal and plant species, and not just outstanding but also ordinary members ([*die*] *Masse der Exemplare*). I would have thought that if Nietzsche uses *Exemplar* to refer to ordinary blades of grass he is not using it to refer only to Kantian creative geniuses, but perhaps Conant thinks that in interpreting Nietzsche's use of a word it is less important to look at Nietzsche's own repeated use of that word a half-page earlier than at its use by another philosopher in another book published eighty years before.[27]

---

[26] James Conant, 'Nietzsche's Perfectionism: A Reading of *Schopenhauer as Educator*', in Richard Schacht (ed.), *Nietzsche's Postmoralism: Essays on Nietzsche's Prelude to Philosophy's Future* (Cambridge: Cambridge University Press, 2001), 181–257.

[27] Conant has the good taste to associate antiegalitarian interpreters of Nietzsche with Hitler. His own interpretation reduces Nietzsche to a writer of banal self-help books, a kind of Deepak Chopra of the nineteenth century.

Nietzsche's acceptance of a maximax principle explains several of his other views, for example, about the value of egoism. He holds that egoism is neither always good nor always bad:

Egoism is of as much value as the physiological value of him who possesses it . . . If he represents the ascending course of mankind, then his value is in fact extraordinary; and extreme care may be taken over the preservation and promotion of his development . . . If he represents the descending course, decay, chronic sickening, then he has little value: and the first demand of fairness is for him to take as little space, force, and sunshine as possible away from the well-constituted. (WP: 373)[28]

Beyond Good and Evil claims not only that lesser individuals must be sacrificed, which could be something forced on them by their superiors, but that they must 'sacrifice themselves' or voluntarily forgo their own perfection (BGE: 265).[29] And *Zarathustra* speaks frequently of sacrificing oneself for the sake of the overman, saying, for example, 'I love him who works and invents to build a house for the overman and to prepare earth, animal, and plant for him: for thus he wants to go under' (Z 1: Prologue 4).[30] Nietzsche's endorsement of egoism by the best is qualified by his claim that they have duties to each other and should treat their peers as they treat themselves (BGE: 260, 265).[31] This might be a tactical recommendation, proposing a bargain with those few others capable of hindering one's perfection. But this is not how Nietzsche presents the issue, speaking simply of 'duties,' 'rights,' and 'equal privileges' among the most perfect. And his whole treatment of egoism precisely fits a maximax principle. If the good of society depends entirely on the good of its few best members, those best members should be mostly egoistic, restraining their pursuit of their own perfection only to acknowledge the similar perfection of their peers, while the majority of members sacrifice themselves entirely for the good of their betters.

If Nietzsche applies a maximax principle across persons, one might expect him to do the same across times, and equate the aggregate perfection in a person's life with the perfection he achieves at his few best moments. But he does not seem to do so. His most striking remarks about the value in whole lives urge people to 'die at the right time,' and especially not to 'die too late,' as apples do that hang on the branch long after they 'taste best' (Z 1: 21).[32] These remarks are inconsistent with a maximax principle, on which once a life's best moments have passed it is a matter of indifference whether other moments follow. Instead, they suggest something like an averaging view across times, which equates the aggregate perfection in a life with its average perfection per moment; this implies that additional moments below a life's previous

---

[28] A lightly edited version of this passage appears in TI IX: 33.
[30] See also Z II: On the Famous Wise Men; Z IV: The Welcome.
[32] See also GS: 281; TI IX: 36; WP: 864.

[29] See also WP: 246.
[31] BGE, 260, 265.

average make it worse. It is probably too much to attribute averaging across times to Nietzsche on the basis of his few remarks about 'free death,' but those remarks do tend in an averaging direction.

Nietzsche's discussions of aggregation bring out more clearly than any other perfectionist's how different aggregative principles are appropriate for perfectionist than for other values. No one would average across times given hedonic values, or say that additional happy moments can make a person's life less good. But many take precisely this line when making perfectionist judgements about careers in sports or the arts, which are often thought to be best if they end not too far past their peak. A similar point applies to maximax across persons. Whereas the idea that society should maximize the happiness of its few happiest members has no plausibility, the parallel view about perfectionist values has real, albeit disturbing, appeal. These values make antiegalitarianism intelligible and even tempting in a way that hedonic values do not. In an earlier discussion I went further, suggesting that just as antiegalitarian principles are more plausible for perfectionist than for hedonic values, so egalitarian principles are less plausible.[33] This may be false: it may be not only logically possible but also morally intelligible to aim at the greatest perfection for the least perfect. Even so, perfectionist values have an affinity for antiegalitarian aggregations that rival values do not. The perfectionist tradition contains many defences of aristocratic inequality, from Plato and Aristotle through Hastings Rashdall and Bertrand de Jouvenel.[34] These defences often turn on factual claims, for example, that people's natural abilities are very different. But one can wonder whether these claims really do support the degree of inequality these writers defend, and whether the perfectionists who cite them may not tacitly be using maximax or a similar principle in arriving at their views. There is nothing at all tacit in Nietzsche's approach: his antiegalitarianism rests on an aggregative principle that directly and explicitly gives most weight to the achievements of the most perfect.

More abstractly, Nietzsche's acceptance of a maximax principle across persons gives his moral view an agent-neutral structure, one where all agents are assigned the same moral goal, so their acts if right will tend to produce the same outcome. There are not different goals for different agents, so the outcome that is best from one person's point of view need not be best from another's; instead, the outcome all should seek is the same. Agent-neutrality is most commonly associated with views like utilitarianism that include all people's goods in their common goal by adding or averaging them. But maximax perfectionism is also agent-neutral, since it assigns everyone the same moral goal of maximizing the perfection of the best. Those who are among the best should

---

[33] Hurka, *Perfectionism*, 79.

[34] Hastings Rashdall, *The Theory of Good and Evil* (London: Oxford University Press, 1907), vol. i, ch. 8; Bertrand de Jouvenel, *The Ethics of Redistribution* (Cambridge: Cambridge University Press, 1951).

pursue that goal in one way, by concentrating primarily on their own perfection, while those who are not best should do so differently, by sacrificing themselves to their betters. But despite this difference their ultimate goal is the same.

Nietzsche's view is not often read as agent-neutral. Most commentators treat it as egoistic, telling each person to seek just his own perfection; this is, for example, an unargued assumption of Alexander Nehamas's *Nietzsche: Life as Literature*.[35] One reason for this assumption may be the belief that perfectionism, and especially those narrow versions grounded in human nature, must be egoistic, because their classical Greek formulations were egoistic. But the claim about Greek perfectionisms is disputable, and it is simply false that perfectionism in general must be egoistic: it can and in its best versions does tell each person to care about others' good as well as his own.[36] A second reason may be Nietzsche's frequent praise of egoism. The praise is usually restricted to egoism by the best individuals—it is only their lives that will be spoiled by altruism. But Nietzsche is so focused on these individuals that it can look as if his praise is for egoism generally. A final reason for the assumption is that the desire claims undergirding Nietzsche's argument that the will to power is essential to humans are egoistic: they say that everyone seeks his own greatest power, not power for others. And the only moral view that can follow from claims of this kind is likewise egoistic. In fact, if the claims were true, a morality telling people to sacrifice their own perfection for the sake of others' could not influence their conduct. Nietzsche's predicament here is similar to that of classical utilitarians such as Bentham, who tried to ground an agent-neutral hedonism in the egoistic psychological claim that everyone desires only his own pleasure. But the latter claim is inconsistent with the former, and later utilitarians such as Sidgwick dropped the psychological egoism and defended agent-neutral moral hedonism on its own. A charitable reading of Nietzsche will do the same. I argued in section 1 that Nietzsche's egoistic claims are not needed for his narrow perfectionism; it now appears that they also contradict his maximax view of social aggregation, at least if that is intended to have action-guiding force. A maximax principle is central to Nietzsche's positive moral view, appearing in works from his earliest to his latest and organizing his claims about the values of egoism and altruism. But it is also obscured by his occasional claims about desire; that is a further reason to ignore those claims.

3. Extent and Organic Unity

Nietzsche's more specific claims about the good value many states of humans: gaiety, courage, unselfconsciousness, pride, overflowing generosity, and more. It is unclear

---

[35] Alexander Nehamas, *Nietzsche: Life as Literature* (Cambridge, MA: Harvard University Press, 1985).
[36] See Hurka, *Perfectionism*, 62–4.

whether all these states can be unified under some more abstract value, either a narrow perfectionist one of will to power or some other. Without settling this issue, I will examine some remarks of Nietzsche's that can unify at least many of his goods and that express a distinctive Nietzschean view of human perfection.

Many of Nietzsche's goods are active, involving the pursuit and especially the achievement of goals rather than mere contemplation of the world. Their further specification requires an account of which goals are most worth pursuing, or whose achievement has most value. Here Nietzsche's approach is distinctively formal. He does not hold that there are substantive goals that perfection requires people to pursue, such as knowledge, virtue, or the creation of beauty. Instead, he evaluates goals in terms of formal qualities, ones that are compatible with many different substantive contents. It is not its specific aim that determines an activity's degree of worth, but how far that aim instantiates certain formal properties. He mentions two such properties, one internal to a goal and the other a matter of its relation to other goals.

The first property is the goal's extent, both in time and in the number of objects or persons it involves. This property naturally connects with ideas about power, since someone who achieves a more extended goal transforms more of the world and so exercises greater power over it. Nietzsche is especially interested in a goal's extent in time. In *The Genealogy of Morals* he sees the chief value of promising as its expressing a 'protracted and unbreakable will,' one through which a person fixes his future behaviour and so makes himself more valuable than 'all more short-willed and unreliable creatures' (GM II: 2). More generally, Nietzsche commends the 'tensing of a will over long temporal distances,' says a great individual can 'extend his will across great stretches of his life,' and looks forward to a new caste that will rule Europe with 'a long, terrible will of its own that would be able to cast its goals millennia hence' (WP: 65, 962; BGE: 208).[37] But he also values a goal's extent across persons. One aspect of power is the ability to impose one's will on others and so determine their behaviour, and the more people one does this to the greater one's exercise of power. Hence the attraction for Nietzsche of a conquering race that 'unhesitatingly lays its terrible claws upon a populace perhaps tremendously superior in numbers but still formless and nomad' (GM II: 17), and of those 'artists of violence and organizers who build states' and who exercise their 'form-giving and ravishing' force on 'some *other* man, *other* men' (GM II: 18).[38] For him the greatest individuals are those creators of new values who fix the general course of life for millions of humans far into the future, and they are marked precisely by the extent of the goals they achieve.

---

[37] See also GS: 356; Z I: 8; BGE: 257; TI IX: 39; WP: 527.

[38] See also WP: 964. The importance of power over others in Nietzsche's account is emphasized in Richardson, *Nietzsche's System*, 28–35.

The second formal property is the degree to which a goal is unified with a person's other goals, so they form a system in which many different ends are pursued as means to a single overriding one. In *The Gay Science* Nietzsche writes,

One thing is needful.—To 'give style' to one's character—a great and rare art! It is practised by those who survey all the strengths and weaknesses of their nature and fit them into an artistic plan until every one of them appears as art and reason and even weaknesses delight the eye . . . In the end, when the work is finished, it becomes evident how the constraint of a single taste governed and formed everything large and small. Whether this taste was good or bad is less important than one might suppose, if only it was a single taste.   (GS: 290)

Beyond Good and Evil expresses a similar idea, saying that what is 'essential' is 'that there should be *obedience* over a long period of time and in a *single* direction' (BGE: 188). And *The Will to Power* uses claims about organization to define power:

Weakness of will: that is a metaphor that can prove misleading. For there is no will, and consequently neither a strong nor a weak will. The multitude and disgregation of impulses and the lack of any systematic order among them result in a 'weak will'; their co-ordination under a single predominant impulse results in a 'strong will'.   (WP: 46)[39]

But Nietzsche does not value just unity of action, as could be found in a life devoted narrowly to a single activity. On the contrary, he heaps scorn on the specialist scholars he finds among European intellectuals, calling them 'nook-dwellers' and 'fragments of humanity'(BGE: 204; TI VIII: 3).[40] Instead, his ideal is a unity that combines diverse elements, so a person's greatness lies in his 'range and multiplicity, in his wholeness in manifoldness' (BGE: 212). It is an ideal of unity-in-diversity, or what is often called organic unity. It requires that a person have a single guiding impulse, one that organizes all his other impulses, but also that those other impulses be varied, individual, and strong. Then his goals combine the two traits of organized unity and individual diversity.

Some may object that this value of organic unity cannot be measured in the way consequentialism requires. This seems to be the suggestion of those who, in commentaries on Nietzsche or elsewhere, describe the value by using literary analogies, speaking of the 'narrative unity' of a life or the unity of a character in fiction.[41] But these analogies are in several ways misleading. Narrative unity is a specific kind of unity with a specific structure, one whose most familiar instances involve rising tension leading to an emotional climax and then a brief denouement. I see nothing in Nietzsche's talk of unity that restricts it to this specifically narrative form. At the same time, the analogy with literary characters is in another respect too permissive.

---

[39] For further remarks about the unity of goals see Z I: 22; BGE: 19, 208; GM, Preface: 2; WP: 334, 387.
[40] See also Z II: 20; BGE: 205; GM III: 23; A: 57; WP: 390, 881.
[41] MacIntyre, *After Virtue*, ch. 15; Nehamas, *Nietzsche*, ch. 6.

I take it that for Nietzsche what unifies a person's impulses must be an end that she herself wills, even if unconsciously, and wills as unifying her impulses. But the unity of a literary character can depend on connections between aspects of her character that she does not will and has no awareness of; this more external unity does not seem sufficient for what Nietzsche calls power. And the analogies' anti-theoretical implications are also misleading. Without attributing it to Nietzsche, let me give a brief sketch of how the value of organic unity can in principle be cardinally measured.[42]

Consider a model of unified action, where a person achieves one goal by achieving two others as means to it, and achieves each of those by achieving two others as means to it. Here the person's goals are hierarchically organized, as in Figure 1.1. And we can measure their organization by stipulating that each goal in this hierarchy has one unit of value in itself, plus an additional unit for every further goal achieved as a means to it. The four goals at the bottom of the hierarchy then have one unit of value each, the two in the middle three units each, and the one at the top seven units, for a total of seventeen units in the hierarchy as a whole. This is more than the seven units of value the person would achieve if he achieved seven unconnected goals (Figure 1.2), and also more than the thirteen units of value in an intermediate structure where six subordinate goals are achieved as a means to an overriding seventh (Figure 1.3). By counting the number of goals subordinate to a given one and taking that to determine its value, this measure neatly captures the value in more complex hierarchies of intention. And it does so even better if it is modified to give more weight to diversity in a unified structure. Instead of counting just the individual goals subordinate to a given one, it can count, either in addition or instead, the number of goals *of different kinds* that are means to that goal. Then, if a goal has ten very similar goals subordinate to it, say, ten pullings of the same lever, it gains at most ten units of value from doing so. But if it has ten subordinate goals of different kinds, it gains ten plus ten equals

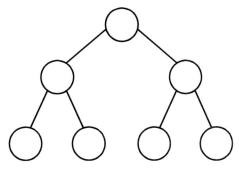

FIGURE. 1.1

[42] For a fuller account see Hurka, *Perfectionism*, chs. 8–10.

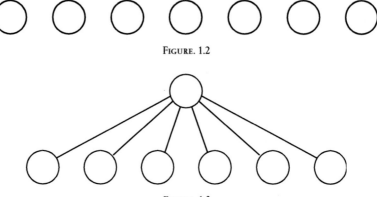

FIGURE. 1.2

FIGURE. 1.3

twenty units, making the more diverse unity better. This account can be modified in further ways, and in any case should not be taken too literally. But it does show how the value of organic unity can at least in principle be measured.

A more serious objection says that if Nietzsche uses only formal measures of perfection, he has to say the instigators of the slave revolt in morality led immensely valuable lives: after all, they profoundly affected millions of people for centuries.[43] Now, Nietzsche does not think the slave revolt had no desirable features. It introduced a new spirituality into human life and also involved a certain devious cleverness—better that, surely, than mere passive resentment of the masters. But he clearly does not consider the instigators of the revolt to be paradigms of excellence, and an account of his view must recognize this fact. There are at least two ways in which a broadly formal account can do so.

The first is to make the value of an activity depend not just on its current properties but also on its origins. If an integrated activity with far-reaching goals issues from strength and self-confidence, as it presumably will in Nietzsche's hoped-for creators of values, it has immense worth. But if it is a product of weakness and resentment, it does not. This move enables the account to deny that the instigators of the slave revolt were immensely valuable, since they acted ultimately from resentment, but will be consistent with the formal approach if the criteria identifying originating motives as weak are themselves formal. This may be Nietzsche's view. He may think resentment is a form of weakness because it is essentially reactive, taking its chief goals from outside the self and being unable to resist doing so, rather than finding them within the self as a truly integrated personality would do.[44] If this is his view, he can condemn action from resentment without using substantive measures of value.

---

[43] I owe this objection to Neil Sinhababu.

[44] Richardson proposes this interpretation; see *Nietzsche's System*, 39–42, 60.

The second way is to make the value of an activity depend in part on the goal to which it is directed. If an integrated, far-reaching activity aims to promote further such activity on the part of the best individuals, as Nietzsche's hoped-for creators' will, it again has immense worth. But if it is designed to hinder such activity by the best, as the slave revolt was, it does not. Here the activity's value is undercut not by its origin but by the value of its intentional object.[45] But the approach is still formal if the evaluation of that object uses only formal measures and an aggregative principle like maximax: if the aim of the slave revolt undercuts its value, it is because that aim involves less of the relevant formal properties in the activities of the only people whose activity matters.

I cannot say that Nietzsche clearly embraces either of these possibilities; he never explicitly addresses why propagating slave values is not only instrumentally but also intrinsically worse than promoting higher ones. But the two show that he can consistently condemn the slave revolt while using only formal and no substantive measures of individual perfection.

Nietzsche's acceptance of these measures connects his view to many others in nineteenth-century philosophy. Organic unity is the chief value in Hegel's ethics and also in those of later Idealists such as F. H. Bradley, whose *Ethical Studies* describes it as the combination of 'homogeneity' and 'specification,' or 'not the extreme of unity, nor of diversity, but the perfect identity of both.'[46] Bradley sometimes combines this good with considerations of extent:

To reduce the raw material of one's nature to the highest degree of system, and to use every element from whatever source as a subordinate means to this object, is certainly one genuine view of goodness. On the other hand, to widen as far as possible the end to be pursued, and to realize this through the distraction and dissipation of one's individuality, is certainly also good.[47]

Similar claims are made by other philosophers of the period who reject Idealist metaphysics but retain a central value of 'personality' involving both the organization of a person's goals and their extension beyond his own states now.[48] Nietzsche's general account of human perfection is therefore absolutely in the mainstream of nineteenth-century philosophy, but his presentation of it has several distinctive features.

First, the Idealists value not only the practical good of achieving goals but also the theoretical one of knowing truths, which they see as involving the same formal properties of mental states. For them the best knowledge is of the most extended states

---

[45] I explore the general idea that love of the good is good and of the evil is evil in Thomas Hurka, *Virtue, Vice, and Value* (New York: Oxford University Press, 2001).

[46] F. H. Bradley, *Ethical Studies*, 2nd edn. (Oxford: Clarendon Press, 1927), 74.

[47] F. H. Bradley, *Appearance and Reality*, 2nd edn. (Oxford: Clarendon Press, 1897), 367.

[48] See, e.g., L. T. Hobhouse, *Liberalism* (London: Oxford University Press, 1911), 111, 122–3, 132; and *The Rational Good* (London: George Allen & Unwin, 1921), 20–1, 39–40, 100.

of affairs and plays the greatest systematizing role, this time by explaining the most other items of knowledge a person has; on both grounds the knowledge of scientific or philosophical principles is especially valuable. In addition, and following earlier perfectionists such as Plato and Aristotle, the Idealists treat knowledge as the greatest good, and in particular as higher than any practical good. Nietzsche firmly rejects this view. He does not develop any parallels between knowledge and achievement, and, far from considering knowledge the greatest good, grants it no intrinsic value whatever. This is most evident in his claim that the falsity of a belief is no objection to it; what matters is only how far the belief is life-promoting and species-cultivating, that is, how far it is instrumental to other goods (BGE: 4). Nietzsche's denial of intrinsic value to knowledge may fit his natural desire claims, which suggest that even a person's choice of beliefs expresses his desire for power.[49] But even apart from that, it gives Nietzsche's view a distinctive cast. Whereas many perfectionists make theoretical or contemplative goods the highest goods, he goes to the opposite extreme of recognizing only practical or conative ones.[50]

Second, the Idealists hold that there is a higher degree of unity in a mind's consciousness of an object than in any physical relationship between things, and more unity still in self-consciousness, where the mind's object is itself. This is why the direction of historical development according to Hegel is toward the full self-consciousness of spirit.[51] But Nietzsche holds that the best activities are unconscious, and that consciousness 'gives rise to countless errors' (GS: 11) and even expresses 'an imperfect and often morbid state in a person' (WP: 289).[52] His reason may be that consciousness detracts from the unity of unconscious drives, by introducing a foreign element that disrupts their smooth functioning.[53] But whereas others use the value of organic unity to affirm the supremacy of conscious states, Nietzsche denigrates those states.

Finally, the Idealists hold that achieving the formal goods of extent and unity necessarily involves acting in a conventionally virtuous way. They have two grounds for this claim, which they do not always clearly distinguish. One is that the entity in which one should seek organic unity is not oneself but something larger, such as one's society. One should identify what Bradley calls one's 'station' in this society and fulfil its 'duties,' all as a means to the society's organic good.[54] The other ground is that even unity in oneself requires conventional virtue. This is Plato's argument

---

[49] See, e.g., WP: 480.

[50] According to Richardson (*Nietzsche's System*, 235) Nietzsche objects to the essentially passive nature of knowledge, the fact that its goal is to mirror or correspond to reality rather than transform it.

[51] For a more recent view identifying consciousness and self-consciousness as higher forms of organic unity, see Robert Nozick, *Philosophical Explanations* (Cambridge, MA: Harvard University Press, 1981), 417.

[52] See also BGE: 191; GM I: 10, GM II: 16; EH II: 9; and WP: 423, 524, 707.

[53] This is suggested in Richardson, *Nietzsche's System*, 204–5.   [54] Bradley, *Ethical Studies*, ch. 5.

in the *Republic*: that an internally unified person will necessarily act justly toward others. The argument is rejected by Aristotle, who holds that a vicious person can be unified around his evil goals. But it is accepted by Bradley, who calls Aristotle's vicious person a 'creature of theory' and holds that a morally bad self can never be properly unified.[55] By so doing he connects his formal value of organic unity with conventionally approved conduct toward others.

Nietzsche rejects both these arguments. Richardson has suggested that Nietzsche's power-ontology should lead him to value organized unity in societies as well as in individuals,[56] but he does not seem to do this. He does not think, for example, that the diversity he values is present in a society where everyone specializes but in a different field; the diversity must characterize individual lives. He here treats individual lives as the morally primary units, the ones where the central values are defined, and the same is true of his concern that people 'die at the right time.' Nor does he think for a minute that a unified life must be conventionally virtuous. His early statement about giving style to one's character says it does not matter whether the taste that governs a person's actions is good or bad so long as it is a single taste (GS: 290). This gives a person complete moral freedom not only in choosing self-regarding projects but also in deciding how to treat others. The same freedom is present in his later discussions of power. If the power Nietzsche values is at least partly power over others, it can be exercised either cruelly, by harming them against their will, or benevolently, by helping them to improve their lives.[57] In itself the concept of power is neutral between these alternatives and therefore neutral between conventional morality and immorality.

Nietzsche here sees more clearly than other perfectionists that formal measures of value are indeed just formal. They do not favour any substantive goals, and certainly not conventionally moral ones, but instead consider only a goal's extent and the process by which it is achieved. What this means is well illustrated by the example of games. In playing a game one pursues an intrinsically trivial goal such as standing atop a mountain or directing a ball into a hole in the ground, while willingly accepting rules that forbid the most efficient means to that goal, such as chartering a helicopter up the mountain or dropping the ball in the hole by hand.[58] Playing the game therefore involves taking complex means to a trivial goal, which makes its value entirely one of process rather than product, journey rather than destination. The same is true on a broader scale of Nietzsche's account of perfection, which likewise values only formal properties of a person's activities and does not pretend that these somehow justify specific substantive projects. In the history of perfectionism this is an important innovation. Most earlier perfectionists do tie a person's practical perfection

---

[55] Ibid. 303–9.   [56] Richardson, *Nietzsche's System*, 50–2.   [57] See, e.g., WP: 769, 784.
[58] See Bernard Suits, *The Grasshopper: Games, Life, and Utopia* (Toronto: University of Toronto Press, 1978).

to substantive goals and, in particular, using arguments similar to Bradley's, to the goals prescribed by conventional morality. But this allows their claims about each person's good to be infected by claims about the right, or about how the person ought all things considered to act. Nietzsche rejects this approach, making claims about the good that concern only that topic and so recognize its autonomy from claims about the right. A perfectionism that follows Nietzsche on this point, and in particular that uses only formal measures of practical perfection, need not as a whole be hostile to the other-regarding elements in everyday morality. Nietzsche's perfectionism is hostile to them, because its maximax aggregative principle implies that for some people the perfection of most others has no intrinsic significance. But a view that uses the same measures of individual perfection can embed them in a more familiar structure where each person is required to care impartially about the good of all; then his pursuit of extended, complex achievements for himself should be constrained by a concern to allow and encourage similar achievements by others. The resulting version of perfectionism captures many other-regarding duties, but does so by deriving them from its form, and more specifically from its claims about whose good each person is to pursue, rather than by building them into its claims about each person's good.

I have said that one of Nietzsche's contributions is to bring out sharply the distinctive features of perfectionism as a moral view. He does so, first, by rejecting the various optimistic tendency claims, thereby giving perfectionism different implications from any view focused on pleasure or the satisfaction of desire. He also does so by recognizing that perfectionist values call intuitively for distinctive aggregative principles, including especially, though disturbingly, antiegalitarian ones. And he does so, finally, by developing an account of individual perfection that is strictly formal and therefore does not incorporate claims about other-regarding duties. Sidgwick said the ancient Greek moral philosophers never properly distinguished between good of self and good of others, or between what will make a person's own life best and how he ought all things considered to act.[59] The same criticism can be made of many later perfectionists, but it cannot be made of Nietzsche, who offers an account of individual perfection that remains within the confines of the good and does not contaminate it with judgements about the right.

I have not claimed that Nietzsche is a completely theoretical philosopher, nor even that his remarks on moral topics are always consistent. He is, after all, Nietzsche. But I have suggested that he often addresses, even if implicitly, the main theoretical questions that arise in a systematic development of perfectionism; that his answers to these questions often show strong tendencies, expressed in different works, toward certain theoretical views; and that these views respond to the distinctive features

---

[59] Henry Sidgwick, *Outlines of the History of Ethics for English Readers*, 5th edn. (London: Macmillan, 1931), 17–28, 197–8.

of perfectionist values by making claims that, while striking, intuitively fit those values. Together these aspects of Nietzsche's moral thought make him, if not a fully theoretical philosopher, then more stimulating for contemporary moral theorists than any earlier figure in the long line of perfectionist writers on ethics.[60]

[60] For helpful comments I am grateful to Neil Sinhababu, who commented on an earlier version of this essay at the 'Morality after Nietzsche' conference, and to Maudemarie Clark, Brian Leiter, and other conference participants.

2

The Will to Power and the Ethics of Creativity

Bernard Reginster

Few of Nietzsche's ideas have been more maligned than his concept of the will to power. Among the various objections it has invited, the deepest and most enduring remains rooted in a tempting interpretation of power in terms of *control* or *domination*: to will power is to seek to control or dominate.[1] The implications of this interpretation (for example, that Hitler's Nazism is a paradigmatic embodiment of the will to power) have proved deeply embarrassing to scholars otherwise favorably disposed toward Nietzsche's ideas.[2] This interpretation is not embarrassing, however, insofar as it is a *descriptive* psychological theory, which presents the desire to dominate as the fundamental human motivation. Although this view is certainly disturbing to those who want to believe that human beings are capable of genuine compassion, for example, it should hardly be embarrassing to Nietzscheans themselves. After all, it is one of those 'terrible' 'un-Christian' truths about which he regularly warns his unsuspecting readers. The view is embarrassing because he also claims that the will to power is a *value*, indeed the 'standard' of a new ethics superior to the prevalent

---

[1] Some of the objections to the concept of the will to power bear on its nature: when it is taken as a cosmological principle, for example, it appears to lack utterly any adequate empirical basis. I do not pronounce on this issue here and focus exclusively on the will to power as it operates in human psychology.

[2] Stern (1979: 120) offers a representative statement of this embarrassment. Even though he acknowledges that the will to power can also assume less disturbing guises, he declares: 'If there is anything in the recent "Nietzschean" era that comes close to an embodiment of "the will to power", it is Hitler's life and political career'.

morality (A 2; WP 391). In this interpretation, for example, Hitler's Nazism is not only a phenomenon he could have predicted, but also one of which he would have approved.

To avoid this sort of embarrassment, scholars have developed three broad strategies. Some have attempted to make the idea of will to power more palatable by downplaying or suppressing its disturbing features. Walter Kaufmann, for example, agrees that the will to power is a will to control, but points out that the control Nietzsche advocates is primarily *self*-control.[3] John Richardson also endorses the view of power as domination, but introduces some crucial qualifications: for instance, he argues that the form of domination favored by Nietzsche is 'mastery,' which precludes troubling forms of coercion or repression, rather than 'tyranny,' which includes them; and he points out that this mastery is primarily a relation among *drives*, rather than among agents.[4] And Maudemarie Clark suggests that the notion of power should be understood not primarily as control and domination, but as the *capacity* to achieve ends. To will power is therefore to seek to acquire or develop certain capacities.[5] Unfortunately, the substantive ethical proposals such qualifications and revisions inspire fall far short of the originality and radicality Nietzsche claims for his 'new values'. His valuation of the will to power boils down to the disappointingly trite praise of personal self-control in the first case; it amounts to the more interesting but hardly more original call for the integration and development of one's personality (through the organization of one's drives into a hierarchy of mastery) in the second case; and it consists of little more than the hackneyed (and purely instrumental) exhortation for the cultivation of one's talents and capacities in the last case.

The second strategy concedes that Nietzsche's ethics of power is disturbingly radical, but finds in his metaethical views, in particular in his rejection of ethical objectivism, a way to mitigate the embarrassment it causes. Value judgments, for him, are 'interpretations' that are only valid from certain contingent perspectives, or they are mere expressions of particular psychological or even physiological proclivities.[6] As a consequence, in commending disturbing ethical views, such as the view that war and domination are good, Nietzsche would merely offer his idiosyncratic point of view, and make for them no claim to objective validity. Even if he makes no claim to objectivity for his new values, Nietzsche still advocates them, however, and he advocates them pointedly for those 'rare' and 'higher' individuals he considers his distinctive audience. Hence, we should still like to understand what he finds so special and appealing about these values. In this respect, the valuation of a crude conception of power as domination hardly seems satisfactory.

---

[3] Kaufmann (1974: 213–16).   [4] Richardson (1996), esp. pp. 28–35.
[5] Clark (1990: 211 ff.).
[6] Nehamas (1985) and Leiter (2002: 138 ff.), develop different versions of this metaethical view and its implications for Nietzsche's substantive ethical proposals. See also Larmore (1996: ch. 4).

A third and final strategy proposes to meet this interpretative challenge by developing an account of Nietzsche's new values that does not depend on the concept of will to power at all. Although this strategy is given various official justifications (the concept of will to power is too vague to be the foundation of a substantive ethics; it does not play an essential role in Nietzsche's ethical thought anyway; it is a parody of traditional forms of ethical naturalism, not intended to be taken seriously; it is merely rhetorical bombast designed to scare away the weak-minded; and so on), it remains often unofficially motivated by the concern to avoid the embarrassment I described earlier. The most successful versions of this last strategy emphasize the value Nietzsche places on creation or creativity. According to Alexander Nehamas' influential interpretation, Nietzsche's new ethics centers on an ideal of self-creation, or the aspiration 'to be the poets of our lives' (GS 299);[7] and Brian Leiter has recently pointed out the importance of creativity, particularly artistic creativity, in the ethical outlook Nietzsche opposes to traditional morality.[8]

I will argue here that this last view gets something right, insofar as the central importance of creativity in Nietzsche's ethical thought is undeniable, but also goes significantly wrong in dissociating creativity from the will to power. In my view, we simply fail to grasp the nature of Nietzsche's ethics of creativity if we regard it as an alternative to one based on the will to power rather than as a paradigmatic manifestation of it. To appreciate the deep and original connection Nietzsche draws between creativity and the will to power, however, I find it necessary to reexamine the latter concept and to develop a new account of it. Once this new account is in place, I believe that we become able not only to understand the basic contours of Nietzsche's ethics of creativity, but also to appreciate why the creative life has, in his view, some of the distinctive and troubling features it has. Accordingly, the present essay comprises two main parts. In Section 1, I develop a new account of the will to power. In Section 2, I show how Nietzsche's ethics of creativity is based on his concept of the will to power, and how some of the most distinctive features he attributes to the creative life have their source in the conception of it in terms of the will to power.

I. The Will to Power

The interpretation of power in terms of domination and control is widespread because it appears strongly suggested by some of Nietzsche's own formulations, among which the most notorious may be the following:

Life itself is *essentially* appropriation, injury, overpowering of what is alien and weaker; suppression, hardness, imposition of one's own forms, incorporation and at least, at its mildest,

---

[7] Nehamas (1985: esp. ch. 6).   [8] See Leiter (2002: 115 ff.).

exploitation—but why should one always use those words in which a slanderous intent has been imprinted for ages? . . . 'Exploitation' does not belong to a corrupt or imperfect or primitive society: it belongs to the *essence* of what lives, as a basic organic function; it is a consequence of the will to power, which is after all the will of life.   (BGE 259)

A close reading of even this provocative passage already suggests that this interpretation is not inevitable: it presents domination and control, in their various forms of 'appropriation,' 'overpowering,' 'exploitation,' and so on, as a common, perhaps unavoidable, *'consequence'* of the pursuit of power, but not necessarily as what this pursuit *consists of*. A proper appreciation of this fact should, in my view, not only enable us to achieve a much deeper understanding of this crucial Nietzschean idea, but also go a long way toward assuaging the enduring embarrassment it has caused to so many scholars.

All the activities Nietzsche associates with the will to power have a common core, which he describes elsewhere in the following terms: 'But all expansion, incorporation, growth is striving against something that resists [*ein Anstreben gegen Widerstehendes*]; movement is essentially tied up with states of displeasure; that which is here the driving force must in any event desire something else [than happiness] if it desires displeasure in this way and continually looks for it.—' (WP 704). The pursuit of power ('expansion, incorporation, growth'), he declares, is 'striving against something that resists.' Since striving against is an effort to overcome, we might say that the will to power aims at the overcoming of resistance. It is 'a desire to overcome, a desire to throw down, a desire to become master, a thirst for enemies and resistances and triumphs' (GM, I 13).

At first glance, this explication does not compel us to think of power in terms other than domination and control, since their pursuit often requires overcoming the resistance of those (or that) one seeks to dominate or control. But closer examination shows that it does. We should first note that the pursuit of the desire to dominate does not, in fact, *necessitate* the overcoming of resistance, even when domination is of other people. As Nietzsche observes, many people actually wish to be dominated and would oppose no resistance to those who seek to subjugate them—namely, those to whom he attributes a 'slavish' disposition (see, e.g., BGE 261; GS 363; A 54). And control could presumably at least sometimes be achieved by circumventing all possible resistance through deception or indoctrination. Insofar as he emphasizes 'striving against something that resists,' Nietzsche already draws a contrast between his concept of the will to power and the mere desire to dominate and control.

Even if the desire to dominate and control were to necessitate it, moreover, the overcoming of resistance would play only a purely instrumental role, so that if domination and control could be achieved without overcoming resistance, this desire would be no less satisfied. But Nietzsche explicitly and insistently maintains that the will to power 'is never satisfied unless it has opponents and resistance [*ohne den Gegner und Widerstand noch nicht satt genug ist*]' (WP 696; cf. 656; A 2). This is the case because the will to power has a distinctive characteristic, which the widespread interpretation entirely overlooks: it is 'a *thirst* for enemies and resistances [*ein Durst nach Feinden und Widerständen*].' This interpretation explains only why my will to power requires that I be prepared to confront and overcome whatever resistance is opposed to its satisfaction, but it does not explain why it should induce me to 'thirst' for such resistance. In other words, the widespread interpretation fails to recognize a crucial ambiguity in the notion of the will to power. It could designate a desire for the satisfaction of which overcoming resistance is a perhaps necessary means. Or it could designate a desire for the overcoming of resistance itself. In the first case, which is the view of power as domination or control, pursuing power requires being prepared to overcome whatever resistance presents itself, but certainly not deliberately seeking it. In the second case, which is the view I think we should favor, pursuing power requires actually and deliberately seeking resistance to overcome.[9]

Thus, power for Nietzsche is not synonymous with domination or control. The explicit contrast between power and happiness in the passage mentioned earlier (WP 704) suggests one important additional qualification. In the conception under which he disparages it, happiness is understood in terms of pleasure, or the absence of pain, which, on the Schopenhauerian version of it he has in mind in this context, requires the satisfaction of all desires as its necessary and sufficient condition (see WWR, I 65). If we keep in mind that happiness so conceived requires that all resistance to that satisfaction has been overcome, then in contrasting power with it, Nietzsche indicates that the will to power is not a will to a *state in which resistance has been overcome*. Since the will to power is not simply a will to *resistance* either, or the desire for a condition in which some striving is perpetually frustrated by resistance or obstacles to its fulfillment (there would be no 'expansion, incorporation, growth' unless the striving were eventually successful), we must conclude that the will to power is a will to the very *activity of overcoming resistance*.

We may now turn to the most perplexing claim Nietzsche makes about the will to power: whoever wills power thereby 'desires displeasure and continually looks for it [*die Unlust will und fortwährend aufsucht*]' (WP 704). I believe that we cannot begin to make sense of this claim without a better grasp of the basic structure of the will to power, particularly its relation to other desires. I follow most recent scholarship in assuming that the will to power is not the only human desire, or the most fundamental desire, to

---

[9] Failure to make sense of this deliberate quest for resistance is the central shortcoming of all interpretations of power in terms of control or domination, including in particular the most sophisticated among these interpretations found in Richardson (1996). It is also a shortcoming of the interpretation of power as capacity, rather than domination, developed in Clark (1990), which also arguably takes a consequence of the pursuit of power to be what this pursuit consists of.

which all other desires are somehow reducible, but that it is one desire among others, albeit one with a special role and significance in human psychological economy. But I depart from the recent scholarship in my conception of the relation the will to power entertains with other desires.[10] My conception is inspired by the interpretation of the will to power as a desire for the overcoming of resistance. Considered in isolation, this desire lacks *determinate content*. It gets a determinate content only from its relation to some *other* (determinate) desire. Something constitutes a resistance only in relation to a determinate end one desires to realize. For example, a recalcitrant puzzle is an obstacle to the desire to understand, and the strength of an opposing player is resistance against the desire to win. Accordingly, the will to power cannot be satisfied unless the agent has a desire for something else than power. The will to power therefore has the structure of a *second-order desire*—it is a desire whose object is or includes another (first-order) desire. It is, specifically, a desire for the overcoming of resistance in the pursuit of some determinate first-order desire.

We can now begin to make sense of the puzzling claim that the will to power 'desires displeasure' or suffering. It will help to consider this claim against the backdrop of Schopenhauer's conception of suffering in terms of frustration or resistance to satisfaction: 'We call its [=the will's] hindrance through an obstacle placed between it and its temporary goal, *suffering* [Leiden]' (WWR, I §56; p. 309). Suffering is the experience of frustration. Schopenhauer is himself both a psychological and an ethical hedonist: the ultimate motivation of human beings is to avoid suffering. In this respect, Nietzsche radically departs from his erstwhile mentor:

Human beings do not seek pleasure and avoid displeasure. . . . What human beings want, what every smallest organism wants, is an increase of power; driven by that will they seek resistance, they need something that opposes it [*aus jenem Willen heraus sucht er nach Widerstand, braucht er Etwas, das sich entgegenstellt*]—Displeasure, as an obstacle to their will to power, is therefore a normal fact . . . ; human beings do not avoid it, they are rather in continual need of it. . . . (WP 702; cf. 656)

The will to power, insofar as it is a desire for the overcoming of resistance, must necessarily also include a desire for the resistance to overcome. Since suffering is the experience of such resistance, then he who desires power *ipso facto* 'desires displeasure.'

That the satisfaction of the will to power requires dissatisfaction is a consequence of its being a desire for the confrontation and overcoming of *resistance*. It is worth pointing out that Nietzsche sometimes attributes a different motivation to the search for resistance. It would be the expression of 'a soul that *has*, but *wants* to want and will [*die habende [Seele], welche ins Wollen und Verlangen will*]' (EH, III 'Thus Spoke Zarathustra'

---

[10] I discuss this difficult issue in detail, and criticize existing interpretations, in Reginster (2006: 126–32).

6), that is to say, of a desire to *desire*. To satisfy this (second-order) desire to have (first-order) determinate desires requires that there be resistance to the satisfaction of the latter since, as Nietzsche remarks, '*wanting* to have always comes to an end with *having*' (GS 363).

And this account of the desire for resistance might suggest that the dissatisfaction it causes need not be a source of displeasure, of a *feeling* of dissatisfaction. The courtly lover, for example, simply wants to enjoy the stirrings of his desire for his beloved, but does not particularly care to satisfy it. Indeed, he defers its gratification for as long as possible, and seems rather disappointed when it can no longer be postponed. He therefore appears able to fulfill his desire to desire, and be thoroughly contented by it.[11] The view of desire on which this interpretation of courtly love rests, however, is simply confused. For it assumes that it is possible to desire to have desires without also being moved to pursue their determinate objects. The confusion bears on the nature of what it is to have a desire: to have a desire just *is* to be moved to satisfy it. I cannot have a desire for some determinate object and be indifferent to its possession. In other words, I cannot have a desire and not somehow suffer from its frustration. Hence, the desire to desire cannot be satisfied without causing the agent significant displeasure, for its satisfaction requires that the agent have an unsatisfied desire.

Nietzsche himself makes this very point about the nature of desire indirectly, I believe, in the following aphorism: 'In the end one loves one's desire and not what is desired' (BGE 175). He famously urges considerable caution in our handling of such aphorisms: we are to read them very 'slowly' (D, Preface 5), indeed to 'ruminate' them (GM, Preface 8), which suggests that their surface meaning should not be taken at face value. The surface meaning of the present aphorism relies precisely on the confused view of desire I am now considering—that we can ultimately want the stirrings of desire, but not care for its object. Careful reading is meant to reveal, I think, that the aphorism cannot be literally true. The desire to have desires (the 'love' of one's desire) is the desire to be stirred by some desire. But one cannot be stirred by a desire unless one actually cares about (one might say 'loves') its determinate object. As a consequence, one cannot 'love one's desire' without also loving 'what is desired.'

So, seeking resistance to the satisfaction of determinate desires is motivated both by the desire to confront and overcome resistance and by the desire to have such determinate desires. The first of these two motivating desires is clearly implied by the will to power understood as the desire for the confrontation and overcoming of resistance. The will to power, to be sure, also requires a determinate desire to confer on this resistance a determinate content. But wanting resistance to the satisfaction of this

---

[11] Some of Nietzsche's own musings about love in GS 363 wrestle with this very issue and the view he describes there finds particular resonance with the medieval ideal of 'courtly love,' which exercised considerable influence on romantic thinkers. See Hunt (1994: 131–44).

determinate desire not just to confront and overcome it but to defer this satisfaction (and thus keep the desire alive) for as long as possible is not so clearly implied by the will to power. We therefore need further explanation.

As it turns out, Nietzsche suggests that it is in the very nature of the will to power that the individual who pursues it might actually be inclined to defer the satisfaction of the determinate desire in connection with which it is pursued. Thus, at the end of a section in which he characterizes the love a man has for a woman in terms that evoke his concept of the will to power, Nietzsche offers the following observation: 'It is actually man's more refined and suspicious lust for possession that rarely admits his "having," and then only late, and thus permits his love to persist' (GS 363). Love is understood here as a 'lust for possession,' and the paradoxical suggestion is that a man should, insofar as he is 'refined' in his pursuit of it, postpone its gratification for as long as possible precisely in order to permit his love to persist. In other words, it would appear that the satisfaction of the will to power should be deferred because it brings about its dissatisfaction. To see how this is possible, we should consider again the structure of this peculiar desire.

The two features of the will to power I have been describing—that its satisfaction requires that the agent desire something else than power, and that its satisfaction implies displeasure—combine to give the will to power a complex, indeed paradoxical structure, of which Nietzsche is keenly aware. The will to power is a will to the overcoming of resistance. Since resistance is always defined in relation to determinate ends, the desire for resistance to overcome cannot be satisfied unless the agent also desires these determinate ends. For obstacles to the realization of these ends will not count as resistance for the agent unless he actually desires these ends. Yet, in willing power, he must also desire resistance to their realization. And so the agent who wills power must want *both* certain determinate ends *and* resistance to their realization: 'That I must be struggle and a becoming and *an end and an opposition to ends* [Zweck und der Zwecke Widerspruch][12]—ah, whoever guesses what is my will should also guess on what *crooked* paths it must proceed' (Z, II 12; first emphasis mine).

A passage from the notebooks articulates an even more radical version of this paradox:

---

[12] The term *Widerspruch* used here usually denotes a conceptual or rational opposition, as in contradicting a claim or rejecting an endorsement. It thus differs from the term *Widerstand*, which Nietzsche uses to denote the resistance to the realization of an end. In the present passage, then, Nietzsche appears to claim that willing power implies endorsing an end and rejecting it at the same time—instead of desiring both the end and obstacles to its realization. Note, however, that willing an end and obstacles to its realization is tantamount to endorsing the end and rejecting it, for one cannot coherently endorse an end and will opposition to its realization. Thus, anticipating the example of a competitive game, I want to win the game, but at the same time, I want strong opponents, who will jeopardize my ability to win the game, and this latter desire may seem to contradict the first.

It is *not* the satisfaction of the will that causes pleasure (I want to fight this superficial theory—the absurd psychological counterfeiting of the nearest things—), but rather the will's forward thrust and again and again becoming master over that which stands in its way. The feeling of pleasure lies precisely in the dissatisfaction of the will, in the fact that the will is never satisfied unless it has opponents and resistance. (WP 696; cf. 656; GS 56)

The language strongly suggests that Nietzsche has Schopenhauer in mind, who holds the view that the 'feeling of pleasure' depends on the satisfaction of desires (WWR, I 58). In this context, the central claim of this passage is, I believe, clear enough: 'the will is not satisfied unless it is [dissatisfied] ("unless it has opponents and resistance").' By contraposition, the claim is that the satisfaction of the will to power implies dissatisfaction. At first glance, this passage simply appears to reproduce the paradox just discussed. The satisfaction of the will to power implies *some* dissatisfaction insofar as willing power implies willing to have determinate desires *and* resistance to their satisfaction. Thus, an agent's will to power is satisfied when he has determinate desires that are dissatisfied (when there is resistance against their satisfaction).

Upon closer examination, however, the present passage invites a stronger reading: the satisfaction of the will to power implies *its own* dissatisfaction. How might we make sense of this stronger version of the paradox? To do so, we must first remember that the will to power is not a bare desire to desire, which would amount to a desire for some determinate end and for resistance to its realization. The will to power is rather the desire for the *overcoming* of resistance in the pursuit of a determinate desire. The will to power will not be satisfied, therefore, unless three conditions are met: there is some first-order desire for a determinate end, there is resistance to the realization of this determinate end, *and* there is actual success in overcoming this resistance. But then, the conditions of the satisfaction of the will to power do indeed imply its dissatisfaction. The overcoming of resistance eliminates it, but the presence of such resistance is a necessary condition of satisfaction of the will to power. Hence, the satisfaction of the will to power implies its own dissatisfaction, in the sense that it necessarily brings it about.

The Greek '*agon*' (contest or competition) (KSA, I, pp. 783–92; cf. D 38; TI, II 8; IX 23) is one of Nietzsche's favorite metaphors to describe the pursuit of power. Nietzsche favors it because it helps to bring out the paradox of will to power. The protagonists of a competitive game are not really playing unless they care about winning and do everything they can to achieve victory. This simply follows from the fact that their motivation for playing the game is the will to power, namely, a desire for the *overcoming* of resistance: if they were to lose, their will to power would be frustrated, since they would have failed to overcome resistance. But in achieving victory they also deprive themselves of a game, frustrating thereby their desire to play: 'Alas, who was not vanquished in his victory?' (Z, III 12[30])

What is the implication of this stronger paradox for the pursuit of power? Nietzsche describes it in the following terms: 'Whatever I create and however much I love it—soon I must oppose it and my love; thus my will wills it.' (Z, II 12) He who wills power must not, strictly speaking, destroy what he has created, or hate what he loved. Rather, he must 'overcome' what he loved or created. His will to power soon induces him to find any given creative achievement, any attained object of a determinate desire, no longer satisfying, no longer enough. The agent in pursuit of power seeks not *achievements*, so to speak, but *achieving*. But he cannot simply undo what he has done and do it again: since the resistance to doing it has been overcome already, overcoming it again would no longer count as genuine achieving. What he needs are fresh, new, perhaps greater challenges. And this explains why the pursuit of power assumes the form of *growth*, or *self-overcoming* (WP 125; cf. 704; Z, II 12).

In claiming that the satisfaction of the will to power brings about its dissatisfaction, then, Nietzsche is not saying that the pursuit of the will to power is self-defeating or self-undermining. It is plainly possible to satisfy the will to power—one only has to engage in the successful overcoming of resistance. What I have called the strong paradox of the will to power is meant to reveal one of its most distinctive features, namely that it is a kind of desire that does not allow for *permanent* (once-and-for-all) satisfaction. Its pursuit, on the contrary, necessarily assumes the form of an indefinite, perpetually renewed striving (cf. GS 310). Insatiability is an essential feature of the will to power.

The analysis of the will to power I have just developed explains why it is tempting, if misleading, to define power in terms of control or domination. Increased control or domination may be natural and frequent 'consequences' of the pursuit of power. Any successful effort to overcome resistance does indeed result in some sort of increased control and domination, be it the domination of an opponent in a competitive game, or the mastery of a skill or discipline. But, as I have argued, it would be a mistake to see in this common and perhaps necessary consequence of the pursuit of power its very essence.[13]

II. The Value of Power and the Ethics of Creativity

For Nietzsche, power is not simply the object of a peculiar desire, it is also a good:

What is good?—All that heightens the feeling of power, the will to power, power itself in man. . . . What is happiness?—The feeling that power *increases*—that a resistance is overcome

---

[13] It is worth noting that Nietzsche himself invites confusion (and indeed, the widespread misinterpretation of power in terms of domination and control) when, in his famous example of GM I, he fails to distinguish between two senses of the desire for 'power'—namely, the (first-order) desire for (political) domination and control and the (second-order) desire for the overcoming of resistance in the pursuit of this first-order desire.

[*dass ein Widerstand überwunden wird*]. *Not* contentment, but more power; *not* peace at all, but war; *not* virtue but proficiency (virtue in the Renaissance style, *virtù*, virtue free of moralic acid).   (A 2)

But what sort of good is power? Nietzsche offers a crucial hint in the following passage:

A tablet of the good hangs over every people. Behold, it is the tablet of their overcomings; behold, it is the voice of their will to power. Praiseworthy is whatever seems difficult to a people; whatever seems indispensable and difficult is called good; and whatever liberates even out of the deepest need, the rarest, the most difficult—that they call holy.   (Z, I 15)

Nietzsche observes here that we take the *difficulty* of an achievement to contribute to its value. And he claims that this is the implication of a commitment to the value of power, understood as the overcoming of resistance. At its core, an ethics whose principle is the will to power is intended to reflect the value we place on what is difficult or, as we might prefer to say, challenging.

Precisely what role does the difficulty of an achievement play in its evaluation? Nietzsche is less than ideally explicit on this issue, but I am inclined to attribute the following view to him: the difficulty of an achievement gives it a *special* and *conditional* value, which he calls 'greatness.' An achievement cannot be *great* unless it was also challenging. To say that greatness is a special value is to say that an achievement could fail to be great, insofar as it was not particularly challenging, but still be valuable in respect to its determinate content. And to say that greatness is a conditional value is to say that an achievement can be great only if it is valuable in respect to its determinate content.

Nietzsche must regard greatness as both a special and a conditional value if he wishes to rule out calling great achievements that are frivolous or appalling simply because they were very difficult (such as, for example, the Holocaust). In implying that the greatness of an achievement is conditioned by the value of its determinate content (that is to say, the value of the object of the determinate first-order desire in terms of which the content of the resistance to be overcome is defined), this view naturally raises the following question: What are the standards bearing on the evaluation of the determinate content of an achievement? Nietzsche is sometimes thought to incline toward the following proposal. The value of a determinate project is a function of the degree of resistance that is likely to arise to its realization: 'You say it is the good cause that hallows even war? I say unto you: it is the good war that hallows any cause' (Z, I 10; cf. WP 674, 855). This would make the degree of difficulty of an achievement a *necessary and sufficient* condition of the degree of its *overall* value, since the latter would now be defined in terms of the former. Supposing that degrees of difficulty could actually be established with adequate precision, it remains very uncertain that this line of argument would necessarily rule out undesirable results. The Holocaust, to use again this most disturbing example, is in fact likely to be far more difficult than the invention of new musical forms or than many scientific discoveries, for instance, in which case it would have to be deemed better overall.

I actually believe that Nietzsche did not offer a developed answer to this question probably because it was not required by what I take to be his overall philosophical project.[14] Accordingly, I will therefore assume here that the difficulty of an achievement is a necessary condition of its being great. It is not sufficient for greatness, however, because the determinate content of the achievement must itself be valuable. But Nietzsche, whose focus is on the value of overcoming resistance, leaves open the question of what standards should be brought to bear on the evaluation of the determinate content of achievements.

The particular value Nietzsche's concept of the will to power is intended to capture, then, is *greatness*. And greatness is for him the fundamental value of an ethics of *creativity*: the 'really great men, according to my understanding,' Nietzsche writes, are 'men of great creativity' (WP 957). To appreciate this claim, we must first understand what he means by creativity. A quick initial analysis reveals that this concept is ambiguous. On the one hand, creativity denotes a special skill or ability possessed by some individuals, something like the inventiveness they display in resolving problems or overcoming difficulties. As such, creativity has an essentially *instrumental* value: it helps us to achieve our ends. Individuals who are creative in this sense are simply good at creative activity, but they do not necessarily value it for its own sake. Such individuals prove creatively resourceful in taking on whatever difficulties might present themselves to them, but they do not necessarily relish them or seek them out. On the other hand, individuals are sometimes said to be creative when they value creative activity *as an end*. The individual who is creative in this sense will deliberately seek out opportunities for creative activity in the form of limitations to challenge, difficulties to overcome, or boundaries to transgress.

We typically attribute creativity to artists, of course, but also to individuals engaged in many other kinds of activity: scientists, scholars, businessmen, politicians, and the like. Nietzsche emphasizes the case of artistic creativity because artists are not simply inventive individuals who overcome limitations or difficulties only when they have to, but because they value creative activity itself and so deliberately look for them. The artist is, by his very nature, creative not only in the first sense but in the second as well, and this is the sense in which creativity is a manifestation of the will to power. Although artists are paradigmatically creative in this sense, I should note that there is no reason why scientists, scholars, businessmen, politicians, and the like, could not be as well.

---

[14] I argue that this project is the overcoming of nihilism, for the realization of which Nietzsche only needs to establish the value of power, in Reginster (2006: 181–2).

To think of creativity in terms of the will to power has a number of surprising practical implications for the life of the creative individual. And a significant portion of Nietzsche's ethical investigations actually consist in uncovering and spelling out these implications. In the remainder of the essay, I propose to examine the most salient (and perhaps also the most disconcerting) among them:

1. The valuation of creativity implies a radical revaluation of the role and significance of suffering in human existence.
2. The valuation of creativity implies a valuation of loss (and of destruction in a qualified sense).
3. The valuation of creativity implies a valuation of impermanence (specifically, the impossibility of a final, once-and-for-all satisfaction).
4. The valuation of creativity implies an acceptance of the inevitability of ultimate failure.

II.1 Creativity and Suffering

Nietzsche argues that the value we grant creativity implies a *radical* revaluation of the role and significance of suffering in human existence: it is not merely unavoidable, nor simply instrumentally valuable, as even Nietzsche's Christian predecessors might concede, but it is valuable for its own sake (cf. WP 1041, 1052; EH, II 10). To appreciate the nature of this radical revaluation, we must attend to the relationship between suffering and creativity. It has almost become a commonplace to regard suffering as a condition of creativity, a commonplace Nietzsche wholeheartedly endorses: 'Creation—that is the great redemption from all suffering, and life's growing light. But that the creator may be, suffering is needed [*dass der Schaffende sei, dazu selber thut Leid noth*]' (Z, II 2). His view is distinctive and original, however, precisely in the manner in which it conceives of the nature of this relation.

The commonplace suggests that suffering is a necessary condition of creativity. Supposing this is so, it is still not clear that this fact would suffice to justify a radical revaluation of suffering. We might, for example, imagine Beethoven (Nietzsche's paradigmatic example of a great creative individual) compelled to suffer for the sake of his creativity because he lived in a conservative society, in which creative individuals were isolated, or even opposed and persecuted. This Beethoven could coherently deplore his suffering, even as he acknowledged its necessity for the sake of creativity, and aspire to a world in which one does not have to suffer in order to be creative. He could, in other words, continue to subscribe to the condemnation of suffering, yet without abandoning his commitment to the value of creativity.

If the value we ascribe to creativity is to underwrite a radical revaluation of suffering, we need a specific explanation for the view that suffering is a necessary condition of creativity. It is tempting to regard creativity as a good that 'redeems' suffering in the sense that it compensates or makes up for it. This rather common view does not require a revaluation of suffering at all, which is still understood as something that is to be deplored and demands compensation. The appeal to the value of creativity underwrites a radical revaluation of suffering only if we assume an altogether different sort of relation between suffering and creativity.

Thinking of creativity in terms of will to power enables us to do just that. If creativity is a paradigmatic instance of the will to power, then suffering, in the form of resistance, proves to be an essential *ingredient* of creative activity. Nietzsche's characterization of creativity in terms of power shows that it is no accident that one must suffer in order to be creative: he who wants to be creative must welcome resistance, and therefore suffering, for overcoming resistance is precisely what creativity *consists in*. Suffering is no longer a necessary evil to which the creative individual must somehow accommodate himself, it is an essential component of his ideal of creativity.

It is precisely insofar as it implies a radical revaluation of suffering that Nietzsche's ethics of creativity underwrites his famed attack on morality. As Nietzsche understands it, morality, paradigmatically the 'morality of compassion' (GM, Preface 5), is predicated upon a wholesale condemnation of suffering (BGE 225; GS 338). As such, it fosters an ethical climate that is essentially inimical to creativity:

Such men of great creativity, the really great men according to my understanding, will be sought in vain today and probably for a long time to come; until, after much disappointment, one must begin to comprehend *why* they are lacking and that nothing stands more malignantly in the way of their rise and evolution, today and for a long time to come, than what in Europe today is called simply 'morality'—as if there were no other morality and could be no other—the aforementioned herd-animal morality which is striving with all its power for a universal green-pasture happiness on earth, namely for security, absence of danger, comfort, the easy life.... The two doctrines it preaches most often are: 'equal rights' and 'sympathy with all that suffers'—and it takes suffering itself to be something that must absolutely be abolished.   (WP 957; cf. Z, I 12; BGE 44, 212; GM, Preface 6)

The revaluation of suffering is grounded in the claim that the difficulty of an achievement, or the fact that it requires overcoming of resistance, is an essential part of what makes it a great achievement. I should add, then, that if the value Nietzsche grants creativity is to justify suffering, then creative achievements must be not only *objectively*, but also *subjectively* difficult—they must be a cause of *felt* suffering. But we cannot assume that what is objectively difficult will always be subjectively difficult as well. Some of Beethoven's musical creations might have been objectively difficult, though relatively easy for someone with his ability. But Nietzsche is considering individuals who live their lives in accordance with his ethics of creativity. Their commitment to creativity will induce these individuals to seek ever greater challenges, some of which will eventually prove subjectively difficult even for those who possess exceptional abilities. And so, suffering proves to be an ineliminable ingredient of the creative life.

The idea that the greatness of an achievement depends upon the degree of its difficulty raises a number of important questions, two of which we need to consider here. The first question is the following: Is the difficulty that contributes to the greatness of an achievement *absolute* or *relative*? Specifically, is that difficulty a function of the strength or weakness of particular agents, or not? Does what is difficult to some who are relatively weak contribute to the greatness of their achievement, if it is not difficult (or not as difficult) to others, who are relatively stronger? Since the difficulty of an achievement consists of the degree of resistance against it, the issue is here simply that of the relation between resistance, on the one hand, and strength and weakness, on the other. We might be tempted to accept two claims about this relation. The first (A) is that resistance is relative to the strength or weakness of the agent—in other words, what is high resistance to a weak agent is low resistance to a strong agent. The second (B) is that strength and weakness designate agents' relative capacities to overcome resistance.

Taken together, these two claims have one problematic implication, namely that no achievement can ever be truly great. Any successful achievement demonstrates that the agent had the capacity to overcome resistance to it. This shows—by B—that the agent was strong. Now, this also shows—by A—that the resistance to this achievement was low, since resistance is relative to the agent's capacity to overcome it. Any achievement that was not difficult is not a great achievement. Hence, no achievement can ever be great.

Nietzsche, who clearly believes that some achievements are genuinely great, must find this implication unacceptable, and therefore reject either A or B. He urges us to reject A, for it has, in and of itself, an unacceptable implication as well, namely that the same achievement could be both great and not great. According to A, what constitutes high resistance for the weak would not constitute high resistance for the strong. Accordingly, the same achievement would be great for the weak (insofar as they would have had to overcome higher resistance for it), but not so great for the strong. Once again, Nietzsche, whose ethical elitism is no secret, would most certainly reject this implication. By contrast, B is eminently plausible, for it is hard to see what strength and weakness could possibly be, if they are not defined in connection with the capacity to overcome resistance: 'The strength of those who attack,' Nietzsche observes, 'can be measured in a way by the opposition they require' (EH, I 7). Hence, we must conclude that resistance is not a function of the strength and weakness of individuals, but should be defined independently of them.

A second important question raised by the ethics of creativity is the following: What sort of difficulty is relevant to value—only the difficulty *intrinsic* to the nature of the achievement, or perhaps also difficulties *extrinsic* to it? By intrinsic difficulty or resistance, I mean resistance that has two characteristics. First, it is *pertinent* insofar as it is created by the specific requirements of the determinate end one pursues. Second, it is *essential*, insofar as it is resistance anyone who engages in the pursuit of this end would have to confront, regardless of his or her particular circumstances. For example, Beethoven's musical achievements had to overcome the intrinsic resistance involved in breaking with traditional harmony, developing new forms of musical expression, struggling to articulate complex new musical ideas, and so on. These difficulties are pertinent, since they belong to the very nature of musical innovation, and also essential since anyone who tries himself at it will have to face them.

By extrinsic resistance, I have in mind two types of obstacles. First, some obstacles are *non-essential*, but still *pertinent* to the pursuit of a determinate end. For example, Beethoven's deafness constituted a resistance to his ability to write music that is pertinent, insofar as it is created by the requirements of musical composition (a mathematician, for example, might not be comparably affected by deafness). But it is also accidental, insofar as it is not an obstacle any composer would have to face. Second, some obstacles are *neither essential nor pertinent* to the pursuit of the determinate end. Obstacles of this sort might include Beethoven's precarious financial situation, his loneliness, the recalcitrance of a conservative public to his innovations, or the opposition of conflicting aspirations to his desire to write music. Do both kinds of resistance make a contribution to the greatness of Beethoven's achievement? And if both do make contributions, are they similar or different? It helps, to get the issue into focus, to consider the following case. Suppose that two composers (Beethoven being one of them) produce roughly similar and equivalent pieces of music (let us assume), but while one managed to compose his piece only through considerable labor, the other produced his with relative ease. Although the content of their creative achievements is identical, producing it proved considerably more difficult for one than for the other. Does this make a difference to the greatness of their respective achievements? How we answer this question crucially depends, I think, on the nature of the difficulty the first composer had to overcome.

It may appear that, because the content of the composition is roughly similar and equivalent, the degree of intrinsic resistance that had to be overcome must also be similar. But matters might not be so simple, for the intrinsic difficulty of an achievement may well *not* be the same for both composers. Thus, it certainly was a greater achievement for Beethoven to write his kind of music *when he did* (given the technical development of his medium, the musical sensibilities of his time, and so on) than it would be for someone *today* to write music of the same kind and quality as Beethoven's (which may explain why we regard mere imitation, however skillful, as a defect in a work of art). This implies that what counts here as the creative achievement might consist of more than just the *end-product* (the particular piece of music), and include something of the *circumstances* of its composition. In this case, we would be inclined, it seems, to treat them as *different* achievements that nonetheless have similar contents. So, the intrinsic difficulty of an achievement may be seen as relative to the circumstances of the achievement, provided we do not include among these circumstances the strength or weakness of the individual achiever.

Suppose now that the intrinsic difficulty was the same for both composers, and that the only difference lay in the degree of extrinsic difficulty they had to confront. Does the fact that one composer had to contend with a higher degree of extrinsic difficulty than the other make his creative achievement greater? The presence of extrinsic difficulty does seem to make a difference: for example, our admiration for Beethoven plausibly grows deeper when we learn of his deafness or loneliness. But what sort of evaluative difference does extrinsic difficulty make? It is unlikely to affect our estimation of Beethoven's *music*, which would presumably not have been any less great an achievement if he had turned out not to be deaf or lonely. But it might well influence our estimation of *Beethoven* himself.

We ought to distinguish between a great creative *achievement* and a great creative *individual*. Thus, Beethoven, unlike the second composer of my example who did not have to contend with deafness or loneliness, had to demonstrate certain qualities of character, such as discipline and perseverance, in order to produce his works. And those qualities make him a great *composer*, in the sense that they show that his existing achievements were not a matter of luck and make him likely to produce further works. The second composer could also be a great composer but, as things stand, we have no reason to think so from the sole fact he composed a relevantly similar and equivalent piece of music, since in so doing he did not have to demonstrate the qualities of character that would prepare him to produce further pieces of comparable quality. To be a great composer, great musical achievements are necessary, but they are not sufficient. The presence of certain qualities of character, which make the achievement more than a mere matter of luck, seems also to be required.

Nietzsche's own analysis of the concept of greatness invites us to distinguish between a great creative achievement and a great creative individual. His paradigmatic exemplars of greatness are undeniably individuals distinguished by their *achievements*: the greatness of a Beethoven or a Shakespeare consists in their challenging successfully musical or poetic conventions, in their expanding the expressive resources of their respective media beyond traditional limits, and (perhaps) in their overcoming the inertial resistance of a public accustomed to the very conventions they shatter. But Nietzsche also suggests that what makes these individuals great is not, or not only, such achievements, but a distinctive condition of their *soul*. In the soul of a great individual, many different drives and points of view are unified and organized into a coherent whole: 'The highest man would have the greatest multiplicity of drives, in the relatively greatest strength that can be endured. Indeed, where the plant "man" shows himself strongest one finds instincts that conflict powerfully (e.g., in Shakespeare), but are controlled' (WP 966; cf. 928, 933; BGE 212; TI, IX 49).

Great creative achievements might be necessary to be a great creative individual, but they do not suffice. The deliberate confrontation of resistance by the creative individual is bound to spawn all kinds of resistance within his soul, including decidedly extrinsic resistance, in the form of fear of isolation, insecurity, discouragement, or conflicting aspirations. For creative greatness to be possible, then, the drives expressed in these forms of resistance must be mastered—the individual must overcome or manage the ever greater psychological tensions his pursuit of ever greater challenges will inevitably generate (cf. BGE 257; cf. Z, III 12[19]). In other words, if a given great creative achievement is to be more than a mere matter of luck, a great creative individual, or an individual with a great soul, is required.

II.2 Creativity and Loss (and Destruction)

The creative individual, according to Nietzsche, must leave behind the products of particular spells of creative activity in order to seek new opportunities for creation: 'Whatever I create and however much I love it—soon I must oppose it and my love: thus my will wills it' (Z, II 12). Curiously, Nietzsche's very terminology here suggests that this opposition to one's realized creative goals will be ambivalent at best: we do not love them less for having to oppose them. This might seem perplexing, for to value creativity is to value less the particular products of creation than creative activity itself. If the good is the activity rather than its final products, then the creator should have no qualm leaving them behind, inasmuch as they mark the end of particular spells of creative activity. Instead, Nietzsche goes so far as to describe the creative life, insofar as it demands the abandonment of old creative achievements, as filled with 'bitter dying', with the experience of *loss*.

This claim does not go without saying. Must the creative individual actually care about the determinate ends of his creative endeavors (the 'works') and, as a consequence, necessarily experience leaving them behind as a loss? Could he not regard the determinate ends in connection to which he exercises his creative faculties as mere opportunities for the bare overcoming of resistance? Could he, for example, relish the difficulties of musical composition, while caring not really about music, but only about exercising his creative faculties? In this view, it would not matter *what* he overcomes resistance *for*, so long as he overcomes resistance. And his desire to overcome resistance would motivate him to pick some determinate end—*any* determinate end—as a mere opportunity for overcoming. He would not experience the technical difficulties of musical composition as resistance because he cares about music, but he would care about music only because it allows him to define some resistance against which he can exercise his creative faculties.

This is a difficult issue, but I can find in Nietzsche two possible grounds for justifying the ambivalence of the creative individual toward his own creative achievements, that is to say, his continuing to love the achievements he must also oppose. First, I have suggested earlier that, for Nietzsche, creative activity requires that I actually *desire* some determinate end besides creativity itself. I do not genuinely participate in the activity of overcoming resistance if I do not care about the determinate end in terms of which the content of that resistance is defined. The metaphor of the *agon*, the competitive game, is illuminating in this respect. When I *contemplate* taking part in such a game, I may care only about participation, about exercising my faculties in playing the game. But genuine *participation* in the game requires that I actually care about winning—indeed, genuine participation in the game is arguably *constituted* by my desire to win.

The same goes, in Nietzsche's view, for creative activity in general: I do not genuinely engage in it unless I care about its determinate end. It may be possible, through some form of psychological manipulation, to induce in myself a desire for some particular end. But the point is that, whatever its source, my desire for that end is a necessary condition of full participation and enjoyment in the activity of overcoming resistance in order to achieve it. The initial desire for this determinate end, and the subsequent efforts deployed in pursuing it presumably presuppose and foster an attachment to it. Hence, the creative individual cannot love creative activity without loving the particular ends of this activity, the works themselves. But his very love of creative activity also requires him to leave behind his creative achievements, to 'oppose' them. The creative individual must both love and leave his creations—he can never rest content with one particular creative achievement without renouncing thereby his commitment to creativity itself.

It is worth remarking that the motivation for surpassing one's own prior creative achievements is not, in the ethics of creativity I am articulating here, a consequence of the *perfectionism* that is so often attributed to Nietzsche.[15] If Nietzsche's ethics of creativity were a perfectionist ethics, then creative individuals should be judged by the degree to which they approximate an ideal of creative perfection, or a maximal standard of achievement. The individual who embraces such an ethics would soon come to see that his existing achievements, though they may themselves be closer to this ideal of perfection than earlier achievements, still fall short of it, and should therefore be destroyed or left behind to make room for new ones that approximate it even more closely.

---

[15] Surprisingly influential in spreading this interpretation of Nietzsche's ethics is Rawls (1971: 25). Rawls is particularly worried by the anti-democratic consequences of the elitism that seems to trail in the wake of this perfectionism. This elitism is also a central concern of those who follow Rawls in attributing perfectionism to Nietzsche. For a critical discussion of this view and a defense of perfectionism in Nietzsche's early essay, *Schopenhauer as Educator*, see Conant (2001).

This perfectionist reading is inspired by Nietzsche's calls for the achievement of 'the *highest power and splendor* actually possible to the type man' (GM, Preface 6), or for the 'enhancement [*Erhöhung*]' of man (BGE 225), and by passages like the following: 'Joy in destruction of the most noble and at the sight of its progressive ruin: in reality joy in what is coming and lies in the future, which triumphs over existing things, however good' (WP 417). The destruction seems here motivated by the hope of a future greater good. Close examination shows that the perfectionist reading of this passage is highly questionable. We should note, in the first place, how destructiveness does *not* seem here motivated by the shortcomings of its objects (which Nietzsche pointedly characterizes as 'the *most* noble,' and 'existing things, *however good*'). And if we ask Nietzsche, in the second place, what 'is coming and lies in the future,' he remains disappointingly elusive: the advent of an undefined 'new dawn' or of the no less enigmatic 'overman.' This apparent lack of determinate content has invited the conjecture that Nietzsche deliberately refrained from advocating a substantive ethics. Much of the argument of the present essay suggests, on the contrary, that interpretations of this sort look for Nietzsche's substantive ethical pronouncements in the wrong places.

We take joy, he declares, 'in what is coming . . . , which triumphs over existing things, however good'—in other words, we enjoy the endless process of overcoming in which the pursuit of the will to power necessarily consists. It is not that existing achievements are not good, and could be improved on, it is rather that our will to power insatiably impels us to move on to further creative opportunities. This focus on the future is thus less an expectation of future perfection than the affirmation of *becoming* itself: 'The affirmation of passing away *and destroying*, which is the decisive feature of a Dionysian philosophy; saying Yes to opposition and war; *becoming*, along with a radical repudiation of the very concept of *being*' (EH, III 'The Birth of Tragedy' 3; cf. TI, X 5). Insofar as great creative individuals, and indeed Nietzsche himself, continue to employ the rhetoric of perfection, it is not a shortcoming of his view, but a crucial requirement of it, that the standard of perfection should remain devoid of determinate content: it represents the indeterminate and ever-receding objective of an essentially insatiable creative impulse that is valued for its own sake.[16]

It is the commitment to creativity, not the commitment to some ideal of perfection, that motivates Nietzsche's creative individual to 'oppose' his existing creative achievements. In fact, if he were motivated by a commitment to perfection, he arguably could not coherently continue to 'love' these achievements, since this

---

[16] I argue for the view that the concept of the 'overman,' which is one of the keystones of the perfectionist reading, operates in just this way in Nietzsche's introduction of it in *Thus Spoke Zarathustra*. I therefore maintain that it is no surprise that perfectionist interpretations of this notion, such as the recent one offered by Gooding-Williams (2001: 65), manage to provide no clear substantive characterization of it. See Reginster (2006: 250–1).

commitment would compel him to focus on their shortcomings. It is because it is motivated by a commitment to creativity itself that the creative individual's opposition to his existing creative achievements remains compatible with his continuing love for them.

Consider, in this connection, Nietzsche's analysis of the peculiar destructiveness he so often associates with creativity. The creative individual must 'destroy' past creative achievements—and to destroy here might plausibly mean to surpass, supplant, or make obsolete, as much as actually to dismantle or annihilate—and he must learn to enjoy this destructiveness, but he must not be motivated by contempt for, or condemnation of, what he destroys: it must be 'joy in destruction *of the most noble*' or in triumphing 'over existing things, *however good.*' (WP 417, my emphases; cf. GM, II 24; EH III, 'The Birth of Tragedy' 3). This is a plausible feature of the creative life: Beethoven did not have to despise Haydn's musical achievements to seek to surpass them, and indeed, as I suggested earlier, he did not require disenchantment with his own earlier works as an inducement to write later ones.

In fact, the commitment to creativity is not simply compatible with the creative individual's continuing love for the achievements he must oppose, it arguably also *demands* it. This brings us to the second ground Nietzsche offers for the claim that the creative individual must love the creative achievements he must also oppose. The greatness of an achievement is a function of the degree or the quality of the resistance it is required to overcome. Accordingly, the great creative individual will seek out great creative challenges, and this often means aiming to surpass existing achievements: the greater the existing achievement, the greater the challenge of surpassing it. Thus, Zarathustra exhorts his disciples to 'have eyes that always seek an enemy' (Z, I 10), but he also gives them the following recommendation: 'For the worthier enemy, O my friends, you shall save yourselves; therefore you must pass by much' (Z, III 12[21]). The worthier the enemy, the greater—or, as Nietzsche also likes to say, the 'nobler'—the achievement of vanquishing him: 'How much reverence has a noble man for his enemies! . . . For he desires his enemy for himself, as his mark of distinction; he can endure no other enemy than one in whom there is nothing to despise and *very much* to honor!' (GM, I 10; cf. III 7; EH, I 7; WP 770). Insofar as he admires the very achievements he surpasses, the creative individual should presumably regard his surpassing them with some measure of ambivalence.

II.3 Creativity and Impermanence

Valuing creativity is valuing a specific type of activity, that of confronting and overcoming resistance. The valuation of this sort of activity implies a valuation of becoming and impermanence: 'there must be much bitter dying in your life, you creators. Thus are you advocates and justifiers of all impermanence' (Z, II 2). The reason for this is once again to be found in Nietzsche's understanding of creativity in terms of will to power. The will to power, remember, has a paradoxical structure: its satisfaction brings about its own dissatisfaction. To satisfy the desire for the activity of overcoming resistance in the pursuit of some determinate end, one must be moved to achieve that determinate end, that is to say, overcome all the resistance to its realization. But once that resistance is overcome, the activity comes to a close, and the desire for this sort of activity finds itself frustrated, and induces the individual to seek out new opportunities for it. The will to power is a kind of desire that does not allow for *permanent* (once-and-for-all) satisfaction. Its pursuit, on the contrary, necessarily assumes the form of an indefinite, perpetually renewed striving, or, as Nietzsche likes to put it, of an indefinite 'becoming.'

It is therefore no surprise that his valuation of the creative life leads Nietzsche to claim to have discovered a 'new happiness' (GS, Preface 3). In its traditional conception, happiness is 'the happiness of resting, of not being disturbed, of satiety, of finally attained unity, as a "sabbath of sabbaths" ' (BGE 200). In contrast, the 'new happiness' of Nietzsche's creative individual not only is not a *state* of rest, tranquility, or satiety, but also, by its very nature, it *cannot be* a state at all, for two reasons. First, this form of happiness is experienced in an *activity*, that of confronting and overcoming resistance. And second, it is in the nature of this happiness to be *impermanent*, since the distinctive activity in which it consists necessarily takes the form of an indefinite becoming. For so soon as the resistance to the realization of some determinate end is actually overcome, the activity comes to end, and so does the happiness it brings.

II.4 Creativity and the Inescapability of Ultimate Failure

The last characteristic of the creative life is that it is bound to end in failure. Creative activity is, for Nietzsche, the primary source of what he calls 'joy.' And of joy he declares: 'You higher men, for you it longs, joy, the intractable blessed one—for your woe, you failures. All eternal joy longs for failures. For all joy wants itself, hence it also wants agony' (Z, IV 19[11]). The will to power of the creative individual induces him to seek ever greater or newer challenges, which are bound to subject him to ever greater or newer risks, and given his limited strengths, lead him ultimately to failure and frustration. For it is inevitable that, under the sway of that will, he should eventually be driven to confront limitations he is not strong enough to overcome, and the resistance of which will break or defeat him. And so, in the end, the pursuit of the creative life not only precludes any final, once-and-for-all satisfaction, it is also destined to end in failure.

The inescapability of ultimate failure is precisely what makes the life of the creative individual a *tragic* life. The *Birth of Tragedy* presented Oedipus as a quintessential tragic hero (BT 9), but Nietzsche eventually came to recognize that the true meaning of tragedy was revealed not so much in that book as in *Thus Spoke Zarathustra*. It is, in my view, no coincidence that 'the tragedy begins [*Incipit tragoedia*]' in a book in which the concept of the will to power and the ethics of creativity are introduced for the first time in their full-fledged form (GS 342). To appreciate how the creative life is also, by virtue of being driven by the will to power, a tragic life, we must first identify some of its relevant features.

We get some useful clues to Nietzsche's mature conception of a tragic life from a consideration of two aspects of the story of Oedipus that *The Birth of Tragedy* downplayed.[17] First, Oedipus' life is tragic because it is doomed to a woeful fate. And second, this woeful fate is sealed by his very own decisions and actions, quite specifically his efforts to escape that fate and live a happy life (themselves motivated by what Sophocles calls his *hubris*). Nietzsche's conception of a tragic life possesses analogous features. Like Oedipus, the creative individual is doomed to a woeful fate. And like Oedipus again, he is driven to this fate by his very quest for happiness. But there are important differences.

In the first place, in Nietzsche's view the instrument of fatality is no longer the agent's *hubris*, his conviction that he can escape his fate, but his *will to power*. And in the second place, while the relation of Oedipus' *hubris* to his ineluctable misery is only *accidentally* necessary, the link of the creative individual's will to power to his own woeful fate is *essentially* necessary. It is only by virtue of contingent historical circumstances that Oedipus' decision to leave Corinth and his adoptive parents led him to Thebes and the fatal altercation with his real father Laios. Under different circumstances (for example, if he had come to learn that Laios was his real father), the same decision might not have had the same consequences. In contrast, it is by its very nature that the pursuit of the will to power by an agent with finite strength eventually drives him to failure. For the will to power is essentially insatiable, and it induces the agent to seek out ever newer and greater challenges, meeting which requires ever greater expenditures of strength, until that ineluctable moment when this strength runs out, the resistance can no longer be overcome, and the challenge remains unmet.

Nietzsche's view seems excessive. Surely, it is possible for some individuals never to confront a challenge they cannot meet. For example, they can circumvent quantitative limitations of strength through qualitative variations in the challenges they choose to confront. Or they may simply die before they meet a resistance they cannot overcome (although death itself, on which Nietzsche says surprisingly little, might be considered the ultimate resistance). However, Nietzsche should be assumed to make a point about the *internal logic* of the pursuit of power by agents endowed with finite strength. For these agents, the *prospect* of ineluctable eventual failure, at least, is very real.

---

[17] Nietzsche is primarily focused here on Sophocles' *Oedipus the King*.

The tragic fate to which his very pursuit of the good life—the creative life—dooms the creative individual is therefore ultimate frustration, or self-destruction in a losing struggle. Nevertheless, this tragic fate belongs to the very heart of what makes the creative life desirable to Nietzsche's Zarathustra: 'I love him who wants to create over and beyond himself and thus perishes' (Z, I 17).

Abbreviations

Reference edition of Nietzsche's works: *Friedrich Nietzsche: Sämtliche Werke, Kritische Studienausgabe*, ed. Giorgio Colli und Mazzino Montinari (Berlin: de Gruyter, 1967–77).

A   *The Anti-Christ*, trans. R. J. Hollingdale (Harmondsworth, England: Penguin Books, 1968).

BGE   *Beyond Good and Evil*, trans. W. Kaufmann (New York: Random House, 1966).

BT   *The Birth of Tragedy*, trans. W. Kaufmann (New York: Random House, 1967).

D   *Daybreak*, trans. R. J. Hollingdale (Cambridge, England: Cambridge University Press, 1982).

EH   *Ecce Homo*, trans. W. Kaufmann (New York: Random House, 1969).

GM   *On the Genealogy of Morals*, trans. W. Kaufmann (New York: Random House, 1969). See also: *On the Genealogy of Morality*, trans. M. Clark and A. J. Swensen (Indianapolis: Hackett Publishing Company, 1998).

GS   *The Gay Science*, trans. W. Kaufmann (New York: Random House, 1974).

TI   *The Twilight of the Idols*, trans. R. J. Hollingdale (Harmondsworth, England: Penguin Books, 1968).

WP   *The Will to Power*, trans. W. Kaufmann and R. J. Hollingdale (New York: Random House, 1968).

Z   *Thus Spoke Zarathustra*, trans. W. Kaufmann (Harmondsworth, England: Penguin Books, 1978).

WWR   A. Schopenhauer, *The World as Will and Representation* i–ii, trans. E. F. J. Payne (New York: Dover Publications, 1969).

References

CLARK, MAUDEMARIE (1990). *Nietzsche on Truth and Philosophy* (Cambridge: Cambridge University Press).

CONANT, JAMES (2001). 'Nietzsche's Perfectionism: A Reading of *Schopenhauer as Educator*', in R. Schacht (ed.), *Nietzsche's Post-Moralism: Essays on Nietzsche's Prelude to Philosophy's Future* (Cambridge: Cambridge University Press), 181–257.

GOODING-WILLIAMS, Robert (2001). *Zarathustra's Dionysian Modernism* (Stanford: Stanford University Press).

HUNT, MORTON (1994). *The Natural History of Love* (New York: Anchor Books, Doubleday).

KAUFMANN, WALTER (1974). *Nietzsche: Philosopher, Psychologist, Antichrist* (Princeton: Princeton University Press).

LARMORE, CHARLES (1996). *The Morals of Modernity* (Cambridge: Cambridge University Press).

LEITER, BRIAN (2002). *Nietzsche on Morality* (London: Routledge).

NEHAMAS, ALEXANDER (1985). *Nietzsche: Life as Literature* (Cambridge, Mass.: Harvard University Press).

REGINSTER, BERNARD (2006). *The Affirmation of Life* (Cambridge, Mass.: Harvard University Press).

RAWLS, JOHN (1971). *A Theory of Justice* (Cambridge, Mass.: Harvard University Press).

RICHARDSON, JOHN (1996). *Nietzsche's System* (Oxford: Oxford University Press).

SOPHOCLES (1982). *Oedipus the King*, trans. R. Bagg (Amherst: University of Massachusetts Press).

STERN, J. P. (1979). *A Study of Nietzsche* (Cambridge: Cambridge University Press).

3

Nietzschean 'Animal Psychology' versus Kantian Ethics

Mathias Risse

1. Introduction

1.1   Characterizing the *Genealogy* as an exercise in 'animal psychology' (GM III, 20), Nietzsche pays tribute to the extraordinary cultural impact of the biological sciences, in particular physiology and evolutionary biology, in the second half of the nineteenth century.[1] While much of his mature thinking applies physiological considerations to traditional philosophical problems, he is especially eager to explain in this manner the development of Christian morality and of what he took to be theories derived from it (Kantian ethics and utilitarianism), as well as the development of the kind of person persuaded by such morality. While I am far from claiming that all that is of interest in Nietzsche can be captured from this standpoint, this perspective on him is still under-appreciated. Elsewhere I offer accounts of *guilt* as part of a reading of the second treatise

[1]   For references to and abbreviations of Nietzsche's works, cf. the beginning of the literature references. I am grateful for discussion to audiences at the Harvard moral and political philosophy workshop; at the conference on 'Moral Theory after Nietzsche,' organized by Brian Leiter at the University of Texas in Austin in February 2003 (special thanks to Matt Evans, my commentator); a Nietzsche session at the Central APA, organized by the North American Nietzsche Society, in Cleveland in April 2003; to an audience at a conference of the British Society for Ethical Theory in Belfast in July 2003 (especially Pekka Väyrynen); and to an audience at a workshop on 'Nietzsche and Naturalism' that I organized at Harvard University in November 2004 with the generous support of the Radcliffe Institute of Advanced Study. Thanks to John Richardson for letting me read his unpublished piece 'Nietzschean and Kantian Freedoms.' Thanks to Matt Evans, Beatrix Himmelmann, Jim Kreines, and Brian Leiter for comments.

in the *Genealogy* (Risse 2001), as well as of *ressentiment*, primarily discussed in the first (Risse 2003*b*). Both pieces are meant to support such a reading of Nietzsche. Taking that reading for granted, this essay develops it by clarifying the relationship between Nietzsche and Kant in light of Nietzsche's physiological, hence naturalistic, ideas about morality.[2]

For our purposes, Blackburn's (1998) account of *naturalism* suffices:

> To be a naturalist is to see human beings as frail complexes of perishable tissue, and so part of the natural order. It is thus to refuse unexplained appeals to mind or spirit, and unexplained appeals to knowledge of a Platonic order of Forms or Norms; it is above all to refuse any appeal to a supernatural order.' (pp. 48–9)

Statements of Nietzsche's naturalistic attitude can be found in BGE 230 and A 14, but anyway, this study explores his more specific interest in physiology, rather than

---

[2] (1) Nietzsche's interest in these sciences can be documented as early as *Human All Too Human*, where he suggests that the relationship between the 'true' world and the world as we perceive it must be explained by 'the physiology and evolutionary history of organisms and concepts' (HAH 10). Already in the First Untimely Meditation (UM I, 7), Nietzsche complains that his contemporaries, including David Friedrich Strauss, are reluctant to design a genuinely Darwinian ethics, seriously and consistently carried through. Nietzsche's engagement with the biological sciences is discussed in detail by Moore (2002); cf. also Leiter (2002: ch. 1). Following Moore, my claim above that the perspective on Nietzsche developed in this study is 'still' underappreciated must be qualified: many of Nietzsche's contemporaries and those who read him in the decades after his death understood him along such lines, to such an extent that Heidegger, in his own Nietzsche interpretation, was aware of the need to demarcate his reading from that one (cf. Moore 2002: 6–7). Leiter has done much to make the naturalistic dimensions of Nietzsche's work visible. (2) Nietzsche's fascination with the 'ascetic ideal' (cf. third treatise of GM) is a concern with what he took to be the 'counter-paradigm' to his physiological one. So far, of course, that paradigm had carried the day. (3) Needless to say, more must be said about the credibility of a naturalistic approach to Nietzsche, where the concern is to make sure that the subjects Nietzsche is mostly interested in can plausibly be accounted for within such an approach without stretching the notion of 'naturalism' too much to accommodate passages that seem to highlight a separation of human beings from nature. To give the reader a sense, a passage of that sort is the following excerpt from GM 3, 28: 'Apart from the ascetic ideal, man, the animal man, had no meaning (*Sinn*) so far. His existence on earth contained no goal . . . the will for man and earth was lacking; . . . the ascetic ideal offered man meaning! It was the only meaning offered so far; any meaning is better than none at all; . . . the tremendous void seemed to have been filled; the door was closed to any kind of suicidal nihilism. But all this notwithstanding—man was saved thereby, he possessed a meaning, he was henceforth no longer like a leaf in the wind, a plaything of nonsense—the 'Ohne-Sinns'—he could now will something; no matter at first to what end, why, with what he willed: the will itself was saved . . . it is and remains a will! . . . And, to repeat in conclusion what I said at the beginning: man would rather will nothingness than not will.' Passages like this suggest a break with nature: if we are animals (which in some sense and to some extent will be undeniable), we are at any rate different from the rest in that we are not merely determined (like a leaf in the wind). This essay does not seek to defend the naturalistic approach to Nietzsche by reconciling it with such passages (which seem to conflict with Nietzsche's rejection of the 'juxtaposition of "man and world"' (GS 346)), but instead explores certain substantive positions that can be ascribed to a Nietzsche understood from the physiological angle, and does so by way of developing stances vis-à-vis Korsgaard's Kant.

his general naturalist commitments, which by themselves do not distinguish him. That is, I take it that Nietzsche is a naturalist mostly through his commitment to a physiology-driven paradigm.

To see why we need clarification especially of the relationship between Kant and a physiologically preoccupied Nietzsche, note that Kantians may wish to dismiss 'animal psychology' as irrelevant for moral philosophy. Morality, they may say, addresses what an agent ought to do: it is a first-person affair, a matter of giving guidance, and takes agents to be practical reasoners. What one ought to do does not turn on the historical or physiological background of morality, and thus third-person explanatory inquiries are irrelevant to it. This objection arises to any inquiry about morality from the third-person explanatory viewpoint and has gained prominence through recent work on the evolution of norms in psychology, biology, and game theory—work that sometimes seems meant to render traditional moral philosophy obsolete. The response cannot be that Nietzsche in particular must be addressing questions different from those of moral philosophy. After all, he wishes to *undermine* views from which this objection is formulated. A closer look is needed to decide whether Nietzsche misses the mark or, far from making contributions irrelevant to moral philosophy, actually undermines the critic voicing such a complaint.[3]

Once we focus on this *objection from the irrelevance of third-person inquiries,* it turns out that the relationship between Nietzsche and Kant must be clarified more generally from a standpoint that takes Nietzsche to apply physiological considerations to traditional philosophical problems. Korsgaard (1996a) illustrates the need for clarification by adding a twist to an assessment of the irrelevance-objection. Classifying her Kantian account as 'naturalistic', she suggests that Nietzsche's way of tying the development of the mind to morality speaks in her support. This move is ingenious as well as puzzling, since for Nietzsche, Kantian ethics is a feeble attempt to reconstruct fragments of the Christian *sittliche Weltordnung* (ethical world-view) without endorsing its argumentative keystone, the notion of God. Yet on Korsgaard's view, Nietzsche succeeds as far as he agrees with Kant, but otherwise mostly demonstrates how human-all-too-human events can obstruct the path to the Kingdom of Ends.[4] So we need a clarification

---

[3] A discussion of this objection does not presuppose that Nietzsche does not address the first-person point of view ('become what you are' at least seems directed at the first-person), or that Kant never asks questions relevant to moral philosophy from a third-person explanatory standpoint (as he does, e.g., in his *Conjectures on the Beginnings of Human History*). The point is, instead, that the reading of Nietzsche sketched above naturally triggers the question of its sheer relevance for moral thought.

[4] The background to this is that Nietzsche ties the development of *ressentiment* to the emergence of the mind itself, and more specifically to the mind becoming self-conscious (cf. Risse (2003b) for an elaboration), and morality in turn emerges from there. Korsgaard derives the Categorical Imperative from the reflective nature of the mind and hence also from its self-consciousness. It is before this background that she believes Nietzsche's (and Freud's) accounts of self-consciousness are in harmony with her own.

of the relationship between Kant and Nietzsche on morality beyond the need for addressing the objection from the irrelevance of third-person inquiries to ensure the independence and distinctness of his approach. The need for such a stance is increased by Hill's (2003) claim that Nietzsche is indebted to Kant to such an extent that we must ask whether this indebtedness 'does not make him a footnote in the history of ideas rather than a daring critic of modernity's most cherished dogmas' (p. 230). Korsgaard and Hill represent two ways of judging the relationship between Kant and Nietzsche that I think we must resist.[5]

This study looks at Kant mostly through Korsgaard's lenses. That restriction will be both controversial and consequential, since Korsgaard's approach to Kant denies that Kant's insistence on the importance of freedom for morality requires substantive metaphysical commitments, of the sort that will be unavailable if transcendental realism is true (i.e., if appearances are things in themselves and there are no grounds for the series of appearances outside that series, not directly accessible to the natural sciences). Korsgaard, that is, develops Kant's ethics in a manner that is free from metaphysical commitments. It is obvious why such an approach to Kant would be controversial; it is consequential because an approach to Kant that considers metaphysical commitments essential would not require as much of the clarification vis-à-vis a naturalistically interpreted Nietzsche that this essay seeks to provide.[6] Moreover, on such an approach to Kant, the objection from the irrelevance of third-person inquiries loses some of its urgency for Kantians. Such a third-person inquiry could find that transcendental realism is true: if so, there could be no freedom of the sort required for Kantian morality, and so clearly a third-person inquiry would have proved its relevance. But at any rate, Korsgaard's view will have to be related to Nietzschean 'animal psychology' even if it were not Kant's, because of its relevance for contemporary ethics (much of which is not too eager to be bound to any particular metaphysical commitments, especially not of the sort required by transcendental idealism), and that relevance does not turn on its pedigree.[7]

This section concludes by summarizing Korsgaard's account, and subsequent sections develop a Nietzschean stance vis-à-vis this account. Section 2 responds to the objection from the irrelevance of third-person inquiries with an objection to the Kantian view, especially its account of the *will*: Kantians cannot dismiss third-person inquiries since they rely on a chimerical understanding of the first-person standpoint

---

[5] Cf. also Risse (forthcoming), which is a joint review of Hill (2003) and Moore (2002).

[6] A different sort of clarification would be needed with regard to the relationship between a Kantian ethics metaphysically interpreted and a non-naturalistic approach to Nietzsche.

[7] To the extent that I work with Kant's texts, I use the *Groundwork*. Differences between the *Groundwork* and the *Critique of Practical Reason* would matter in Section 3: but with many others, I think the second *Critique* assumes too much and does not offer argumentative improvements over passages in the *Groundwork* where an argument actually given fails.

to which such inquiries are allegedly irrelevant. Section 3 objects to another part of the Kantian view and leads to a comparison of Nietzschean versus Kantian notions of freedom. While 'freedom' is central for both Kant and even a Nietzsche championing biological sciences they endorse very different conceptions of freedom. Section 4 links these threads and discusses Nietzsche and Kant's views on the unity of agency. Section 5 is a brief conclusion. I hope that these discussions demonstrate the philosophical richness and distinctness vis-à-vis Kant of Nietzsche *qua* philosopher endorsing a physiology-driven paradigm.[8]

1.2　Let me introduce some core elements of Korsgaard's (1996*a*) account. Her goal is to show how obligation is grounded in the reflectiveness of self-consciousness, and it is in virtue of this connection that she regards her account as *naturalistic*. The guiding idea is that the capacity to value rests on the reflective nature of the mind: what the mind can and must value, and thus what it is morally permitted, forbidden, or obligated to do, is constrained thereby. To begin with, it is in virtue of being reflective that a human being can and must view her desires and impulses from a position of deliberative detachment. In virtue of being reflective, a human being is the kind of creature that can and must act for reasons. To be able to make choices and thus to act for reasons presupposes a conception under which the agent values himself and finds his life worth living. Otherwise he would be in the position of Buridan's famous ass: he would not know how to choose to act on some desire rather than any other. This conception is what Korsgaard calls the agent's *practical identity*. While reasons express an agent's identity, obligation stems from what is inconsistent with it. For a practical identity to pertain to a *unified* decision-maker operating over a range of phenomena, there must be a principle governing her choices to guarantee that similar choices are made under similar circumstances. Otherwise, the agent's choices would be a set of disconnected phenomena. Thus the reflective nature of the agent's consciousness forces her choices to be governed by a law.

So far we have said nothing about other agents. To make the connection, note that what these considerations, properly expanded, aim to show is that agents have a practical identity only in virtue of being animals capable of reflection, which is what makes them human. Our humanity, then, is the source of our ability to bestow value on anything. Thus we must value our humanity if we are to value anything. But since we must value our humanity, we must not only value it in ourselves, but also

---

[8] I am not aware that Nietzsche uses the actual formulation 'physiology of morality' in his published writings; it does, however, appear in the notes, cf. VII 2, 27 [14] and V 1, 6 [123]; moral states are called physiological states in V 1, 6 [445]; cf. also VII 1, 3 [1], p 99. He is more explicit in his published writing when it comes to aesthetics: in *Nietzsche contra Wagner, Where I offer Objections*, aesthetics is called 'nothing but a kind of applied physiology.' In GM III, 8 Nietzsche announces plans for a 'physiology of aesthetics' and says that this is an area that has so far remained entirely underexplored.

in others. This entails that no rational being should ever be used merely as a means, and not as an end. Otherwise, a rational agent could be used merely as a means to something that has value only because rational agency confers it. This is a practical perversity at best, and possibly a kind of contradiction. Moral agency, on this view, is shaped by considerations of consistency.[9]

This account is developed from a first-person viewpoint, answering the question 'What ought I to do?' by advising the agent to make up her mind while respecting constraints imposed by her rational nature. Any approach to morality not developed from this viewpoint fails to answer that question and is deficient from the standpoint of Kantian morality (which is the objection from the irrelevance of third-person inquiries). We can now also see how this account is intertwined with Nietzsche's. In both accounts, the emergence of morality is intimately tied to the development of the mind, and more specifically to the emergence of self-consciousness. That is why Korsgaard appeals to Nietzsche. For Korsgaard, the route leads from the development of self-consciousness to the emergence of reflexivity and reflectivity, and from there to the demands of reason as captured by the Categorical Imperative. That is, it is because the agent is self-conscious that she starts thinking about herself and her reasons and then finds that, *qua* rational decision-making, she cannot help but act in accordance with the Categorical Imperative. Nietzsche, however, while sharing Korsgaard's view that the emergence of self-consciousness is crucial to the development of morality, denies the various steps that lead from the emergence of self-consciousness to the requirement that a rational agent abide by the Categorical Imperative. Instead, he argues that the development of self-consciousness leads to *ressentiment*: a mind that is already angry because it arose from the oppression of instincts turns its anger against itself as soon as it becomes aware of itself, and the resulting state of mind is *ressentiment*. When that state of mind is present, Christianity arises eventually, of which then, in turn, Kantian ethics is merely a feeble and half-hearted imitation.[10] To sort out the relationship between Kant and Nietzsche (understood as a philosopher working in a physiological paradigm) in more detail is the goal of this study.

2. The Will

2.1   Let us develop Nietzschean responses to the Kantian picture. Focusing on the notion of will, this section objects to that picture drawing on Nietzsche's view of the

---

[9] This is the Formula of Humanity version of the Categorical Imperative; see Korsgaard (1996*b*: ch. 4), and also Wood (1999: ch. 4). Many details remain to be filled in, but the subsequent discussion does not turn on such details.

[10] Cf. Risse (2003*b*) for more details on this account.

mind. This discussion shows why the objection from the irrelevance of third-person inquiries fails.

Consider the following account of the functioning of the mind in GS 333:[11]

Since only the last scenes of reconciliation and the final accounting at the end of this long process rise to our consciousness, we suppose that *intelligere* must be something conciliatory, just, and good—something that stands essentially opposed to the instincts, while it is actually nothing but a *certain behavior of the instincts toward one another*. For the longest time, conscious thought was considered thought itself. Only now does the truth dawn on us that by far the greatest part of our spirit's activity remains unconscious and unfelt. . . . *Conscious* thinking, especially that of the philosopher, is the least vigorous and therefore also the relatively mildest and calmest form of thinking; and thus precisely philosophers are most apt to be led astray about the nature of knowledge.

As Thiele (1990) says, on this view the 'Platonic opposition between reason and passion is fractured into the opposition between multiple passions, each with its own capacity for reason and will to dominate' (p. 256). What is characteristic of a human mind is not the possession of reason, but instead, 'by what rank order the innermost drives of his nature are related to each other' (BGE 6), or, as Nietzsche puts it in *Dawn*, 'the totality of drives which constitute [a person's] essence' (D 119). In particular, a person's inner life fails to include an entity reviewing desires and deciding which ones to endorse as reasons. Instead, Nietzsche talks about the soul as a 'societal structure (*Gesellschaftsbau*) of many drives and affects' (BGE 12, cf. BGE 19). If some desire is disregarded for another desire to be adopted into a maxim (as Kant has it), the relevant process fails to be reason-based choosing; instead, '[t]he will to overcome an emotion is ultimately only the will of another emotion or of several others' (BGE 117). Much of this happens without the agent's awareness. The mind is the 'unknown world of the subject' (which is the title of D 116), and filled with 'phantoms and will-o'-the-wisps' (TI, 'Errors', 3).

A remark on Wagner in the *Fourth Untimely Meditation* illuminates this view:

The dramatic element in Wagner's development is quite unmistakable from the moment when his ruling passion became aware of itself and took his nature in its charge: from that time on there was an end to fumbling, straying, to the proliferation of secondary shoots, and within the most convoluted courses and often daring trajectories assumed by his artistic plans there rules a single inner law, a will by which they can be explained. (UM IV, 2)

Wagner never *endorsed* a conception of his life and then followed it. Instead, a certain drive became dominant, forcing unity on his personality.[12] Because of the sheer

---

[11] Cf. Parkes (1994), Thiele (1990: 51 ff.), and Richardson (1996: ch. 1.4), for the drive constitution of the human mind to be discussed in this paragraph.

[12] Instincts can be influenced by choices, but in roundabout ways; cf. the illuminating discussion in D 109.

complexity of the mind decisions are made in ways different from deliberative detachment. As Richardson (1996: 47), puts it: '[A] person is formed of a vast network of power balances, struck at a hierarchy of levels,' and a person's life is shaped by how these balancing processes turn out.

These ideas are typical of what Nietzsche regarded as implications of the naturalistic world-view for traditional areas of philosophical inquiry. We must be careful, however, to assess how this account of the mind applies to the Kantian view, and how it may contribute to a response to the objection from the irrelevance of third-person inquiries. One may say Nietzsche talks about matters without any bearing on the Kantian picture. Korsgaard's view in particular does not depend on any theoretical view of the mind, especially not on there being a *physiologically* identifiable organ called 'the will.' Instead, it depends on the practical consideration that agents *perceive* themselves as making choices, as obviously they do. A crucial component of making such choices is the capacity for deliberative detachment. Speculations about the physiological constitution of the mind, or its origins, seem beside the point, just as the objection from the irrelevance of third-person inquiries says: they do not address questions that moral philosophers in the Kantian tradition should be concerned with.

2.2   Yet appearances are deceptive. Our capacity for such detachment, thus the core of the Kantian view, is precisely what Nietzsche's physiological speculations question. The point is best made in contrast with Kant's notion of the will. Will, for Kant, 'is a faculty of choosing only that which reason, independently of inclination, recognizes as practically necessary, i.e., as good' (G 4:412). As Wood (1999) explains (while also illustrating that nothing turns on understanding the will as a *physiological* organ), the will

is the activity of determining one's practical faculty to seek an end that has been set according to a maxim or practical principle. The basic activity in willing is the adoption of normative principles for the regulation of our conduct. Desires involve the representation of objects (or states of affairs) whose existence we would experience as agreeable. But ends are possible states of affairs to whose actualization we are actively directing our powers. Willing an end is therefore quite different from merely wishing for something, since willing involves the subjection of one's actions to a norm and, to the extent that one acts on the norm, also the summoning of the agent's power to produce it through actions chosen as appropriate means.   (pp. 53–4)

Two points matter for us: first, the will is a *single* capacity, distinct from desires; second, that capacity is action-guiding, whereas desires come to be so by being 'incorporated' into maxims. This second point is a thesis about the relationship between will and desires that Wood, following Allison (1990), calls the *Incorporation Thesis*.[13]

---

[13] As Kant says in his *Religion within the Limits of Reason Alone*, 'an incentive can determine the will to an action only insofar as the individual has taken it up into his maxim (has made it into a general rule,

Nietzsche denies that there is a will with such properties. He replaces this picture with an aggregate structure within which there is no single will but a complex set of minor wills attached to various mental entities. This much is suggested in the passage from BGE 117 quoted above, which mentions 'the will of another emotion or of several others': the notion of will, then, as Nietzsche uses it, merely captures the idea that mental entities have an urge to be realized. This move modifies the meaning of 'will' as Nietzsche, as well as the physiologists who inspired him, use the term. As he puts it: 'The old word "will" only serves to denote a resultant, a kind of individual reaction that necessarily follows upon a multitude of partly contradictory, partly harmonizing affects:—the will does not "effect" anything any more, does not move anything any more' (A 14). What Nietzsche denies in particular through denying the Kantian view of the will is that there are 'mental raw materials' (desires, inclinations, instincts, or drives) that affect actions through being incorporated into maxims.[14] With the Kantian notion of the will discarded, it seems, such entities are viewed as directly leading to action. It is by rejecting a notion of will characterized by the properties of the Kantian notion that Nietzsche denies the Kantian idea of detachment: neither is there a *single* capacity that would *do* the detaching, nor is there an opposition between mental raw materials and an entity detached from them. Nietzsche's picture allows detachment from any given set of desires, but rules out a viewpoint allowing for detachment from all desires at once.

The insistence on the possibility of such detachment shows how Kant is trapped in the Christian legacy. As Christianity postulates a soul to hold individuals accountable, so Kant postulates the capacity for deliberative detachment to impose moral constraints on choice. Both the Christian soul and the Kantian will are characterized by their singularity and opposition to other internal entities, and both are ideas of an 'inner chooser' and thus flawed on similar grounds.[15] In *The Blank Slate*, the psychologist

according to which he will conduct himself' (R 6:24). Note that Cartesian transparency is not part of the Kantian picture of agency. While Nietzsche frequently insists that the mind is largely unknown to us, such remarks would put him more in opposition to Descartes than to Kant.

[14] Nothing depends on carefully distinguishing between desires, inclinations, instincts, and drives. What matters is that they stand in opposition to the Kantian will as explained above.

[15] As Nietzsche says in the *Genealogy*, '[T]here is no such substratum; there is no *being* behind doing, effecting, becoming; *the doer* is merely a fiction added to the doing' (GM I, 13). It is wrong that no interesting account of deliberation could accompany Nietzsche's picture of the mind. Just as the Categorical Imperative comes with an account of deliberation, so does Nietzsche's dictum 'become what you are.' Nietzschean deliberation cannot be concerned with applying objective principles to the agent's situation, since there would be no such principles. But to the extent that objective principles lose their importance, introspective deliberation, concerned with understanding who the agent is and why he has felt motivated to do what he did (an endeavor that is also possible, of course, on the Kantian account), becomes more important, as does deliberation concerned with choosing actions that allow the agent to become who she is.

Steven Pinker, discussing the soul, writes that 'science is showing that what we call the soul—the locus of sentience, reason, and will—consists of the information-processing activity of the brain, an organ governed by the laws of biology' (2002: 224). It is that thought which Nietzsche tried to grasp, working with what biology he had access to.

2.3 We can now respond to the objection from the irrelevance of third-person inquiries. The point can be made by way of contrast with Korsgaard's discussion of determinism (cf. Korsgaard 1996a: 95). Suppose you take part in a scientific experiment and know that your every move is determined by 'the system.' You know you cannot beat the system, and attempts to do so are also predetermined. Second-guessing the system makes no difference. To do anything, you must ignore the fact that you are predetermined, and act as if you were not. Crucially, while you need not (and have no reason to) believe you are free, you must choose *as if you were*. The truth of determinism, from a practical standpoint, makes no difference to how you go about deciding what to do, and thus is irrelevant to the practical standpoint. Let us not quarrel with this now (as we will do, to some extent, in the next section) but use it to draw a contrast between this account of the irrelevance of determinism to practical agency, on the one hand, and the unavailability of a similar account of the irrelevance of third-person inquiries, on the other.

This contrast can be developed as follows. Note first that, if Nietzsche's view of the mind is correct, Kantians would be engaged in a decision-making process based on an illusionary understanding of the mind. They would persistently *misunderstand* mental events by assuming our deliberations are conducted from a single standpoint detached from desires, while in fact, different desires become dominant in the process of deliberation until one is strong enough to trigger action, or is the strongest when action is required. Next note that the truth of determinism is irrelevant from a practical standpoint because it does not affect how we should characterize the decision-making process as such: the decision process itself is the same regardless of whether determinism is true or false. That is, the agent could answer questions about what reasons prompted her to act in certain ways in the same way, regardless of any views about determinism. Yet according to Nietzsche's attack on the Kantian notion of the will, we are deceived precisely about what that process *is*, and thus this attack does affect how we should characterize the decision-making process. That is, agents would systematically give wrong answers to questions about why they acted the way they did, and would do so because they are deceived about their own decision-making process. Exploring that decision process is the subject of third-person inquiries, which is why, by way of contrast with the truth of determinism, they matter to the practical standpoint.

The Kantian picture focuses on the notion of the will, understood as a single entity detached from all desires. While that is the picture the Nietzschean stance attacks, Kantians like to account for the philosophical soundness of their moral psychology by appealing to the fact that it is confirmed by introspection: do we not undoubtedly perceive ourselves as taking the standpoint of deliberative detachment? If so, will this not be enough to render the Kantian machinery applicable? But if Nietzsche is right, outcomes we may perceive as obtained from a standpoint of deliberative detachment really emerge from a struggle of desires, and what detachment is involved may be detachment from sets of desires at a time but not, as the Kantian picture has it, detachment from all desires at the same time. That is, there may be a sense in which some mental entities can be detached from others (and thus in which the agent herself can be said to be so detached), but, absent the Kantian notion of the will, there is no sense in which the agent herself can be detached from all her desires at once. So any introspection that conveys the impression that such detachment is involved is, on the Nietzschean account, purely epiphenomenal with respect to the resultant action. While the phenomenology as such may strike the agent as real enough, it makes no difference whatsoever to the decision-making process. This, at any rate, is implied by the Nietzschean stance on the mind (which in turn is a third-person inquiry), and if that stance is correct it would indeed have an impact on how agents would need to answer questions about why she acted the way she did. Third-person inquiries, then, are not irrelevant to the practical standpoint.

But how could it be explained, so one may ask now, that the agent's introspection would so systematically deceive him about the nature of his own decision process? Why do we perceive ourselves as deliberatively detached although we are not? Different answers are available. First of all, one may question the Kantian account of the phenomenology. Without pushing this point far, it seems fair to say that internal turmoil and conflict among desires that is not actually 'resolved' but rather 'terminated' at some point is as real as any perception of deliberative detachment. Second, one may leave the phenomenology unquestioned and wonder why we came to have it. One possible answer would be that we learn to think of our inner lives in a certain way within a culture that believed in souls and thus misguided us on a large scale about who we are; and such misguidance would have been facilitated by the fact that we literally look at the world through one pair of eyes and thus from a single standpoint, which seems to render it all too plausible that there is a kind of 'inner eye' (such as the Kantian will) that allows for a similar perspective on our inner lives. What Nietzsche argues is that this is not so.

So, by way of contrast with the truth of determinism, we have seen that third-person inquiries are not irrelevant to decision-making and thus to the practical standpoint. The truth of determinism is irrelevant to decision-making because the decision-process as such is unaffected by it, and thus neither are any answers that an agent would have to give to questions about why she acted the way she did. What third-person inquiries deliver is not irrelevant because they could deliver the result that the decision-making really occurs in a way that is very different from what we perceive it to be, and if so, this would affect what an agent would need to say in response to questions about why she acted in certain ways. That is, if Kantians insist that for their purposes it suffices that we do introspectively perceive ourselves as making choices from a standpoint of deliberative detachment, then the response is that we must be justified in taking the phenomena at face value by not having good reasons to think they are chimerical; but on the Nietzschean view, we do have such reasons. Third-person inquiries, then, could deliver the result that the phenomenology of decision-making is irrelevant to decision-making itself, and if that is so, then an appeal to the phenomenology of decision-making cannot itself be used to show that third-person inquiries are irrelevant. Not enough has been said to establish the actual correctness of the Nietzschean view, but we can conclude that this third-person inquiry does matter to moral philosophy as Kantians conceive of it. The sort of detachment at the core of the Kantian argument is unavailable if Nietzsche is right, which not only shows how third-person inquiries are relevant to the practical standpoint after all, but also entails that any theorizing is in jeopardy that builds on the availability of such detachment, as does Korsgaard's view introduced in Section 1.[16]

3. Freedom

3.1 Let me introduce an objection to a different part of the Kantian view that draws on Kant and Nietzsche's respective notions of freedom. To prepare the ground, we consider an objection to the derivation of the Categorical Imperative that by itself is not especially Nietzschean. Recall that the steps in the derivation of the formula-of-humanity version are, first, to derive that an agent must value her own humanity from the fact that she values anything, and second, to show that she must value humanity in everybody, lest she drew an untenable distinction. However (this is the objection), the fact that I value certain things only permits the inference that I must value *my having the capacity to value*, or *my partaking of humanity*. What *you* must value is *your* having the capacity to value, or *your* partaking of humanity. I must value the capacity to value, or to set ends, *insofar as it is a capacity that I possess*, and you must value that capacity insofar as it is a capacity *you* possess. I must value all aspects of the capacity

---

[16] Similar concerns about the Kantian picture of agency arise within the sentimentalist tradition of Hume and Smith; cf. Blackburn (1998: ch. 8).

to value that pertain to my being able to value anything, and so must you, *mutatis mutandis*. I do not need to value your capacity to value, and vice versa, and neither you nor I must value the capacity to value *per se*. Neither a perversity nor a contradiction arises if *I* am using *you* as a means to ends that have value because *I* have conferred it upon them. Instead, the argument demonstrates how you become *intelligible* to me as an agent, how I come to see your actions as more than mere events, namely by coming to realize that, in a fundamental way, we are alike. But while shared humanity creates enough community between us to make us intelligible to each other, this also exhausts the community thus created.[17]

The Kantian response is that this objection mischaracterizes the starting point of the derivation of the formula-of-humanity version of the Categorical Imperative.[18] That starting point is not the sheer fact that individuals *value*, but that they value things *in a specific way*, to wit, by regarding them as 'good.' Goodness, however, for Kant, is a rational concept. 'This means two related things,' as Korsgaard (1996b) explains:

First, reason must determine what is good. On this basis, Kant argues in the *Critique of Practical Reason* that if the end were set by inclination and reason determined only the means, then only the means could be called 'good' (C2 62). Thus, if an end is good, it must be set by reason; and if an action is done under the full direction of reason, then the end must be good. Second, and correlatively, if an end is deemed good it provides reasons for action that apply to every rational being. . . . If one's end cannot be shared, and so cannot be an object of the faculty of desire for everyone, it cannot be good, and the action cannot be rational.   (p. 115)

The starting point of the Kantian argument is that I *make something good by means of rational choice*. So if the objection is that I cannot infer a general appreciation of the value-bestowing ability from the observation that I myself *value* something, the response is that I can indeed infer such an appreciation of the good-making ability

---

[17] At this point I should also briefly mention GS 335, the passage in which Nietzsche rejects the Categorical Imperative because it treats all human beings as relevantly similar although they are not. I do not believe, however, that that way of engaging Kantians on the merits of the Categorical Imperative is a particularly fruitful one.

[18] Another response is that it makes little sense to say that I appreciate, say, athletic talent only insofar as I possess it; so how could this be true for the capacity to set ends? Yet if I say I value athletic talent, I mean I value it for its own sake. In that case it does not matter in whose person it is embodied: it is the talent that I admire. However, in the present context it would be question-begging to say one values the capacity to set ends for its own sake. That is what the Kantian needs to show and the Nietzschean denies. Or one may say I am drawing irrelevant distinctions and am plainly irrational in valuing something in me that I do not value in you, namely the capacity to set ends. However, I am not doing that at all. I value the capacity to set ends *per se* neither in you nor in myself. What I value in myself is relevantly different from what you value in yourself: in my case it is my ability to set ends, in your case it is your ability to do so.

from the observation that I *make something good* and thus value it in a specific manner. 'Good-making' as a rational activity makes this claim true.[19]

3.2 In comes Nietzsche, and it is at this point that our discussion of the formula-of-humanity version of the Categorical Imperative turns into an objection to the Kantian picture developed in 1.2 from the Nietzschean standpoint. The Nietzschean objection is to wonder whether agents ever make anything good as required for the Kantian response, that is, whether they are capable of doing so, and if so, why they would. In response Kantians must explain the work done by the notion of freedom in their argument. Recall the structure of the *Groundwork*: the first section derives the moral law from perceived moral common sense and the second from a theory of the will, but only the third shows that the will can and must be motivated by a moral law (whose form is developed in the first two sections) and derives the proposition that the will is under that law from the proposition that it regards itself as free. According to Kant, the agent is justified in postulating freedom (and must do so to regard herself *as* an agent) because at the theoretical level she cannot know whether she is free. Freedom of the will is inconsistent with acting heteronomously. So 'willing' must be captured in terms of 'making good' as explained by Korsgaard. For agents to value anything differently means for them to be motivated heteronomously.

There is a twofold Nietzschean response to this appeal to freedom of the will. To begin with, following from Section 2, the idea of freedom attached to 'the will' is an illusion, since the Kantian will itself is. So dependency on one's desires fails to appear as heteronomous, as this is plausible only if there is a contrast between 'will' and 'desires' with autonomy pertaining to the former. Yet if this were all there was to the Nietzschean stance on freedom of the will, there would be space for *some* notion of freedom of the individual—it just would not be freedom of the *will* in its Kantian conception. Many contemporary philosophers agree with Kant's deontological approach without endorsing his idea of the autonomous will and hence the account of freedom that accompanies it. One such view is Scanlon's (1988) compatibilist account of freedom according to which

[w]hat is required [for moral responsibility] is that what we do be importantly dependent on our process of critical reflection, that that process itself be sensitive to reasons, and that later stages of the process be importantly dependent on conclusions reached at earlier stages. But there is no reason, as far as I can see, to require that this process itself not be a causal product of antecedent events and conditions.   (Scanlon 1988: 176)

This approach allows for a notion of freedom without tying it to the Kantian will (and the accompanying notion of autonomy). But Nietzsche denies (and

---

[19] As Wood (1999: 127) points out, the argument requires us to concede that setting an end for ourselves involves ascribing objective goodness to it.

this is the second response, which is entirely independent of the discussion of the will in Section 2) that individuals have freedom *and* that they have reason to think of themselves as having freedom. Before I elaborate, note what this means with regard to the irrelevance-objection. Against Kantians, we showed that Nietzsche's theory of mind (thus a third-person explanatory inquiry) is relevant because the Kantian enterprise of building morality on consistency considerations turns on the existence of a mental entity that can engage in consistent or inconsistent activity (the will). Other moral theories turn on no such thing but share much substance with Kantians. While Nietzsche's objections to the Kantian theory of the will do not speak to such theories, his rejection of freedom of the individual *does*.

3.3   To elaborate this second way of rejecting the Kantian conception of freedom, note that Nietzsche is a determinist: 'The single human being,' he says, 'is a piece of *fatum* from the front and from the rear, one law more, one necessity more for all that is yet to come and to be' (TI, 'Morality as Anti-Nature', 6). Free will is among the prejudices of the philosophers discussed in the first book of *Beyond Good and Evil*. The will is neither free nor unfree, but merely strong or weak (BGE 21; cf. BGE 231). Unlike Kantians, Nietzsche finds the question of freedom of the will not theoretically unsolvable (cf. first *Critique*, Third Antinomy). He conceives of human beings as physiological units subject to the usual laws of nature, finding no room for freedom of the will as Kantians understand it.[20]

Embracing an incompatibilist stance, Nietzsche thinks that determinism gives agents reason *not* to think of themselves as free. As far as he is concerned, compatibilists like Scanlon maintain an untenable 'juxtaposition of "man and world"' to support a notion of freedom of choice and responsibility in the face of determinism, that is, 'an attitude of man as a *world-negating* principle, of man as the measure of the value of things, as judge of the world who in the end places existence itself upon his scales

---

[20]   There is room for dispute about whether Nietzsche should be taken to be a determinist, or as Leiter (1998) suggests, a causal essentialist. Determinism, as Leiter defines it, is the view that for any event *E* at time *t*, *E* is necessary given the totality of facts prior to *t*, together with the laws of nature. Causal essentialism is the view that for any substance (e.g., a person) there are essential properties that non-trivially determine the space of possible trajectories of that substance, which is consistent both with there being and with there not being any laws of nature. (As Leiter is careful to point out, the notion of substance used here is meant to be free from traditional metaphysical baggage.) Leiter suggests that Nietzsche is better understood along such lines. However, Leiter would agree that this claim is meant to capture Nietzsche's style of argument rather than to assume that Nietzsche's texts contain detailed remarks that allow us to ascribe this distinction to Nietzsche himself. I do think that the passage in TI, 'Morality as Anti-Nature', 6, quoted above much resembles the definition of determinism presented here, and thus will continue to refer to him as a determinist. But nothing hangs on this dispute for the purposes of this study.

and finds it wanting' (GS 346). As opposed to that, Nietzschean agents are fatalists, appropriately understood. A passage from the *Twilight* illustrates that view:

What alone can be *our* doctrine? That no one *gives* man his qualities, neither God, nor society, nor his parents and ancestors, nor *he himself*. (The nonsense of the last idea was taught as intelligible freedom by Kant, perhaps by Plato already.) *No one* is responsible for man's being there at all, for his being such-and-such, or for his being in these circumstances or in this environment. The fatality of his essence is not to be disentangled from the fatality of all that has been and will be. Man is *not* the effect of some special purpose, of a will, and end; nor is he the object of an attempt to attain an 'ideal of humanity' or an 'ideal of happiness' or an 'ideal of morality.' It is absurd to *devolve* one's essence on some end or other. We have invented the concept of 'end:' in reality, *there is* no end . . . One is necessary, one is a piece of fatefulness, one belongs to the whole, one *is* in the whole; there is nothing which could judge, measure, compare, or sentence our being, for that would mean judging, measuring, comparing, or sentencing the whole. *But there is nothing beside the whole.* That nobody is held responsible any longer, that the mode of being may not be traced back to a *causa prima*, that the world does not form a unity either as a sensorium or as 'spirit'—*that alone is the great liberation*; with this alone is the innocence of becoming restored. The concept of 'God' was until now the greatest *objection* to existence. We deny God, we deny the responsibility in God: only *thereby* do we redeem the world.   ('The Four Great Errors', 8)

This passage expresses Nietzsche's effort to come to terms with the loss of the Christian *sittliche Weltordnung* and the impossibility of related ethical theories.[21] Unlike existentialists, Nietzsche does not deny that there is such a *Weltordnung* and that *therefore* individuals are in an appropriate sense on their own. Far from finding freedom through being left to her own devices, the person who endorses Nietzsche's doctrine conceives of herself as embedded into a causal web comprising the whole universe. As Nietzsche says at the beginning of this passage, we are what we are, and holding us responsible or guilty is pointless. As Nietzsche puts it in *Dawn*, he offers a perspective in which causes do not turn into sins and consequences do not turn into hangmen (D 208).[22] What we may seem accountable for occurs because of qualities that nobody has given us and that we have not chosen either. 'Men were considered 'free' so that

---

[21] I discuss this in more detail in Risse (2003a); see also Leiter (1998). What matters is that the Nietzschean fatalist is a determinist who thinks that this determinism has considerable implications for agency.

[22] While exploring this point further would take us too far afield, note that such a perspective can be developed using what Leiter (1998) calls Nietzsche's 'Doctrine of Types,' according to which each individual has a fixed psycho-physical constitution defining him as a type of person. Facts about one's type explain one's beliefs and values. As Nietzsche says, 'Moralities are the sign languages of affects' (BGE 187), or earlier, in D 119, 'our moral judgements and evaluations . . . are only images and fantasies based on a physiological process unknown to us.' Since there is a richness of such types, any universal 'Thou Shalt' is misguided (TI, 'Morality as Anti-Nature', 6). Morality and religion tend to disregard this supervenience-relationship between type-facts and facts about beliefs and values. For that reason, Nietzsche refers to them as the realm of imaginary causes and imaginary effects (A 15).

they might be judged and punished—so that they might become *guilty*' (TI, 'Four Great Errors', 7). Unlike *ressentiment*, which emerges as a consequence of socialization as such, and like guilt, the belief in freedom of the will emerges from a particular historical power struggle and can be overcome.[23]

How impressed should compatibilists be with Nietzsche's incompatibilist stance and his blatant dismissal of their position?[24] This is one of those points where Nietzsche gives us little more than the sketch of an (albeit intriguing) philosophical position. As in the case of his view on the mind discussed in Section 2, he shows little concern to discuss his views in a way that might persuade those whose initial outlook differs from his. Frequently, his views entail that an opposing view must go wrong *somewhere*, but fail to advance beyond such a claim. At the same time, all these matters have since been up for substantial philosophical discussion, often much richer in sophistication than Nietzsche's views. Still, this study seeks to argue for the relevance and distinctness (vis-à-vis Kant) of Nietzsche's views, and these goals can be met even while much remains inconclusive.

Instead of trying to supply more argument where Nietzsche did not supply any, let me illustrate the radical nature of his view by casting it in vocabulary familiar from the work of Thomas Nagel (see e.g., Nagel 1979). Nagel distinguishes an internal and an external point of view, two perspectives from which we see ourselves in the world. From the internal point of view we regard ourselves as agents. We do not regard our actions and characters merely as fortunate or unfortunate episodes (Nagel 1979: 37); rather, we understand them in ways that let us ascribe them *to ourselves* in a way that allows for the application of terms such as guilt, shame, pride, or responsibility. At the same time we may understand that our actions and character are events in the world, and that after sufficient pressing nothing is left to be ascribed to ourselves in a way that renders such vocabulary applicable. That is the external point of view. Nagel believes we are unable to see ourselves merely as portions of the world. But accepting this external point of view to the exclusion of the internal one is precisely Nietzsche's doctrine: in its light Nagel emerges as another theorist insisting on an untenable 'juxtaposition of "man and world." '

To illustrate the radical nature of Nietzsche's view in a different way, consider how the Kantian and the Nietzschean view differ in their responses to *moral luck*.

---

[23] Nietzsche claims that Christianity (hence the form of guilt that came along with it) will perish as morality (GM, third treatise, sec. 27, cf. also GS 357). He even envisages a time frame, thinking that 200 years after writing the *Genealogy* should suffice for this development to begin. Note HAH I 39 about the prospects for freedom and responsibility: 'The feeling [of freedom and responsibility] is something one can disaccustom oneself to, and many people do not feel it at all in respect of actions which invoke it in others. It is a very changeable thing tied to the evolution of morality and culture and perhaps present in only a relatively brief span of world-history.' For the views on guilt and *ressentiment*, cf. Risse (2001).

[24] On this subject, cf. Leiter (2002: 88–101).

The challenge posed by moral luck is that we treat individuals as objects of moral judgment although a significant share of what they do depends on factors beyond their control. The Kantian response is to devise a view that lets us continue to see each other as objects of moral judgments, first by allowing each of us to see herself as free and then by urging a transfer of that attitude towards others. Since all this turns on the rationality of wills, it is in virtue of that rationality that we see ourselves as agents in a deterministic world, and even create a sense of moral objectivity compatible with it. For Nietzsche, that stance denies that we are embedded into the world as he suggests we are: it solves the problem by creating a fictitious reality. As opposed to that, Nietzsche claims that '[w]hat justifies man is his reality,' and that '[n]othing offends the philosopher's taste more than man, insofar as man desires' (TI, 'Skirmishes', 32). His response to moral luck is to embrace things as they are and suspend judgments that have become untenable, rather than to salvage them by deceiving ourselves.

3.4 I must qualify Nietzsche's denial of freedom in an important way. For many Nietzsche is *the* philosopher of freedom and self-creation, and it is the prominence he gives these themes, along with a similar prominence that freedom obtains for Kant, that makes it tempting to suggest, as Hill (2003) does, that Nietzsche 'thinks there is something fundamentally right about Kant's account of agency as an arena of conflict between self-made laws and passions, and of freedom as the capacity to impose these laws upon oneself. This power is what makes human action qualitatively different from animal behavior' (Hill 2003: 217). We should resist this view, and to do so I must show how his insistence on freedom can be preserved (as it must) even from the viewpoint that thinks of Nietzsche as exploiting insights from the biological sciences to answer traditional questions of philosophy.

There is a sense of freedom that Nietzsche endorses, but a sense very different from Kantian freedom of the will, one that is rather revisionary compared to notions of freedom that Nietzsche ascribes to philosophers, moralists, or theologians. A hint towards the presence of such a sense of freedom is in Beyond Good and Evil, 19, where Nietzsche says that '[t]hat which is termed "freedom of the will" is essentially the affect of superiority in relation to him who must obey.' To explore further this notion of freedom and to illuminate how it finds room within his otherwise deterministic and non-compatibilist position, let us briefly look at another determinist, namely Spinoza. Turning to Spinoza will help us understand how Nietzsche can rightly be for many the philosopher of freedom, creativity, and self-creation, appropriately modified, while also being a determinist and fatalist. Plausibly, the key to reconciling these apparently conflicting views must be a highly revisionary notion of freedom.[25]

[25] My presentation of Spinoza's views follows Della Rocca (1998).

Admired by Nietzsche as well as by Nietzsche's idol Goethe, Spinoza offers an account that is most useful for our purposes. To begin with, Spinoza distinguishes complete from partial causes. A cause is a complete cause of an effect if no reference to any other cause is required to explain the effect. Otherwise, it is a partial cause. This terminology leads to a distinction between activity and passivity: something is active to the extent that it is the complete cause of something else and passive to the extent that it is merely a partial cause of something else. So activity and passivity are defined relative to cause–effect relations; corresponding notions for objects or events can then be defined derivatively, that is, in terms of the cause–event relations in which this object or event is involved. Activity and passivity are matters of degree, as indicated by the 'to-the-extent' formulations. Using those notions, Spinoza defines an *increase in power* as an increase in activity. As Della Rocca puts it, 'a thing's power of acting increases to the extent to which it becomes less dependent on external things in the production of some effect' (1993 1230). For reasons that do not concern us, Spinoza claims that each thing strives to increase its power: that is, figuratively speaking and using Spinoza's picture of causality, each thing aims to increase the number of causal chains that run through it and aims to increase the number of such chains in which it is at least close to being a complete cause for the effect.

So, indeed, Spinoza's theory allows us to make sense of the notion of freedom that Nietzsche endorses in a manner consistent with Nietzsche's physiology-shaped approach. Freedom, in such a model, can be accounted for in terms of degrees of power: an agent has the more freedom the more power he has. Spinoza offers a conception of freedom that allows us to see Nietzsche as a philosophical champion of freedom while also seeing him as a determinist, fatalist, and champion of a physiological approach to traditional philosophical problems; at the same time, Spinoza's conception also makes sense of several remarks on freedom that Nietzsche makes. Within the confines of this approach, Spinoza could subscribe to an appropriate version of Nietzsche's dictum that there is neither a free nor an unfree will, but merely a strong or a weak will (BGE 21), to the idea that '[t]hat which is termed 'freedom of the will' is essentially the affect of superiority in relation to him who must obey' (BGE 19), and to the claim that freedom of the will 'is the expression for the complex state of delight of the person exercising volition, who commands and at the same time identifies himself with the executor of the order' (BGE 19). Consider, finally, a telling discussion of Goethe in TI, 'Skirmishes of an Untimely Man', 49, a passage that is not only Spinozistic, but mentions Spinoza:

Goethe . . . He bore the strongest instincts within himself: the sensibility, the idolatry of nature, the anti-historic, the idealistic, the unreal and revolutionary (the latter being merely a form of the unreal). He sought help from history, natural science, antiquity, and also Spinoza, but, above all, from practical activity . . . What he wanted was *totality*; he fought the mutual extraneousness of reason, senses, feeling, and will; he disciplined himself to wholeness, he *created* himself. In the middle of an age with an unreal outlook, Goethe was a convinced realist: he said

Yes to everything that was related to him in this respect. . . . Goethe conceived a human being who would be strong, highly educated, skillful in all bodily matters, self-controlled, reverent towards himself, and who might dare to afford the whole range and wealth of being natural, being strong enough for such freedom; the man of tolerance, not from weakness but from strength . . . ; the man for whom there is no longer anything that is forbidden—unless it be weakness, whether called vice or virtue. Such a spirit who has *become free* stands amid the cosmos with a joyous and trusting fatalism, in the *faith* that only the particular is loathsome, and that all is redeemed and affirmed in the whole—*he does not negate any more.*

Two points stand out: first, Goethe has *become free* in a way reminiscent of Spinoza's increase-in-activities account, and second, that Goethe became free is mentioned along with the fact that he was a fatalist. So Spinoza's account of freedom shows how Nietzsche can be a champion of freedom while rejecting the notion of freedom that is the starting point for Kantian ethics, and while being properly characterized as a deterministic and fatalistic philosopher who applies physiological considerations to traditional philosophical problems.[26]

4. Unity of Agency

4.1   Inquiries about the unity of agency ask what it is about an agent that allows her to think of herself as *one* agent. The correlative ideal of unity of agency will be realized if the respective form of unity of agency is achieved to perfection. This subject also illuminates differences between Kantian ethics and Nietzschean 'animal psychology' and is thus the third topic we discuss by way of developing a Nietzschean response vis-à-vis Korsgaard's Kant. This subject also turns on results from Sections 2 and 3 and thus ties together the different threads of the discussion in this study.

Unity of agency, on the Kantian view, comes about in two ways. First, there is a single standpoint from which deliberation is conducted, and second, the adoption of principles ensures that agents act consistently across situations. So it is through the presence of the will and its activities, hence through his rationality, that an agent can think of himself as one. What the *Groundwork* calls a *holy will* can be regarded as the ideal pertaining to this conception of unity. A will is holy if it always follows objective principles and does what is good without being constrained by recalcitrant desires. Finite wills either do not always follow objective principles or, if they do, need to overcome such resistance. Still, the Categorical Imperative guides each rational mind to approximate that ideal. Deliberation seeks to assess what the Categorical Imperative demands in a situation that calls for moral choice.

---

[26] Note, though, that this study does not make claims about the similarities between Nietzsche's views and those of Spinoza beyond what is summarized in this sentence.

However, Sections 2 and 3 threaten to undermine this conception of unity. Section 2 questions whether there is a will as envisaged by Kantian moral psychology. Section 3 observes that the derivation of the formula-of-humanity version of the Categorical Imperative rests on operations of 'good-making' through rational choice that apply to the will only if it is free; however, Nietzsche questions the availability of any conception of individual freedom of the sort permitting applications of the good-making operation to the will (or that would render it more than optional for the will to 'make good' in this sense). If all this is correct, the Categorical Imperative cannot be derived any more.[27] So the Kantian conception of unity (and the holy will as its ideal) comes under fire from two directions. First, since there is no Kantian will, the idea of not letting one's agency be shaped by desires is uncompelling. Second, since the Categorical Imperative can no longer be derived, consideration for others does not constrain deliberation as much as Kantians claim. Such considerations lead towards a different picture of unity of agency.

4.2   Since on Nietzsche's view there is no Kantian will, that will cannot allow the agent to think of himself as one. Instead, what creates unity, I submit, is the joint presence of desires or instincts in the same body, with shared memories and cognitive apparatus. This is a very different conception of unity. Where in the Kantian conception the physical oneness of the agent is mirrored by the stipulation of one 'inner chooser,' this oneness, in the Nietzschean conception, is matched by an internal multiplicity, a 'societal structure of many drives and affects' (BGE 12, cf. BGE 19). What unites those 'drives and affects' is their joint presence in one body with shared memories and cognitive abilities.

This conception of unity itself is philosophically not particularly interesting, but comes with an ideal of unity that *is*. That ideal (the counterpart to the holy will) is one of physiological and mental *Wohlgeratenheit*—well-turned-out-ness. The ideally unified agent, on this account, is physiologically and mentally balanced, stable, and well-rounded. This ideal is one of physiological cofunctionality within an organism: everything works well together. We must see this ideal before the background of Nietzsche's views on the development of self-consciousness. Self-consciousness, as GM II 16/17 explains, emerges through the oppression of instincts, a painful process that is the physiological root of the subsequent *ressentiment* many feel because such oppression puts them in an unbalanced state (cf. Risse 2003*b*). So the ideal of *Wohlgeratenheit* captures organic unity in the presence of self-consciousness. Although self-consciousness is often accompanied by inner turmoil, some individuals succeed at integrating an

---

[27] One may adopt the strategy Kant chose in the second *Critique*: to *stipulate* crucial components of this picture. But the Nietzschean response to such stipulations is a plain denial. If Kant thinks certain postulations are facts of reason, Nietzsche would explain why we might be deluded into thinking so.

array of different components into a whole—those are the ones that turned out well.[28]

This ideal appears in *Ecce Homo*, where Nietzsche describes himself:

What is it, fundamentally, that allows us to recognize *who has turned out well*? That a well-turned-out person pleases our senses, that he is carved from wood that is hard, delicate, and at the same time smells good. He has a taste only for what is good for him; his pleasure, his delight cease where the measure of what is good for him is transgressed. He guesses what remedies avail against what is harmful; he exploits bad accidents to his advantage; what does not kill him makes him stronger. Instinctively, he collects from everything he sees, hears, lives through, *his* sum: he is a principle of selection, he discards much. He is always in his own company, whether he associates with books, human beings, or landscapes: he honors by *choosing*, by *admitting*, by *trusting*. He reacts slowly to all kinds of stimuli, with that slowness which long caution and deliberate pride have bred in him: he examines the stimulus that approaches him, he is far from meeting it halfway. He believes neither in 'misfortune' nor in 'guilt': he comes to terms with himself, with others; he knows how to *forget*—he is strong enough; hence everything *must* turn out for his best.   (EH, 'Wise', 2)

What unifies an agent is captured in terms of health and sanity. *Wohlgeratenheit* is the opposing notion to the character shaped by guilt and *ressentiment*: the person who turned out well is not at odds with the world in the manner of that character, but rests and finds strength in himself. For Nietzsche, the ideal of unity is wholeness, the successful integration of different streaks within one personality into one pattern, the absence of overwhelming internal turmoil. Elsewhere, Goethe is discussed in a manner that reflects this idea: 'What he wanted,' says Nietzsche in a passage we already quoted in 3.4,

was *totality*; he fought the mutual extraneousness of reason, senses, feeling, and will (preached with the most abhorrent scholasticism by Kant, the antipode of Goethe); he disciplined himself to wholeness, he *created* himself. In the middle of an age with an unreal outlook, Goethe was a convinced realist: he said Yes to everything that was related to him in this respect. . . . Goethe conceived a human being who would be strong, highly educated, skillful in all bodily matters, self-controlled, reverent towards himself, and who might dare to afford the whole range and wealth of being natural, being strong enough for such freedom; the man of tolerance, not from weakness but from strength . . . ; the man for whom there is no longer anything that is forbidden—unless it be weakness, whether called vice or virtue.   (TI, 'Skirmishes of an Untimely Man', 49)

This passage emphasizes the integration of different influences and parts of the personality that make Goethe a person of *Wohlgeratenheit*. The Kantian conception and

---

[28] Consider a healthy animal organism without self-consciousness. Such an organism may be characterized as one in which everything functions well together. Nietzschean *Wohlgeratenheit* reproduces this idea as an ideal of agency at the level where organisms have become self-conscious, with all the problems that entails.

its correlative ideal are 'too superficial,' taking seriously only the conscious and thus a relatively unimportant level of the mind, and even that in an unsatisfactory way.

One facet of Nietzsche's ideal unity of agency is the ability to maintain a healthy self-centeredness and self-assuredness, the ability to 'draw a horizon around oneself,' to take up a phrase Nietzsche uses in *Untimely Meditations* II, 1 claiming that '[e]very living being can only be healthy, strong, and fertile within a horizon.' The recognition all rational beings are due within Kantian morality is disregarded: recognition of others may undermine one's unity, at least if conceived as obligatory. For Nietzsche, the practical identity of a person who turned out well is shaped by facts about himself, physiological and psychological needs, which determine what actions benefit him.[29] In a passage in the *Antichrist* that is unusually informative about his disagreements with Kant, Nietzsche writes:

One more word against Kant as moralist. A virtue must be *our own* invention, *our* most necessary self-expression and self-defense: any other kind of virtue is merely a danger. Whatever is not a condition of our life *harms* it. . . . 'Virtue', 'duty', the 'good in itself,' the good which is impersonal and universally valid—chimeras and expressions of decline, of the final exhaustion of life . . . The fundamental laws of self-preservation and growth demand the opposite—that everyone invent *his own* virtue, *his own* categorical imperative . . . Nothing ruins us more profoundly, more intimately, than every 'impersonal' duty, every sacrifice to the Moloch of abstraction . . .   (A 11)

As opposed to the Kantian ideal, Nietzsche's does not focus on consistency. On the contrary, unity may sometimes have to be obtained by preventing deliberations from going where consistently they would go, especially if the relevant kind of consistency is interpersonal consistency, just as unity may sometimes have to be obtained by closing off bits of one's past from awareness if they bring up hurtful memories.[30]

One reason why the person of *Wohlgeratenheit* succeeds in obtaining peace of mind is because he is a fatalist: not a fatalist whom this doctrine commits to inactivity, but one who endorses a *'joyous and trusting fatalism,'* the attitude for which Goethe is praised in TI, 'Skirmishes', 49. Goethe, who was not only creative, but created himself drawing on a splendid range of sources, who was a healthy, well-rounded, stable and strong personality capable of resting in himself, is also applauded for his ability to find strength through comprehending and appreciating his place within the causal web of the universe that relieves him of thoughts of responsibility, blame, and guilt. To the extent that Nietzsche's ideal of unity is fatalistic, it seeks to terminate (to

[29] For this reason, the adjective 'healthy' is frequently apt to capture Nietzsche's recommendation for character development.

[30] Thiele (1990: 61) also discusses why consistency is not a virtue for Nietzsche. Note that this does not mean that deliberation cannot play any role: it must play a role for assessing who you are.

make use of another passage quoted earlier) 'the juxtaposition of "man and world"',
that is, an attitude 'of man as a "world-negating" principle, of man as the measure
of the value of things, as judge of the world who in the end places existence itself
upon his scales and finds it wanting' (GS 346). Thus Nietzsche's ideal is subtle. On
the one hand, the unified agent rests in himself in ways in which the person of guilt
and *ressentiment* does not. (Guilt and *ressentiment*, after all, are feelings of excessive and
unhealthy other-directedness.) On the other hand, the person who turned out well
also conceives of herself as embedded in a causal web comprising the whole universe
(cf. TI, 'Errors', 8). Characteristically for Nietzsche's ideal, this second feature operates
in support of the first: the person who turned out well can safely rest in himself *because*
he is conscious of being part of a causal web that allows for no feelings of guilt and
blame.

5. Conclusion

This study seeks to contribute to a better understanding of Nietzsche as a philosopher
concerned to apply physiological considerations to traditional philosophical problems
and in that sense committed to naturalism. It has done so by clarifying the relationship
between a Nietzsche so understood and Kant as interpreted by Christine Korsgaard,
and has done that, in turn, by formulating objections from such a Nietzschean stance
to Korsgaard's Kant.

First, we have objected to the Kantian picture of the mind, especially Kant's
conception of the will. Doing so has not merely shown a major difference between
Kant's and Nietzsche's respective theories of the mind, but also provided Nietzscheans
with a response to what we have called the objection from the irrelevance of third-
person inquiries to the practical standpoint. For if Nietzsche's view of the mind and
his objection to Kant on that count are correct, that irrelevance objection itself will
be based on a chimerical understanding of the mind and thus could not be raised
any longer, or at any rate would meet a ready Nietzschean response. Second, we
have explored a standard objection to the derivation of the formula-of-humanity
version of the Categorical Imperative, one that by itself has nothing to do with any
Nietzschean ideas. However, the Kantian response to that objection appeals to the
notion of freedom, and it is to that notion to which there is a Nietzschean objection.
That objection is to the idea that individuals have any reason to think of themselves
as free. If they have no such reason, as Nietzsche urges, Kantians cannot defend the
derivation of the formula-of-humanity version of the Categorical Imperative. And
third, finally, we have looked at Kant's and Nietzsche's respective ideas of unity of
agency. If the arguments in Section 2 and 3 succeed (that is, the first two objections

to the Kantian picture), then *ipso facto* an argument against the Kantian conception of unity of agency is forthcoming. We have developed that argument in Section 4. Even if not all of these arguments will persuade those who already have Kantian inclinations, I hope they show at least Nietzsche's philosophical distinctness vis-à-vis Korsgaard's Kant and the intellectual richness of his thought when interpreted in the context of physiology.

Literature

Works of Nietzsche are from the *Kritische Studienausgabe*, edited by Giorgio Colli and Mazzino Montinari, dtv/de Gruyter, second edition 1988. I use the usual abbreviations for the works in English translation:

A	*Antichrist*
BGE	*Beyond Good and Evil*
D	*Dawn*
EH	*Ecce Homo*
GM	*On the Genealogy of Morality*
GS	*Gay Science*
HAH	*Human All Too Human*
TI	*Twilight of Idols*
UM	*Untimely Meditations*
WS	*The Wanderer and his Shadow* (part of *Human, All too Human* II)
Z	*Zarathustra*

I use in general the translations by Walter Kaufmann (of Kaufmann and R. J. Hollingdale, for UM, A, TI, and D), except for GM, where I use Clark/Swensen; however, I have modified the translations at various points and do not in general document precisely where.

References

ALLISON, H. (1990). *Kant's Theory of Freedom* (Cambridge: Cambridge University Press).

BLACKBURN, S. (1998). *Ruling Passions* (Oxford: Oxford University Press).

DELLA ROCCA, M. (1998). 'Spinoza', section IV of V. Chappell, M. Della Rocca, and R. Sleigh, 'Determinism and Human Freedom', in M. Ayers and D. Garber (eds.), *Cambridge History of 17th Century Philosophy* (Cambridge: Cambridge University Press).

HILL, R. KEVIN (2003). *Nietzsche's Critiques: The Kantian Foundations of his Thought* (Oxford: Oxford University Press).

KORSGAARD, C. (1996a). *The Sources of Normativity* (Cambridge: Cambridge University Press).

—— (1996b). *Creating the Kingdom of Ends* (Cambridge: Cambridge University Press).

LEITER, B. (1998). 'The Paradox of Fatalism and Self-Creation', in C. Janaway (ed.), *Willing and Nothingness: Schopenhauer as Nietzsche's Educator* (Oxford: Oxford University Press).

—— (2002). *Nietzsche on Morality* (New York: Routledge).

MOORE, G. (2002). *Nietzsche, Biology, and Metaphor* (Cambridge: Cambridge University Press).

NAGEL, T. (1979). 'Moral Luck', repr. in Nagel, *Mortal Questions* (Cambridge: Cambridge University Press).

PARKES, G. (1994). *Composing the Soul: Reaches of Nietzsche's Psychology* (Chicago: University of Chicago Press).

PINKER, S. (2002). *The Blank Slate: The Modern Denial of Human Nature* (New York: Penguin).

RICHARDSON, J. (1996). *Nietzsche's System* (Oxford: Oxford University Press).

RISSE, M. (2001). 'The Second Treatise in *On the Genealogy of Morality*: Nietzsche on the Origin of the Bad Conscience', *European Journal of Philosophy* 9: 55–81.

—— (2003a). 'Nietzsche's "Joyous and Trusting Fatalism"', *International Studies in Philosophy* 35/3, 147–63.

—— (2003b). 'Origins of *Ressentiment* and Sources of Normativity.' *Nietzsche-Studien* 32: 142–70.

—— (forthcoming). 'In Defense of Nietzsche's Distinctness: Reflections on Gregory Moore's *Nietzsche, Biology, and Metaphor*, and Kevin Hill's *Nietzsche's Critiques: The Kantian Foundations of his Thought*.' To appear in the *European Journal of Philosophy*.

SCANLON, T. (1988). 'The Significance of Choice', in S. McMurrin (ed.), *The Tanner Lectures on Human Values*, viii (Salt Lake City: University of Utah Press).

THIELE, L. (1990). *Friedrich Nietzsche and the Politics of the Soul: A Study of Heroic Individualism* (Princeton: Princeton University Press).

WOOD, A. (1999). *Kant's Ethical Thought* (Cambridge: Cambridge University Press).

4

The Case for Nietzschean Moral Psychology

Joshua Knobe and Brian Leiter

I. Introduction

Moral psychology is the branch of ethics directly concerned with the psychology of the kind of agency we exercise in acting morally. Moral psychology asks whether such agency is psychologically possible, what motivations it requires, what the source of those motivations might be, and what the emotive and cognitive mechanisms are by which they translate into actions. Until fairly recently (e.g., Doris 2002; Nichols 2004; Prinz forthcoming), Anglophone philosophers writing about moral psychology have tended to approach these questions 'from the armchair,' and without regard to pertinent empirical findings about human psychology.[1]

Indifference to empirical findings is probably not unrelated to a second striking feature of the moral psychology literature, namely, that the field has been so dominated by a small number of historical figures, the two most prominent being Aristotle and Kant.[2] From Aristotle has come to us the tradition of virtue ethics,[3]

---

[1] Moral psychologists influenced by Freud, like Deigh (1996), are also an exception to the inattention to empirical psychology, though even Deigh does not spend time investigating the empirical evidence for Freudian moral psychology. But the Freudian theory is an empirical one, and support does exist (e.g., Westen 1998).

[2] Humean views have also been influential, and, in fact, have certain structural similarities to Nietzsche's, but we shall leave for another occasion consideration of how they fare by the lights of empirical psychology.

[3] See, e.g., Hursthouse (1999), Swanton (2003).

which emphasizes the importance of stable characterological dispositions to act in morally appropriate ways, dispositions which it is the task of a sound moral education to inculcate in children. From Kant, by contrast, has come the rationalist tradition in moral psychology,[4] according to which reason is the source of moral motivation, and the mechanism for moral action is one in which rational agents legislate for themselves certain principles on the basis of which they consciously act.

Our goal in this essay is to add a neglected figure to this debate, namely Nietzsche, and to show that a fair reading of the relevant empirical sciences strongly favors the broad outlines of his moral psychology as against the Aristotelian and Kantian traditions. We shall largely follow the account of Nietzsche's moral psychology in Leiter (2002), which makes the interpretative case for the reading relied on here. Our primary concern in this essay is not interpretative, but philosophical: to show that neglect of Nietzsche in moral psychology is no longer an option for those philosophers who accept that moral psychology should be grounded in *real* psychology.

Admittedly, not all philosophers accept that constraint on their moral psychology. Indeed, some contend that issues in moral psychology are not really empirical ones at all. Thus, certain Kantians might say: 'Kant's theory is not intended as a psychological hypothesis. It should be understood rather as a statement of the conditions of the possibility of moral agency. Hence, if we find that no one actually meets the conditions set out by the theory, we should not conclude that the theory itself was mistaken. Instead, we should conclude that no one ever truly is a moral agent.' Let us call philosophers who adopt such a posture *Above-the-Fray Moral Philosophers.* Such philosophers are indeed invulnerable to the empirical results: they tell us how moral agents *ought* to be, and they are indifferent to how moral agents actually are or can be. We reject such an approach in this essay. We assume that *ought implies can* is a reasonable aspiration in moral psychology; indeed, that *ought implies realistically can* is an even better aspiration (see, e.g., Flanagan 1991). We assume with most moral philosophers (including many Kantians) that there are agents who perform morally valuable acts, and thus the question for moral psychology is *not* merely a question about the *possibility conditions* for such psychology, but how this psychology *actually works*.

II. Three Views in Moral Psychology

The Aristotelian and Kantian traditions in moral psychology are historically complex and philosophically rich. Our ambition, plainly, is not to do justice to the history or even all the philosophical permutations. Rather, we want to extract certain *core*

---

[4] See, e.g., Nagel (1970), Darwall (1983).

and *distinctive* elements of these traditions, ones that are, on almost any rendering, important to the views so named, and which, at the same time, involve or presuppose psychological claims that admit of empirical evaluation. Just as there are a multitude of 'Humean' views in ethics and action theory that are traceable to Hume, but do not necessarily have the full texture of Hume's actual views, so too, we claim, there are Kantian and Aristotelian views in moral psychology that are traceable to their distinguished historical forebears, but which we do not claim are Kant's or Aristotle's *precise* views. What we do claim, in each case, is that the views in question are important views in moral psychology *to the present* and that these views do not fare well when compared to the, hitherto, under-appreciated 'Nietzschean' approach to moral psychology.

A. Aristotle

In the Aristotelian tradition of moral psychology, morally good agents are *virtuous* agents, that is, agents possessed of stable dispositions to act in morally appropriate ways as different situations require. The agent who acts morally, according to Aristotle, has three attributes: 'he must act knowingly, next he must choose the actions, and choose them for themselves, and thirdly he must act from a firm and unalterable character' (*NE* 1105^{a}29–33).

But Aristotle does not merely suggest that moral action stems from a certain type of character; he also advances a series of specific hypotheses about the nature and origin of that type of character. In particular, he claims that good character consists in certain *habits* (*NE* 1103^{a}25), that these habits are acquired during *childhood* (*NE* 1103^{b}25), and that the key to their acquisition is proper *upbringing* (*NE* 1095^{b}5–10). Ultimately, then, we are left with a definite picture of how virtuous character is acquired. This picture says that people are encouraged to perform certain virtuous behaviors during childhood and that they gradually come to acquire the corresponding dispositions, leading eventually to a full-fledged possession of the relevant virtue.

Richard Kraut (2001) provides a more nuanced discussion of this hypothesis:

All free males [according to Aristotle] are born with the potential to become ethically virtuous and practically wise, but to achieve these goals they must go through two stages: during their childhood, they must develop the proper habits; and then, when their reason is fully developed, they must acquire practical wisdom (*phronēsis*). This does not mean that first we fully acquire the ethical virtues, and then, at a later stage, add on practical wisdom. Ethical virtue is fully developed only when it is combined with practical wisdom (1144b14–17). A low-grade form of ethical virtue emerges in us during childhood as we are repeatedly placed in situations that call for appropriate actions and emotions; but as we rely less on others and become capable of doing more of our own thinking, we learn to develop a larger picture of human life, our deliberative skills improve, and our emotional responses are perfected. Like anyone who has developed a skill in performing a complex and difficult activity, the virtuous person takes pleasure in exercising his intellectual skills. Furthermore, when he has decided what to do, he does not have to contend with internal pressures to act otherwise. He does not long to do something that he regards as shameful; and he is not greatly distressed at having to give up a pleasure that he realizes he should forego.

'To keep such destructive inner forces [or pressures] at bay,' notes Kraut, 'we need to develop the proper habits and emotional responses when we are children, and to reflect intelligently on our aims when we are adults.'

This 'process of training' through which a virtuous agent is produced is not, as John Cooper emphasizes, 'purely mechanical':

Aristotle holds that we become just (etc.) by being repeatedly made to act justly (etc.). . . . [S]ince he emphasizes that the outcome of the training is the disposition to act in certain ways, knowing what one is doing and choosing to act that way, the habituation must involve also . . . the training of the mind. As the trainee becomes gradually used to acting in certain ways, he comes gradually to understand what he is doing and why he is doing it: he comes, to put it vaguely, to see the point of the moral policies which he is being trained to follow, and does not just follow them blindly.   (Cooper 1975: 8; citations omitted)

Of particular importance for our purposes are two features of Aristotle's moral psychology of the virtuous agent: first, the morally good agent, properly raised, must have 'a firm and unalterable character'; second, this type of character is typically the product of *childhood upbringing*.[5] Although there has been a great deal of excellent work on the proper interpretation of Aristotle's account of the origin of virtue, there has been surprisingly little discussion of the question whether or not Aristotle's views are actually correct. Our concern here will be with this latter question. We want to know whether there actually is any evidence for the view that people's dispositions are shaped primarily by childhood upbringing or whether people's dispositions might arise through some other process entirely.

B. Kant

In the Kantian tradition of moral psychology, moral obligations are grounded in principles that each agent consciously chooses. But it is not enough for an agent

---

[5] Although these two themes have been central to the 'Aristotelian' tradition within contemporary moral psychology, Aristotle himself appears to have had a more complex and multi-faceted view. He attributes the development of character to a broad process of 'acculturation' (*trophē*) which includes more than just treatment from one's caregivers, and he mentions at a number of points that there are innate differences between individuals in their capacity for virtue, even to the point of suggesting that women and slaves are not capable of true virtue regardless of their childhood experiences. Since modern philosophers working in the tradition of Aristotelian moral psychology have no reason to accept Aristotle's view about who has the potential to be virtuous, we may assume that a credible modern Aristotelian moral psychology must be committed to the proposition that everyone is potentially 'brought up' properly such that they can become virtuous agents.

simply to perform behaviors that happen to accord with these moral principles. If an agent's behavior is merely the product of emotion or habit, then no matter how well that behavior fits with her moral principles, she can never truly be acting morally. Genuine moral action must actually be chosen *because* it is morally right. Or, as Kant famously puts it, genuine moral action is not merely *in accordance with* duty; it is done *out of* duty.

Here is how J. B. Schneewind usefully summarizes the Kantian view:

> At the center of Kant's ethical theory is the claim that normal adults are capable of being fully self-governing in moral matters. In Kant's terminology, we are 'autonomous.' Autonomy involves two components. The first is that no authority external to ourselves is needed to constitute or inform us of the demands of morality. We can each know without being told what we ought to do because moral requirements are requirements we impose on ourselves. The second is that in self-government we can effectively control ourselves. The obligations we impose upon ourselves override all other calls for action, and frequently run counter to our desires. We nonetheless always have a sufficient motive to act as we ought. (Schneewind 1992: 309)

So on the Kantian view of moral psychology, (1) agents impose moral requirements on themselves, and (2) these self-imposed requirements are motivationally effective. In order for the self-imposition of moral requirements to be genuinely autonomous it must presumably be a conscious process of self-imposition. And for these consciously imposed principles to be motivationally effective it must be the case that conscious moral principles are motivationally effective.[6]

C. Nietzsche

The Nietzschean account of moral psychology differs from the Aristotelian and Kantian accounts along almost every dimension. What is decisive is not upbringing, particular habits, or conscious choice; what matters most are heritable psychological and physiological traits.

Of course, Nietzsche would not deny that people have habits and conscious moral principles (nor would he deny that environment is an important influence on development, a point to which we return below). The only question is about

---

[6] We take Schneewind's summary, and the points we emphasize, to comport reasonably well with more elaborate treatments of Kantian ethics and moral psychology, such as that in Korsgaard (1996). So, e.g., Korsgaard says that for Kant, 'principles of practical reason' are 'principles that govern choice' (p. xii) and that Kant demonstrates 'the reality of moral obligation' in the *Critique of Practical Reason* by appeal to 'our consciousness of the moral law and its capacity to motivate us whenever we construct maxims. We are conscious of the law not only in the sense that it tells us what to do, but in the sense that we know we *can* do what it tells us, no matter how strong the opposing motives' (p. 26).

whether these factors actually play any important role in the etiology of people's moral behavior. So, for example, Nietzsche would say that people do have conscious moral principles but that these principles have only a limited impact on the behaviors they actually end up performing. More typically, people *first* perform certain behaviors and *then* develop principles that serve to justify the behaviors they have already performed. The most important factors in the origin of moral behavior are people's basic psychological and physiological traits; the conscious moral principles largely serve as *post hoc* justifications for behaviors that would have been performed either way.

Under the influence of several decades of postmodern readings, these central aspects of Nietzsche's moral psychology have often been neglected. In consequence, they deserve a bit more exposition than we have accorded to the Aristotelian and Kantian views, whose broad outlines are widely recognized. To begin, we should remember that Nietzsche was very much influenced by the idea, popular among German Materialists in the 1850s and after, that human beings are fundamentally bodily organisms, creatures whose physiology explains much of their conscious life and behavior (see generally Leiter 2002: 63–71). Nietzsche adds to this Materialist doctrine the proto-Freudian idea that the unconscious psychic life of the person is also of paramount importance in the causal determination of conscious life and behavior.[7] Thus, Nietzsche accepts what we may call a 'Doctrine of Types' (Leiter 2002: 8), according to which,

Each person has a fixed psycho-physical constitution, which defines him as a particular *type* of person.

These 'type-facts', for Nietzsche, are either *physiological* facts about the person, or facts about the person's unconscious drives or affects. The claim, then, is that each person has certain largely immutable physiological and psychic traits that constitute the 'type' of person he or she is. While this is not, of course, Nietzsche's precise terminology, the ideas are familiar enough from his writings.

A typical Nietzschean form of argument, for example, runs as follows: a person's theoretical beliefs are best explained in terms of his moral beliefs; and his moral beliefs are best explained in terms of natural facts about the type of person he is (i.e., in terms of type-facts). So Nietzsche says, 'every great philosophy so far has been . . . the personal confession of its author and a kind of involuntary and unconscious memoir'; thus, really to grasp this philosophy, one must ask 'at what morality does all this (does *he*) aim?' (BGE 6).[8] But the 'morality' that a philosopher embraces simply bears

---

[7] Nietzsche's 'official' view seems to be that physiology is primary, but he mostly concentrates on psychological claims, most obviously because he is no physiologist!

[8] We cite Nietzsche's texts using the standard English-language acronyms as follows: *Daybreak* (D); *The Gay Science* (GS); *Beyond Good and Evil* (BGE); *On the Genealogy of Morality* (GM); *Twilight of the Idols* (TI);

'decisive witness to *who he is*'—i.e., who he *essentially* is—that is, to the 'innermost drives of his nature' (BGE 6). Indeed, this explanation of a person's moral beliefs in terms of psycho-physical facts about the person is a recurring theme in Nietzsche. '[M]oralities are . . . merely a sign language of the affects' (BGE 187), he says. 'Answers to the questions about the *value* of existence . . . may always be considered first of all as the symptoms of certain bodies' (GS P:2). 'Moral judgments,' he says are, 'symptoms and sign languages which betray the process of physiological prosperity or failure' (WP 258). '[O]ur moral judgments and evaluations . . . are only images and fantasies based on a physiological process unknown to us' (D 119), so that 'it is always necessary to draw forth . . . the *physiological* phenomenon behind the moral predispositions and prejudices' (D 542). A 'morality of sympathy,' he claims, is 'just another expression of . . . physiological overexcitability' (TI IX:37). *Ressentiment*—and the morality that grows out of it—he attributes to an 'actual physiological cause [*Ursache*]' (GM I:15). Nietzsche sums up the idea well in the preface to the *Genealogy*: 'our thoughts, values, every "yes," "no," "if" and "but" grow from us with the same inevitability as fruits borne on the tree—all related and each with an affinity to each, and evidence of one will, one health, one earth, one sun' (GM P:2).

We can see Nietzsche's Doctrine of Types clearly at work in his discussion of the 'error of confusing cause and effect,' in sections 1 and 2 of 'The Four Great Errors' section of *Twilight of the Idols*, which is devoted to debunking the idea of free will. The crux of this first error can be summarized simply: given two regularly correlated effects E1 and E2 which have the same 'deep cause,' we confuse cause and effect when we construe E1 as the cause of E2, missing altogether the existence of the deep cause that *really* explains them both. Let us call this error 'Cornarism' after the (now) famed example Nietzsche invokes:

Everybody knows the book of the famous Cornaro in which he recommends his slender diet as a recipe for a long and happy life . . . I do not doubt that scarcely any book (except the Bible, as is meet) has done as much harm . . . The reason: the mistaking of the effect for the cause. The worthy Italian thought his diet was the *cause* of his long life, whereas the precondition for a long life, the extraordinary slowness of his metabolism, the consumption of so little, was the cause of his slender diet. He was not free to eat little *or* much; his frugality was not a matter of 'free will': he became sick when he ate more.   (TI IV: 1)

In other words, what explains Cornaro's slender diet *and* his long life is the same underlying fact about his metabolism. Cornaro's mistake was to prescribe his diet for all without regard for how individuals differed metabolically, metabolism being the relevant type-fact in this context.

The Will to Power (WP). Roman numerals mark chapters, Arabic numerals refer to sections, not pages. Translations—with occasional minor emendations by Leiter—are by Maudemarie Clark and Alan Swenson, R. J. Hollingdale, and/or Walter Kaufmann.

Even if we grant Nietzsche all the facts as he presents them, this would not suffice for a *general* attack on free will unless the error involved in Cornarism extended beyond cases such as diet and longevity. But that is exactly Nietzsche's contention, since in the very next section he saddles morality and religion quite generally with Cornarism. According to Nietzsche, the basic 'formula on which every religion and morality is founded is: 'Do this and that, refrain from that and that—then you will be happy! Otherwise . . .' Cornaro recommended a slender diet for a long life; morality and religion prescribe and proscribe certain conduct for a happy life. But, says Nietzsche, '[A] well-turned out human being . . . *must* perform certain actions and shrinks instinctively from other actions; he carries the order, which he represents physiologically, into his relations with other human beings and things.' So morality and religion are guilty of Cornarism: the conduct they prescribe and proscribe in order to *cause* a 'happy life' are, in fact, *effects* of something else, namely the physiological order represented by a particular agent, one who (as Nietzsche says) '*must* perform certain actions,' just as Cornaro *must* eat a slender diet (he is 'not free to eat little *or* much'). That one performs certain actions *and* that one has a happy life are themselves both effects of the physiological order. If we grant Nietzsche the Doctrine of Types, then there is indeed reason to think that Cornarism is a feature of morality too, since morality fails to recognize the crucial role of type-facts in determining what one does, even what morality one accepts.

All this being said, it is important to recognize that Nietzsche's view is *not* that type-facts determine *everything* (his is not some nineteenth-century vulgar biologistic determinism) (cf. Leiter 2002: 91–101). Type-facts radically circumscribe possible developmental trajectories, but the environment (for Nietzsche, especially the *moral* environment) is quite significant in determining the outcomes. Think of some seeds from a tomato plant. No amount of environmental input will yield an apple tree from those seeds, yet the 'environment' (the amount of water, sun, pests, etc.) will affect which of the trajectories possible for a tomato plant—wilting, flourishing, or any of the stages in between—will be realized. Yet still the fact is that the *type* tomato is the only possible outcome, even though the particular token of a tomato we get may vary quite a bit.

We may now summarize the implications of the Nietzschean view for moral psychology: individuals are simply born with a certain psycho-physical package of traits (the person's distinctive type-facts); these type-facts play a powerful (but not exclusive) role in determining one's behavior and values, though a far more powerful role than education or upbringing or conscious choice; indeed, a person's crucial conscious choices and values are themselves explicable in terms of these type-facts. *That* one is a 'moral' agent is explained by one's biological inheritance, the type-facts; *that* one is not a moral agent is similarly explained.

D. Three Views in Moral Psychology: Summing Up

Thus far, we have been presenting three rival views in moral psychology. Our goal now is to figure out which of these three views provides the best account of how people actually come to perform moral behaviors. In addressing this question, we make use of an extremely straightforward methodology: we turn to studies that directly measure the extent to which different factors appear to be influencing behavior.

While the issue here is an empirical one, we should also emphasize that it is not the kind of issue that could ever be resolved by a single crucial experiment. In essence, the problem here is that none of the three views can be refuted by a single isolated case. Virtue ethicists in the Aristotelian tradition do not typically claim that *everything* about a person's character was determined by the way in which he or she was brought up. Nor does Nietzsche need to say that *everything* about a person's character is determined at birth. The three positions differ primarily in their understanding of what *typically* happens in cases where a person performs a behavior deemed valuable. Our question is whether the existing empirical evidence favors one of these positions over the others.

III. The Empirical Evidence in Moral Psychology

To address this question, we turn to the literature in empirical psychology. We will proceed by reviewing psychological research that will enable us to assess the plausibility of the Aristotelian, Kantian, and Nietzschean assumptions about what people are like. The evidence strongly suggests, we shall argue, that the Nietzschean view is far more likely to be correct than either of the others.

We should emphasize that the empirical results we will be discussing here are not those of a few maverick scientists drawing on some small number of scattered experiments. Rather, we will be focusing on some of the major lessons of personality and social psychology, replicated in numerous experiments using a wide variety of methodologies and subject pools. Occasionally, we will describe a specific experiment and report its results, but the importance of these specific experiments is not that they themselves provide evidence for the theories discussed but rather that they serve as *examples*—giving the reader a sense for the kinds of techniques and results to be found in the relevant literatures. In addition to descriptions of specific experiments, we therefore rely heavily on reviews that summarize large numbers of relevant studies. Thus, to take just one example, we briefly mention a paper by Feingold (1992) on the impact of attractiveness on personality. That paper is a review of more than ninety studies including a total of more than *fifteen thousand* subjects. What makes Feingold's theory convincing is the fact that such a wide variety of studies have converged on a single basic result. The same could be said of each of the other theories we discuss.

In sections (A) and (B), we adduce empirical evidence that supports the broad outlines of the two central features of Nietzschean moral psychology: first, that individuals are simply born with a certain psycho-physical package of traits (the person's distinctive type-facts); and second, that heritable traits play a powerful role in determining behavior and values. In sections (C) and (D), we consider empirical evidence at odds with essential presuppositions of the Aristotelian and Kantian approaches: first (*contra* Aristotle), that character is shaped by upbringing; and second (*contra* Kant), that conscious principles determine action.

A. Type-Facts and Heredity (For Nietzsche)

As we have seen, Nietzsche puts forward the view that a person's traits are determined, to a great extent, by factors (type-facts) that are fixed at birth. This view has gone more or less unexplored in the contemporary philosophical literature on moral psychology. (No one suggests, e.g., that the secret to becoming a compassionate person might lie in part in inheriting a genetic propensity for compassion.) And yet, although the Nietzschean view has not found much favor among philosophers, it is receiving an ever-growing mountain of support from empirical studies.

The most important evidence here comes from studies in behavioral genetics. Typically, these studies are conducted either by looking at twins (comparing monozygotic to dizygotic) or by looking at adopted children. The results of such studies are as consistent as they are shocking. Almost every personality trait that has been studied by behavioral geneticists has turned out to be heritable to a surprising degree. So, for example, a recent review of five studies in five different countries (comprising a total sample size of 24,000 twins) estimates that genetic factors explain 60 percent of the variance in extraversion and 50 percent of the variance in neuroticism (Loehlin 1992).

It is difficult to convey just how astoundingly high these numbers are, but perhaps one can get a better sense for the issue by considering the effect sizes obtained in some classic social psychology experiments. The Festinger and Carlsmith (1959) study of cognitive dissonance found an effect that explained 13 percent of the behavioral variance; the Darley and Batson (1973) study of bystander intervention and the diffusion of responsibility found an effect that explained 14 percent of the behavioral variance; the Milgram (1975) study of obedience and proximity showed an effect that explained 13 percent of the behavioral variance.[9] These are among the most

---

[9] Note for the statistically inclined: No effect sizes are reported in the original papers, but Funder and Ozer (1983) have shown that it is possible to compute additional analyses based on information that

influential and important experiments in all of social psychology. In each case, the fact that researchers were able to explain 13–14 percent of the variance led to a veritable revolution in our understanding of the relevant phenomena. Now consider, by contrast, the fact that behavioral geneticists routinely find effects that explain *50 percent* of the variance in trait measures. Effect sizes of this magnitude are beyond the range that would previously have been considered possible.

Having said that, we should emphasize that it would be a mistake to attach too much importance to the exact percentages obtained in these studies. On the one hand, adoption studies generally yield lower heritabilities than twin studies do, and one might therefore suspect that the true heritabilities are lower than those reported here. On the other hand, our ability to measure traits is quite limited, and one might therefore suspect that we would obtain even higher heritabilities if we could develop a more accurate trait measure. Whatever the resolution of these various difficulties, it seems clear that most traits have extremely high heritabilities.

Here we should pause to avert a potential misunderstanding of what it means for a trait to be 'heritable.' When we say that a trait is heritable, we do not mean that it is produced entirely by a person's genes, without any intervention from the environment. All we mean is that the differences between different people's scores on this trait can be explained in part by differences in those people's genetic material. This effect may not be direct. Differences in people's genes might lead to differences in their environments, which in turn lead to differences in their scores on certain traits. Often the result will be a self-reinforcing cycle in which early behaviors that express a given trait lead the person to possess that trait to ever greater degrees. For example, a person's initial extraverted behavior might leave her with a reputation for extraversion, which in turn makes her even more extraverted.

At least in principle, then, it is possible that heritable differences in personality are caused by heritable differences in some non-psychological characteristic. For example, it might turn out that heritable differences in physical appearance lead to differences in treatment by parents and peers, which in turn lead to differences in personality traits (Hoffman 1991). In actual fact, however, it is highly unlikely that any substantial portion of the variance in personality traits can be explained in this way. To take one striking example, physical attractiveness appears to have almost no impact at all on personality: it explains around 2 percent of the variance in dominance, 0 percent of the variance in sociability, 2 percent of the variance in self-esteem, and so forth (Feingold 1992).

Of course, the impact of genetics is not confined to morally neutral traits like extraversion and neuroticism; it also extends to traits that lie at the heart of moral

the authors do report. (All effect sizes given here are calculated by taking the square of the relevant correlation coefficient.)

psychology. Consider the tendency to use violence (what psychologists sometimes call 'aggressive antisocial behavior'). A number of studies have examined the causes of violent behavior among children, and all show a strong influence of genetics. One recent study using 1,523 pairs of twins found an heritability of 70 percent (Eley et al. 1999). Other studies yield percentages that are lower but still surprisingly high—60 percent (Edelbrock et al. 1995), 49 percent (Deater-Deckard and Plomin 1999), and 60 percent (Schmitz et al. and 1995). These huge effect sizes cannot plausibly be ascribed to experimental artifacts or measurement error. Clearly, genetic factors are playing a substantial role in the etiology of certain kinds of violence.

Studies like these confirm the commonsense view that morally relevant traits, like most other traits, are the product of not only environmental factors but also of heredity. This is the view we find assumed (commonsensically enough) in the works of Nietzsche. 'It is simply not possible that a human being should *not* have the qualities and preferences of his parents and ancestors in his body,' as Nietzsche quips, 'whatever appearances may suggest to the contrary' (BGE: 264).

Subsequent philosophical work, in both the Aristotelian and Kantian traditions, has more or less ignored the role of heredity, focusing either on environmental factors like culture and upbringing, or ignoring questions about the genesis of motivation altogether. Yet all available evidence points to the view that heredity plays a major role in the development of morally relevant traits, and if we want our moral psychology to be defensible and empirically sound, we need to grapple seriously with the philosophical issues this evidence raises. Of the historical figures we are considering, only Nietzsche has come to terms with the issue.

B. Type-Facts and Fatalism (For Nietzsche)

Thus far, we have been concerned with questions about how people come to have certain traits rather than others. But Nietzsche also makes very strong claims about the *importance* that these traits—however they are acquired—actually have in people's lives. A person's character, he seems to suggest, has a substantial and pervasive impact on the whole course of that person's life. This claim may seem so banal and obviously correct as not even to be worthy of discussion. In actual fact, however, aspects of it have been the object of a long-standing controversy within social and personality psychology.

Personality psychologists have performed numerous studies in which subjects first engage in some task designed to measure their personality traits (typically, filling out a questionnaire) and then are given an opportunity to perform a behavior that ought to be influenced by those traits. One surprising result of such studies is that correlations between a trait measure and an actual behavior rarely exceed 0.30. In other words, the trait measure rarely allows us to explain more than 9 percent of the variance in the behavior.[10] This is an extremely important finding, and it has been discussed in detail by both personality and social psychologists.

In his groundbreaking discussion of the phenomenon, Mischel (1968) suggested that perhaps broad traits do not really exist at all. The suggestion was that it might be more accurate to posit only extremely narrow traits (e.g., a tendency to cheat in exams by copying other people's answers) and stop looking for broad traits like 'extraversion' and 'neuroticism.' This suggestion spurred a great deal of debate throughout the 1970s (e.g., Bem and Allen 1974; Jones and Nisbett 1972), but that debate is now over. Almost all psychologists now believe that broad traits do exist.[11] The key question is how important they are—whether they actually have a large impact on people's behavior or whether they turn out to be far less powerful than certain subtle situational forces.

This issue is surprisingly complex. Ross and Nisbett (1991) have offered sophisticated arguments for the view that traits have only a small impact on behavior, but Funder and Ozer (1983) and Epstein (1979) have offered arguments of equal sophistication for the view that traits can have quite large impacts on behavior.

To get a sense for the complexity of the issue, consider what would happen if we tried to predict a basketball player's performance using some measure of his or her ability. Clearly, our predictive power would depend in part on how much of the player's behavior we were trying to predict. If we tried to predict the player's success in getting one particular randomly selected rebound, our measure of ability would give us only very limited predictive power. (The most important factor would be the difficulty of that particular rebound.) On the other hand, if we were trying to predict the quality of the player's overall performance across the course of an entire season of play—including numerous different kinds of tasks performed in a wide variety of situations—our ability measure would probably prove extremely useful. So should we say that ability has only a small impact on performance or that it has a very large impact? Ultimately, our answer will depend on the precise nature of our concern:

---

[10] Note on statistics: Although results in behavioral genetics are normally reported as percentages of variance, results in personality psychology are normally reported as correlation coefficients. For the sake of consistency, we therefore transform each correlation coefficient (r) into a coefficient of determination (r^2), which is equal to the percentage of variance explained. The reader can obtain correlation coefficients by taking the square root of each percentage of variance given in the text.

[11] By 'broad traits,' we simply mean traits that produce a wide variety of different types of behavior. Belief in the existence of broad traits should be carefully distinguished from what Doris (2002) has called *globalism*—namely, belief in the existence of traits that are stable, evaluatively integrated, and yield consistent behavior. (A trait that explains, say, 9 percent of the variance in a wide range of morally relevant behaviors could be extremely broad but would not yield consistent behavior and would therefore provide no evidence at all for globalism.) When we say that the existence of broad traits is no longer a matter of controversy in social and personality psychology, we certainly don't mean to imply that all psychologists are globalists. Far from it: as we shall see, trait-relevant behaviors are often surprisingly inconsistent.

whether we are concerned with success on one particular occasion or with success over the course of a whole season.

As Epstein (1979) has argued, a similar conundrum arises in the domain of moral psychology. For example, suppose we wanted to know whether a broad trait of 'honesty' can be used to predict the degree to which children will engage in a broad array of different kinds of honesty-related behaviors. If we try to predict just *one* such behavior on the basis of one other behavior, we obtain a correlation that explains only 5 percent of the behavioral variance. However, if we look at the overall honesty that a child shows across a whole battery of tests and then try to predict the honesty that the same child will show in another battery of tests, we obtain a much higher correlation—this time, explaining a full 81 percent of the variance (Hartshorne and May 1928).

So should we say that traits have only a small impact on behavior or that they have a very large impact? Here again, the answer will depend on the nature of our concern: whether we are concerned with one particular behavior or with a long sequence of behaviors performed over the course of many years. Doris (2002) and Harman (1999) have argued that traditional virtue ethics can only be tenable if we have some way to predict specific behaviors on the basis of broad personality traits. This is a powerful argument—and one for which we have considerable sympathy—but the issue remains controversial. A number of philosophers have argued that virtue ethics can still be viable even in the face of the Doris–Harman critique (see, e.g., Kamtekar 2004; Merritt 2000; Sabini and Silver 2005; Sreenivasen 2002).

Our aim here is not to resolve this controversy but rather to emphasize that the problem Doris and Harman have identified for virtue ethics does not also apply to Nietzsche's account. Since Nietzsche is interested in the *structure of a life*, and not in isolated, particular instances of conduct, it would seem that Epstein's approach offers strong support. What matters for Nietzsche is that heritable traits structure the *course of a life*, not that they enable one to predict any particular instance of conduct in that life. That was clear enough in the case of Cornaro discussed earlier: what was at issue was explaining his *overall diet* in terms of type-facts, not every bit of food he consumed. Or as Nietzsche puts it elsewhere, 'Wherever a *cardinal* problem is at stake, there speaks an unchangeable "this is I" ' (BGE: 231; emphasis added). Or similarly: 'Our *most sacred convictions* . . . are judgments of our muscles' (WP: 314; emphasis added). It is the *central* features of moral belief and action—the recurring ones that mark the distinctive features of a life—that Nietzsche wants to understand in terms of type-facts, not any particular belief or action on any particular occasion. As we shall see in a moment, though heritable traits may not predict people's behavior on any individual occasion, a wide variety of studies show that they do have a quite substantial impact on the long-run path of an individual's life.

C. The Role of Upbringing (Against Aristotle)

In contrast to Nietzsche, philosophers working in the Aristotelian tradition tend to assume that upbringing plays a major role in the shaping of people's character traits. Here it is essential to distinguish two related claims. First, there is the bland and relatively uncontentious claim that a person's environment has an important influence on his or her character. Second, there is the more specific and largely unsubstantiated claim that character is shaped by *upbringing*, i.e., by the ways in which a person is treated by his or her parents or caregivers. This latter claim is usually put forward without argument, but as we shall see, recent empirical research gives us quite substantial reasons to be suspicious of it.

In thinking about this issue, it may be helpful once again to consider what percentage of the variance in personality traits is explained by each of a number of different factors. We saw above that heredity explains around one-third to two-thirds of the variance in most traits, with the rest presumably explained by environmental factors. Our question now is: Of the variance explained by the environment, how much is explained by upbringing and how much is explained by other environmental factors?

To begin with, we should note that socialization researchers have uncovered numerous correlations between childrearing practices and personality development (e.g., in the classic studies of Baumrind 1967; 1991). In other words, it can be shown that children who have been raised in particular ways tend to have particular personality traits. But the existence of correlations is not in question here; the only question is about whether particular childrearing practices actually *cause* people to have particular personality traits. For example, it is widely assumed that there is a correlation whereby people who are beaten as children tend to be more violent as adults. One possible explanation of this correlation would be that childhood beatings actually cause people to develop more violent personalities. But there are other plausible interpretations. It could be that certain people have more violent personalities even as children and that these people are more likely to misbehave and then to be beaten by their parents. Alternatively, it could be that a genetic propensity for violence is passed down from parents to children and that, since violent people are especially likely to have violent parents, such people are especially likely to be beaten as children.

The key contribution of behavioral genetics to this question has been in distinguishing between variance explained by the *shared environment* and variance explained by the *non-shared environment*. The 'shared environment' is made up of those aspects of the environment that are shared by all children growing up in the same family, while the 'non-shared environment' is made up of those aspects of the environment that differ even between two children growing up in the same family. Thus, suppose that two children are brought up by the same parents but have different peer groups. The traits of the parents would then be part of the shared environment, while the traits of the peers would be part of the non-shared environment. We can now ask how much of the variance in personality traits is explained by the shared environment. The surprising answer is: *very little* (only 5 percent to 10 percent in most studies). This is truly a shocking result, but it has been replicated in an enormous variety of studies and is now the basis of a wide-ranging consensus among researchers (see, e.g., Bouchard 1994; Loehlin 1992; Plomin and Daniels 1987).

To see the force of this finding, it may be helpful to engage in a quick thought experiment. Suppose we know that a given child is going to be adopted by a pair of particularly kind, loving and open parents. What should we predict about the development of this child's personality? The answer appears to be that our knowledge of the parents gives us almost no predictive power at all. If these parents adopt three different children, those three children will be hardly any more similar than three randomly selected individuals.

As usual, the findings obtained for morally neutral personality traits hold for morally relevant personality traits as well. We noted above that one recent study finds that 70 percent of the variance in children's aggressiveness is explained by genetic differences. That same study finds that only 5 percent of the variance is explained by the shared environment (Eley et al. 1999). But as the authors themselves point out, this result is methodologically suspect, since the study had parents themselves assessing the degree to which their children behaved violently. When the violence of children is assessed by their teachers, heredity accounts for 49 percent of the variance and shared environment has no impact at all (Deater-Deckard and Plomin 1999). Of course, results like these do not call into question the widespread assumption that there is a correlation whereby violent parents are especially likely to rear violent children—but they do suggest another possible interpretation of that correlation. Perhaps the observed correlation has almost nothing to do with parents serving as 'bad role models' or 'perpetuating a cycle of violence.' The effect might be almost entirely genetic, the product of genetic similarity between parents and children.

Reading the works of behavioral geneticists, it is easy to get the impression that no study has ever found the shared environment to have a substantial impact on anything of importance. But that is not quite right. Some studies have indicated a substantial impact of shared environment; it's just that the vast majority of studies have shown no substantial impact, and even when shared environment does have a substantial impact, this impact is usually far smaller than that of either heredity or non-shared environment.

For a case in which shared environment really has sometimes been shown to make a difference, let us consider the study of criminality. As one might expect, there is a correlation whereby criminal parents are more likely to have criminal children. But what explains this correlation—nature or nurture? To find the answer, we can look at studies of adopted children. Our question will be whether criminality in the children is best predicted by criminality in the adoptive parents or by criminality in the biological parents. A number of early studies using this methodology found that criminality in the biological parents predicted criminality in the children but that criminality in the adoptive parents had no significant impact (Schulsinger 1972; Crowe 1974). Later studies, however, did show that children of criminal adoptive parents had somewhat higher rates of criminality. This is an important victory for the significance of shared environment. Yet, even here, the importance of genetics ends up dwarfing the importance of shared environment. To give one striking example, Cloninger and colleagues showed that children of criminal adoptive parents did have higher rates of criminality, but they also showed that children of criminal biological parents were *twice* as likely to become criminals as were children of criminal adoptive parents (Cloninger et al. 1982). Thus, of the total explained variance, 59 percent was explained by the criminality of the biological parents and only 19 percent was explained by the criminality of the adoptive parents.

In light of the repeated failure of shared environment to explain a large portion of the variance in personality, we seem forced to choose between three possible views. One view would be that parental treatment has only a very small impact on the development of personality, with other environmental factors playing a much more important role (Harris 1995; 1998). A second view would be that, although the similar treatment received by children raised together has very little impact, the respects in which such children are raised differently actually do have considerable impact (Plomin and Daniels 1987). A third would be that the very same kinds of parental treatment can have radically different impacts on different kinds of children (Maccoby and Martin 1983). The debate among these three views continues to rage on—with considerable theoretical sophistication (and a fair amount of animosity) being shown on all sides.

In sum, we have overwhelming evidence that heredity plays a major role in the shaping of personality, whereas the claim that upbringing plays a major role is contentious at best. It is, of course, correct that psychologists have not studied the role of upbringing with respect to the specifically Aristotelian virtues such as 'courage,' but it is reasonable to assume that if upbringing has little effect on morally relevant behaviors like criminality, it probably has little impact on the more fine-grained virtues that interested Aristotle. Hence, it may somehow be possible to vindicate Aristotle's moral psychology against its Nietzschean rival, but in light of the empirical evidence, there is plainly no reason for optimism that the Aristotelian account is more plausible.

D. Conscious Decision and Behavior (Against Kant)

Recall that on the Kantian view, moral agents impose motivationally effective moral requirements upon themselves. This process of rational moral self-legislation is presumably a conscious one, and thus we must presume that these consciously imposed moral 'laws' have a substantial impact on behavior. On the Nietzschean view, by contrast, conscious beliefs play no such role in moral (or immoral) agency. People's behaviors are determined not so much by their conscious beliefs as by certain underlying type-facts.

To see the key difference between these two views, consider the case of a professor who devotes a great deal of time to her students. One explanation of the professor's behavior would be that she has a conscious belief about the importance of devoting time to one's students and that she is acting on that belief. This is the type of explanation that Nietzsche wants to reject; it is the mundane analogue of Cornaro's self-understanding, according to which it was his 'free' choice to follow a certain kind of diet that explained his long life. A second type of explanation would be that the professor is simply the type of person who feels compelled to help her students and that, although she may have various conscious beliefs about how she ought to live, these beliefs have very little impact on the way she actually treats other people. It is this sort of explanation that one frequently finds in Nietzsche's works and that we saw illustrated, earlier, in Nietzsche's account of Cornaro.

At least at first glance, it may seem that one way to decide between these two types of explanations would be to see whether there were substantial correlations between certain types of conscious attitudes and certain types of behaviors. For example, we could check whether there was a correlation between the degree to which professors believed they were obligated to spend time with their students and the degree to which those professors actually did spend time with their students. After all, it does appear that we would have a certain kind of *prima facie* evidence that attitudes were influencing behavior if we found a substantial correlation here.

It should be clear, however, that this sort of test is not sufficient to settle the question. The mere existence of a correlation plainly does not establish causality. Just as it is possible that people's attitudes influence their behavior, it is possible that people's behaviors influence their attitudes. Thus, it might turn out that certain professors just happen to be the kinds of people who spend time with their students (for reasons that have nothing to do with their conscious beliefs) and that these professors then come to have the belief that they have an obligation to spend time with their students as a result of the fact that they are already performing the relevant behavior.

Accordingly, we proceed in two steps—beginning with the question whether conscious attitudes are *correlated* with behavior and then asking whether conscious attitudes actually *cause* behavior.

We begin, then, with the question of correlation. In the early decades of the twentieth century, most researchers simply assumed that attitudes were highly correlated with behavior. It was assumed, for example, that any program that decreased racist attitudes would thereby also decrease racist behavior. This initial assumption was called into question by the influential work of LaPiere (1934). LaPiere went on a long car trip with a Chinese couple. Along the way, he took careful notes about how his companions were treated at each of the hotels and restaurants they visited. Despite the widespread prejudice against Chinese people in America at the time, LaPiere found that he and his companions were generally treated quite well and that they were refused service on only one occasion. Later, he wrote to all 250 hotels and restaurants listed in his notes, asking the employees whether or not they would be willing to serve Chinese guests. Over 90 percent of respondents said that they would not serve Chinese, in spite of the fact that they had just done exactly that. This finding seemed to suggest that attitudes and behavior were not quite as closely linked as had previously been thought.

The ensuing decades saw an enormous profusion of studies testing the degree to which attitudes and behavior were correlated. The results of this initial wave of research were extremely surprising. In almost every domain studied, the correlation between attitudes and behavior was shockingly low. By 1969, Wicker was able to draw on a wide variety of studies for the influential review in which he argued that there was little convincing evidence for a substantial attitude–behavior correlation (Wicker 1969).

Wicker's review served as a challenge to the next generation of researchers. The goal was to find specific circumstances in which attitudes truly were substantially correlated with behavior. As it happened, researchers were quite successful at this task—devising ever more clever ways to create a situation in which attitudes and behavior were correlated. (To give one particularly striking example, it has been shown that behavior is more highly correlated with attitudes when subjects are looking at themselves in a mirror (Carver 1975).) In a summary of this next generation of research, Kraus reviewed eighty-eight studies and showed that the attitude–behavior correlation was explaining, on average, 14 percent of the total variance (Kraus 1995).

As might be expected, there has been a fair amount of debate about whether a correlation of this size should be regarded as large or small (e.g., McGuire 1985; Kraus 1995). But the size of the correlation is not our primary concern here. Our concern is with the question whether or not attitudes actually *cause* behavior. If we find, for example, that there is a substantial correlation between attitudes toward a given race and actual behavior toward that race, we still cannot be sure whether the attitudes are causing the behavior, the behavior is causing the attitudes, or some third factor is causing both the attitudes and the behavior.

In fact, systematic experiments suggest that a substantial portion of the observed correlation is due to the impact of behavior on attitudes rather than other way around. For a simple example, consider the results reported in Fendrich (1967). Subjects were (a) given a questionnaire regarding their attitudes toward black people and (b) asked to participate in a meeting of the National Association for the Advancement of Colored People (NAACP), a civil rights group advocating for the interests of black people. The key question was whether there would be any correlation between subjects' attitudes (as measured by the questionnaire) and their behavior (actual participation in the meeting). There were two conditions in the experiment. In one condition, subjects were *first* given the questionnaire and *then* asked to participate in the meeting. In this first condition, there was no significant correlation between attitude and behavior—indicating that, whatever attitude was measured by the questionnaire, that attitude had very little impact on people's actual attendance at NAACP meetings. The second condition was exactly the same as the first, except that the order of the tasks was reversed: subjects first decided whether or not to attend the meeting and then filled out a questionnaire regarding their attitudes toward black people. In this second condition, there was a significant and substantial correlation between attitude and behavior. The overall pattern of the results thus points to a surprising conclusion. In this experiment at least, it appears that attitudes had very little impact on behavior *but that behavior had a substantial impact on attitudes*. In particular, subjects appeared to be modifying their attitudes toward black people in such a way as to justify a prior decision to attend or not to attend a meeting of a civil rights organization.

Fendrich's experiment is just one of the many that have demonstrated the surprising impact of behavior on attitudes. In a typical experiment of this type, psychologists find some way to manipulate subjects into performing a behavior that goes against their pre-existing attitudes. The result—as psychologists have found again and again—is that subjects modify their attitudes to fit the behavior they have been manipulated into performing. The examination of this phenomenon has been a major preoccupation of the field of social psychology, and a number of competing theories have been proposed to explain it (Aronson 1969; Bem 1972; Festinger 1957; Steele 1988). Although there is no clear consensus as yet, the dominant view seems to be that people are motivated to believe that their own behaviors are justified and that they therefore tend to adopt attitudes that justify the behaviors they have already performed.

Given that the correlation between attitudes and behavior is not overwhelmingly high and that a substantial portion of this correlation can be explained in terms of the impact of behavior on attitudes (rather than the other way around), a number of researchers have concluded that attitudes actually have only a very minimal influence on behavior. So, for example, Haidt (2001) has argued that, although people often have conscious attitudes regarding very general moral questions, these attitudes actually have little impact on people's feelings about the rightness or wrongness of specific acts. Perhaps people's feelings about specific acts are derived not from their conscious moral attitudes but rather from a set of non-conscious mental states (Wilson 2002). Thus, it might be thought that the degree to which an individual discriminates against black people is affected, not so much by that individual's conscious attitudes regarding black people in general, as by certain purely non-conscious prejudices over which the person's conscious attitudes have little causal influence.

In light of the empirical data, it seems rather improbable that conscious principles, adopted on Kantian grounds, would actually motivate most people to act. By the same token, though, the empirical evidence does not show that there are *no* moral agents who act on the basis of consciously adopted moral principles. The problem for the Kantian, however, is that there is no reason to think that the class of people (however small) who do act on the basis of consciously chosen principles is coextensive with the class of people who perform actions that otherwise comport with deontological principles, even if they do not act on the basis of those principles. To be sure, such agents may lack the kind of motivation (e.g., respect for the moral law) Kant himself thought morally significant, but they may well be agents whose conduct otherwise manifests respect for the dignity and autonomy of other persons and comports with the categorical imperative. What the evidence from empirical psychology suggests is that Kantians, insofar as they follow Kant in treating motive as morally decisive, are likely to have to treat as immoral a lot of apparently moral individuals because of the largely unrealistic demands of Kant's moral psychology.

IV. A Puzzle about Moral Diversity on the Nietzschean View of Moral Psychology

Suppose Nietzsche is right that individuals are simply born with a certain psycho-physical package of traits (the person's distinctive type-facts), and that these type-facts play a powerful role in determining one's central behavior and values, a far more powerful role than education or upbringing or conscious choice. Suppose, in short, that the fact *that* one is a morally good agent is to a large extent explained by one's biological inheritance (the type-facts), and *that* one is not a morally good agent is similarly explained. This explanation seems to fly in the face of the apparent diversity of moral opinions across cultures. So, for example, most Americans think it is acceptable for a woman to walk down the street with her hair exposed, while in some Islamic countries, people would disagree. Canada and Spain have recognized a legal right to gay marriage—reflecting a kind of moral consensus in those societies—while in the United States, leading political figures, including the President, have expressed resolute opposition to the morality of such unions. Examples like this could, of course, be multiplied *ad nauseam*, and it is reasonable to think that they reflect the pervasive influence on moral opinion of non-biological differences, that is, differences in culture and environment of some sort. Surely it is incredible to think that there is a difference in biological 'type-facts' that makes people of different cultures differ in their views about gay marriage or women who expose their hair!

Nothing in the preceding argument should be construed as endorsing this latter incredible proposition. As we emphasized earlier in discussing the notion of 'heritable' traits, the choice is *not* between 'genes' and 'environment.' Environmental factors *of course* play an important role.[12] The real issue concerns how we individuate the morally relevant attitudes and how we explain them. At a certain level of cultural specificity, one must necessarily recognize that certain 'moral' views are not biologically determined: the view that women should not expose their hair in public, for example, is obviously in large part a product of culture and environment. But the crucial question, for our purposes, is what more *general* moral attitude underlies the specific views which manifest environmental and cultural influences. If the Nietzschean view has bite, it must be at this more general level.

When Nietzsche observes, for example, in the *Genealogy* that 'the earth is the *ascetic planet par excellence*, a nook of discontented, arrogant, and repulsive creatures who could not get rid of a deep displeasure with themselves, with the earth, with all life and who caused themselves as much pain as possible out of pleasure in causing pain' (GM III:11), and then tries to offer an explanation for why this kind of 'ascetic ideal' should be so prevalent,[13] he necessarily abstracts away from all the many culturally particular manifestations of asceticism, whether it is Islamic or Orthodox Jewish proscriptions on women's dress and appearance in public, or American Baptist prohibitions on dancing and drinking, or Catholic views of 'original sin.' Nietzsche thinks there is a psychology (and a kind of psycho-biology) of asceticism that is adequate to explaining why 'the earth is the ascetic planet,' even though the psychological story told will not illuminate the local differences in how the ideal expresses itself. In other words, the suggestion is that each particular ascetic practice is the product of a complex interaction between certain type-facts (which yield a general drive toward asceticism) and certain cultural constructs (which determine the specific form in which this drive will express itself).

Recent work in social and personality psychology lends some support to this basic perspective. Consider the concept of *need for closure* (Kruglanski and Webster 1996).

---

[12] Note that our certainty about the importance of culture does not conflict with our doubts about the importance of upbringing. The key question is whether the transmission of culture takes place primarily through *upbringing* (i.e., through the activities of the caregivers who bring us up) or through other sources (peers, television, etc.). The evidence we reviewed in section III.C. seems to suggest that upbringing actually plays a surprisingly small role here.

[13] See the account in Leiter (2002: 254–63).

People who are high in need for closure (NFC) feel a strong need to arrive at very definite views. They tend to be intolerant of ambiguity and uncertainty, preferring always to have an answer to the questions at hand. In American culture, high-NFC people are more likely to be conservative than liberal (Jost et al. 2003), more likely to be accountants than artists (Webster and Kruglanski 1994). It seems, however, that high-NFC people do not perform the very same kinds of behaviors in all cultures. What one finds is rather that high-NFC people tend to believe strongly in the traditional values of whichever culture they grew up in. Thus, high-NFC people in America tend to subscribe to traditional American values, whereas high-NFC people in China tend to subscribe to traditional Chinese values. Under certain conditions, one therefore finds that high-NFC people in China perform exactly the *opposite* sort of behavior from what we find in high-NFC people in America (Chiu et al. 2000). Here we seem to have a case of exactly the pattern described above—a complex interaction between an underlying type-fact (which yields a drive for quick answers to complex questions) and certain features of the cultural context (which determine the specific form in which this drive expresses itself).

Cases like this one illustrate the promise of Nietzschean moral psychology. It is not that we expect to find certain type-facts that are correlated, in all possible cultural contexts, with the very same specific behaviors. Rather, the type-facts serve (along with various other factors) to produce certain basic drives, but the precise form in which these drives express themselves will often be determined in large part by the cultural context.

V. Conclusion

We have been concerned with three rival views in moral psychology—one that emphasizes habits acquired through childhood upbringing, one that emphasizes conscious moral principles, and one that emphasizes heritable psychological traits. Philosophers have devoted considerable time and thought to the first two of these views, and partisans of each view have shown great theoretical sophistication in clarifying the relevant concepts and working out the key ethical implications. But this philosophical ingenuity is never accompanied by any empirical evidence showing that the factors under discussion actually play any important role in people's lives, and when one looks to the empirical literature, one finds shockingly little evidence that either childhood upbringing or conscious moral principles have a substantial impact on people's moral behavior. It seems likely, then, that much of the recent work on these issues has been taken up with an attempt to work out the implications of a moral psychology that is not actually instantiated in many real human beings.

By contrast, the third view—the one that we find in Nietzsche—garners support from a growing body of empirical evidence. This evidence suggests that heritable psychological traits influence many aspects of people's lives, including their moral behavior. What we need now is an investigation into the philosophical implications of this psychological account (see, e.g., Leiter 2002). Such an investigation would, in many ways, resemble the projects we find in the Aristotelian and Kantian traditions, but it would differ in that it would be concerned with the implications of a hypothesis that seems quite likely to turn out to have a sound basis in empirical reality.[14]

References

ARONSON, E. (1969). 'The Theory of Cognitive Dissonance: A Current Perspective', in L. Berkowitz (eds.), *Advances in Experimental Social Psychology*, iv (New York: Academic Press), 2–34.

BAUMRIND, D. (1967). 'Child Care Practices Anteceding Three Patterns of Preschool Behavior', *Genetic Psychology Monographs* 75: 43–88.

BAUMRIND, D. (1991). 'The Influence of Parenting Style on Adolescent Competence and Substance Use', *Journal of Early Adolescence* 11: 56–95.

BEM, D. J. (1972). 'Self-Perception Theory', in L. Berkowitz (ed.), *Advances in Experimental Social Psychology*, vi (New York: Academic Press), 1–62.

BEM, D. J., and ALLEN, A. (1974). 'On Predicting Some of The People Some of the Time: The Search for Cross-Situational Consistencies in Behavior', *Psychological Review* 81: 506–20.

BOUCHARD, T. J. (1994). 'Genes, Environment and Personality', *Science* 264: 1700–1701.

CARVER, C. S. (1975). 'Physical Aggression as a Function of Objective Self-Awareness and Attitudes toward Punishment', *Journal of Experimental Social Psychology* 11: 510–19.

CHIU, C. Y., MORRIS, M. W., HONG, Y. Y., and MENON, T. (2000). 'Motivated Cultural Cognition: The Impact of Implicit Cultural Theories on Dispositional Attribution Varies as a Function of Need for Closure', *Journal of Personality and Social Psychology* 78: 247–59.

CLONINGER, C. R., SIGVARDSSON, S., BOHMAN, M., and KNORRING, A. (1982). 'Predisposition to Petty Criminality in Swedish Adoptees', *Archives of General Psychiatry* 39: 1242–7.

COOPER, JOHN M. (1975). *Reason and Human Good in Aristotle* (Cambridge, Mass.: Harvard University Press). Page references are to the reprint edition (Indianapolis: Hackett, 1986).

CROWE, R. (1974). 'An Adoption Study of Antisocial Personality', *Archives of General Psychiatry* 31: 785–91.

[14] This was a fully collaborative project; authors are listed alphabetically. We are deeply grateful to John Doris both for the stimulus of his published work and for many hours of conversation on these topics. The essay has benefited from comments and suggestions from Julia Annas, Thom Brooks, Joshua Greene, Gilbert Harman, Richard Holton, Susan James, Peter Jones, Rachana Kamtekar, Graham Long, Richard Posner, C. D. C. Reeve, Hagop Sarkissian, and Kevin Timpe; as well as from audiences at the University of London, the University of Newcastle upon Tyne, and Arizona State University.

DARLEY, J. M. and BATSON, C. (1973). 'From Jerusalem to Jericho: A Study of Situational and Dispositional Variables in Helping Behavior', *Journal of Personality and Social Psychology* 27: 100–8.

DARWALL, STEPHEN. (1983). *On Impartial Reason* (Ithaca: Cornell University Press).

DEATER-DECKARD, K., and PLOMIN, R. (1999). 'An Adoption Study of the Etiology of Teacher Reports of Externalizing Problems in Middle Childhood', *Child Development* 70: 144–54.

DEIGH, JOHN (1996). *The Sources of Moral Agency: Essays in Moral Psychology and Freudian Theory* (Cambridge: Cambridge University Press).

DORIS, JOHN M. (2002). *Lack of Character: Personality and Moral Behavior* (Cambridge: Cambridge University Press).

EDELBROCK, C., RENDE, R. D., PLOMIN, R., and THOMPSON, L. A. (1995). 'A Twin Study of Competence and Problem Behavior in Childhood and Early Adolescence', *Journal of Child Psychology and Psychiatry* 36: 775–85.

ELEY, THALIA, LICHTENSTEIN, PAUL, and STEVENSON, JIM (1999). 'Sex Differences in the Etiology of Aggressive and Nonaggressive Antisocial Behavior: Results from Two Twin Studies', *Child Development* 70: 155–68.

EPSTEIN, SEYMOUR (1979). 'The Stability of Behavior: On Predicting Most of the People Much of the Time', *Journal of Personality and Social Psychology* 37: 1097–1126.

FEINGOLD, ALAN (1992). 'Good-Looking People Are Not What We Think', *Psychological Bulletin* 111: 304–41.

FENDRICH, JAMES (1967). 'A Study of the Association among Verbal Attitudes, Commitment and Overt Behavior in Different Experimental Situations', *Social Forces*, 45: 347–55.

FESTINGER, L. (1957). *A Theory of Cognitive Dissonance* (Stanford, CA: Stanford University Press).

FESTINGER, L., and CARLSMITH, J. M. (1959). 'Cognitive Consequences of Forced Compliance', *Journal of Abnormal and Social Psychology* 58: 203–10.

FLANAGAN, O. (1991). *Varieties of Moral Personality* (Cambridge, MA: Harvard University Press).

FUNDER, D. C., and OZER, D. J. (1983). 'Behavior as a Function of the Situation', *Journal of Personality and Social Psychology* 44: 107–12.

HAIDT, J. (2001). 'The Emotional Dog and its Rational Tail: A Social Intuitionist Approach to Moral Judgment', *Psychological Review* 108: 814–34.

HARMAN, GILBERT (1999). 'Moral Philosophy Meets Social Psychology: Virtue Ethics and the Fundamental Attribution Error', *Proceedings of the Aristotelian Society* 99: 315–31.

HARRIS, JUDITH RICH (1995). 'Where is the Child's Environment? A Group Socialization Theory of Development', *Psychological Review* 102: 458–89.

—— (1998). *The Nurture Assumption: Why Children Turn Out the Way They Do* (New York: Free Press).

HARTSHORNE, H. and MAY, M. A. (1928). *Studies in Deceit* (New York: McMillan).

HOFFMAN, LOIS (1991). 'The Influence of the Family Environment on Personality: Accounting for Sibling Differences', *Psychological Bulletin* 110: 187–203.

HURSTHOUSE, ROSALIND (1999). *On Virtue Ethics* (Oxford: Oxford University Press).

JONES, E. E. and NISBETT, R. E. (1972). 'The Actor and the Observer: Divergent Perceptions of the Causes of Behavior', in E. E. Jones, D. E. Kanouse, H. H. Kelley, R. E. Nisbett, S. Valins, and B. Weiner (eds.), *Attribution: Perceiving the Causes of Behavior* (Morristown, NJ: General Learning Press), 79–94.

Jost, J. T., Glaser, J, Kruglanski, A. W., and Sulloway, F. J. (2003). 'Political Conservatism as Motivated Social Cognition', *Psychological Bulletin* 129: 339–75.

Kamtekar, R. (2004). 'Situationism and Virtue Ethics on the Content of Our Character', *Ethics*, 114: 458–91.

Korsgaard, Christine (1996). *Creating the Kingdom of Ends* (Cambridge: Cambridge University Press).

Kraus, Stephen (1995). 'Attitudes and the Prediction of Behavior: A Meta-Analysis of the Empirical Literature', *Personality and Social Psychology Bulletin* 21: 58–75.

Kraut, Richard (2001). 'Aristotle's Ethics', in E. Zalta (ed.), *The Stanford Encyclopedia of Philosophy*. URL: http://plato.stanford.edu/entries/aristotle-ethics/

Kruglanski, A. W., and Webster, D. M. (1996). 'Motivated Closing of the Mind: "Seizing" and "Freezing" '. *Psychological Review* 103: 263–83.

LaPiere, R. (1934). 'Attitudes vs. Actions', *Social Forces* 13: 230–7.

Leiter, Brian (2002). *Nietzsche on Morality* (London: Routledge).

Loehlin, J. C. (1992). *Genes and Environment in Personality and Development* (Newberry Park, CA: Sage).

Maccoby, E. E., and Martin, J. A. (1983). 'Socialization in the Context of the Family: Parent–Child Interaction', in E. M. Hetherington (ed.), *Handbook of Child Psychology*, iv: *Socialization, Personality, and Social Development* (New York: Wiley).

McGuire, W. J. (1985). 'Attitudes and Attitude Change', in G. Lindzey and E. Aronson (eds.), *The Handbook of Social Psychology* (New York: Random House), 238–41.

Merritt, M. (2000). 'Virtue Ethics and Situationist Personality Psychology', *Ethical Theory and Moral Practice* 3: 365–83.

Milgram, S. (1975). *Obedience to Authority* (New York: Harper Colophon).

Mischel, Walter (1968). *Personality and Assessment* (New York: Wiley).

Nagel, Thomas (1970). *The Possibility of Altruism* (New York: Oxford University Press).

Nichols, Shaun (2004). *Sentimental Rules: On the Natural Foundations of Moral Judgment* (New York: Oxford University Press).

Plomin, Robert and Daniels, Denise (1987). 'Why are Children in the Same Family So Different from One Another?', *Behavioral and Brain Sciences* 10: 1–16.

Prinz, Jesse (2006). *The Emotional Construction of Morals* (Oxford: Oxford University Press).

Ross, Lee, and Nisbett, Richard (1991). *The Person and the Situation: Perspectives of Social Psychology* (New York: McGraw Hill).

Sabini, John and Maury Silver (2005). 'Lack of Character? Situationism Critiqued', *Ethics* 115: 535–62.

Schmitz, S., Fulker, D. W., and Mrazek, D. A. (1995). 'Problem Behavior in Early and Middle Childhood: An Initial Behavior Genetic Analysis', *Journal of Child Psychology and Psychiatry* 36: 1443–58.

Schneewind, J. B. (1992). 'Autonomy, Obligation, and Virtue: An Overview of Kant's Moral Philosophy', in Paul Guyer (ed.), *The Cambridge Companion to Kant* (Cambridge: Cambridge University Press).

Schulsinger, F. (1972). 'Psychopathy: Heredity and Environment', *International Journal of Mental Health* 1: 190–206.

Sreenivasen, G. (2002). 'Errors about Errors', *Mind* 111: 47–68.

STEELE, C. M. (1988). 'The Psychology of Self-Affirmation: Sustaining the Integrity of the Self', in L. Berkowitz (ed.), *Advances in Experimental Social Psychology*, xxi (New York: Academic Press), 261–302.

SWANTON, CHRISTINE (2003). *Virtue Ethics: A Pluralistic View* (Oxford: Oxford University Press).

WEBSTER, D. M. and KRUGLANSKI, A. W. (1994). 'Individual Differences in Need for Cognitive Closure', *Journal of Personality and Social Psychology* 67: 1049–62.

WESTEN, DREW (1998). 'The Scientific Legacy of Sigmund Freud: Toward a Psychodynamically Informed Psychological Science', *Psychological Bulletin* 124: 333–71.

WICKER, A. W. (1969). 'Attitudes vs. Actions: The Relationship of Verbal and Overt Behavioural Responses to Attitude Objects', *Journal of Social Issues* 22: 41–78.

WILSON, T. (2002). *Strangers to Ourselves: Discovering the Adaptive Unconscious* (Cambridge, MA: Harvard University Press).

5

Ressentiment, Value, and Self-Vindication: Making Sense of Nietzsche's Slave Revolt

R. Jay Wallace

In its broad outlines the account of the origin of modern morality that Nietzsche offers in the first essay of his *Genealogy* (GM) is reasonably clear. The account begins with the postulation of two different schemes of value, organized around the pairs of opposites good/bad and good/evil, which are associated respectively with the contrasting personality types of the noble and the slave. Characteristic of the slavish personality structure are the negative affects of hatred and *ressentiment*, which, deprived of a natural outlet, become pent up and fester within the psyche of the powerless until reaching "monstrous and uncanny proportions" (GM, I.7).[1] The slave revolt begins when these sentiments "become creative and give birth to values" (GM, I.10), initiating an historical process through which the universalistic, Christianized values of good and evil largely come to supplant the aristocratic values of good and bad.

Though this story is clear enough in its general outlines, however, it is not at all clear how exactly the psychological processes the story describes are really supposed to work. The crux is the causal relation that is posited between the *ressentiment* of the powerless slaves and the new table of values to which that psychic force allegedly

---

[1] Parenthetical references in the text will be to sections of Nietzsche's *On the Genealogy of Morals* (GM); other references to texts by Nietzsche will be given in notes. Quotations from the *Genealogy* will follow the Kaufmann and Hollingdale translation: Friedrich Nietzsche, *On the Genealogy of Morals*, trans. Walter Kaufmann and R. J. Hollingdale, ed. Walter Kaufmann (New York: Vintage, 1989).

gives rise. There is a natural way of thinking about this causal nexus—the strategic interpretation, as I shall call it—that makes sense of the basic idea that *ressentiment* should give rise to the erection of a new table of values, in an event that might accurately be described as a revolt. But I shall argue that the causal links postulated by this interpretation are ultimately untenable, yielding a narrative that is riddled with paradox at the level of both psychic mechanism and social process. We need a different, non-strategic way of understanding how *ressentiment* could eventuate in Nietzsche's slave revolt, and the main aim of my essay will be to develop such an interpretation. To do so, it will be necessary to think systematically about the nature of *ressentiment*, and about the psychological situation of those who are subject to this emotion in a conceptual landscape defined by the aristocratic values of good and bad. The key to understanding how a new table of values might emerge under these conditions, I shall argue, is to acknowledge the profound human need for a distinctive kind of self-conception, one that I shall refer to as vindicatory. The *ressentiment* of the powerless leads them to internalize a new evaluative scheme that makes sense of their basic emotional orientation to the world. This expressive relation between emotion and value, I shall argue, is the crux for understanding Nietzsche's striking claim that the *ressentiment* of the weak is one of the main sources of modern moral consciousness.

Nietzsche's writings are among the most important documents in our philosophical tradition that grapple with issues in what we now call moral psychology. But not all of his reflections in this vein seem to me to be of equal value. His exploration of asceticism in modern moral consciousness, for instance, has less relevance today than in Nietzsche's own time, as social morality in the western world has moved away from the Victorian emphasis on instinctual self-denial as an end in itself. Some have celebrated Nietzsche's reflections on the will as examples of a laudably minimalistic or naturalistic approach to understanding the psychological preconditions of morality.[2] But this part of Nietzsche's ethical writing strikes me as overrated: there are ways of interpreting rational agency and volition that avoid his objections, and that seem superior to the mixture of epiphenomenalism and psychological determinism that he appears to recommend.[3] The real strength of Nietzsche's moral psychology lies in his insight into the pathological deformations of personality associated with modern moral consciousness, especially where they involve the interplay of emotional forces and evaluative ideals. The account of the emergence of the good/evil table of value out of the *ressentiment* of the powerless is a brilliant example of this tendency in Nietzsche's

---

[2] See Bernard Williams, "Nietzsche's Minimalist Moral Psychology", as reprinted in his *Making Sense of Humanity* (Cambridge: Cambridge University Press, 1995), 65–76.

[3] See, for instance, my *Responsibility and the Moral Sentiments* (Cambridge, Mass.: Harvard University Press, 1994). Nietzsche flirts with epiphenomenalism at *Twilight of the Idols*, VI.3, e.g., while characterological determinism is evident in GM, Preface, sec. 2 and throughout *Ecce Homo*.

polemical critique of modern morality, one that should repay the effort at critical reconstruction that it is my aim in this essay to provide.

1. The Strategic Interpretation

I want to begin by sketching an interpretation of the psychic mechanisms involved in the slave revolt that seems to me to be implicit in much work on this topic. I am tempted to say that the account I shall describe is the default interpretation of the slave revolt, in part because it gives a clear sense to Nietzsche's characterization of this episode in cultural history as a "revolt", in part because it captures at least some aspects of the complex historical process that Nietzsche is concerned to understand. But the default interpretation cannot be the whole truth about the slave revolt, for reasons that I shall also try to explain.

The psychological force that drives the slave revolt, on any account of it, is the *ressentiment* of the slaves. The strategic interpretation understands this emotional orientation primarily in terms of its aim. *Ressentiment* is a negative affect of hatred on the part of the powerless toward their oppressors, involving the desire to strike out against them, in ways that will harm them and deprive them of their cultural and social advantages. The slave revolt may then be thought of strategically in relation to this fundamental aim, as an undertaking that is precisely calculated to harm the powerful. The inferior position of the powerless means that they are unable to pursue this goal directly, through actions that are immediately damaging to the interests of the powerful. So they resort to a more indirect strategy, erecting a new table of values as a devious way of undermining the position and advantages of the people they despise.

There are several considerations that speak in favor of this strategic reading of the slave revolt. For one thing, Nietzsche himself often writes about the events involved in the slave revolt in strategic terms. He describes the invention of the Christian ethic of love, for instance, as part of a "truly grand politics of revenge" on the part of the Jewish people (GM, I.8), suggesting that it was a calculated effort to strike a blow against the oppressors of Israel. To the extent that this political characterization is accurate, the slave revolt must involve activities on the part of at least some of its proponents that are conceived of strategically in relation to the goal of harming the powerful masters. The strategic interpretation takes this political dimension of Nietzsche's account to capture the defining moment of the slave revolt, which consists essentially in activities undertaken with the aim of subverting the power and position of those whom the powerless hate.

Furthermore, understanding the slave revolt in these strategic terms fits with other things that Nietzsche prominently says about it. Thus *ressentiment* plausibly involves the desire to inflict harm on those at whom it is directed, so the aim that is central to the strategic interpretation is one that *ressentiment* may be understood to supply. According to the strategic interpretation, *ressentiment* becomes "creative" when the desire to achieve that aim finally becomes insistent enough to lead to action. And insofar as the actions in question are undertaken with the aim of inflicting harm on the powerful, they can be characterized accurately as a form of revolt. They are attacks on the politically and socially powerful, which are expressly calculated to undermine their position and to harm their central interests.

In these respects, then, the strategic interpretation would seem to recommend itself, as a natural way of understanding the processes that Nietzsche is describing in the first essay of the *Genealogy*. But the interpretation cannot ultimately be sustained; I want to identify three insuperable difficulties that arise when we think about the slave revolt in the terms that it suggests. First, there is a basic problem that is encountered when we try to make sense of the intentions with which the new table of values was erected. The strategic account interprets this as an activity whose goal is to land a blow against the strong and powerful. It is very hard to understand, however, why anyone would choose to pursue this goal by a strategy so feckless and obscure as the erection of a new table of values. This strategy is reasonable only if the new evaluative scheme is something whose articulation and propagation is likely to damage the interests of the politically and socially powerful. But why should the weak believe that the evaluative activities in which the slave revolt consists would have this effect? If the powerful are truly powerful, they could be expected simply to ignore the evaluative scheme that is proposed as an alternative to their own, or perhaps to suppress attempts on the part of the weak to advocate in its defense. The strategic interpretation requires that the weak understand the erection of a new table of values in the logic of instrumental rationality, as a course of action that is effective relative to the goal of revenge against the powerful. But unless they are massively deluded, it seems highly unlikely that they would be able to think of their actions in these terms. Doing so simply does not seem to make much sense.

For similar reasons, the strategic interpretation renders mysterious the historical effects of the slave revolt, as Nietzsche describes them. At the end of the seventh section of the first essay in the *Genealogy* Nietzsche famously remarks that the slave revolt in morality has a history of two thousand years, which we are no longer able to see clearly precisely because it has been victorious. If we think about the revolt in the terms which the strategic interpretation provides, then its victory or success should consist in revenge, where this in turn involves harm or damage to the powerful, of a kind that perhaps eventually leads to their virtual elimination. But why should the erection of a new table of values have had this effect? One would think the truly powerful would simply brush aside the new evaluative rhetoric of the slaves, or crush politically the weak and slavish people who resort to such rhetoric in daily life. In short, the considerations that make it mysterious why the weak would think of their actions as effective means of revenge against the powerful equally render mysterious the postulated success of those actions over the centuries.[4]

There is a third difficulty, however, that is even more serious than the first two problems I have described. This is that the slave revolt becomes a self-undermining process if we conceptualize it in the terms that the strategic interpretation proposes. To this point I have spoken of the slave revolt as involving the erection of a new table of values, as if this were a mere act of rhetoric or transparent propagandizing. But it is clear that Nietzsche does not understand the revolt in such superficial terms as these. It occurs, he says, when *ressentiment* becomes creative and gives birth to values, and this process involves more than merely the invention of a new discourse or set of evaluative terms. Values come into existence only to the extent that a new discourse of value is internalized and taken seriously, as a framework for organizing life and experience. An evaluative framework of this kind leads one to prefer some things to others, shaping one's deliberations about action, and providing a basis for criticizing social institutions and individual behavior. But the erection of a new table of values, to the extent it is undertaken with the aim of exacting revenge against the powerful, would precisely fail to give rise to values in this sense.

To see this, we need only note that the new values are supposed to take root in precisely the population whose members are subject to pent-up hatred and *ressentiment*. The strategic interpretation takes these emotions to supply the powerless with a goal—the destruction of the noble class—that the invention of new values is calculated to bring about. But the strategic understanding of the revolt on the part of the slaves undermines the very processes that the revolt itself is supposed to consist in. We can speak of the invention of new values only insofar as the scheme organized around the opposition between good and evil comes to be internalized by the slaves, as a comprehensive framework of the sort described above. A scheme that the slaves themselves understand in strategic terms, however, cannot really play this role in their lives. To the extent the scheme is viewed strategically, as an instrument of revenge, it cannot function as a fundamental framework for preference, deliberation, and criticism. And to the extent it plays these roles, it cannot be viewed by the agent whose experience it fundamentally shapes as a device that is calculated to bring about revenge.[5]

---

[4] For a clear statement of this problem, see Mark Migotti, "Slave Morality, Socrates, and the Bushmen: A Reading of the First Essay of the *Genealogy of Morals*", *Philosophy and Phenomenological Research* 58 (1998), 745–79. In sec. 2 below I shall offer a different response to the problem from the one Migotti favors.

[5] Similar questions about the slave revolt are raised by Rüdiger Bittner, "*Ressentiment*", in Richard Schacht (ed.), *Nietzsche, Genealogy, Morality. Essays on Nietzsche's "Genealogy of Morals"* (Berkeley: University of California Press, 1994), 127–38. Bittner develops his objection in the language of agency, suggesting that

It might be thought that these difficulties can be avoided if we postulate—as Nietzsche's text would seem to allow—that the strategic calculation involved in the slave revolt occurs at the level of unconscious psychic processes. Perhaps the slaves are not really aware that they embrace the evaluative scheme of good and evil as a way of achieving revenge against the powerful. In that event they might fully internalize those values while remaining ignorant of the strategic goals that the process of internalization was originally calculated to achieve. I would agree that Nietzschean *ressentiment* operates beneath the radar of consciousness in the slave revolt, and also that there are conflicts and tensions between the unconscious forces that sustain modern morality and the content of the values in which that morality consists. But these facts do not suffice to remove the problem I have been attributing to the strategic interpretation. For one thing, the unconscious motives at work on the strategic interpretation still involve the aim of achieving revenge against the powerful, and it remains obscure why the slavish should believe at any level, conscious or unconscious, that their invention of a new table of values is likely to advance this aim. (This is a further application of the first objection canvassed above.)

Moreover, it seems implausible to suppose that the unconscious processes at work in Nietzsche's account of the slave revolt follow the linear logic of instrumental rationality that is central to the strategic interpretation. Those in the grip of *ressentiment* and hatred may well have desires to harm and thwart the powerful that they are not fully aware of, at the level of conscious reflection. But it would be peculiar if unconscious forces of this kind operated to sustain the values of modern morality through calculations centered on the relation between means and ends. Unconscious processes tend to follow more primitive logics of association, expression, and symbolic representation. The question is: how exactly might such unconscious processes be involved in the Nietzschean narrative of the origins of modern morality?

2. The Expressive Interpretation

The strategic interpretation sees the meaning of the slave revolt as lying in its instrumental relation to an end that is given by *ressentiment*. The aim it attributes to *ressentiment*, namely to inflict harm on the hated masters, seems one that genuinely belongs to it. But *ressentiment* is more than merely a desire to inflict harm or suffering on someone. How exactly *ressentiment* goes beyond a mere desire to harm is not

---

it undermines the idea that the slave revolt is the result of a creative act on the part of the slaves (cf. pp. 133–4). I agree with him about this (understanding action to be behavior undertaken through the logic of strategic rationality), but disagree that it tells against Nietzsche's story (rather than a common interpretation of that story).

something that Nietzsche himself spells out very explicitly.[6] To make sense of the role Nietzsche ascribes to this emotion, we need to supplement the letter of his texts with an independent examination of a phenomenon to which he is drawing attention, situating *ressentiment* more precisely in relation to other social sentiments and reactions. By attending systematically to the circumstances that plausibly nurture this complex emotional phenomenon, I shall argue that we can arrive at a more satisfactory understanding of the causal role of *ressentiment* in generating and sustaining the new evaluative framework of good and evil.

Ressentiment can be understood as a general emotional orientation of the person. It emerges under conditions in which people find themselves systematically deprived of things that they want very much to possess, without any prospects for improvement in this respect. But systematic deprivation is not sufficient for the emergence of *ressentiment*. If everyone was equally subject to a condition in which he is denied coveted goods—as for instance in a natural emergency, such as a devastating famine or earthquake—the result might be a tendency to feelings of rage, frustration, and depression in the populace at large, but not the kind of focused hatred characteristic of *ressentiment*. For the latter emotions to emerge, there need to be some people who are singled out from the rest in not being deprived of the coveted goods, and who are publicly known not to be deprived. The ur-context of *ressentiment* is one in which some people have things that you very much desire, but that you lack and feel yourself unable ever to obtain. Thus Nietzsche's slaves are systematically excluded from enjoying many of the desirable things that the masters in their society have in abundance, including status, material possessions, and above all political power and influence.[7] *Ressentiment* is fundamentally occasioned by invidious comparisons of this kind.

In the circumstances that give rise to it *ressentiment* bears some similarity to envy, which is also about a person's lack of access to goods that others are conspicuously

---

[6] In GM, I.10, where the concept is first explicitly introduced, Nietzsche characterizes *ressentiment* as a reaction against a hostile external world, and he contrasts the "reactive" mode of evaluation to which to *ressentiment* gives rise with the self-affirmation involved in aristocratic evaluation. Drawing on these passages, Brian Leiter suggests that the "core elements" of *ressentiment* include "a negative, evaluative reaction to an external state of affairs that is unpleasant but which one cannot address through physical action"; see his *Nietzsche on Morality* (London: Routledge, 2002), 204. But this characterization is at once obscure (what is an "evaluative reaction"?) and underdescribed. Not every negative reaction to an unpleasant and unyielding stimulus counts as *ressentiment*. To arrive at an illuminating account of the moral psychology of *ressentiment*, we need to think more systematically about the distinctive features of the emotion and the circumstances in which it emerges, drawing on Nietzsche's texts, but going beyond them to arrive at a fuller picture.

[7] I take it here that one of the most important desiderata for an account of *ressentiment* is the fact that Nietzsche associates it paradigmatically with the outlook of the slavish. We should therefore expect that its origin and structure would reflect features that are distinctive of the position of slaves within a culture, and comparative structural deprivation seems highly salient in this connection.

able to enjoy. But envy does not have the quality of intense and focused malice that distinguishes *ressentiment*. It seems perfectly possible to envy someone their wealth or professional good fortune, say, without wishing them ill or feeling any particularly negative affect toward them personally. Envy of this variety might be structured by the thought "I'm just as good or deserving as he is" and one can entertain this thought without believing that the target of envy is unworthy or undeserving in any way; nor does this emotion require one to feel hostility or hatred toward the person who is envied. These latter forms of focused negative affect, which seem very much characteristic of Nietzschean *ressentiment*, emerge under circumstances that structurally prevent a person from ever coming to enjoy the desired goods that the more fortunate have access to in abundance.[8] Ordinary envy might well be assuaged by one's coming into possession of the desirable items that one formerly lacked, as when a person finally wins the raise or the professional standing that she took herself all along to deserve. Envy grows into *ressentiment* when ordinary rectification of this kind is (believed to be) impossible, because one is systematically prevented by one's nature or one's circumstances from acquiring the things that one so covetously desires.

Nietzsche shows great psychological insight in his assumptions about the transformation that envy undergoes under conditions that involve structural deprivation of this kind. The intensification of hatred into which envy grows becomes focused specifically on the persons who are comparatively privileged; though it is occasioned by relative disadvantage, it is no longer really about the fact of relative disadvantage, but about the individuals who are advantaged, whom the unfortunate come to despise. But why should envy come to assume this quality of personal hatred under conditions of this kind? What explains its transformation into an affect that is essentially focused and personal in the way I have described? This question may not have any very deep or illuminating answer. The process through which ordinary envy turns into the kind of personal animus involved in *ressentiment* cannot plausibly be traced to any further emotion or complex of ideas. It seems to me a primitive mechanism, one that can perhaps be understood to reflect our deeply social nature, our nearly obsessive concern for our relative standing within local and less local communities. Under

---

[8] Compare Bernard Reginster, "Nietzsche on *Ressentiment* and Valuation", *Philosophy and Phenomenological Research* 57 (1997), 281–305, at p. 286. A more extensive treatment, which also emphasizes the structural conditions that give rise to *ressentiment*, is Max Scheler, *Das Ressentiment im Aufbau der Moralen* (Frankfurt am Main: Vittorio Klostermann, 1978), ch. 1. In GM, I.10 Nietzsche entertains tentatively the possibility that noble types might occasionally be subject to feelings of *ressentiment*, remarking that such feelings will immediately be discharged by the noble person who is subject to them, and so fail to fester and grow. This might appear to be at odds with the suggestion that *ressentiment* grows out of structural deprivation. But we can imagine that the masters Nietzsche is here thinking of are only selectively deprived of things that they desire (e.g., a given sexual partner or political office), in ways that are compatible with lack of deprivation in many other domains of their life and experience.

conditions of structural deprivation, in which we permanently lack access to what Rawls calls the social bases of self-respect, the ordinary tendency to envy may be transformed into something quite different: an intensely personal loathing of those who are more fortunate than we are.

This focused emotional orientation toward the fortunate involves the desire to lash out at them that was discussed in the preceding section of this essay. The strategic interpretation correctly attributes desires of this kind to the slavish types in whom *ressentiment* flourishes. But it goes wrong in its account of the relation between such desires and the new table of values to which *ressentiment* gives rise. The fundamental emotional dynamic of the slave revolt is not the selection of means to an end that is set by one's desires. It is the *expression* of one's negative emotional orientation toward the powerful, in the embrace of an evaluative framework that makes sense of that basic orientation.[9]

To understand this emotional dynamic, we need to reflect on the situation of the powerless in the period immediately preceding the invention of the new table of values. *Ressentiment* has festered within these people for years, building up to the point where it becomes the dominant emotional orientation of their lives. This involves a concentration of hatred and hostility directed toward the people in their society who are powerful, successful, and outwardly flourishing. At the same time, the evaluative framework that is available under these cultural conditions characterizes the objects of this concentrated negative affect as precisely good in a superlative degree. In the terms of the evaluative schema of good and bad, it is the aristocratic masters who are paradigms of positive value, and the characteristics that distinguish them from the rabble—their superior discernment, independence, confidence, and so on—are singled out for praise and celebration. So the powerless find themselves in a conceptual situation in which the negative affect that dominates their emotional lives is directed at individuals whom they themselves seem compelled to regard as exemplars of value and worthy of admiration. This is a highly unstable combination of attitudes, one which is antithetical to the slaves' ability to make sense of their own deepest emotional experience.

In my view, the slave revolt should be understood as a response on the part of the slavish to this psychic tension.[10] The weak are subject to attitudes that color their

---

[9] Similar ideas are sometimes vaguely hinted at in the secondary literature. For example, in *Nietzsche on Morality*, 202–4, Brian Leiter describes the slave revolt as a "projection" of the *ressentiment* of the slaves. See also Bittner, "*Ressentiment*", 133–4, who remarks that suffering and *ressentiment* might give rise to new moral convictions in something like the way a disease gives rise to symptoms. But neither Leiter nor Bittner offer any detail about how exactly the new table of values might be understood as the projection or symptom of an emotion such as *ressentiment*. It is the burden of my essay to try to work out in clear terms this central Nietzschean idea.

[10] In *Das Ressentiment im Aufbau der Moralen* Scheler also treats the slave revolt as a response to psychic tensions in the self; see, e.g., pp. 32–4. A similar approach is developed by Reginster in "Nietzsche on *Ressentiment* and Valuation", who emphasizes the tension between the repressed desire for power of the

experience of the social world, in ways that cannot be reconciled with the dominant ethical ideology that they themselves have so far accepted. So they come to embrace a new and more congenial scheme of values. This new evaluative scheme is the expression of their underlying *ressentiment*, insofar as its adoption can be explained in terms of that emotional orientation, which is postulated to be prior to it in the order of causation. *Ressentiment* becomes creative and gives birth to values when the tensions that attend it lead the powerless to adopt and internalize a wholly new evaluative framework. The causal nexus linking *ressentiment* to this new framework does not follow the logic of means/end rationality, but the more archaic pattern of emotional self-interpretation. The slaves adopt the scheme of values organized around good and evil, because doing so enables them to make sense of their experience of the world, which is mediated by the sentiments of hatred and *ressentiment*. If the masters are evil, then hatred of them becomes a response that is merited by its object, and the latent tensions in the world-view of the slaves are thereby resolved.

This way of understanding the causal role of *ressentiment* in the slave revolt—the expressive interpretation, as I shall call it—has several immediate advantages. For one thing, it makes very good sense of some of the more prominent strands in Nietzsche's reflections about the slave revolt. Nietzsche emphasizes repeatedly, for instance, that the negative pole is basic in the morality of good and evil, and he contrasts the resulting scheme in this respect with the more affirmative morality of good and bad. The concept of evil, Nietzsche says, is "the original thing, the beginning, the distinctive *deed* in the conception of a slave morality" (GM, I.11, p. 40; cf. GM, I.10). This fits well with the idea that the slavish scheme has its origin in the need to make sense of the essentially hostile affect of *ressentiment*. The problem to which the new morality is a response is the fact that this hostile orientation is directed at objects that have heretofore been regarded as superlatively good. What is required, in light of this problem, is a different way of conceptualizing the landscape of value, one that represents the objects of *ressentiment* as worthy of this kind of negative orientation. By coming to see them as evil, one can experience one's own deep hostility as something that is appropriate to its object, and to the extent this is the case the category of evil is indeed the "original thing . . . in the conception of a slave morality." It is the original thing in the sense that the invention of this category is what most basically resolves the psychic tension to which the slave revolt is a response.

Furthermore, the expressive interpretation attributes a plausible causal role to the unconscious forces of hatred and *ressentiment*. These are pictured as combining with the

aristocratic priests and their inability to satisfy that desire overtly, a tension that is crystallized in their experience of shame; see, e.g., Reginster, "Nietzsche on *Ressentiment* and Valuation", 286–7, 296–7. But Scheler and Reginster give an account very different from mine of how tension is released through the slave revolt, one that remains wedded to the structures of instrumental rationality, and that ultimately treats the new values as pieces of false consciousness.

prevailing ethical framework of good and bad to create a situation of acute psychic tension and instability. The powerless might not be fully aware that they are in the grip of *ressentiment*, but the focused and intense hatred it involves will inevitably color their experience profoundly, in ways that sit very uneasily with the dominant ethical ideology of good and bad. Under these circumstances their whole emotional orientation toward the social world will be fraught with latent tension and conflict; it will not cohere with the values that they themselves accept and attempt to live by, and this tension and conflict will be experienced as forms of anxiety, discomfort, and alienation. The contribution that the new table of values makes is essentially to resolve this acute psychic discomfort, something that is likely to be experienced by the weak as profoundly satisfying. This is the primitive dynamic of self-interpretation to which I earlier referred, and the supposition that unconscious processes might operate in accordance with this dynamic has the ring of truth to it.[11]

This is one respect in which the account I have proposed seems clearly superior to the strategic interpretation, with its postulation of unconscious calculation about means and ends. But Nietzsche clearly does use the language of strategic agency in his discussions of the slave revolt. To take just one example, the "revaluation of values" in which the slave revolt consists is characterized by him as "an act of the most spiritual revenge" (GM, I.7, p. 34), a characterization that suggests calculation with the aim of striking out against the masters. How is this tendency in Nietzsche's theory to be reconciled with the expressive interpretation, which understands the slave revolt in fundamentally non-strategic terms?

To answer this question, we need first to think about Nietzsche's suggestion that the erection of a new table of values amounts to a revolt. This political language acquires a straightforward meaning on the strategic interpretation, which represents the powerless as engaged in a course of action whose avowed aim is to strike a blow at the masters, and hence as a kind of uprising. The expressive interpretation, by contrast, treats the erection of new moral values in non-strategic terms, as in the first instance a response to psychic tensions internal to the outlook of the slavish. A psychological process of this kind would not seem to be political in its overt meaning or in the

---

[11] To the extent the internalization of new values relieves the anxiety and discomfort of the slavish masses, it might be described as a means to that end. It does not follow from this, however, that the expressive processes I have postulated operate through the logic of instrumental *rationality*. A process implicates this form of rationality when its operation requires the agent to conceptualize their actions in terms of the relation between means and ends (either consciously or unconsciously). The expressive processes I have described, however, do not require the agent to think about them in this way. The slaves adopt new values because doing so helps them to make sense of their emotional experience, thereby relieving a condition of psychic distress; but they do not need to be aware, at any level, that the adoption of new values will bring about this effect. (I am indebted to Herlinde Pauer-Studer for pressing me to be clearer about this point.)

intentions with which it is carried out. But it might nevertheless inadvertently be a process of great political significance, carrying political meanings in its effects if not in its intent, and this is the way I would suggest we think about Nietzsche's talk of revolt. The response to the pent up tension that the powerless experience is their invention of a new ethical vocabulary, where this is to be understood not as a cynical rhetorical display, but as the acceptance and internalization of a new evaluative framework for organizing their responses to the world. To take this step, under the conditions that prevail at the time of the slave revolt, is in effect to challenge the authority of the masters to be the final arbiters in questions of value. Their verdicts about what is good and bad are no longer taken as valid or regulative for the responses of everyone, and to the extent this is the case their superior standing in normative questions will have been called into question. By challenging the normative authority of the masters in this way, the slaves may be thought of as having initiated a revolt, even if it was not their conscious or implicit aim to do so.

In the preceding section I raised the question of how the slave revolt could possibly have succeeded over time, in the way Nietzsche clearly believes that it has. If the revolt is the attempt to strike out directly against the masters by erecting a new evaluative scheme, it is hard to understand how it might have been successful on its own terms; the superior position of the masters should have ensured their immunity to the effect the slaves were—however obscurely—aiming to achieve. On the alternative interpretation I have proposed, the central moment of revolt is not the immediate attempt to inflict physical or psychic harm on those who are powerful, but rather the challenge to their normative authority that is implicit in the acceptance of a radically new evaluative framework. If this is what the revolt essentially consists in, however, then we get a very different and more intelligible account of its eventual success. The challenge to the authority of the masters will have been successful when they are no longer taken to be the final arbiters in questions of value. For this condition to be achieved, it is only necessary that more and more people come over time to internalize the new table of values organized around the concepts of good and evil. How this might occur is not at all difficult to understand. Supposing that the new values really do fit well with the psychic structures characteristic of pent-up *ressentiment*, it is only natural that they would take firm root among the oppressed and frustrated masses in urbanized European culture, coming eventually to be the dominant evaluative schema for individual deliberation and social criticism.

In thinking about this historical process, there is no need to suppose, initially at any rate, that the strong types should themselves accept the new values of the slavish masses, in a process akin to religious conversion. This would represent a direct capitulation to slave morality, something that would indeed be hard to make sense of as the deliberate act of a genuinely higher nature. Nevertheless the cultural authority of the strong will effectively be undermined, and their broader interests thereby damaged, when the alternative value system they espouse has been eclipsed and marginalized through the dominance in the population at large of modern, Christianized morality.[12] Moreover, once this process has been set in motion, we may suppose that it will have further, indirect effects over time on the ability of those with the native capacity for distinction to realize their true potential. Thus Nietzsche suggests that the ideological parameters of modern life, in which a large majority have taken to heart a system of values that supports leveling, democratic, egalitarian policies and practices, are inimical to the emergence and development of higher individuals.[13] Under these social conditions, there will be fewer and fewer truly distinguished specimens of humanity, the natural successors to the aristocratic nobles of an earlier era. Furthermore, such higher types as are able to emerge will lack the confidence of their predecessors; their thinking will inevitably be corrupted by the ethical orthodoxy under which they came to maturity, which will leave traces in their own evaluative outlook.[14] These outcomes are for Nietzsche a potential source of nihilistic despair about modern culture, and at least one basis for his multifaceted criticism of the slave morality that is prevalent in that culture (cf. GM, I.11, I.12).[15]

With this account of the slave revolt in hand, let us now return to the issue of Nietzsche's strategic descriptions of the processes in which the revolt consists. The most important thing to note about this issue is that Nietzsche distinguishes clearly between the masses of *ressentiment*-filled slaves, and a smaller group, the so-called priestly aristocracy, whose relation to the slavish masses is complicated. On the one

---

[12] The slave revolt does, then, eventually inflict harm on the masters, as the strategic interpretation maintains, insofar as it undermines their cultural authority. But the expressive interpretation supplies the mechanism whereby this kind of harm is gradually inflicted, a mechanism that is missing when the revolt is thought of exclusively in terms of strategic rationality. This mechanism operates without our needing to suppose that the masses deliberately aim to inflict harm on the masters through their adoption of the new value scheme.

[13] Nietzsche clearly assumes that modern European culture has a leveling and egalitarian tendency that is inimical to the development of higher specimens of humanity; see GM, I.12, on "the diminution and leveling of man" (p. 44), also the "Anmerkung" at the end of the first essay of the *Genealogy*, with its discussion of the effects of an evaluative scheme on "producing a stronger type" of human being (p. 56). It is not perhaps entirely clear why the democratizing values of modernity should have had this effect; one could imagine that a hereditary aristocracy would lead the rulers over time to become decadent and effete, while a culture that gives opportunities to everyone might tend to encourage genuine innovation and continual renewal (in spiritual and intellectual domains, at any rate, if not necessarily on the battlefield).

[14] See for instance GM, III.14, where the masses are described as having "poison[ed] the consciences of the fortunate with their misery" (p. 124), making them ashamed of their good fortune; also GM, I.16, where it is said to be the decisive mark of the higher natures in contemporary culture to be "divided in this sense and a genuine battleground of these opposed values" (p. 52).

[15] For a persuasive and comprehensive treatment of this important theme in Nietzsche's philosophy, see Bernard Reginster, *The Affirmation of Life. Nietzsche on Overcoming Nihilism* (Cambridge Mass.: Harvard University Press, 2006).

hand, the priests are described as having an emotional orientation to the social world that has much in common with the powerless masses. It is in them, for instance, that hatred is said to have grown to "monstrous and uncanny proportions" (GM, I.7, p. 33), a hatred that stems primarily from their impotence vis-à-vis the noble warrior class. In this respect, then, the aristocratic priests would seem to share with the masses the kind of *ressentiment* that is rooted in a situation of irremediable structural deprivation. On the other hand, the priests are precisely unlike the powerless masses in constituting an aristocracy of their own. They are a group apart from the masses, being superior to them in qualities of mind and character, in ways that make it fitting to speak of them in the language of nobility.

Now it is striking that Nietzsche's strategic descriptions of the slave revolt apply primarily to the activities of the priestly aristocracy. Thus it is the Jewish priestly class that is said to have practiced a "secret black art of truly grand politics of revenge, of a farseeing, subterranean, slowly advancing, and premeditated revenge" in advancing the new table of values (GM, I.8, p. 35; cf. GM, I.7). This can be reconciled with my expressive interpretation of the slave revolt in the following way. We may suppose that it is a reflection of the superiority of the priestly aristocracy that its members take a clear-eyed, strategic attitude toward the processes in which the slave revolt basically consists. Those processes involve the acceptance and internalization of a new set of values, on the part of a populace whose deepest emotional experience is thereby rendered intelligible. I have argued that this emotional dynamic would not succeed if the powerless masses viewed the new table of values in strategic terms, as something to be advocated solely as a way of striking a blow against the master class. The aristocratic priests, I now want to suggest, grasp the susceptibility of the masses to this dynamic, and exploit it expressly for the purpose of undermining the power and position of the warrior class. That is, without really accepting the new table of values themselves, they cynically advocate on its behalf, in the expectation that the values will catch on over time among the masses who join with them in resenting the power of the political aristocracy.[16] There is, in other words, a strategic dimension to the slave revolt, but strategic rationality does not capture the primary psychological dynamic in which that revolt consists. It is rather a secondary or parasitic phenomenon, which characterizes the thinking not of the masses in whose psyches the revolt takes place, but only of an elite group, the priestly aristocracy.

[16] Contrast Reginster, "Nietzsche on *Ressentiment* and Valuation". Reginster takes the psyche of the priests to be the primary site at which the slave revolt takes place, and he supposes that it leads the priests to be deeply self-deceived about the nature of their own real values; see pp. 289, 291, 297. By contrast, I take the priests to be initiators and facilitators of a process that takes place elsewhere, in the psyches of the slavish, and to be free from self-deception about their values and aims as they play this role. This interpretation fits better the overt strategic language Nietzsche deploys in talking about the role of the aristocratic priests.

In at least one respect, however, it may be misleading to characterize the strategic calculations of the priestly class as a secondary phenomenon in relation to the slave revolt. Nietzsche often represents the priestly nobility as the driving force behind the revolt. In section I.7 of the *Genealogy*, for instance, he says that it was the Jews ("that priestly people") "who, with awe-inspiring consistency, dared to invert the aristocratic value-equation" (p. 34), a statement which suggests that the priests played the leading role in the revaluation of values. Similarly, in *Beyond Good and Evil* (sec. 261) Nietzsche apparently denies that the slaves have it in them to create values, suggesting that this is uniquely the prerogative of those who are by nature masters. But this strand too can be reconciled with my interpretation. We may suppose that it was the priests who originally thought to invert the noble values of good and bad, articulating for the first time a different way of conceptualizing the landscape of value. To the extent this is the case, we may say that they created the new values, and that their act of creation is temporally prior in the chain of events in which the slave revolt consists. At the same time, however, this act of creation would not have succeeded in bringing new *values* into existence unless there were other people in the world who were emotionally primed to internalize the new evaluative vocabulary that the priests had invented. It is for this reason that I described the role of the priests as secondary. Their genius can be said to consist in the invention of an ideology that is precisely calculated by them to mesh with the emotional orientation of the oppressed masses. They thus deliberately set in motion and nurture the expressive processes through which the slaves come to embrace a new evaluative scheme, processes that constitute, strictly speaking, the true birth of new values.[17]

This account of the role of the ascetic priests attributes to them a devious plan to achieve genuine revenge against the masters whom they hate, a revenge that involves harming the masters, and undermining their comparative cultural authority and political and social advantages. At times, however, Nietzsche appears to describe the revenge that is involved in the slave revolt in less literal terms. Of the psychic force that becomes creative and gives birth to new values, for instance, he says that it is "the *ressentiment* of natures that are denied the true reaction, that of deeds, and compensate themselves with an imaginary revenge" (GM, I.10, p. 36). Here he seems to be talking about the very force that is at work in the expressive dynamic I have been discussing in this section, the *ressentiment* of the masses that leads them to embrace the new values of good and evil. In what sense can their doing this be characterized as compensation for their literal impotence, through a revenge that is merely imaginary?

---

[17] To the extent the aristocratic priests are engaged in this strategy of premeditated revenge, their activities can straightforwardly be characterized as a revolt, insofar as they are aimed at undermining the power of the masters. Thus the multifarious processes in which the revolt consists will involve both overt and covert political meanings.

There is nothing particularly mysterious about the idea that thoughts and fantasies can provide psychic gratification for a person whose options for action are in reality limited. Gratifications of this kind belong to the archaic logic of unconscious processes, which operate in accordance with assumptions about the "omnipotence of thought" that are characteristic of infantile mental life. We all experience pleasures that reflect the continuing latent operation of these patterns of thinking in adult life, as for instance when we indulge in sadistic fantasizing about someone who has done us wrong, or daydream about the victory of the political party that we have been working in vain to support all these years. It would be no surprise if the unconscious *ressentiment* of the masses provided a source for archaic satisfactions of this kind, involving an imaginary revenge against the powerful who are the objects of this focused negative affect.[18]

The more interesting question is why the internalization of the new table of values should provide an occasion for the operation of this kind of mental process. To do so, it would need to involve a representation of the powerful in thought, as suffering the kind of harm or comeuppance that might be imagined as revenge. But it is not at all clear why Nietzsche might have thought that the slave revolt itself involves representations of this sort. As a result of the revolt the slaves come to think of the powerful masters as supremely evil, but to think of them in these terms is not to represent them (either consciously or unconsciously) as having been harmed or undermined in any way.[19] Perhaps Nietzsche supposes that the powerless are dimly aware of their new moral scheme as a challenge to the authority of the masters; building on this dim awareness, they might imagine themselves to be striking out against the masters in doing something that eventually will undermine their superior position. This is reminiscent of the strategic interpretation, with the difference that the act of harming the masters is not part of a postulated unconscious calculation, but rather something that is fantasized about by the slaves.[20]

A different and more likely possibility is that the element of fantasized revenge is not so directly connected to the acceptance of new values in which the slave revolt consists. After all, in the passage quoted above Nietzsche does not strictly say that

---

[18] Contrast Bittner, "*Ressentiment*", 132–3. Bittner suggests that this kind of fantasizing can provide psychic gratification only when agents are (temporarily) unaware that they are fantasizing. But this seems to me to be untrue to experience, perhaps underestimating the extent to which infantile patterns of mental activity leave traces in adult life.

[19] A person can be evil and still, by all outward measures, flourishing.

[20] This way of understanding Nietzsche's talk about imaginary revenge would entail that elements of strategic thinking infect the outlook of the slavish masses themselves (at least at the level of fantasy), not merely that of the priestly aristocracy. It would not follow, however, that the expressive interpretation would thereby have been supplanted. On the contrary, the mechanism whereby the fantasized revenge is enacted precisely presupposes the susceptibility of the masses to the expressive processes I have described.

the slave revolt itself is a form of imaginary revenge, only that it is the result of the kind of *ressentiment* that compensates for impotence through such revenge. Perhaps Nietzsche is merely noting that the same psychic force that becomes creative in the slave revolt also finds expression in other forms of modern Christianized thought, ones that involve fantasies in which the powerful are brought low and made to suffer. The most obvious example would be Christian stories about damnation and the last judgment, such as the remarkable passage from Tertullian that Nietzsche quotes extensively toward the end of the first essay of the *Genealogy* (GM, I.15). On this reading, which I myself would favor, the element of imaginary revenge is not really integral to the slave revolt itself, but rather a by-product of the unconscious psychic forces that are primarily at work in the creation of new values, and further evidence of their pervasive presence and operation.

3. Value and Emotion

The expressive interpretation seems to me to make good sense of the central processes that Nietzsche is describing in the first essay of the *Genealogy*. But there are large philosophical questions that the interpretation raises, questions that need to be grappled with before we can really take seriously the account Nietzsche is offering of the role of *ressentiment* in giving birth to new moral values. In this section I shall address four sets of issues.

A first question concerns the primacy of *ressentiment* vis-à-vis value. Nietzsche's genetic story assumes that the powerless are subject to *ressentiment* before they embrace the values that are organized around the pair of opposites good and evil. This emotional orientation becomes pent up in the psyches of the weak, growing ever more intense until it finally gives birth to new values in the slave revolt. It is the priority of *ressentiment*, its temporal precedence and logical independence from modern values, that enables us to explain the acceptance of those values by appeal to this emotional state. But it is not clear that we can really make sense of *ressentiment* as an emotional condition that is independent of an evaluative framework or point of view.

There are in fact two aspects to this potential difficulty. One is the general concern that *ressentiment*, like many emotional states or conditions, makes sense only against the background of an evaluative commitment of some kind or other. Pride, for instance, presupposes that one takes oneself to have done or produced something that is good and worthy of admiration, while shame is an emotional response to an aspect of oneself that one views with dismay, as vicious, or disfigured, or base. If *ressentiment* is like these emotions in presupposing an evaluative framework, then it may be doubted whether we can appeal to it to account for the adoption by the slaves of the values through which they view the world. A second and related aspect of this problem is that some of the specific values potentially associated with *ressentiment* seem at odds with the new values that the emotion is said to give rise to. Thus it seems that we experience *ressentiment* toward people when they are in a conspicuously good way in comparison to ourselves, and when we feel that we are prevented from realizing the goods that they exhibit or manifest in a striking degree. This suggests that the target of *ressentiment* must be conceptualized in positive terms, as possessing things or properties that are worthy of admiration and pursuit. But this positive evaluation of the targets of *ressentiment* is precisely at odds with the negative assessment of them that is integral to the morality of good and evil. To express the problem as a paradox, *ressentiment* appears to presuppose the very values that are repudiated in the slave revolt; but then the new table of values that is internalized by the slaves would preclude them from feeling the very sentiment that is supposed to find expression in their act of revolt.[21]

These problems can be illustrated by looking at two emotions that are superficially similar to Nietzschean *ressentiment*, namely resentment and envy. Resentment is a reactive sentiment that is bound up with our tendency to hold people morally accountable for their actions. Its distinctive feature—at least this is what I have elsewhere argued[22]—is its connection to moral demands. In the paradigm cases, one resents other people when one believes that they have wronged one, doing something that violates a moral obligation to which one holds them in one's interpersonal relations. If this is right, however, then resentment is an essentially moral sentiment, presupposing the acceptance of moral standards on the part of the agent who is subject to the emotion. An emotion with this structure clearly cannot be called on to explain the agent's fundamental moral outlook, since an outlook of that kind is implicated in the emotion itself. Similarly, many episodes of common envy seem to be occasioned by one's awareness of the person envied as good or admirable in some way or other. One envies the person who is supremely confident in social situations (when one is not oneself), or who is sharp or clever or successful or unusually attractive. Here the danger is that the emotion is bound up with a positive evaluative assessment of its target, in a way that is at odds with the superlatively negative evaluation in which the emotion finds expression in the slave revolt.

---

[21] Reginster, in "Nietzsche on *Ressentiment* and Valuation", takes the opposite response to the paradox from the one I would favor. He affirms that noble-valuation is built into the experience of *ressentiment*, and denies that the new values are genuinely accepted by the priests in whom the slave revolt takes place, who are said to be deceived about what they really value (see e.g. pp. 296–7). By contrast, I deny that *ressentiment* really presupposes the acceptance of the aristocratic values repudiated in the slave revolt.

[22] See *Responsibility and the Moral Sentiments*, ch. 2. The distinctions between Nietzschean *ressentiment* and moralized resentment appear to be overlooked in Robert C. Solomon, "One Hundred Years of *Ressentiment*: Nietzsche's *Genealogy of Morals*", in Schacht (ed.), *Nietzsche, Genealogy, Morality*, 95–126, esp. pp. 103, 115–18.

But Nietzschean *ressentiment* is precisely unlike both resentment and ordinary envy in these respects. As interpreted in the preceding section, it is a kind of focused hatred that grows out of a situation of structural comparative deprivation, and its essential features are psychically primitive by comparison with both moralized resentment and common envy. To be subject to this sentiment, one needs to conceptualize oneself as lacking access to things that other people in one's social world conspicuously possess, where this is experienced as a kind of deprivation. Deprivation might in turn appear to be an evaluatively laden concept, implying that the things one lacks access to are good or valuable along some dimension. But it does not need to be evaluatively colored in this way. To experience oneself as deprived in comparison to others it is enough that there are things that one simply desires to possess, things that other people have and that are unattainable for oneself. In these terms, the psychic structure of Nietzschean *ressentiment* might involve a susceptibility to elemental desire or longing, the kind of brute urge observable in young children when they strike out at their siblings or make off with their playmates' toys. If it makes sense to attribute such primitive desires to adult human beings, then a conceptual framework will be in place that will make possible the kinds of experiences that give rise to Nietzschean *ressentiment*. There is no need to postulate that the slavish evaluate the powerful as genuinely good, still less need we assume that they take themselves to have been wronged by those whom they come to hate, in the style characteristic of moralized resentment.[23]

The crux, then, is the idea that the powerless masses are subject to a kind of longing or desire to possess things that is intelligible independently of evaluative concepts and attitudes. If this idea is plausible, then we can make sense of their *ressentiment* as a phenomenon that is primary vis-à-vis the value system that the emotion is invoked to explain. Now I myself do not believe that ordinary, conscious desire really is intelligible apart from an evaluative point of view.[24] But we should recall that Nietzschean *ressentiment* is not among the surface phenomena of mental life; it is

---

[23] A different possibility is that those in the grip of *ressentiment* view the powerful as *possessing* things of value, without necessarily *being* good or admirable themselves (for instance, in the dimension of ethical assessment of character). This kind of evaluative framework would seem compatible with, and so leave room for, the extreme negative assessment of the masters that is involved in the new table of values to which *ressentiment* eventually gives rise. I doubt, however, that tensions within the evaluative outlook of the slaves would entirely be eliminated by this way of understanding *ressentiment*. In terms of the new table of values, among the things that make the powerful evil are precisely their possession of traits and qualities that the weak presumably covet themselves (including, above all, power and strength); cf. GM, I.7, also the parable of the lambs and the birds of prey in GM, I.13. So if *ressentiment* involves essentially a positive evaluation of those traits and qualities, it will be at odds with the new forms of assessment to which it itself is supposed to give rise.

[24] See my "Addiction as Defect of the Will. Some Philosophical Reflections", as reprinted in Gary Watson (ed.), *Free Will* (Oxford: Oxford University Press, 2003), 424–52. See also T. M. Scanlon, *What We Owe to Each Other* (Cambridge, Mass.: Harvard University Press, 1998), ch. 1.

rather an unconscious state of mind, which colors the agent's experience of the world without reaching to the level of full conscious awareness. It seems to me quite likely that the desiderative states operative at this unconscious level of psychic functioning are states of archaic bare striving to possess, states that do not imply the acceptance or application of evaluative concepts on the part of the agent in their grip. If this right, however, then psychic structures would seem to be in place that render intelligible the kind of *ressentiment* that Nietzsche's explanatory narrative requires. The experience of structural deprivation that is essential to *ressentiment* can be made sense of in terms of the frustration of archaic desire, and the priority of *ressentiment* vis-à-vis evaluation that Nietzsche assumes can thus be maintained.

A second set of questions about Nietzsche's account concerns the gratification that I have suggested would be occasioned by the acceptance and internalization of new values on the part of those in the grip of *ressentiment*. The idea is that these values would speak to an unconscious need to which the powerless are subject, enabling them to make sense of their basic emotional orientation to the social world, as one that is appropriate to its immediate object. But this idea may seem to sit uneasily with a different strand in Nietzsche's account of modern morality, his depiction of it as a kind of pathology. It seems clear that Nietzsche views the Christian morality of good and evil, especially in its asceticized form, as a fundamentally unhealthy psychic formation, one that is inimical to the forces necessary to sustain life itself, and a cause of exquisite suffering and torment. The evaluative framework of good and evil allows the powerless to characterize their hated enemies in superlatively negative terms. But its requirements, especially in the "moralized" and "ascetic" guise they assume over time, also become instruments for rechanneling aggressive energies back against the self who is their original subject (GM, II.21, III.15). These energies, which first come on the scene as responses to suffering (GM, III.15, p. 127), thus become co-opted into a psychic economy that intensifies the suffering to which they originally were a response, leading Nietzsche to describe asceticized Christian morality as "the true calamity in the history of European health" (GM, III.21, p. 143; cf. GM, II.19).[25]

This interpretation of modern moral consciousness as a profound pathology, a device for the internalization of aggressive instincts that intensifies the suffering of those who are in its grip, may seem hard to reconcile with the idea that the same evaluative framework originally served to gratify a psychic need on the part of the slaves. But in fact these aspects of modern morality are not really incompatible with the expressive account I have been developing. Nietzsche himself is always alert to

[25] These processes are unhealthy, I take it, for the masses who accept the ideology of ascetic morality, increasing their suffering and inhibiting in them the very instincts necessary to sustain life itself. To characterize modern morality in these terms, as a form of psychic pathology, is of course not to say that the masses could realistically do any better.

the ways in which a single phenomenon can bear multiple meanings, having causal consequences (for instance) that are multifaceted, and that ultimately work at cross purposes. In the case at hand the supposition would be that a phenomenon that originates in the satisfaction of a psychic need might at the same time, through an instantiation of the law of unintended consequences, be disadvantageous in relation to other psychic processes, and hence a source of both gratification and suffering. Thus modern moral values might be adopted because they enable the weak to make sense of their emotional experience of the world, even though those same values become co-opted into a system for intensifying the torment of the agent who is in their grip.

Given the deleterious consequences Nietzsche attributes to the Christianized morality of modernity, it would in fact be highly peculiar if it did not gratify some psychic need on the part of the masses who have embraced it, and the drive to make sense of one's emotional situation seems well-suited to play this role. Nietzsche invokes a similar drive at the end of the third essay of the *Genealogy*, noting that the incorporation of ascetic ideals into Christian morality enables the suffering to make sense of their condition, presumably as one that is deserved on account of their inherently sinful nature (GM, III.28).[26] On my interpretation, essentially the same drive (or "will") to understand and to attach meaning to one's situation is at work in the original transformation of *ressentiment* into a new evaluative scheme.

In both contexts in which it appears to play a role, the need for meaning operates in a distinctive way. In particular, it does not give rise to a clear-eyed or scientific understanding of the psychic forces actually at work in the people who seek to make sense of their situation in the world; their internalized aggression and *ressentiment* remain, to a large extent, beneath the surface of consciousness. What happens, instead, is that the powerless masses are led to think about themselves in terms that are essentially evaluative, and that therefore provide a kind of vindication of their most fundamental ways of experiencing the world. Thus suffering acquires a meaning under the ascetic interpretation of morality, becoming a cosmically just condition, one that is peculiarly fitting for the profoundly sinful natures we take ourselves to be.[27] Similarly, the interpretation of the powerful masters as embodiments of evil enables the slavish masses to make sense of their emotional experience, insofar as the immediate object of their *ressentiment* can be thought of in terms that render this powerful sentiment peculiarly appropriate. The evaluative self-conception that is made possible by these forms of moral consciousness I shall call vindicatory, since its

---

[26] See also *Thus Spoke Zarathustra*, I.15, and *The Gay Science*, sec. 1.

[27] Here it is perhaps misleading to speak of self-vindication, insofar as ascetic morality precisely serves to characterize the person who accepts it as pervasively sinful. This moral outlook nevertheless provides a value-laden vindication of some aspect of the situation of the self in the world, in this case the experience of suffering. It is in this broader sense that the notion of "self-vindication" should be construed.

point is to provide a kind of justification for the conditions of life that are characteristic of the suffering masses.

This aspect of Nietzsche's position, however, raises a third set of questions. For one thing, there is something puzzling about the claim that the evaluative scheme of good and evil provides a vindication of the slaves' emotional experience. For the new values to which the slave revolt gives rise have a content that condemns the very emotion that originally motivated them and that continues to sustain them over time. This is the aspect of Nietzsche's narrative that has led some to see it as delivering the materials for a kind of internal critique of modern moral consciousness. Thus from the standpoint of one committed to such Christian values as patience, humility, pacifism, and justice, it would presumably be an embarrassment to learn that the psychic forces that sustain these very commitments amount to forms of personal hatred and *ressentiment*. Far from vindicating the slave's emotions, the new table of values actually appears to undermine their moral legitimacy.

This is correct as far as it goes, but it is not grounds for rejecting the expressive account. The inconsistency it reveals is not a feature of my interpretation of the slave revolt, but of the outlook of the slaves in whom the expressive processes take place. Thus it is a matter of surface paradox rather than psychic impossibility that the values embraced in the slave revolt should provide a basis for criticizing the very emotions that gave rise to those values in the first place.[28] The emotional experience of the slaves is vindicated through the adoption of values that brand the hated masters as evil. But those same values, if consistently applied in an exercise of honest self-assessment, would lead the slaves to lament their original susceptibility to the feelings of *ressentiment* that so deeply color their experience.[29] That the evaluative and emotional structure they inhabit is unstable in this way is part of what makes their predicament so highly problematic, on Nietzsche's account of it. There is no way for them to satisfy completely their desire for self-vindication while confronting the whole truth about their own emotional situation.

But why is it that human beings need self-vindication of this kind? What accounts for the drive to make sense of one's condition and orientation in evaluative terms, as one that is appropriate, or just, or fitting? I am not certain that there is a good Nietzschean answer to this question, at the end of the day. It might simply be a contingent psychological fact that many people need to understand themselves in this way, as subject to conditions that can be made sense of through the lens of an

---

[28] Nietzsche's account of ascetic ideals in the third essay of the *Genealogy* exhibits this same kind of complexity. There the need that is gratified in ascetic morality, namely the need to inflict harm, serves only to increase the suffering of the agent to which that need itself originally was a response.

[29] This is presumably part of what keeps the psychic forces of *ressentiment* and hatred beneath the radar of consciousness.

evaluative framework. As an empirical generalization this would seem to be a plausible hypothesis, which receives some confirmation from such common phenomena as psychological rationalization. The alacrity with which people grasp at specious justifications for their political preferences and personal behavior is remarkable, and suggests the operation of a deep need to think of oneself in terms that provide vindication for one's attitudes and behavior.

But is this psychic need really so prevalent a feature of human life? Consider the outlook of the priestly aristocracy. I have suggested that the members of this class should be understood as taking an essentially cynical attitude toward the slave revolt that they foment in the masses. Without themselves accepting the new values of good and evil, they encourage the powerless to accept and internalize those values, seeing this as part of a strategy to undermine the masters over time. This strategic orientation of the priests to the slave revolt seems to assume that they are able to accept their hatred of the masters for what it is, without needing to accept the vindicatory self-narrative to which the ordinary masses cling. They are simply people who despise the powerful masters, for no other and no better reason than that the masters are in possession of things that they too would like to possess, but that they have no access to. And so they strike out against the masters, acting strategically with the aim of inflicting harm on them and eventually undermining their superior position entirely.

Indeed, it seems plausible to assume that the ability to understand and accept their true emotional orientation on its own terms, without seeing it as justified by or appropriate to its circumstances, may be a sign of the higher nature of the priests in comparison to the powerless masses. They form a kind of aristocracy precisely insofar as they are not driven to internalize an evaluative rationalization of their essentially hostile emotional experience of the world. It would not be quite accurate, however, to conclude from this that the priests feel no need whatsoever to accept a vindicatory interpretation of themselves. Nietzsche in fact writes as if the need for this kind of self-conception were a fairly universal feature of human psychology, treating it as perhaps the most fundamental manifestation of the will to power that he virtually identifies with life itself. Thus even the original valuations of the aristocratic warrior class, through which the scheme of values good/bad is articulated, are described as serving as instruments of self-glorification.[30] Similarly, insofar as the priests are able to see themselves as striking a strategic blow against the hated masters, they will be able to make sense of their experience in terms of the aristocratic values that they continue

---

[30] See *Beyond Good and Evil*, sec. 260. Nietzsche here (and also in sec. 261) contrasts the active mode of valuation of the masters with the passive or receptive mode that is characteristic of the slaves, a contrast that might appear to suggest that the slavish mode of valuing things is heteronomous, and entirely indifferent to any need for self-vindication. But the later sections of the third essay of the *Genealogy* make clear that the will for meaning is equally at work in the valuations of the masses in modern culture, however passive or perverted those valuations might be in other respects.

to accept. Their hatred might not ultimately be justified by intrinsic features of its object, but because they take positive action against the masters, they can understand themselves as exhibiting the kind of self-assertion and strength that the noble table of values precisely celebrates. Their good fortune by comparison with the slaves consists in part in their ability to construct a vindicatory narrative of their own situation in the world while retaining a kind of clarity about their own psychic needs and emotions that is missing in the benighted masses.

A final set of questions I want to touch on concerns the metaphysics of value that Nietzsche's account of the creative dimension of *ressentiment* requires. Nietzsche's immediate interest, it seems clear, is in the relation of evaluative structures to the emotions and experiences of the person who accepts them. Values are not thought of as systems of propositions that might be considered true or false representations of an independent domain of evaluative fact; rather they are interpreted as expressions of distinctive personality types, and assessed by reference to their effects on the persons who accept and internalize them. This general way of approaching questions about value is suggestive of a kind of anti-realism, which denies that there are any independent facts of the matter about values or norms. And Nietzsche has in fact been interpreted along these lines, as (for instance) an anti-realist about (non-prudential) value, who holds that there are no objective facts about good and evil, because such facts are not needed to explain the psychological phenomena that Nietzsche is primarily interested in.[31] Raymond Geuss offers a pithy statement of this outlook in the following summary of Nietzsche's metaethical position:

In the final analysis there is just the mass of human individuals and groups exercising power or being dominated, succeeding or failing at various projects, and, at a slightly eccentric angle to this world of direct action, a flux of admiration of various things by various people and of disgust at various things by various people who have or have not tried and have or have not succeeded in influencing their own reactions of admiration and disgust.[32]

There are numerous passages in Nietzsche's writings that hint at a metaethical position of this kind. But I am not convinced that these passages should be taken completely

---

[31] See Leiter, *Nietzsche on Morality*, 146−55.

[32] Raymond Geuss, "Nietzsche and Morality", 191. Geuss goes on to suggest that the flux of admiration and disgust "gives rise to a wide variety of different 'oughts' " (p. 191). But the acknowledgement of local and contingent "Verbindlichkeiten" of this kind is actually in tension with the metaethical picture that Geuss ascribes to Nietzsche. Either there is, in the "final analysis", just a flow of attitudes such as admiration and disgust, or there is in addition to such natural psychological facts a set of distinctively normative or evaluative claims about what variously situated individuals have reason to do. The fact that "Verbindlichkeiten" are local and contingent rather than universal does not make them part of the natural flux of human attitudes and reactions. (The difference here is that between an anti-realist position which holds that there are no true claims about what anyone has reason to do, and an "internalist" position which allows for such truths, but holds that reasons are conditioned by the desires and attitudes of the agent who has them.)

at face value. It is not obvious to me that Nietzsche was really interested in offering a consistent theory of the metaphysics of value, a worked-out position that might be assigned a precise position on the landscape of metaethical views. His dismissive remarks about objectivity in the realm of value can often be read as polemical invitations to attend to the role of evaluative outlooks within the economy of human drives and purposes. When he writes, for instance, that "nature is always valueless, but has been *given* value at some time",[33] he is, strictly speaking, saying that there are no mind-independent facts about value; but his *aim* in saying this is to get us to think about the psychological process of investing things with value.

Furthermore, this interest in the moral psychology of value is in the service of a more comprehensive critique of modern morality, and it is hard to reconcile these critical purposes of Nietzsche's with a literal anti-realism about reasons and values. At least part of his critique of modern morality focuses on its deleterious consequences for the emergence and development of genuinely higher types of humanity, people who can inspire confidence in the species, and counteract thereby the tendency to nihilism in contemporary culture. This critical argument becomes completely banal, however, if we attribute to Nietzsche himself an anti-realist conception of the evaluative and normative domains. According to this kind of metaethical position, there is nothing that is genuinely and independently valuable, or worthy of choice, admiration, and pursuit; there are merely the preferences and desires that different people happen to have at different times and for different things. We might be able to say that contemporary morality is bad *for* the higher specimens of humanity, insofar as it is deleterious to their interests and their flourishing. But we cannot say either that these "higher" types really are superior examples of human nature in themselves, or that it is an objectively good thing that they should come into being and flourish. Nietzsche himself simply happens to admire the kinds of people he refers to as higher types, and so his criticism of modern morality comes down to the charge that it frustrates the satisfaction of his own preferences concerning the development of the species (preferences that he presumably hopes his readers will share).[34] If this is what his critique amounts to, however, then an appropriate response would be, "So what?" Why should anyone care whether modernity is hospitable to the contingent preferences and desires of Nietzsche and his targeted readers (as opposed, say, to the preferences of the masses)? The whole critical animus of his account seems to make sense only if we take the distinction between higher and lower types objectively, as

---

[33] *The Gay Science*, sec. 301.

[34] Leiter pretty much embraces an interpretation of Nietzsche's critical project in just these terms, in *Nietzsche on Morality*, 149–50. He recognizes that this reading may not seem to comport with Nietzsche's unqualified critical conclusions, but dismisses this tendency in Nietzsche as rhetorical excess; see *Nietzsche on Morality*, 153–5.

marking a genuine distinction of rank in regard to the development of human nature and potential, and only if we take it to be an objectively good thing that genuinely higher natures should be able to come into existence and flourish.[35]

For these reasons, I think it is difficult to attribute to Nietzsche himself a straightforwardly anti-realist conception of (non-prudential) value and reasons for action. How exactly his critique of modern morality can be reconciled with his occasional anti-realist pronouncements is a problem, to which I do not have a worked-out solution (beyond suggesting that these pronouncements can be read as polemical invitations to think about value as a psychological phenomenon). Leaving aside the issue of Nietzsche's own metaethical views, however, it seems plain that Nietzsche does not think that people in general hold an anti-realist conception of the good. His own account of our evaluative practice and our emotional experience suggests that we take values to be objective in the way that anti-realism denies, so that if he is an anti-realist about this domain, his view will amount to a kind of error theory. This can be seen very clearly by reflecting on his account of the slave revolt, as I have reconstructed it in this essay.

Consider the role of values in relation to the *ressentiment* of the slavish masses. I have characterized this relation as one of expression, and the language of expression might seem to comport well with a noncognitivist interpretation of evaluative discourse. But the details of the expressive account I have developed in fact preclude such an interpretation. *Ressentiment* finds expression in the slave revolt through the postulated need for vindicatory self-understanding. The adoption of a new table of values satisfies this need, however, only on the assumption that the new values capture independent facts of the matter about genuine distinctions of merit. The emotional orientation of the slaves is vindicated in the relevant sense when it can be experienced by the slaves as one that is uniquely appropriate to its object, insofar as the object is taken to be

---

[35] Against this, it might be said that it overlooks the distinction between metaethical reflection about moral discourse and its metaphysical commitments, and the first-order "moralizing" that goes on when we deploy moral discourse in practice. Nietzsche's critical animadversions on modern morality serve to express his strong attitudes about the development of the human species, and there is nothing in an anti-realist view that would preclude such moralizing discourse from being as vigorous as one might please. (Compare Simon Blackburn, *Ruling Passions* (Oxford: Oxford University Press, 1998)—though Blackburn is a "quasi-realist", not an unvarnished anti-realist about morality.) But I think the question remains as to why the rest of us should take Nietzsche's vigorous moralizing seriously, if it really functions as the anti-realist presumes. Furthermore, Nietzsche himself does not distinguish hermetically between first-order moralizing and metaethical reflection. His apparently anti-objectivist pronouncements are sprinkled throughout the works in which he is conducting his critical examination of the value of moral values, and this makes it seem very artificial to ignore them for purposes of thinking about that critical project. Given the integral relation of those pronouncements to Nietzsche's critical project, we cannot take them as straightforward statements of an anti-realist metaethical view, for the integration of such statements into his polemic would seem at cross-purposes to his critical intentions.

evil. The sense of vindication thus operates on the supposition that the values that are affirmed in the revolt are prior to and independent of the emotional stances that they are taken to validate. We might put this by saying that the expressive dynamic at work in the slave revolt requires that the slaves themselves do not understand the values they embrace in expressive terms.

Of course it is possible that people are mistaken to view their values in this objective way. Nietzsche could himself favor an anti-realist position, even while granting that values are generally *taken* by people to be objective; in that event, as I noted above, his position would have the shape of an error theory. But it is an interesting consequence of this that Nietzsche's account of the creative aspect of *ressentiment* can to some extent be detached from larger issues in metaethics about the objectivity of value. As long as one is prepared to concede that evaluative discourse carries a claim to objective validity, one will be in a position to take seriously Nietzsche's story about the way in which *ressentiment* gives rise to new values. This means that even those of us who are not attracted to an anti-realist account of value might be able to take on Nietzsche's central insights about the role of the emotions in relation to evaluative consciousness.

In the contemporary world, those insights seem likely to have their primary relevance not in relation to the universalistic morality of the Enlightenment, but in connection with such phenomena as religious fundamentalism and nationalistic self-assertion. Countless people live today under conditions of structural comparative deprivation of the kind that gives rise to Nietzschean *ressentiment*, and the inarticulate hatred that builds up under these conditions makes them easily susceptible to evaluative ideologies of a distinctive sort. These ideologies—conservative fundamentalism in the United States, militant Islamism in the Middle East and Asia, revanchist nationalism in parts of the old Soviet empire—may be inimical to the true interests of the people who embrace them. But they nevertheless speak to a need that Nietzsche identified, the need for a vindicatory interpretation of one's own basic emotional situation and experience.[36] The contemporary successors to Nietzsche's ascetic priests, it seems to me, are the populist politicians, preachers, and imams of revenge, who exploit the *ressentiment* of the masses for their own transparently cynical purposes. And

---

[36] The expressive function of these contemporary ideologies is, in fact, more obvious than is the case with the more generalized morality of modernity that Nietzsche was considering. Hatred is closer to the surface in these ideologies, and they do not shrink from calling explicitly for revenge against those who are condemned as evil infidels, historical enemies of our people, liberal elitists, etc. This makes them less interesting from a psychological point of view—less complex, paradoxical, self-undermining, and so on—but perhaps even more dangerous.

Nietzsche's account of the slave revolt can help us to understand the psychic forces that render so many people vulnerable to the ministrations of this new priestly class.[37]

[37] I received much stimulating feedback on earlier versions of this essay from audiences at the Humboldt University in Berlin, the University of Vienna, and the University of Canterbury in Christchurch. Brian Leiter provided helpful comments on the penultimate draft. I owe a special debt to Bernard Reginster for extensive and constructive suggestions about an early version of the essay, and in general for many stimulating discussions over the years about Nietzsche's moral psychology. Work on this project was conducted with the generous support of a Research Award from the Alexander von Humboldt Foundation.

6

Guilt, Bad Conscience, and Self-punishment in Nietzsche's *Genealogy*

Christopher Janaway

I. Cruelty that Turns Back

The Second Treatise of *On the Genealogy of Morality*, entitled ' "Guilt," "Bad Conscience," and Related Matters', has been comparatively poorly served by extended commentary.[1] The essay admittedly follows a winding path even by Nietzsche's standards, but I hope to reveal a central train of thought from which its many byways branch off. The central train of thought is that having a bad conscience or feeling guilty is a way in which we satisfy a fundamental need to inflict *cruelty*. This is achieved by turning the exercise of cruelty *inwards*, upon the self rather than others, and by interpreting such cruelty as a legitimate form of *punishment* of oneself.

In *Ecce Homo* Nietzsche sums up GM II as follows:

The *second* inquiry offers the psychology of the *conscience*—which is *not*, as people may believe, 'the voice of God in man': it is the instinct of cruelty that turns back after it can no longer

---

[1] It is perhaps symptomatic of the slight attention GM II has generally received that the Introduction of the excellent edition by Clark and Swensen (1998) includes only a single paragraph of commentary on the essay, contrasted with a whole section devoted to each of GM I and GM III. Some recent exceptions to the general neglect are: Ridley (1998: chs. 1–2); Risse (2001); Ridley (2005); Risse (2005); May (1999: ch. 4); Leiter (2002: ch. 7); Soll (1994); Havas (1995: ch. 5).

discharge itself externally. Cruelty is here exposed for the first time as one of the most ancient and basic substrata of culture that simply cannot be imagined away.[2]

Not the voice of God, but a human instinct. Each of GM's three essays, I would argue, illustrates a point that Nietzsche makes towards the beginning of *Beyond Good and Evil*: 'The fundamental belief of metaphysicians is *the belief in oppositions of values*'. Metaphysicians ask: 'How *could* anything originate out of its opposite?' But, Nietzsche counters, 'It could even be possible that whatever gives value to those good and honorable things has an incriminating link, bond, or tie to the very things that look like their evil opposites; perhaps they are even essentially the same.'[3] GM I provides a good example of this: morality is founded on a fundamental opposition between 'good' and 'evil', but that essay locates the origin of the moral description 'good' in just the same kind of drive to dominate as is abhorred under the description 'evil'. In GM II likewise we start with morality's tacit assumption that cruelty is an evil thing, whereas feeling guilty and having a bad conscience about one's actions, especially those that spring from natural instincts, is something good: the opposite of cruelty, and therefore (by a metaphysician's false inference) something with a different or higher origin. The essay tells us that feeling guilty or having a bad conscience is a more perverse and disguised way *of inflicting cruelty*. Feeling guilty is insidiously, incriminatingly, related to cruelty, and is even the same as it in essence.

GM II is structured around two central thoughts concerning cruelty and its 'turning back' against the self. The first, which Nietzsche calls 'an old powerful human-all-too-human proposition', might be put as follows:

(A) Because of an instinctive drive, human beings tend to gain pleasure from inflicting suffering.[4]

We might call this the 'pleasure-in-cruelty' thesis. The second thought, which I shall state also in my own formulation, posits a psychological process which Nietzsche calls *Verinnerlichung* or internalization:

(B) When the instinctive drives of a socialized human individual are prevented from discharging themselves outwardly, they discharge themselves *inwardly, on the individual him/herself*.[5]

Nietzsche's 'own hypothesis' concerning the origin of 'bad conscience', a pivotal hypothesis of the whole essay, makes use of both these thoughts and might be expressed thus:

---

[2] EH, 'Genealogy of Morals'. My emphasis on the word *not* is introduced to reflect the emphasis present in the German text.

[3] BGE 2.   [4] See GM II, 6.   [5] See GM II, 16.

(C) Because human beings have an instinctive drive that leads them to gain pleasure from inflicting suffering, human beings subjected to the restrictions of civilized society, and so constrained to internalize their instincts, satisfy their instinctive drive *by inflicting suffering on themselves.*

In Nietzsche's own words:

Hostility, cruelty, pleasure in persecution, in assault, in change, in destruction—all of that turning itself against the possessors of such instincts: *that* is the origin of 'bad conscience'.[6]

We might pause to consider the idea of experiencing pleasure in making oneself suffer. Nietzsche does not need to claim that human beings feel pleasure in *undergoing* suffering. That might also be true sometimes, but, if it is, Nietzsche does not use it here. He relies on the proposition that human beings find pleasure in *inflicting* suffering on themselves. We are gratified as instigators, agents, of suffering in his account, not as its recipients. The relevant proposition thus has the same interesting form as one of Nietzsche's pithier epigrams in *Beyond Good and Evil*: 'Anyone who despises himself will still respect himself as a despiser.'[7] Being despised is unpleasant and distressing, and being despised by oneself instead of by another presumably does not alter that fact; but in so far as one identifies with the subject of the despising relation, to some extent split off from oneself as its object, one can stand in a positive affective attitude to oneself, that of respecting. Compare the thought in GM II. Self-inflicted suffering is, like any suffering, a painful and negative experience. But a pleasure or gratification is possible for one who identifies with the inflicter of suffering, to some extent split off from him- or herself as the suffering object.

A pre-echo of this position is found in *Daybreak*, 113:

the *ascetic* and martyr . . . feels the highest enjoyment by himself enduring . . . precisely that which . . . his counterpart the *barbarian* imposes on others on whom and before whom he wants to distinguish himself. The triumph of the ascetic over himself, his glance turned inwards which beholds man *split asunder into a sufferer and a spectator* [my emphasis] . . . this is a worthy conclusion and one appropriate to the commencement: in both cases an unspeakable happiness at the sight of torment!

Here the ascetic enjoys as spectator 'precisely that which' the barbarian enjoys inflicting on others: the two are the opposite ends of a single continuum or 'ladder'. The barbarian enjoys seeing another suffer, the ascetic enjoys seeing a sufferer suffer, but the sufferer is himself. Asceticism is a more sophisticated form of enjoying-seeing-suffering, and to sustain it one must be 'split asunder', identifying with the spectator of suffering rather than merely with the sufferer. That this passage talks of spectating suffering rather than inflicting it, as I have done so far, does not affect the essential

---

[6] GM II, 16.   [7] BGE 78.

point. Both the pleased spectator and the pleased inflicter are cruel. And in GM II Nietzsche often treats them in one breath. His original statement of the point I expressed as (A) is 'Seeing-suffer feels good, making-suffer even more so',[8] and he further plays up the role of spectatorship by dwelling on cruelty 'as festival' and on the public enactment of punishments. I shall retain the formulation given in (A) because, as I shall argue, in the inward turn from ordinary cruelty to bad conscience around which the whole of GM II coheres, it is pleasure in *inflicting* suffering on oneself that must be present.

Finally, is it plausible that Nietzsche would hold that the drives of human beings are so constituted that there is such a pervasive tendency towards pleasure in being cruel? He elsewhere makes clear his view that human beings do not have a basic drive towards pleasure as such—compare the unpublished note in which he says 'What man wants, what every smallest part of a living organism wants, is an increase of power. Pleasure or displeasure follow from the striving after that'.[9] Rather, the constancy of the need to inflict cruelty has a deeper explanation: 'Above all, a living thing wants to *discharge* its strength—life itself is will to power.'[10] And in GM II Nietzsche confirms that the force that leads to acts of dominance and state-building 'is basically the same force that here, inwardly ... creates for itself the bad conscience ... namely that *instinct for freedom* (in my language: the will to power).'[11] So simply as living creatures we seek to discharge our strength, and when the opportunity to discharge it outwardly is denied, we discharge it inwardly. Our earlier (A) and (C) should therefore be replaced by:

(A') Because of the instinctive drive of all living things to express power, human beings tend to gain pleasure from inflicting suffering.[12]

(C') Because human beings have the instinctive drive of all living things to express power, which leads them to gain pleasure from inflicting suffering, human beings subjected to the restrictions of civilized society, and so constrained to internalize their instincts, satisfy their instinctive drive *by inflicting suffering on themselves.*

As Ivan Soll has argued, psychological hedonism, 'the theory that the deepest motive of all human behaviour is the attainment of pleasure and the avoidance of pain',[13] is false for Nietzsche, and to be replaced by the doctrine of will to power. Pleasure is merely a by-product, the subjective result of the natural discharge of power. This, however, does not prevent Nietzsche from emphasizing the pleasure involved in inflicting suffering and the transference of this pleasure to the case of self-inflicted suffering. The vocabulary of pleasure, joy, satisfaction, or feeling good in relation to cruelty is prevalent throughout the essay.[14]

---

[8] GM II, 6.   [9] Published in WP 702.   [10] BGE 13 (see also 23, 259).
[11] GM II, 18.   [12] See GM II, 6.   [13] Soll (1994: 169).
[14] See section 5: 'the creditor is granted a certain *feeling of satisfaction* as repayment and compensation,—the feeling of satisfaction that comes from being permitted to vent his power without a second

II. Some questions of interpretation

GM II raises numerous large-scale issues of interpretation which make it difficult to go into detail beyond the level of the 'mission-statement'. Such issues should not be multiplied beyond necessity, so I shall mention just the following: (1) Is 'bad conscience' a form of the 'conscience' that Nietzsche attributes to the 'sovereign individual' in the essay's opening sections? (2) Are 'consciousness of guilt' and 'bad conscience' two separate phenomena, or one and the same? (3) Is the process of internalization of the instincts which Nietzsche describes as the 'origin of bad conscience' already an instance of 'bad conscience' or merely a precondition for it? (4) What is the process of 'moralization' which results in a particularly Christian form of bad conscience towards the end of the essay?

In sections 1–3 the 'sovereign individual' is 'the human being who *is permitted to promise*', in virtue of the memory developed by a prior history of pain-infliction, but also in virtue of the exceptional aristocratic strength to maintain a single will unchanged over time and to 'uphold it even against accidents, even "against fate" '. The 'consciousness of this rare freedom, this power over oneself and fate' Nietzsche calls the sovereign individual's *conscience*. However, section 4 begins with a question that introduces, seemingly for the first time, the topics contained in the essay's title: 'But how then did that other "gloomy thing," the consciousness of guilt, the entire "bad conscience" come into the world?' Taken simply on its own, this sentence suggests clear answers to two of our questions of interpretation, namely (1): Is 'bad conscience' a form of the 'conscience' that Nietzsche attributes to the 'sovereign individual' in the opening sections? Answer: No, it is an 'other' thing. And (2): Are 'consciousness of guilt' and 'bad conscience' two separate phenomena, or one and the same? Answer: They are the same, announced here as a single topic for investigation. Nothing Nietzsche says about the sovereign individual in sections 1–3 implies that he or she must feel guilty or suffer from a bad conscience. And nothing from section 4 onwards

---

thought on one who is powerless, the carnal delight "*de faire le mal pour le plaisir de le faire*," the enjoyment of doing violence'; section 6: '*cruelty* constitutes the great festival joy of earlier humanity ... Seeing-suffer feels good, making-suffer even more so—that is a hard proposition, a central one, an old powerful human all-too-human proposition'; section 7: 'this pleasure in cruelty needn't have actually died out, but ... it would need a certain sublimation and subtilization'; section 16: 'Hostility, cruelty, pleasure in persecution, in assault, in change, in destruction: all of that turning itself against the possessors of such instincts: *that* is the origin of "bad conscience" '; section 18: 'this uncanny and horrifying-pleasurable work of a soul compliant-conflicted with itself, that makes itself suffer out of pleasure in making suffer ... and we know ... what kind of *pleasure* it is that the self-less, the self-denying, the self-sacrificing feel from the very start: this pleasure belongs to cruelty'; section 22: 'a kind of madness of the will in psychic cruelty that has absolutely no equal: the *will* of man to find himself guilty and reprehensible to the point that it cannot be atoned for'.

(the sovereign individual not as such being mentioned again) implies that those who suffer from bad conscience are sovereign individuals.[15] Guilt, or bad conscience, is a condition in which we fall well short of any ideal Nietzsche entertains. I suggest that we can grasp the central train of thought of GM II from section 4 onwards without trespassing further into an elucidation of the sovereign individual.

But are 'consciousness of guilt' and 'bad conscience' the same thing for Nietzsche? A contemporary reader of Nietzsche might well have expected the terms to be more or less synonymous. For example, Nietzsche's former friend and collaborator, Paul Rée, in his book on the origin of conscience published two years earlier, had written that the knowledge or consciousness which blames us for our own wrongdoing is called 'punishing conscience, also pang of conscience, or guilt-consciousness', adding that 'if one nevertheless wanted to make a distinction between pangs of conscience and guilt-consciousness, it can only reside in duration. Guilt-consciousness is a longer pang of conscience.'[16] Later in his essay Nietzsche also sometimes appears to treat the two as equivalent:

Punishment is supposed to have the value of awakening in the guilty one the *feeling of guilt*; one seeks in it the true *instrumentum* of that reaction of the soul called 'bad conscience,' 'pang of conscience.'... Precisely among criminals and prisoners the genuine pang of conscience is something extremely rare.... But if we think, say, of those millennia *before* the history of man, then one may unhesitatingly judge that it is precisely through punishment that the development of the feeling of guilt has been most forcefully *held back*.[17]

It is hard to follow this passage except on the assumption that 'feeling of guilt', 'bad conscience', and 'pang of conscience' are being equated. Then, when using the conception of internalization to give his 'own hypothesis on the origin of the "bad conscience"', Nietzsche appears content to switch to talk of 'this whole development of guilt consciousness'.[18] Finally, the 'man of bad conscience' who achieves the maximum of internalization of cruelty tortures himself with the painful feeling of '*guilt* before God'.[19]

Recent writers (May 1999, Risse 2001, and Leiter 2002) have stated that there is an important Nietzschean conceptual distinction between bad conscience and guilt consciousness, though there appears no clear consensus across the accounts as to the nature of the distinction. At least two commentators, Risse and May, agree that the true target of Nietzsche's critique is bad conscience in its moralized and Christianized form, which is indeed *a pervasive feeling of guilt*: one feels a mental pain because one represents oneself as perpetually failing to fulfil an obligation or state of indebtedness

---

[15] Risse gives an account of the development of guilt and bad conscience in GM II, and all but apologizes (2001: 56) for not dealing with sections 1–3. On my view he would have little need to apologize for that.

[16] Rée (1885: 212).   [17] GM II, 14.   [18] GM II, 19.   [19] GM II, 22.

which one conceives oneself to stand in towards the all-powerful God (an anguished state presented with inimitable eloquence in GM II, 22).

On Risse's account the distinction between bad conscience and the feeling of guilt is as follows. After centuries of Christianity, we now have 'bad conscience *as a feeling of guilt*', which is the notion Nietzsche wishes to uncover in the essay as a whole, 'but in section 17, Nietzsche talks about an *older form* of the bad conscience that *precedes* Christianity and is not connected to guilt at all. This older form arises through the internalization of instincts and is a remote ancestor of the bad conscience as a feeling of guilt.'[20] In sum, for Risse, 'late' bad conscience—Nietzsche's true target for criticism—is identical to the feeling of guilt, while 'early' bad conscience is not yet guilt, but is simply the internalization of cruelty. One might point out, on the other hand, that Nietzsche frequently talks of internalization in various qualified ways as 'the *origin* of bad conscience' or 'bad conscience *in its beginnings*', or '*animal's* "bad conscience"'[21] all of which are compatible with internalization's being simply a preliminary and necessary component of bad conscience, not bad conscience as such.[22]

So it is hard to assert either that Nietzsche consistently distinguishes bad conscience from the feeling of (or consciousness of) guilt, or that he sees bad conscience as consisting *simply* in internalization of instincts, lacking a further component present in guilt. But rather than pursuing these issues, I shall proceed under the following assumptions: (1) internalization of the drive to express power and hence to inflict cruelty is one crucial component in the genesis of guilt-consciousness; (2) such internalization is not identical to guilt-consciousness proper; (3) guilt-consciousness proper is the most fully developed form of bad conscience and the true target of Nietzsche's critique.

III. What Explains Guilt-Consciousness?

We reached the idea that, because of a standing human tendency to gain pleasure from inflicting suffering and an enforced incapacity to inflict it outwardly, human beings who are subjected to the conditions of a settled society gain pleasure from inflicting

---

[20] Risse (2001: 58).   [21] GM II, 16, 17 and GM III, 20. My emphases.

[22] Nietzsche sometimes discusses guilt in a similar way. In GM III, 20 he refers back to the discussion of the 'animal psychology' of internalization and glosses it with 'there the feeling of guilt first confronted us in its raw state as it were'. Priests exploit this already existing kind of guilt-feeling by reinterpreting it as 'sin', he says, 'for thus reads the priestly reinterpretation of the animal's "bad conscience" (cruelty turned backwards)'. Here Nietzsche describes the state of internalization of the instincts indifferently as 'bad conscience' and as 'guilt'.

suffering on themselves. Internalization of cruelty means that we must discharge power somehow by inflicting suffering upon ourselves in a manner that produces gratification. But there are plenty of imaginable ways in which such a mechanism could work without the suffering being specifically that of feeling *guilty*. Human beings, when faced with society's confines, could have aggressed against themselves by inflicting the pain of *fear* on themselves, becoming afraid of one another or of the untamed natural environment or of some imagined predatory beings. Or they might have made themselves suffer from painful *jealousy* of other beings whose instincts did not need to be curbed. Or they might have suffered from crippling *shame* or been *angry* at their own impotence. These would all have been ways (compatible with our propositions (A'), (B), and (C')) in which to 'torture' or 'persecute' themselves. So even if we accept that internalization of hostile instincts dictates that socialized human beings must gratify themselves through self-inflicted suffering, we still do not have to accept that such human beings must feel guilt, have guilt-consciousness, or indeed that they must suffer the pangs of bad conscience in any usual sense. And that creates a gap for Nietzsche to bridge. If the internalization of cruelty is not yet the feeling of guilt, then how do we reach there from here?

A potentially even more serious problem for the overall train of thought in GM II is that Nietzsche gives what looks like a quite different explanation of the origin of the feeling of guilt: 'The feeling of guilt . . . had its origin . . . in the oldest and most primitive relationship among persons there is, in the relationship between buyer and seller, creditor and debtor.'[23] One of the main sources of explanatory energy for the whole essay is the repeated play on *Schuld, Schulden, Schuldner* (guilt, debt, debtor), at its most salient in Nietzsche's thought that 'that central moral concept "guilt" had its origins in the very material concept "debt" '.[24] One is a debtor when one is under an obligation, such that something is rightly claimed by someone as a conventional equivalence for a detriment one has caused them. But if *this* is the origin of the consciousness of guilt, why give us also the apparently quite separate hypothesis that consciousness of guilt originates in internalization of the instincts of hostility? The two explanations are not only distinct but of different kinds, the one invoking a psychological process supposed to occur in each individual as a consequence of the adaptation of the instinctual nature of humans to a socialized environment, the other a cultural regularization of exchange between individuals.

And finally there is a further difficulty. The debtor–creditor relationship operates independently of any *feeling* of guilt by those party to it—as Nietzsche points out with great clarity. If one is punished as a debtor, it is essential that one suffers a pain which is, according to some institutional rule, equivalent to the harm inflicted on

[23] GM II, 8.   [24] GM II, 4.

one's creditor. But throughout the majority of human history—Nietzsche makes clear—arousing the *feeling* of guilt has been neither the purpose nor the characteristic effect of punishment. My standing in what we can call 'objective guilt',[25] my *being* guilty, in the sense of someone's having the right to pay back some punishment to me, is emphatically independent of my having any *feeling* or *consciousness* of guilt: 'no other "inner pain" ' need be felt than sorrow and fear over one's impending ruin. That one suffers at the hands of one's creditor may present itself to one only as a matter of grave misfortune, little different from facing 'a plummeting, crushing boulder against which one can no longer fight.'[26]

So our difficulties have been compounded. Nietzsche appears to give two independent explanations for the origin of guilt-consciousness. And of the would-be explanations—internalization of instincts and the debtor–creditor relationship—neither on its own takes us near to the explanandum.

IV. Self-Punishment

If we are to regain coherence for the central train of thought in GM II, the 'two explanations' of the origin of guilt-consciousness must be parts of a single more subtle story. This can be the case, I suggest, if at some stage the cruelty that is internalized takes the form of a putative redress for transgression or payment of what is owed—if, in other words, we fulfil our alleged instinctive need to inflict suffering by conceiving the pain inflicted on ourselves as legitimate, because rightfully inflicted as a *punishment*. A further advantage of this reading, I maintain, is that the notion of *inflicting suffering on oneself because one conceives it as legitimate that one suffer* goes some way towards a believable characterization of the feeling of guilt.

We must, incidentally, say something about the role of punishment in GM II. One of the most substantial and convincing aspects of the essay is Nietzsche's reconstruction of the birth of punishment as a legitimation of cruelty by the introduction of equivalences between harms incurred and degrees of suffering owed to the perpetrators of harm (sections 4–15). Nietzsche leads us down something of a blind alley, since in sections 14 and 15 we discover that punishment was neither the direct origin of, nor a deliberate instrument towards, making people feel guilty. But, given the richness and prominence of the material on punishment, the essay

---

[25] A succinct statement by Card (1998: 139) is helpful here: ' "Guilt" is ambiguous between emotional self-punishment for having wronged others (internal guilt; guilt feelings) and the fact or finding of a transgression (objective guilt; a verdict)'.

[26] GM II, 14.

achieves more cohesion if punishment plays a role, albeit relatively indirectly, in the development of guilt-consciousness.[27]

The reading of GM II that I wish to defend is, schematically, as follows: the consciousness of guilt is a means of punishing oneself, and punishment originates in the debtor—creditor relationship; hence it makes sense for Nietzsche to say that consciousness of guilt originates in the debtor—creditor relationship. But self-punishment is also a form of self-cruelty or self-persecution, an outlet (or inlet) for the instinctive drive of living beings to dominate over something. Hence, if consciousness of guilt is a form of *self-punishment*, then Nietzsche can intelligibly claim both that it originates in internalization of the instincts and that it originates in the debtor—creditor relationship.

It may help to put the same point in another way. Nietzsche talks of internalizing cruelty, or reversing its direction: the self replaces others as the object on which suffering is inflicted. But in the passages on punishment he talks also of the legitimation of cruelty: 'Through his "punishment" of the debtor the creditor participates in a *right of lords*: finally, he, too, for once attains the elevating feeling of being permitted to hold a being in contempt and maltreat it as something "beneath himself" . . . The compensation thus consists in a directive and right to cruelty.'[28] So internalization and legitimation are two processes by which the expression of cruelty may be modified. If we think of them as two dimensions of transformation we arrive at the following schema:

	non-legitimated $\rightarrow$	legitimated
non-internalized	(*a*) simple cruelty to others	(*c*) punishment of others (conceived as rightful recipients of suffering)
$\downarrow$ internalized	(*b*) simple cruelty to self	(*d*) punishment of self (conceived as rightful recipient of suffering)

There is a standing need to express power and hence to inflict cruelty, which adapts to socialization by inflicting the suffering on the self. Then there is the debtor—creditor relationship, which interprets the infliction of suffering as rightful or permitted. In the transformation from (*a*) to (*c*) the primitive standing need to inflict cruelty co-opts

---

[27] Leiter (2002: 225—6) calls the material on punishment 'somewhat tangential' to GM II's argument. Risse (2001: 57—8) points out that punishment already plays another role, in that it coerces the populace's internalization of their instincts in GM II, 16.

[28] GM II, 5.

the institutional debtor—creditor relationship so as to legitimate cruelty towards others, giving permission to despise and maltreat them. My suggestion is that in the transformation (b) to (d) the same primitive standing need to inflict cruelty co-opts the debtor—creditor relationship so as to legitimate the internalized version of itself. We are being cruel to ourselves because, given our instincts as living beings, we are driven to be cruel to something, but we interpret the self-cruelty as deserved and rightful, as punishment of ourselves by ourselves. We give ourselves permission to despise and maltreat ourselves.

Why should we do this? Because of a further need thematized in the *Genealogy* as a whole, the need to give meaning to suffering. Nietzsche observes that 'what actually arouses indignation against suffering is not suffering in itself, but rather the senselessness of suffering'.[29] The relation between a primitively existing suffering and an interpretation imposed upon it appears in Nietzsche's substantive discussion of punishment as a series of reinterpretations of, or givings of meanings to, the relatively permanent 'drama' of inflicting a measured amount of cruelty (GM II, 12—13). See also the discussion in GM III, 20, where the priest imposes upon the basic suffering that arises from 'animal psychology' a 'reinterpretation . . . into feelings of guilt, fear, and punishment' so that the self-torturing human is to seek 'the cause of his suffering . . . in *himself*, in a *guilt* . . . he is to understand his suffering itself as a *state of punishment*.' As a way of giving meaning to a self-inflicted suffering that has to occur when our nature as living beings is subjected to socialization, we interpret that suffering as deservedly inflicted upon ourselves—an interpretation which, as we shall see, motivates the subsequent invention of reasons to regard ourselves as deserving to suffer.

I have argued so far that (b) and (c) in our schema are insufficient for the feeling or consciousness of guilt. In (d) we have in play both the adaptive mechanism of internalization and an interpretation which applies to self-cruelty the conception of punishment. I now want to suggest that (d) is at least a plausible candidate as an analysis of the feeling or consciousness of guilt.

What differentiates the feeling of guilt from other kinds of psychological pain? It must be the way the subject represents herself: she must at least take herself to have done harm, to have transgressed, usually against some other agent, in such a way as to violate an obligation she accepts herself to be under. To feel guilty requires an inner suffering that one represents as undergone because one has departed from what one believes one ought to do, in a way that is likely to cause anger or resentment from others,[30] and would permit them to despise or maltreat one. Something Nietzsche does not explicitly provide for in his analysis—but which must be there nevertheless

---

[29] GM II, 7. See also GM III, 28.
[30] See Williams (1993: 89—90); Gibbard (1990: 126—40); Rawls (1971: 445, 484).

for guilt to occur—is the conception of oneself as a transgressor in one's own eyes. I cannot feel guilty unless I believe that there is something I have done which I truly ought not to have done, that I have violated an obligation that I conceive myself genuinely and rightly to be under. If one represents oneself as having transgressed an obligation that one was genuinely under, one may regard oneself as a *worthy* or *rightful* object of anger and indignation, and hence of external punishment. It is plausible that the internal feeling of guilt is a process whereby some putatively permitted or rightful punishment is exacted already by means of a partial identification with those whom one conceives as angered by one's transgression. As Bernard Williams has put it, feeling guilty involves the internalization of a figure who is an ideal 'victim' or 'enforcer' (in contrast to shame which internalizes the figure of the watcher or witness).[31] One allows oneself to be punished *by oneself* on behalf of those one pictures either as harmed or as charged with punishing the transgressive harm. Assuming for now that this is approximately correct, then if Nietzsche puts forward self-punishment as a characterization of the feeling of guilt, he makes, if not a full analysis of the phenomenon, at least a claim about it with some plausibility.

A noteworthy feature of Nietzsche's account is that the need to inflict cruelty on oneself comes first, the incentive to conceive oneself as a legitimate recipient of cruelty comes second as a way of giving meaning to self-cruelty, and the invention of reasons why one deserves cruelty comes last in the story. We interpret ourselves as 'transgressors' or 'sinners' in order to make our suffering meaningful in that we can conceive it as rightful or permitted. We thus make suffering meaningful in order to perpetuate our primitive cruelty to ourselves, in order to satisfy our even more primitive need to inflict suffering, in order to continue to satisfy our natures by discharging power.

By the time Nietzsche reaches the end of his narrative and his true analysandum—the moralized Christian form of bad conscience which is a pervasive guilt-consciousness—it is clear that the subject of this state is indeed a self-punisher. The Christian has a concept of God as judge and executioner, which fulfils 'the *will* of man to find himself guilty and reprehensible to the point that it cannot be atoned for; his *will* to imagine himself punished without the punishment ever becoming equivalent to the guilt'.[32] This God is part of a very ambitious interpretation of suffering: one punishes oneself because one interprets one's self-cruelty as a punishment that one deserves for being inherently unworthy in the sight of God. On this theistic interpretation there exists a world-order containing a divine or absolute being of whom we are not worthy, and before whom we are wrongdoers; so we will always do wrong, so we will always feel guilty. Nietzsche reverses the direction of explanation: we need to be cruel to ourselves, so we invent the notion

---

[31] Williams (1993: 219).   [32] GM II, 22.

of ourselves as wrongdoers in order to legitimate the self-cruelty; then in order to sustain the notion of ourselves as wrongdoers we resort to a metaphysical picture in which we are bound to transgress against something absolute that is placed there for that very purpose. Cruelty is the base: the rest is interpretation in the service of giving meaning to the suffering we cannot help giving ourselves once society boxes us in.

V. Christian Bad Conscience

Section 19 of GM II begins a final assault on the development of the 'sickness' of bad conscience, promising to explain how it reached its 'most terrible and most sublime pinnacle'. Nietzsche takes up the debtor–creditor relation again, and tells how in earlier times human communities interpreted themselves as indebted to figures in their distant past, the ancestors who founded their clan. Over time these ancestors are conceived as ever more powerful and the clan's indebtedness to them as greater and harder to pay off. The ancestor eventually becomes transfigured into a god. Nietzsche then presents the Christian god as the end-point of this process: 'The rise of the Christian god as the maximum god that has been attained thus far . . . also brought a maximum of *Schuldgefühl* into appearance on earth.'[33]

Even now Nietzsche alerts us that we do not yet have an account of the 'moralization' of the concepts "*Schuld*" and "duty" '.[34] Nietzsche's glosses on 'moralization' are brief and confusing, so that it is much easier to describe the end-result of this process than the process itself. He does appear, however, to make the maximal Christian God a presupposition of the process.[35] We have already referred to section 22's devastating description of Christian self-torment. The end-result of moralization is that God is conceived as an absolute and all-powerful being to whom one is indebted for everything, but to whom it is impossible to discharge one's obligations or make adequate reparation. In Christianity man 'erect[s] an ideal—that of the "holy God"—in order, in the face of the same, to be tangibly certain of his absolute unworthiness.' In particular, man's 'natural and inescapable animal instincts' are the

---

[33] GM II, 20. *Schuldgefühl* is most naturally translated as 'feelings of guilt', as by Clark and Swensen. Risse (2001: 61–2) urges the translation 'feelings of indebtedness', because of his view that feelings of guilt do not predate the Christian God for Nietzsche—but see the discussion below.

[34] GM II, 21. Clark and Swensen have 'guilt' for *Schuld* here. Risse argues for 'debt' as the right translation—again see below.

[35] See GM II, 21: moralization of the concepts *Schuld* and *Pflicht* is 'their being pushed back into conscience, more precisely the entanglement of *bad* conscience with the concept of god'; and 'faith in our "creditor," in God' is a 'presupposition' of the moralized concepts. On 'moralization' and the elusive notion of 'pushing back', see Risse (2001: 63 ff.), and May (1999: 70 ff.).

antithesis of the perfect God. As Risse puts it, 'man's nature is full of dispositions to violate the divine order'.[36] In this conception it belongs to the human essence to be transgressive against absolute values, and so the consciousness of guilt is in-built, perpetual, and profound.[37]

Section 22 marks a magnificent rhetorical climax to the essay (presumably this is what Nietzsche later meant by GM II's *tempo feroce* . . . in which everything rushes ahead in a tremendous tension'[38]); but notice too how carefully Nietzsche recapitulates the earlier features of his psychological narrative and incorporates them in the picture of the Christian self-torturer:

> that will to self-torment, that suppressed cruelty of the animal-human who had been made inward, scared back into himself . . . who invented the bad conscience in order to cause himself pain after the *more natural* outlet for this *desire to cause pain* was blocked,—this man of bad conscience has taken over the religious presupposition in order to drive his self-torture to its most gruesome severity and sharpness. Guilt before *God*: this thought becomes an instrument of torture for him.[39]

There is still the standing tendency towards pleasure-in-cruelty. But we must inflict suffering on ourselves, because our drive to cruelty has undergone internalization. But in order to continue inflicting suffering on ourselves meaningfully, we must interpret ourselves as transgressors in a debtor–creditor relationship who are granted the permission rightfully to despise and maltreat ourselves, to inflict self-punishment. And in order thus to interpret ourselves we must fabricate a creditor residing in another realm of values which absolutely guarantees that we continue to deserve punishment. In short, we use the invention of God as an elaborate and disguised way of being intensely cruel in perpetuity.

VI. Guilt Without God?

So how, for Nietzsche, does the feeling of guilt relate to belief in a single all-powerful God? Mathias Risse puts forward the following analysis of the development of bad conscience in GM II:

> We have followed Nietzsche through his discussion of the two elements from which the current meaning of bad conscience descends, the bad conscience as the result of the internalization of instincts and the indebtedness to the gods. . . . [The] third element is *Christianity*, and it is through

---

[36] Risse (2001: 65).

[37] In May's formulation: 'moralization is defined . . . by the idea that one's human nature is essentially and undischargeably guilty and *hence defective*' (1999: 70–1).

[38] EH, 'Genealogy of Morals'.   [39] GM II, 22.

the interaction of Christianity with the early form of the bad conscience [internalization—C.J.] and the indebtedness that the bad conscience as a feeling of guilt arises.[40]

This would give Nietzsche quite an extreme position: no one has feelings of guilt until the advent of Christianity. And it is a surprising position, given our analysis so far. If feeling guilty is self-punishment, one might expect it to be possible for someone who (a) conceives himself to have obligations of some kind, (b) conceives himself to be legitimately punished for transgressing his obligations, and (c) has undergone internalization of the hostile instincts, planting the punishing agency within. Hence the conditions for guilt-consciousness or guilty bad conscience are present before the Christian world-picture arrives, indeed before any concept of a god.

Certainly Nietzsche believes that bad conscience persists once the conception of the maximum god perishes,[41] and explicitly urges the reader to try feeling guilty about his or her yearnings to side with the transcendent against the natural human inclinations.[42] This, however, is not inconsistent with the idea that human beings had this general capacity to feel guilt only once they became believers in some monotheistic religion. But does Nietzsche really hold that? First, as we have said, it seems an implausible position, but secondly, as Aaron Ridley has pointed out,[43] we can construct a much more plausible Nietzschean narrative in which an already existing propensity to feel guilt—whose psychological and institutional origins we have seen traced in the internalization of instinctual drives and the debtor–creditor relationship—is subsequently exploited to particular ends by Christianity. When in GM II, 22 our belief in God functions to push our 'self-torture to its most gruesome severity', what is being intensified is most naturally taken to be the general propensity to feel guilty. This fits with Nietzsche's emphasis in 'Guilt before *God*: this thought becomes an instrument of torture for him', and the idea that man here fulfils a pervasive 'will to find himself guilty and reprehensible'. Therefore, the presence of guilt-feelings prior to the belief in the Christian God is not only possible in Nietzsche's account, but needed to make sense of it.[44]

---

[40] Risse (2001: 63).   [41] See GM II, 21

[42] GM II, 24. This point is urged against Risse's reading by Ridley (2005: 38).

[43] Ridley (2005: 40).

[44] Risse (2005: 46–7) has countered criticisms by saying that the guilt-consciousness that arises solely with the belief in the Christian God is 'existential guilt', as opposed to the more ordinary responsive attitude which he calls 'locally reactive guilt', guilt felt concerning some particular act of putative transgression by the agent. In these terms, however, Nietzsche's account is best read as explaining the origins of locally reactive guilt in internalization and the debtor–creditor relation, and the subsequent intensification of locally reactive guilt into existential guilt by means of the Christian metaphysical picture.

VII. The goodness of guilt

What then of 'moralization'? A simple but unremarked characteristic of 'moralizing' a concept is making it fit to take its place in an overall conception of the morally good. This suggests that in the final step of Nietzsche's narrative 'feeling guilty' and 'having a bad conscience' become part of what the morally good person does or is. Earlier in the narrative human beings cannot be said to have regarded the self-cruelty and self-punishment into which they fell as anything particularly good *per se*. Suffering in this way began as an enforced psychological adaptation, then became a kind of burden or sickness. There were good, even spectacularly good consequences of internalization: Nietzsche mentions the development of the inner mental life, creativity, beauty, and the promise of self-overcoming.[45] But implicit in his account is that no one prior to Christianity conceived self-cruelty or self-punishment as a good *per se*.

It is, I suggest, the supposed *goodness* of feeling guilty that Nietzsche thinks requires metaphysical underpinning. This provides a clearer sense in which moralization of guilt presupposes an 'entanglement with the concept of god', as Nietzsche says in GM II, 21.[46] It is a good thing to punish myself if I deserve punishment in principle and essentially. And the Christian conception of the self and its place in the world—the infinite all-valuable divine order and the pernicious animal self in perpetual transgression against it—provides the guarantee of punishment's being wholly deserved. Moralization is the elevation of feeling guilty into a virtue, its incorporation into what the morally good individual is or does, into a conception of the kind of person one should want to be, by means of the rationalizing metaphysical picture in which the individual's essential instinctual nature *deserves* maltreatment, because it stands in antithesis to an infinite creditor.

Why is the self-punishment of feeling guilty construed as a good? Because our natures are conceived as evil. Why are our natures conceived as evil? Because of their animal drives towards aggression and cruelty. But what is feeling guilty? An outlet—or again an inlet—for these same drives. If we find the story credible, we may incline towards a wry smile at the expense of the inflated Christian conception of the good. And if, as Nietzsche says in *Ecce Homo*, a new truth becomes visible in his essay, it must be a version of his 'opposites' point from *Beyond Good and Evil*: 'what gives value to that good and honorable thing, bad conscience, has an incriminating link to

---

[45] See GM II, 16, 18.

[46] Ridley (2005) and Risse (2005) disagree on whether the 'moralization' of the concept *Schuld* presupposes belief in the Christian God; yet both take the moralization in question to be the transformation of indebtedness into guilt-feeling. I have followed Ridley in arguing that that transformation does not require belief in God. But I take moralization to be something that happens to guilt-feelings further down the track, and to be a process in which the concept of God is indeed implicated.

what looks like its evil opposite, the drive towards inflicting cruelty; perhaps they are even essentially the same.'

References

Works by Nietzsche

Beyond Good and Evil, trans. Judith Norman (Cambridge: Cambridge University Press, 2002).

Ecce Homo, trans. Walter Kaufmann (New York: Vintage Books, 1967).

On the Genealogy of Morality, trans. Maudemarie Clark and Alan J. Swensen (Indianapolis: Hackett, 1998).

The Will to Power, trans. Walter Kaufmann (New York, Vintage Books, 1968).

Other Works

CARD, CLAUDIA FALCONER (1998). 'Rectification and Remainders', in Edward Craig (ed.), *The Routledge Encyclopedia of Philosophy*, vii (New York/London: Routledge), 139.

GIBBARD, ALAN (1990). *Wise Choices, Apt Feelings: A Theory of Normative Judgement.* (Oxford: Clarendon Press).

HAVAS, RANDALL (1995). *Nietzsche's Genealogy: Nihilism and the Will to Knowledge.* (Ithaca and London: Cornell University Press).

LEITER, BRIAN (2002). *Nietzsche on Morality* (London: Routledge).

MAY, SIMON (1999). *Nietzsche's Ethics and his 'War on Morality'* (Oxford: Clarendon Press).

RAWLS, JOHN (1971). *A Theory of Justice* (Cambridge, Mass.: Harvard University Press).

RÉE, PAUL (1885). *Die Entstehung des Gewissens* (Berlin: Carl Duncker).

RIDLEY, AARON (1998). *Nietzsche's Conscience* (Ithaca and London: Cornell University Press).

——— (2005). 'Guilt before God, or God Before Guilt? The Second Essay of Nietzsche's *Genealogy*', *The Journal of Nietzsche Studies* 29: 35–45.

RISSE, MATHIAS (2001). 'The Second Treatise in *On the Genealogy of Morality*: Nietzsche on the Origin of the Bad Conscience', *European Journal of Philosophy* 9: 55–81.

——— (2005). 'On God and Guilt: A Reply to Aaron Ridley', *The Journal of Nietzsche Studies* 29: 46–53.

SOLL, IVAN (1994). 'Nietzsche on Cruelty, Asceticism, and the Failure of Hedonism', in R. Schacht (ed.), *Nietzsche, Genealogy, Morality* (Berkeley: University of California Press), 168–92.

WILLIAMS, BERNARD (1993). *Shame and Necessity* (Berkeley: University of California Press).

Part II

Metaethics

7

Honest Illusion: Valuing for Nietzsche's Free Spirits

Nadeem J. Z. Hussain

1. Introduction

There is a widespread, popular view—and one I will basically endorse—that Nietzsche is, in one sense of the word, a nihilist. As Arthur Danto put it some time ago, according to Nietzsche, 'there is nothing in [the world] which might sensibly be supposed to have value.'[1] As interpreters of Nietzsche, though, we cannot simply stop here. Nietzsche's higher men, *Übermenschen*, 'genuine philosophers', free spirits—the types Nietzsche wants to bring forth from the human, all-too-human herds he sees around him with the fish hooks, as he says, of his books—seem to engage in what looks like *valuing*. These free spirits are supposed to *revalue* the old values—revaluing, as is clear from the texts, is not simply to remove the old values from circulation (Nietzsche uses '*umwerten*' and not '*entwerten*')—and they are supposed to create *new* values. And, of course, Nietzsche himself, free spirit that he is, takes on the task of revaluing all values and seems to assert many a strident evaluation. So we need to say more here. What are Nietzsche and his free spirits up to when they engage in what looks, for all the world, like a practice of valuing? What is the practice of valuing Nietzsche is recommending for his free spirits?

---

[1] Arthur C. Danto, *Nietzsche as Philosopher* (New York: Columbia University Press, 1965), 33. This is not, however, the orthodoxy in the Anglo-American secondary literature on Nietzsche. I turn to this issue later in the essay.

I will argue for two claims:

(i) First, we end up facing an interpretive puzzle when we attempt to explain how Nietzsche's free spirits are supposed to engage in a practice of valuing.

(ii) Second, we can solve the interpretive puzzle by taking Nietzsche's free spirits to be engaged in a fictionalist simulacrum of valuing.

2. The Interpretive Puzzle

2.1 Interpretive Constraints

Nietzsche makes a range of claims about values, valuing, and the tasks and nature of his free spirits and higher men. Any interpretation of Nietzsche needs to take account of these claims; these claims form, as I shall call them, interpretive constraints. The interpretive puzzle I will focus on is generated by a particular set of interpretive constraints:

(1) A central task of Nietzsche's free spirits is the creation and revaluation of values.

Nietzsche, 'free spirits', 'higher men'—the new and genuine philosophers—are the ones 'who write new values on new tablets' (Z P).[2] Nietzsche insists that we must 'reach' towards 'new philosophers': '[T]oward spirits strong and original enough to provide the stimuli for opposite valuations and to revalue and invert "eternal values" ' (BGE 203). The task is not simply to create new objects, actions, states of affairs, and persons that are valuable given existing values. This would be merely to create more value but not to create new values.[3]

(2) Nietzsche's free spirit 'conceives reality *as it is*'[4]

---

[2] In citing Nietzsche's texts I have basically followed the guidelines of the North American Nietzsche Society; I use the following standard English title acronyms: *The Antichrist* (A), *Beyond Good and Evil* (BGE), *Ecce Homo* (EH), *Gay Science* (GS), *On the Genealogy of Morals* (GM), *Human, All Too Human* (HH), *Philosophy in the Tragic Age of the Greeks* (PTA), *Twilight of the Idols* (TI), *Will to Power* (WP), *Zarathustra* (Z). References to Z and TI list abbreviated chapter title and section number. The translations, where available, are listed in the Bibliography. All other translations are mine. Roman numerals refer to major parts or chapters. Arabic numerals refer to sections. For the German text I refer to the *Kritische Studienausgabe* (Berlin: de Gruyter, 1980) (KSA) and *Kritische Gesamtausgabe: Werke* (Berlin: de Gruyter, 1967–78) (KGW). For Nietzsche's correspondence I refer to *Sämtliche Briefe: Kritische Studienausgabe in 8 Bänden* (Munich: de Gruyter, 1986) (KSB).

[3] See also GS 55, 320, 335; Z:1 'On the Three Metamorphoses', 'On the Thousand and One Goals'; BGE 211; TI P; AC, in particular 13; EH 'Destiny' 1; WP 260, 972, 979, 999. See Richard Schacht, *Nietzsche* (London: Routledge, 1983), 466–9.

[4] EH 'Destiny' 5: 'concipirt die Realität, *wie sie ist*'. See also GS 2, 110, 283; Z 2 'The Stillest Hour':2; BGE 230; A 50; EH 'Destiny' 3; WP 172.

Nietzsche claims that for many of us, and perhaps for all of us some of the time, 'untruth'—having false or inaccurate beliefs—is 'a condition of life' (BGE 4). Such false beliefs are necessary in order for us to continue living. However, one of the central features of the 'higher men' that sets them apart is precisely their ability, in a sense that will need explication, to face up to the truth: 'How much truth does a spirit *endure*, how much truth does it *dare?* More and more that became for me the real measure of value. Error (faith in the ideal) is not blindness, error is *cowardice*' (EH P:3). The question for Nietzsche is to what extent his free spirits can 'incorporate' truth in their lives (GS 110).[5]

Now, in order to make sense of what the creation of values in (1) might come to, we need a better sense of what it is for something to be valuable according to Nietzsche. Here we come to our third interpretive constraint, the one that does indeed make our interpretive puzzle come into focus.

(3) Nietzsche's nihilism: Nietzsche claims that nothing has value in itself and therefore all claims of the form '*X* is valuable' are false.

I am here, obviously, ascribing to Nietzsche a sweeping error theory about evaluative claims and it will take a bit of interpretive work to justify this particular interpretive constraint. In the case of moral values and moral judgments, the textual evidence is fairly straightforward:

My demand upon the philosopher is known, that he take his stand *beyond* good and evil and leave the illusion of moral judgment *beneath* himself. This demand follows from an insight which I was the first to formulate: that *there are altogether no moral facts*. Moral judgments agree with religious ones in believing in realities which are no realities. Morality is merely an interpretation of certain phenomena—more precisely a misinterpretation. Moral judgments, like religious ones, belong to a stage of ignorance at which . . . 'truth,' . . . designates all sorts of things which we today call 'imaginings.' (TI, 'Improvers', 1)

I will take such textual evidence to be sufficient to ascribe to Nietzsche an error theory about moral claims. For the purposes of this essay, an error theory about morality need involve only the following claim: the beliefs expressed by moral judgments are false because they involve believing in moral facts when in fact there are none. We can use Nietzsche's own analogy with religious judgments to provide an example of an error theory about something other than moral claims. An error theory about

---

[5] This ideal for Nietzsche's higher men is compatible with the possibility that some degree of falsification may be ineliminable from our beliefs including those of the higher men. For an extended discussion of Nietzsche's metaphysics and epistemology, see Nadeem J. Z. Hussain, 'Nietzsche's Positivism,' *European Journal of Philosophy* 12/3 (2004): 326–68.

religion would claim that religious judgments express beliefs that are false because they involve believing in certain entities, such as God, that do not exist.[6]

However, the explicitly error-theoretic claims in Nietzsche's texts do tend to occur only where morality in some narrow sense seems to be the topic. For non-moral evaluations, we often get passages of the following form: 'Whatever has *value* in our world now does not have value in itself, according to its nature—nature is always value-less, but has been *given* value at some time, as a present—and it was *we* who

---

[6] According to traditional typologies of the metaethical domain, an error theory is a conjunction of two claims, one semantic and the other substantive. The first claim is that of cognitivism. Moral claims are truth-apt; they are true or false. Moral judgments are then taken to express beliefs. The second claim is that such moral claims, and thus the relevant beliefs, are systematically false. Given the truth-conditions moral claims have, it turns out that the world is not the way these claims say it is. Cognitivism here is to be contrasted with non-cognitivism. Staying for now with the traditional typologies, a non-cognitivist account claims that moral judgments express a conative state, perhaps some pro-attitude, rather than a cognitive state such as belief. Moral claims then are not truth-apt. They never were about moral facts. It makes as little sense to assess them for truth or falsity as it does to assess commands for truth or falsity (for surveys of such traditional topologies, and worries about them, see Geoffrey Sayre-McCord, in Geoffrey Sayre-McCord (ed.), 'Introduction: The Many Moral Realisms,' in *Essays on Moral Realism* (Ithaca and London: Cornell University Press, 1988), 1–21, and Stephen Darwall, Allan Gibbard, and Peter Railton, 'Toward *Fin de siècle* Ethics: Some Trends,' *The Philosophical Review* 101/1 (1992): 115–89).

Given this traditional typology, to claim that Nietzsche is an error theorist would then involve ascribing to him a particular view about the semantics of moral discourse, namely, cognitivism. This would appear to conflict with Leiter's claim that 'there are inadequate textual resources for ascribing to [Nietzsche] a satisfying answer' to questions about the semantics of moral claims (Brian Leiter, 'Nietzsche's Metaethics: Against the Privilege Readings,' *European Journal of Philosophy* 8/3 (2000): 278). Thus 'there are simply not adequate grounds for "assigning" to Nietzsche a view on such subtle matters as whether ethical language is primarily cognitive or non-cognitive' (279). Leiter suggests that ascribing any view on these matters to historical figures would be anachronistic (278). However, as long as we stay within the traditional typology, it does not make much sense to claim that Nietzsche could be a non-cognitivist. After all, such a traditional non-cognitivist would not draw the conclusion that there is something wrong with moral judgment from the claim that there are no moral facts, since moral judgments never were about moral facts in the first place.

Contemporary non-cognitivists often reject the traditional typology. Such a non-cognitivist would provide an account according to which it was perfectly fine to take moral claims as truth-apt and moral judgments as expressing beliefs (see, for example, Simon Blackburn, *Spreading the Word: Groundings in the Philosophy of Language* (Oxford: Clarendon Press, 1984) and Simon Blackburn, *Essays in Quasi-Realism* (New York and Oxford: Oxford University Press, 1993)). Indeed, it would be fine to claim that there are moral facts. Of course, the account of such talk turns out to be rather more complicated than we perhaps originally thought. Once we leave the traditional typology behind and consider the possibility of such contemporary non-cognitivist positions, then I agree with Leiter that we lack adequate grounds for assigning Nietzsche a view on such matters. However, for the purposes of this essay, the important point to note is that such a contemporary non-cognitivist could be an error theorist too. Such a non-cognitivist could in principle claim that the beliefs expressed by moral judgments are false because they involve believing in moral facts when in fact there are none. We can thus ascribe an error theory to Nietzsche without 'assigning' him a view on semantic issues.

gave and bestowed it' (GS 301).[7] The claim that nothing has value in itself occurs repeatedly in Nietzsche's texts. 'In themselves', says Nietzsche, things are not 'beautiful, attractive, and desirable' (GS 299). Now such passages are not obviously to be construed along error-theoretic lines. We could use them to ascribe to Nietzsche a subjectivist realism.[8] I use the term 'realism' here in a way that is perhaps not so common outside of discussions in metaethics. A metaethical theory is realist if it provides a cognitivist account of the claims in question and takes the truth-conditions not to be systematically or inescapably false.[9] The account would be a kind of subjectivism because it takes the truth-conditions of evaluative claims as involving some essential reference to an agent's states. That is to say, claims of the form 'X is valuable' are true, but in virtue of the object, state of affairs, what-have-you, standing in certain relations to agents. An agent falls under some such relation in virtue of being in some state or having some property. Something is valuable in virtue of, for example, our having certain attitudes towards the thing. As long as we had the requisite attitudes towards the relevant objects, evaluative claims could be straightforwardly true.

The proposed subjectivist realist reading does not, however, square with certain themes in Nietzsche's texts. At work in Nietzsche's texts is a distinction between theoretical nihilism and practical nihilism.[10] Theoretical nihilism is the belief in valuelessness, or as Nietzsche often puts it, goallessness.[11] Practical nihilism is the practical consequence in most agents of the belief, usually only a tacit belief, in valuelessness or goallessness. Practical nihilism consists of a range of psychological and sociological phenomena. Now it is certainly true that Nietzsche is extremely concerned about the rise of practical nihilism, but theoretical nihilism is something that he does indeed seem to endorse:

It is only late that one musters the courage for what one really knows. That I have hitherto been a thorough-going nihilist, I have admitted to myself only recently: the energy and radicalism with which I have advanced as a nihilist deceived me about this basic fact. When one moves

[7] See also HH 4; D 3; GS 115; BGE P, 107; Z:1 'On the Thousand and One Goals', 1 'On the Afterworldly'; WP 428. Cf. Z P:9, 1 'On the Flies of the Market Place'; WP 972.

[8] It is some such interpretation of Nietzsche that I take to be defended in Harold Langsam, 'How to Combat Nihilism: Reflections on Nietzsche's Critique of Morality,' *History of Philosophy Quarterly* 14/2 (1997): 235–53.

[9] A realist can, of course, think that most moral judgments in the past, and even perhaps most moral judgments today, are false. However, to be a realist about our moral discourse a theorist must think that at least some central moral claims are indeed true. Or at least this is how I shall use the term 'realist' in order to distinguish moral realists from error-theorists. In making just this point, Sayre-McCord emphasizes that a moral realist must be committed to a 'Success Theory' in contrast to an 'Error Theory' (Sayre-McCord, 'Introduction', 10). In any case, the argument of the essay does not turn on how we should settle such terminological issues.

[10] See, for example, WP 4 [11] See, for example, HH I:33, WP 2.

toward a goal it seems impossible that 'goal-lessness as such' is the principle of our faith. (WP 25)[12]

Perhaps more problematic for the proposed subjective realist reading of Nietzsche is that he does often raise problems for evaluation in general. Thus he says that 'all evaluations are premature and are bound to be' (HH I:32). 'The falsity of human [evaluative] judgments,' says Nietzsche, occurs with 'absolute necessity' (HH I:32).[13] This is because they involve a '*necessary* injustice' (HH I:P:6). He says, 'You shall learn to grasp the *necessary* injustice in every For and Against' (HH I:P:6): 'You shall learn to grasp the sense of perspective in every value judgement—the displacement, distortion and merely apparent teleology of horizons ... the quantum of stupidity that resides in antitheses of values and the whole intellectual loss which every For and Against costs us' (HH I:P:6).

Now, whatever we may think is the right way to make sense of what Nietzsche is saying here in detail, and I will come back to that in a moment, two things are clear. First, worries about evaluative judgments are not just restricted to moral judgments in some narrow sense of moral. All evaluative judgments involve some kind of mistake *necessarily*. There appears to be something involved in evaluative judgments *qua* evaluative judgments that is problematic. Of course, moral evaluative judgments could suffer from some additional problem, perhaps that they are false. However, and this brings us to the second point, it seems that a subjective realism about non-moral evaluations would have trouble with such passages. After all, if indeed evaluative claims have the proposed subjective truth-conditions, then they do not get the world wrong. They do not seem to involve any essential intellectual loss.

These considerations force us to reinterpret the passage from the *Gay Science*, and other similar passages, that suggested the subjective realism in the first place. Why would Nietzsche repeatedly insist that nothing is valuable 'in itself' if it was not to suggest some kind of subjectivist realism? The answer is that Nietzsche thinks that our evaluations of things involve judgments that things are valuable in themselves. It is in order to undermine our evaluative judgments that Nietzsche emphasizes that things do not have value in themselves.

Indeed this way of interpreting Nietzsche allows us to make sense of certain things he says about values and valuing. First, it helps us make sense of his use of the metaphor of value being 'given' as a 'present' (GS 301)[14]—elsewhere he talks of 'placing values in

---

[12] See also, for example, HH I:33 on the 'ultimate goallessness of man'.

[13] The context of this passage makes clear that Nietzsche is talking about all evaluative judgments.

[14] 'Was nur *Werth* hat in der jetzigen Welt, das hat ihn nicht an sich, seiner Natur nach,—die Natur ist immer werthlos:—sondern dem hat man einen Werth einmal gegeben, geschenkt, und *wir* waren diese Gebenden und Schenkenden!' (GS 301).

things'.[15] A present, once given, is possessed by that which receives the present. When something is placed in some other thing, it is now *in* the other thing. Things appear to have value *in* themselves but this is not because they are in fact valuable in themselves but in virtue of us. Nietzsche is making the typical error-theorist's explanatory claim: things appear as if they are valuable in themselves, but that appearance is generated by us.

Second, we can now explain Nietzsche's talk of a necessary injustice involved in all evaluative judgments. The necessary injustice involved in all value judgments is an injustice against other possible objects of valuing. We take this object as demanding that it be valued. We take this demand as arising from something in the object that distinguishes it from other objects. What we take as distinguishing it from other objects is that it is valuable in itself. In fact, however, it is not valuable in itself. It is not any more valuable in itself than any other object. Our treatment of these other objects, of other evaluations involving these other objects, is thus 'unfair' and 'unjust'. However, an evaluation in favor of some other alternative would simply in turn be unjust to everything else. Evaluations are thus necessarily unjust.

The error theory about evaluative judgments expressed by interpretive constraint (3) thus allows us to make sense of what Nietzsche has to say about values and valuing as he finds them. This error theory succeeds in accounting for a greater range of texts than the proposed subjective realist option we have considered.[16]

---

[15] 'Werthe legte erst der Mensch in die Dinge' (Z:1 'On the Thousand and One Goals').

[16] Two points: First, the argument against ascribing subjective realism to Nietzsche can be constructed in a more painstaking manner. We could take as a premise that Nietzsche explicitly only claims that things are not valuable in themselves. We could then attempt to look for the relations between agents and objects (states of affairs, actions, etc.) that we could use to come up with a subjective realist set of truth-conditions for evaluative claims. As it turns out, it is not at all easy to see how to do this. One would normally use an agent's pro-attitudes to construct such truth-conditions; however, Nietzsche bemoans the fact that pro-attitudes themselves are constituted by evaluative judgments. It is this that makes us 'from the very beginning illogical and thus unjust beings . . . this is one of the greatest and most irresolvable discords of existence' (HH I:32). There is a discord because we cannot exist, so Nietzsche says, without pro- and con-attitudes. However, if having some set of pro-attitudes towards an object were sufficient to make it the case that the object is valuable, then surely Nietzsche would not speak with such a despairing tone. This comes in the end as no particular surprise given what Williams calls Nietzsche's 'minimalist moral psychology' (see Bernard Williams, 'Nietzsche's Minimalist Moral Psychology,' *European Journal of Philosophy* 1/1 (1993): 4–14). The moral psychological resources in Nietzsche's texts for constructing such a subjective realist account do not give us much to work with.

Second, the ascription of an error theory about evaluative judgments to Nietzsche may seem to be in tension with the fact that he himself repeatedly makes evaluative judgments and that he seems to think his 'free spirits' should also engage in evaluation. This indeed is very much part of the interpretive puzzle that I am at this point attempting to lay out and that I will solve later in this essay.

Let us now turn to the final interpretive constraint:

(4) There is a close connection drawn in Nietzsche's works between art, the avoidance of practical nihilism, and the creation of new values.

The last interpretive constraint, and, as I shall eventually argue, the key to the eventual solution to our interpretive puzzle, is a close connection drawn in Nietzsche's works between art, the avoidance of practical nihilism, and the creation of value. The connection between art and his solution to the undermining of values is a persistent theme in Nietzsche's writings. Let me give you a quick survey. This begins of course with his famous statement in *The Birth of Tragedy*: 'it is only as an *aesthetic phenomenon* that existence and the world are eternally *justified*' (BT 5. This claim is repeated in BT 24). Such a role for art remains central to Nietzsche's thought even though he gives up the Schopenhauerian metaphysics and romanticism of the view defended in *The Birth of Tragedy*.[17] In his notes from the period right after *The Birth of Tragedy*, we see him returning again and again to the thought that art might be an antidote or a response to the threat of practical nihilism generated by the natural sciences and their depiction of the world as lacking value in itself.[18]

In his book *Human All-Too-Human*, right after the discussion of the necessary injustice involved in valuing that I considered above, Nietzsche says that someone who clearly realized the 'goallessness' of man might well see 'actions acquire in his own eyes the character of useless squandering', but, Nietzsche suggests, it is the poets, who faced with this goallessness will know how to 'console themselves' (HH I:33).

In a section of *The Gay Science* entitled '*What one should learn from artists*', Nietzsche asks, 'How can we make things beautiful, attractive, and desirable for us when they are not? And I rather think that in themselves they never are.' His answer is 'that we should learn from artists' how to deal with this lack of value in our lives (GS 299). Similarly, we hear an echo of the position expressed in *The Birth of Tragedy* at the end of Book II of *The Gay Science*:

Our ultimate gratitude to art. —If we had not welcomed the arts and invented this kind of cult of the untrue, then the realization of general untruth and mendaciousness that now comes to us through science ... would be utterly unbearable. *Honesty* would lead to nausea and suicide. But now there is a counterforce against our honesty that helps us to avoid such consequences: art as the *good* will to appearance.... As an aesthetic phenomenon existence is still *bearable* for us. (GS 107)

---

[17] See Nietzsche's own critiques of *The Birth of Tragedy* in BT 'Attempt at Self-Criticism' and EH 'Books' BT.

[18] See Daniel Breazeale (ed.), *Philosophy and Truth: Selections from Nietzsche's Notebooks of the Early 1870's* (Atlantic Highlands, NJ: Humanities Press International, 1979) for a useful selection.

Similarly in the *Genealogy of Morals*, Nietzsche demands an opposition to the ascetic ideal. This opposition cannot come from science since 'it never creates values.' However, art 'is much more fundamentally opposed to the ascetic ideal than is science', since in 'art . . . the *lie* is sanctified and the *will to deception* has a good conscience' (GM III:25). So the suggestion is that art, in some way that will need to be explicated, does help in the creation of new values.[19]

2.1.1 The Puzzle Itself

Given the way I have set matters up, at this point it is perhaps already clear what the interpretive puzzle is, and even, perhaps, what I am going to claim is the solution. One straightforward way of putting the puzzle is this. Given interpretive constraint (1) it seems as if Nietzsche's free spirits are supposed to engage in valuing and create values. However, given interpretive constraint (3), there do not seem to be any values. We might think that perhaps Nietzsche's free spirits are simply supposed to have false beliefs. They are supposed to believe that things are valuable in themselves even though such beliefs are false. This would, perhaps, be an achievement, since after all, intentionally getting oneself to have false beliefs is, as we know, a delicate business that requires, so to speak, much skill. But I think this interpretation runs into interpretive constraint (2), namely, that Nietzsche's free spirits and higher men are distinguished by their ability to face up to reality. I take a systematic holding of false beliefs to be a failing in this regard. If there is another way to manage to do something we might want to call creating values that avoids buying into an ideology, then surely Nietzsche's free spirits would take this option. So the interpretive puzzle is how can we make sense of the importance of values and valuing in Nietzsche's higher men and free spirits—including, importantly, himself—while staying within our interpretive constraints?[20]

---

[19] See also, for example, GS P:301; TI 'Skirmishes', 24.

[20] It is also useful to draw a distinction between what one might call an 'internal' and an 'external' interpretive puzzle. The internal interpretive puzzle is generated by interpretive constraints derived from Nietzsche's texts. As always with interpretations, even if we do find an account of what it is for free spirits to value that coheres with these interpretive constraints, if this interpretation does not seem philosophically plausible, then there will be some defeasible pressure to come up with another interpretation of Nietzsche's texts. A version of the principle of charity would be in play. The 'external' grounds that would generate such pressure would be various platitudes about values and valuing that we tend to hold (I borrow the talk of 'platitudes' here from Michael Smith, *The Moral Problem* (Oxford: Blackwell, 1994)). Now, of course, we need to be prepared that Nietzsche would reject some of these platitudes or radically reinterpret them. Surely Nietzsche is precisely the kind of thinker for whom we need to leave open such a possibility. Nonetheless, if too many of these platitudes are rejected, the worry will be that Nietzsche is simply changing the subject on us.

Such platitudes would include the following. There is a distinction between valuing and wanting (see, for example, Harry Frankfurt, 'Freedom of the Will and the Concept of a Person,' *Journal of*

3. The Solution to the Interpretive Puzzle

The central thought in my solution to the interpretive puzzle is that valuing, in Nietzsche's recommended practice, involves the generation of 'honest illusions'. It can be thought of as a form of make-believe, pretending, or, the non-Nietzschean phrase adopted here, 'regarding . . . as': S values X by regarding X as valuable in itself while knowing that in fact X is not valuable in itself.[21] The motivation for this interpretive strategy arises, perhaps not surprisingly, from what I have called interpretive constraint (4), namely, the suggestion in Nietzsche's texts that there is some close connection between art, avoiding practical nihilism, and the creation of values.

I will proceed by ruling out some natural suggestions for solving the interpretive puzzle. I will motivate my solution by attempting to understand how our interpretive constraints fit into Nietzsche's larger concerns and by considering a range of textual evidence.

It is perhaps best to begin with Nietzsche's controversial psychological claims about his contemporaries and his worries, as I have already mentioned, about practical nihilism.[22] The recognition, conscious or unconscious, that nothing is valuable in itself causes certain kinds of desires and drives to lose their force. The drives and desires in question are those fundamental drives and desires that provide us with the kind of psychological unity required to give our lives continuity and structure—required to give an overall direction to our lives. The threat that such drives and desires will lose their force, or that we might not be able to acquire them, is the threat of what

---

Philosophy 68/1 (1971): 5–20; Gary Watson, 'Free Agency,' in Gary Watson (ed.), Free Will (Oxford: Oxford University Press, 1982), 81–95; and Smith, Moral Problem, 133–47). Judging, or the claim, that something is valuable involves some kind of practicality or internalist constraint (see, for example, Stephen L. Darwall, 'Internalism and Agency,' in James E. Tomberlin (ed.), Philosophical Perspectives (Ridgeview: Atascadero, 1992), 155–74; Darwall, Gibbard, and Railton, 'Toward Fin de siècle Ethics,' 115–19, and Smith, Moral Problem, 147–8). Valuing plays a particular kind of regulative role in an agent's practical deliberations. Valuing has some special connection to autonomy. Finally, valuing involves some appeal to a source of normativity or authority (see Christine Korsgaard, The Sources of Normativity, ed. Onora O'Neill (Cambridge: Cambridge University Press, 1996)).

Dealing with the external interpretive puzzle is a task that I will not take up in this essay.

[21] I will begin by focusing on how Nietzsche's free spirits could reproduce a simulacrum of the existing practices of valuing. As we shall see, this already involves the creativity of art. We will then see how this creativity can be deployed to produce new values. So for now I will just talk of the generic act of regarding X as valuable and not of specific kinds of value.

[22] Nietzsche's claim is expressed here in terms of the psychological dispositions and attitudes of his contemporaries in order to leave open the question of whether we now have the same dispositions and attitudes.

Nietzsche calls practical nihilism.[23] Nietzsche appears to think that practical nihilism can show up in many different forms: on the one hand, in the form of psychological structures that lack unity and coherence; on the other hand, in the form of the 'last men' famously depicted in his *Zarathustra*.[24] The 'last men' retain some kind of psychological unity but only in virtue of taking themselves as pursuing a thin notion of happiness definable in a way that does not seem to them to rest on a more substantive and problematic notion of the good, and thus leading shallow, uninspired, insipid, and mundane lives.[25]

If we are right that Nietzsche holds such a view about the psychological tendencies and the practice of valuing of his contemporaries, then perhaps we can read Nietzsche as simply insisting that the higher men rise out of this practical nihilism by believing that things are valuable in themselves. However, as I have already pointed out, it appears hard to square this suggestion with our second interpretive constraint. Perhaps we could require that the higher men believe that things are valuable in themselves while knowing that in fact that is not the case. But is this kind of willed self-deception psychologically possible? Could Nietzsche really be asking his higher men to do this?

This is the kind of reading of Nietzsche that Bernard Yack adopts. Yack raises worries similar to mine:

Hegel argues that we cannot resurrect the kind of culture Nietzsche longs for because we know that our objects are not infinitely valuable. Nietzsche agrees that we know this, but he argues that, given this knowledge and the knowledge of what makes a culture healthy, we must impose such limitations upon ourselves, knowing all the while that they are without any inherent justification.[26]

Yack often reads Nietzsche as suggesting that the free spirits actually have to forget that the world has no value in itself. However, as Yack points out, Nietzsche at times

---

[23] 'What does nihilism mean?...The aim is lacking; "why?" finds no answer' (WP 2). The term 'nihilism' itself plays different roles in different contexts in Nietzsche's texts. Thus certain values can be nihilistic in that they persuade men to pursue a path that involves a denigration of this life for the sake of *nothingness*! Of course, one does not say "nothingness" but "beyond" or "God," or "*true* life," or Nirvana, salvation, blessedness' (A 7).

[24] Z P:5.

[25] To provide a justification for Nietzsche's claims here would require assessing Nietzsche's claims about the role that judgments of value play in the economy of the drives and desires that according to him constitute the self. Nietzsche also takes himself as having an essentially historical explanation for the presence of these psychological tendencies. He takes humans as having developed a need for regarding what we do in our lives as being justified by something beyond our own inclinations, desires, and drives (GS 1).

[26] Bernard Yack, *The Longing for Total Revolution: Philosophic Sources of Social Discontent from Rousseau to Marx and Nietzsche* (Princeton: Princeton University Press, 1986), 341. This is not, of course, to suggest that Hegel is reacting to Nietzsche.

seems to suggest that a free spirit does not actually forget but indeed is able to have in his consciousness both the thought that the world is valueless and the psychological states required to value things. Yack makes the stronger claim that for Nietzsche '[t]he whole virtue of self-forgetfulness that Nietzsche praises, however, lies in its being *willed*.'[27] But Yack asks, 'How can one will forgetfulness, while remembering what and why one must forget?'[28] Yack points to arguments by Elster in order to suggest that such forgetfulness cannot be willed.[29] The worry is that Nietzsche would be requiring his higher men to carry out an impossible task.

It is, however, important to remember that there is a whole range of notions that can be referred to by such terms as 'forgetfulness' and 'self-deception'. This range of notions is often ignored by interpreters who ascribe to Nietzsche a single usage of terms such as forgetfulness. At one extreme there is the suggestion in Nietzsche of the particularly strong claim that there are truths humans just cannot know if they are to survive, or, as is sometimes suggested, if they are to develop in certain ways. In a weaker form, this is often expressed as a claim that there are truths which weaker humans cannot face up to. It is hard to see how one could argue for the stronger claim. After all, would not the philosopher need to know the truths in order to claim that such and such particular truths are those that are bad for us? A charitable reading of Nietzsche would take him as arguing for the following version of the strong claim: there are some truths or other, specified schematically, unknown to all including Nietzsche, that we cannot afford to know. An argument for the weaker claim would not have the same air of paradox surrounding it as long as it were understood that the philosopher presenting the argument was one of the stronger humans. At other times it appears that the suggestion is that there are truths we can know and even in our cooler moments of reflection allow ourselves to dwell on; however, we cannot allow them to be the centre of our focus and still function in our daily lives. Here the issue is not quite self-deception but rather an issue of the centrality of certain thoughts to one's conscious life. We can know certain truths some of the time but at other times we must learn to 'forget' them. The talk of forgetfulness in this sense suggests that perhaps they still can be in our memory 'somewhere' and recalled later, or just that we cannot dwell on them even if we have not in some stronger sense forgotten them.

Such suggestions, however, do not yet fully appreciate, I want to claim, the importance of Nietzsche's references to art. What is special, for Nietzsche, about art is that it is honest about its use of illusion. Art is in the business of generating honest illusions. In fact, Nietzsche thinks that when compared to the status of the

---

[27] Yack, *Total Revolution*, 352–3.   [28] Ibid. 341.

[29] Ibid. He refers to Jon Elster, *Sour Grapes: Studies in the Subversion of Rationality* (Cambridge: Cambridge University Press, 1983), 44–52.

empirical sciences within Kant's conception of the world, art 'alone is now honest'.[30] In the *Genealogy of Morals*, Nietzsche demands an opposition to the ascetic ideal. What is important to note is that Nietzsche says that the opposition to the ascetic ideal cannot come from science since 'it never creates values'. However, art 'is much more fundamentally opposed to the ascetic ideal than is science', since in 'art . . . the *lie* is sanctified and the *will to deception* has a good conscience' (GM III:25). Art understands that its illusions are illusions without the illusions themselves being undermined.[31] For example, we see a water jug in a painting. We are aware that before us there is only oil paint on canvas. We can come to know that, say, the precision of the illusion—the way the water jug seems to nestle into the carpet resting on the table—is created by a technique of colouring that when viewed up close presents an image that is out of focus but comes into focus when we step back. We can see the illusion even while knowing that it is an illusion.

Now what this requires is being able to master what Nietzsche calls the 'knowledge drive'.[32] Being overly concerned with knowledge, with knowing what is really in front of us, can result in our being unable to see an illusion. This may strike us as implausible in the case of representational art. After all, it is in fact rather hard to see a painting of a person just as a surface of coloured patches. The point is better illustrated by the illusion of seeing a cloud as an elephant, Gestalt figures, or seeing the once popular SEEING EYE™ images.[33] Too much concern with the facts will, as a matter of psychological fact, tend to destroy the illusion.[34]

---

[30] LP 73, TL 184.

[31] See LP 46. See also TL 184. 'We possess *art* lest we *perish of the truth*' (WP 822).

Art can fail to be *honest* illusion. This is what prevents Nietzsche from being inconsistent when he complains that with Wagner 'the musician now becomes an actor, his art develops more and more as a talent to *lie*' (CW 7). As it becomes clear both in *CW* and in Nietzsche's own notes referred to in *CW*, the problem is not illusion and lying itself, but whether or not the artist and the viewer of the art are aware that illusion and lying are present. The distinction is between art as honest illusion and art as dishonest illusion. Nietzsche's critique of Wagner, Liszt, and Victor Hugo is a critique of art as *dishonest* illusion, and not a critique of the importance of art or illusion. For Schacht's mistaken conclusion that Nietzsche's critiques of Wagner's art implies that Nietzsche no longer regards the centrality of illusion in art as valuable, see his, *Nietzsche*, 514–15.

[32] LP 46. See also TL 184.

[33] These are the pictures that look like a dense pattern of coloured patches without any representational import. Looking at the surface—actually, looking through the surface—in a particular way results in one's perceiving a three-dimensional image. The effect is quite striking. For most people it takes much concentration and practice to see the image, and some claim to be simply incapable of seeing the image.

[34] Cf. 'The relevant general principle is that evidence of the falsity of a proposition imposed forcefully on one's consciousness makes it difficult to imagine vividly that the proposition is true' (Kendall Walton, *Mimesis as Make-Believe: On the Foundations of the Representational Arts* (Cambridge: Harvard University Press, 1990), 15).

Nietzsche clearly thinks that such a mastering, or at least appropriate placing, of the knowledge drive is possible. In his discussion of the structure of our drives towards truth and knowledge, he suggests approvingly that to part of our basic drives

belongs the occasional will of the spirit to let itself be deceived, perhaps with a capricious intimation of the fact that such and such is *not* the case, that one merely accepts such and such a delight in all uncertainty and ambiguity, a jubilant self-enjoyment in the arbitrary narrowness and secrecy of some nook, in the all too near, in the foreground, in what is enlarged, diminished, displaced, beautified. (BGE 230)

We need to prevent a concern with knowledge from dominating the way in which we interact and approach the world. Without mastering the knowledge drive we will fail to see the illusions of art.

But what does the possibility of art as honest illusion in Nietzsche tell us about valuing for his free spirits? The connection between art and valuing is that art allows us to see how we can regard something as valuable even when it is in fact not valuable, and we know that it is not valuable. If art can generate honest illusions, then by investigating art we might see how we can make something appear valuable.[35] From art we could learn how to *regard* something *as* valuable in itself even when we know that it is not valuable in itself. Thus my solution to the interpretive puzzle is that Nietzsche's recommended practice for his free spirits is a simulacrum of valuing. Nietzsche's recommended practice is a form of make-believe or pretence. Nietzsche's free spirits pretend to value something by regarding it as valuable in itself while knowing that in fact it is not valuable in itself.

Before we turn to a further analysis of this suggestion, allow me to pile up some more textual evidence in its favor. This will also allow me to add some more flesh to the skeletal view just presented. Nietzsche makes the above connection between art and valuing most clearly in *The Gay Science*. Consider the end of the 1886 preface to *The Gay Science*.[36] Nietzsche says that those that have returned from 'the sickness of severe suspicion' do not pursue what others call pleasure and art:

No, if we convalescents still need art, it is another kind of art . . . There are a few things we now know too well, we knowing ones: oh, how we now learn to forget well, and to be good at *not* knowing, as artists!

And as for our future, one will hardly find us again on the paths of those Egyptian youths who endanger temples by night, embrace statues, and want by all means to unveil, uncover, and put into a bright light whatever is kept concealed for good reasons. No, this bad taste, this

---

[35] The reason for expressing this in phenomenological terms will become clear in a moment.

[36] I emphasize the date of the preface to suggest that the views on art in *The Gay Science* are not in some way idiosyncratic to *The Gay Science*. The preface was written in the autumn of 1886 at around the same time that Nietzsche was having *Beyond Good and Evil* published.

will to truth, to 'truth at any price,' this youthful madness in the love of truth, have lost their charm.

...

Oh, those Greeks! They knew how to live. What is required for that is to stop courageously at the surface, the fold, the skin, to adore appearance, to believe in forms, tones, worlds, in the whole Olympus of appearance. Those Greeks were superficial—out of profundity. And is not this precisely what we are again coming back to, we daredevils of the spirit who have climbed the highest and most dangerous peak of present thought and looked around from up there—we who have looked down from up there? Are we not precisely in this respect, Greeks? Adorers of forms, of tones, of words? And therefore—artists?   (GS P:4)

Now again we could read this passage along Yack's lines as a suggestion to forget completely the knowledge we have gained, in particular, the knowledge that the world is without value. However, this would not explain why being an *artist* is so essential for Nietzsche, and thus why we have 'to be good at *not* knowing, as artists!' The above interpretive solution, where art allows us to see how we can regard things as valuable even when we know that they are not valuable, opens up the possibility of another interpretation of this phrase. Not to know something 'as an artist' is to prevent the drive to knowledge, 'the will to truth', from becoming so dominant that we fail to be able to experience the evaluative illusion. But that, as we saw earlier, is not simply to forget what we know.

But why do we have to be artists rather than just appreciators of art? Seeing an evaluative illusion only seems to require the latter. However, if regarding things as valuable is meant to form the basis for a practice of valuing in everyday life, and not just in art proper, then we, or at least Nietzsche's free spirits, have to learn to regard things in our lives, and even our lives as a whole, as valuable. In these domains we have to create our own evaluative illusions. Thus we have much to learn from artists, but in the end we have to go beyond them. Nietzsche expresses this point as follows in an aphorism entitled 'What one should learn from artists':

How can we make things beautiful, attractive, and desirable for us when they are not? And I rather think that in themselves they never are. Here we should learn something from physicians, when for example they dilute what is bitter or add wine and sugar to a mixture—but even more from artists who are really continually trying to bring off such inventions and feats. Moving away from things until there is a good deal that one no longer sees and there is much that our eye has to add if we are still to see them at all; or seeing things around a corner and as cut out and framed; or to place them so that they partially conceal each other and grant us only glimpses of architectural perspective; or looking at them through tinted glass or in the light of the sunset; or giving them a surface and skin that is not fully transparent—all that we should learn from artists while being wiser than they are in other matters. For with them this subtle power usually comes to an end where art ends and life begins; but we want to be the poets of our life—first of all in the smallest, most everyday matters.   (GS 299)

It is the example of art that (i) shows us the psychological possibility of regarding things as valuable even when we know that they are not, and (ii) provides a source for techniques that, suitably refined, could help us succeed in regarding things as valuable outside the domain of art proper. Without the example of art we might have failed to see a way out of the problems generated by our coming to know that nothing in the world is valuable in itself. As Nietzsche puts it at the end of Book II of *The Gay Science*:

Our ultimate gratitude to art.—If we had not welcomed the arts and invented this kind of cult of the untrue, then the realization of general untruth and mendaciousness that now comes to us through science—the realization that delusion and error are conditions of human knowledge and sensation—would be utterly unbearable. *Honesty* would lead to nausea and suicide. But now there is a counterforce against our honesty that helps us to avoid such consequences: art as the *good* will to appearance. We do not always keep our eyes from rounding off something and, as it were, finishing the poem; and then it is no longer eternal imperfection that we carry across the river of becoming—then we have the sense of carrying a *goddess*, and feel proud and childlike as we perform this service. As an aesthetic phenomenon existence is still *bearable* for us, and art furnishes us with eyes and hands and above all the good conscience to be *able* to turn ourselves into such a phenomenon. (GS 107)[37]

This passage brings us to a central feature of the interpretive strategy proposed here. It is important to see Nietzsche as making a phenomenological claim about the practice of valuing in which he finds his contemporaries engaged. Evaluations 'color' things. Things in the world are experienced, in some sense, as having their value in them.[38] Thus Nietzsche says:

The extent of moral evaluations: they play a part in almost every sense impression. Our world is *colored* by them.

---

[37] There is a complexity here that I am avoiding. Art is central for Nietzsche from the very beginning. It is in *The Birth of Tragedy* that we get Nietzsche's famous statement: 'it is only as an *aesthetic phenomenon* that existence and the world are eternally *justified*' (BT 5. This claim is repeated in BT 24). Art remains central to Nietzsche's thought; however, Nietzsche's position on art changes. Nietzsche's views on art in *The Birth of Tragedy* are tied up with Schopenhauerian metaphysics and an accompanying romanticism that he later repudiates. See Nietzsche's own critiques of *The Birth of Tragedy* in BT 'Attempt at Self-Criticism' and EH 'Books' BT.

There is another, perhaps more important, complexity that I am also avoiding. Nietzsche's suggestions about the importance of art, and given my interpretation, the importance of artistic illusions can also be read as a defence of the importance of illusions or fictions in general. This might include cases that we would not regard as cases of evaluative illusion. I will not try here to work out the degree to which Nietzsche might be concerned with what we would call purely descriptive illusions; however, what is perhaps important to point out in any case is that for Nietzsche much of what we might take to be descriptive illusions would indeed be evaluative illusions. For further discussion, see Hussain, 'Nietzsche's Positivism'.

[38] 'When we speak of values, we speak with the inspiration, with the way of looking at things, which is part of life' (TI 'Morality', 5). See also Frithjof Bergmann, 'The Experience of Values,' *Inquiry* 16 (1973).

We have invested things with ends and values: therefore we have in us an enormous fund of latent force: but by comparing values it appears that contradictory things have been accounted valuable, that *many* tables of value have existed (thus nothing is valuable 'in itself'). (WP 260)

According to the interpretive strategy suggested here, this phenomenological claim is supposed to be true of our experiences, or at least the experiences of Nietzsche's contemporaries, when engaged in the practice of valuing. In the practice of valuing Nietzsche wants to recommend for his free spirits, this phenomenology, in some form or other, will have to be saved even though his free spirits no longer believe that anything has value in itself. The suggestion here is that, again, art shows us how we can recreate this phenomenology more honestly.[39]

Imaginative play shares similar features with art. And play, too, is central in much of Nietzsche. In play, as in art, it is the creative, imaginative, wilful production of, and relishing of, illusion that is often central. In the first of Zarathustra's speeches, 'On the Three Metamorphoses', Nietzsche tells a parable about the development of the human spirit: 'how the spirit becomes a camel; and the camel, a lion; and the lion, finally, a child' (Z:1 'On the Three Metamorphoses'). The camel is the stage of the spirit in which the spirit accepts the weight of traditional schemes of valuation. Nietzsche asks:

My brothers, why is there a need in the spirit for the lion? . . .

To create new values—that even the lion cannot do; but the creation of freedom for oneself for new creation—that is within the power of the lion. . . . To assume the right to new values—that is the most terrifying assumption for a reverent spirit that would bear much. (Z:1 'On the Three Metamorphoses')

And then:

But say, my brothers, what can the child do that even the lion could not do? Why must the preying lion still become a child? The child is innocence and forgetting, a new beginning, a game, a self-propelled wheel, a first movement, a sacred 'Yes.' For the game of creation, my brothers, a sacred 'Yes' is needed: the spirit now wills his own will, and he who had been lost to the world now conquers his own world.   (Z:1 'On the Three Metamorphoses')

The final stage is that of the child. The child goes beyond the lion not merely by rejecting old values but by being capable of creating new values. The suggested reading here is that the child is to be understood as capable of forgetting not just old schemes of valuations, but also that the child, in a manner similar to the artist, can engage in the 'forgetfulness' of imaginative play and thus create a new 'game' of valuing. The

---

[39] See also GS 301, TI 'Skirmishes', 24.

child 'wills his own will' by picking a new evaluational 'game' rather than allowing his own will to be guided by an externally given scheme of evaluations.[40]

Let me add a couple of more comments about the kind of pretence I think Nietzsche requires of his free spirits. Nietzsche presents us with a particular job description for regarding something as valuable, a job description that the free spirits' regarding of things as valuable must fulfil in order for them to avoid practical nihilism. The free spirits need to save the phenomenology of valuing. The pretence thus needs to generate the right kind of phenomenology. Successfully regarding something as valuable in itself requires experiencing it as an end that stands above and beyond my other desires and inclinations. There must be the appropriate connection to my action. There must be the appropriate intensity of emotion and motivation.[41] The pretence must succeed in providing me with a sense that my life has a goal and purpose. The phenomenology is thus not a matter simply of how things stand out to us in the visual field. Or, if it is, then this standing out is in part a matter of having certain kinds of emotive and motivational reactions to things.

Is there any reason to think some kind of pretence can give us all this? And if not, does some interpretive principle of charity work against the interpretation I am suggesting here? At this point we can usefully draw on Ken Walton's discussions of make-believe. In imaginative play, successfully regarding a pile of wood as the *Bismarck* under fire requires, or at least when one is, as we say, 'into' the game, engaging in certain actions, or pretend actions—ducking from the incoming shells (just tennis balls, of course), yelling at your gunners to fire back, and so on. It also requires certain physical responses: the increased heart beat, the sweating of palms, and an intense exclusive concentration. We may even want to talk about the perceptual phenomenology of the child. The pile of logs and the tennis balls have a kind of salience that they do not have to someone not engaged in the game. In fact, as we grow older we often lose the ability to regard the pile of planks as the *Bismarck* under fire. For the adult this can take some serious effort. For adults, on the other hand, the engagement with novels, movies, and art is if anything more emotionally intense than the child's. If we focus on make-believe, in particular the case where we treat

---

[40] Cf. WP 797. Presumably 'picking' and not 'choosing'; the choice of evaluative pretence could not itself be determined by an evaluative fact of the matter about which pretence a free spirit should pick.

[41] This is not to say either that having a 'quasi' emotional state for every real emotional state (see the discussion of 'quasi fear' in games of make-believe in Kendall L. Walton, 'Fearing Fictions,' *The Journal of Philosophy* 75/1 (1978): 5–27), or that carrying out some action analogous to each action the agent who believed that *a* is *F* would carry out, is required in order to regard *a* as *F*. Indeed the idea that there is a straightforward scale of attitudes, emotions, and actions by which one comes closer and closer to what one would do if one believed that *a* is *F* seems mistaken (for this point, see J. L. Austin, 'Pretending,' *Aristotelian Society: Supplementary Volume* (1958), 261–78). Besides other norms that constrain the kind of game one plays—the 'intensity' with which one pretends—the aim of playing the game will certainly determine the kind of pretence one engages in.

ourselves as props in a game, then we may have reason to think that Nietzsche's job description for the kind of pretence his free spirits are supposed to engage in could be satisfied.[42]

Let me summarize and repeat what considering art and imaginative play is supposed to show us. Art and imaginative play each allow us to regard certain things as something else even when we know they are not. Both art and imaginative play involve a kind of make-believe. The examples of art and imaginative play are, according to Nietzsche, supposed (i) to show us the psychological possibility of regarding things as valuable even when we know that they are not, and (ii) to provide a source for techniques that, suitably refined, could help us succeed in regarding things as valuable outside the domain of art or imaginative play proper. Nietzsche's free spirits, with the help of art, are to engage in a simulacrum of valuing by regarding things as valuable in themselves while knowing that they are not.[43]

4. The Secondary Literature

Let me turn now to an inevitably brief, all-too-brief, discussion of some of the relevant secondary literature. The secondary literature does not tend to take up directly the particular interpretive puzzle I have focused on here, namely, the question of how Nietzsche's free spirits are supposed to value. As we saw, this involves getting clear on Nietzsche's metaethics, both the metaethical account of existing practices of valuing and the account of what is supposed to be the replacement practice for his free spirits.

---

[42] Though we are props in the make-believe that is not yet to say that we would engage in a prop-oriented make-believe. I think it is most plausible to take the kind of make-believe involved to be a content-oriented make-believe. For the distinction between these two forms of make-believe, see Kendall L. Walton, 'Metaphor and Prop Oriented Make-Believe,' *The European Journal of Philosophy* 1/1 (1993): 39–56. Teasing out the exact kind of make-believe involved will have to await another occasion.

[43] Much more needs to be said here, of course, to make the full case for this interpretation. We would need to see how this interpretive strategy would deal with what I have called in a previous note the external interpretive puzzle. The proposed solution to the interpretive puzzle also leads to some natural questions about Nietzsche's overall position. Why do Nietzsche's free spirits need to engage in a simulacrum of valuing and why is it so important for them to face up to the truth? A full account needs to be able to provide answers to these questions which can fit with the proposed interpretive solution.

Finally, we need an articulation of what differences would emerge in practice between the original practices of valuing and the proposed fictionalist replacement. For now I can only make some suggestions in this direction. I take Nietzsche's thought to be that a particular kind of seriousness and gravity that is part of traditional morality could not be regenerated within a fictionalist practice of valuing. Instead his free spirits would be 'more ticklish and malicious, with a more delicate taste for joy, with a tenderer tongue for all good things, with merrier senses, with a second dangerous innocence in joy, more childlike and yet a hundred times subtler than one has ever been before' (GS P:4).

When it comes to discussing Nietzsche on values and valuing, the secondary literature focuses on Nietzsche's normative claims. What is the normative basis of his evaluative judgments against morality and his claims that certain types of persons are better than others? Here the Anglo-American secondary literature has almost developed an orthodoxy. The claim usually defended is that Nietzsche regards, in some sense, the degree of power as the ultimate standard of value. I will call this the *Will-to-Power Interpretation* (WPI). As Walter Kaufmann puts it 'quantitative degree of power is the measure of value'.[44]

There is indeed evidence for some such evaluative standard in Nietzsche's texts. He says in his book *Antichrist*:

What is good? Everything that heightens the feeling of power in man, the will to power, power itself.

What is bad? Everything that is born of weakness.   (A 2)[45]

When we turn to Nietzsche's unpublished notes we find such a fundamental evaluative standard mentioned at least twice.[46] Now, as is perhaps obvious, WPI does

---

[44] The versions of this standard that individual commentators subscribe to involve some variations, but, as can be seen from the following quotes, WPI captures the basic thrust. 'Power, then, is the standard of value which Nietzsche affirms with all the eloquence at his command' (George Allen Morgan, *What Nietzsche Means* (New York: Harper, 1965), 118). The 'quantitative degree of power is the measure of value' (Walter Kaufmann, *Nietzsche: Philosopher, Psychologist, Antichrist*, 4th edn. (Princeton, NJ: Princeton University Press, 1974), 200). There is 'one standard about which Nietzsche does not take a relativist position. He evaluates the worth of persons on the basis of a single standard: the degree to which they have attained what he calls power' (Lester H. Hunt, *Nietzsche and the Origin of Virtue* (London and New York: Routledge, 1991), 131). 'Nietzsche's advice: maximize power' (John Richardson, *Nietzsche's System* (New York and Oxford: Oxford University Press, 1996), 148). See also John T. Wilcox, *Truth and Value in Nietzsche: A Study of His Metaethics and Epistemology* (Ann Arbor: The University of Michigan Press, 1974), 194–6, and Schacht, *Nietzsche*, 349, 98.

[45] Cf. Z:1 'On the Thousand and One Goals'.

[46] There are nonetheless some worries about the textual evidence for WPI. As Leiter points out, it is hard to understand on this reading of Nietzsche 'why he says almost nothing about will to power—and nothing at all to suggest it is his "fundamental principle"—in the two major self-reflective moments in the Nietzschean corpus: *Ecce Homo*, where he reviews and assesses his life and work, including specifically all his prior books (EH III); and the series of new prefaces he wrote for *The Birth of Tragedy*, *Human, All Too Human*, *Dawn*, and *The Gay Science* in 1886, in which he revisits his major themes. That this putative 'fundamental principle' merits no mention on either occasion strongly suggests that its role in Nietzsche's thought has been greatly overstated' (Leiter, 'Nietzsche's Metaethics', 285). Indeed much of the textual evidence for both WPI and Nietzsche's arguments for it are drawn, as Leiter points out, from the *Nachlass* (Leiter, 'Nietzsche's Metaethics', 287). For worries about the overuse of the *Nachlass*, see Leiter, 'Nietzsche's Metaethics', 287; Bernd Magnus, 'The Use and Abuse of *The Will to Power*', in Robert C. Solomon and Kathleen M. Higgins (eds.), *Reading Nietzsche* (New York: Oxford University Press, 1988), 218–35; R. J. Hollingdale, *Nietzsche: The Man and His Philosophy*, ARK edn. (London: Routledge and Kegan Paul, 1985), 166–72, 82–6. For a defence of using the *Nachlass*, see Richard Schacht, *Making Sense of Nietzsche: Reflections Timely and Untimely* (Urbana and Chicago: University of Illinois Press, 1995), 117–25.

not immediately present itself as an alternative to my attempt to solve my interpretive puzzle, nor is it presented in the secondary literature as such.[47] I can accept that Nietzsche, self-declared free spirit that he is, has a fundamental evaluative standard, if that standard is taken to be part of Nietzsche's own evaluative pretence. Nietzsche regards the maximization of power as valuable while knowing that it is not.

In the spirit of searching for competing interpretations, we can nonetheless ask whether the will-to-power interpretation suggests an alternative solution to the interpretive puzzle. The secondary literature sometimes does suggest that WPI can be taken as a metaethical view.[48] Nietzsche would then be committed to a reductive realism. He is saying not merely that what is good is power, but rather that what *it is* to be good is to be powerful.

What on such an account would it be for the higher men to create values? And how would this be connected to art and illusion? The answer is not immediately obvious, but perhaps we can see how a story might go. Let's say we could give a reductive account in psychological terms of the attitudes of valuing—say of finding something beautiful. And let us say that having this attitude towards things enhances in some sense our power. To be beautiful is just to be regarded in the appropriate way. And then perhaps Nietzsche's free spirits create new values in the sense of creatively coming up with new attitudes to take towards things. Perhaps this even requires the illusions of art since it is not objects themselves, but rather an object viewed in a certain illusory way that we can have these new attitudes towards. These new values are still consistent with the reductive realism, perhaps, because the value of these new values turns on their instrumental usefulness to enhancing power.

Now this all may be a long row to hoe, but perhaps we have some sense of how such an interpretation might fulfil interpretive constraints (1), (2), and (4). This interpretation will however have a hard time satisfying constraint (3). On this interpretation it appears that power is something in nature—in the world—valuable in itself despite the fact that Nietzsche clearly says that nothing in our world or in nature has value in itself (GS 301).

Perhaps there is still a way out for this version of WPI. Power, as I have been reading Nietzsche, is a property of agents. What is being enhanced is something in us. If we are not, in some relevant sense, in the world or in nature, then Nietzsche's claims that nothing in nature or in the world has value in itself would not apply to the property of power or our will to power. But this runs up against a repeated emphasis in Nietzsche on 'naturalizing' our account of man. He describes his task as follows:

---

[47] This is in part because the authors concerned do not take Nietzsche to be as thoroughgoing an error-theorist as I do.

[48] This is perhaps the case in Richardson, *Nietzsche's System*.

To translate man back into nature; to become master over the many vain and overly enthusiastic interpretations and connotations that have so far been scrawled and painted over that eternal basic text of *homo natura*; to see to it that man henceforth stands before man as even today, hardened in the discipline of science, he stands before the *rest* of nature, in intrepid Oedipus eyes and sealed Odysseus ears, deaf to the siren of old metaphysical bird catchers who have been piping at him all too long, 'you are more, you are higher, you are of a different origin!' (BGE 230)

So it is hard to see Nietzsche as using the term 'nature' in a way to exclude agents. If that is right, then the claim that nothing in nature has value in itself would surely apply to features of agents too. And so a realist reduction of good to power seems hard to square with Nietzsche's claim that there is nothing in nature that has value in itself.[49]

5. Conclusion

Let me conclude by summarizing what I hope to have shown. I hope to have argued convincingly that there is an interpretive puzzle we face when we attempt to explain how Nietzsche's free spirits are supposed to create values. The interpretive puzzle was generated by four interpretive constraints that I listed and provided some textual evidence for. I then suggested that we can use the fourth interpretive constraint as a basis for developing an interpretive solution to our puzzle that takes as central the possibility of honest illusions. Nietzsche's free spirits engage in a simulacrum of valuing by regarding things as valuable in themselves while knowing that they are not.[50]

Historical Postscript

The argument in the form presented above has been in circulation for a while and has been fortunate enough to have already received some published response. Responding to the criticisms of Lanier Anderson and John Richardson would require comparative

---

[49] The discussion in the above section does not, of course, do full justice to the range of positions expressed in the secondary literature nor to the range of positions one could develop out of material present in the secondary literature. For reasons of space, full consideration will have to await another occasion.

[50] Thanks to Elizabeth Anderson, Frithjof Bergmann, Steve Darwall, John Doris, Don Herzog, and David Hills who commented on an earlier version of this essay. Thanks to R. Lanier Anderson, Maudemarie Clark, Sarah Darby, Brian Leiter, Bernard Reginster, John Richardson, Mathias Risse, Bob Solomon, Ken Walton, and Allen Wood for very useful conversations about this essay. Thanks also to audiences at the philosophy departments of Ohio State University, The University of Pittsburgh, and Wellesley College.

assessments of their interpretations of the same stretches of Nietzsche's texts with my above interpretation.[51] For reasons of space these tasks cannot be taken on here. Instead I will use this postscript to respond to Brian Leiter's charge of anachronism. He writes:

> Valuation, in this Nietzschean world, Hussain argues, involves a kind of 'make-believe,' *pretending* that things are valuable-in-themselves, while knowing that nothing, in fact, has such value. There is a pressing philosophical question here—whether 'make-believe' about value really could suffice for valuing—but also an interpretive problem: does Nietzsche *really* think that moral judgments express *beliefs*, that is, truth-apt propositional attitudes which then requires [sic] fictionalist treatment? It would be astonishing if any 19th-century philosopher were to have a *clear* answer to such a question.[52]

Whether or not my interpretation is anachronistic depends on two things: what kind of fictionalist view I am ascribing to Nietzsche and what kind of fictionalist views it is plausible to think a nineteenth-century philosopher could have. I will start by reviewing the kinds of fictionalism that were present in the nineteenth century. The presence of these fictionalist views shows, I shall argue, that ascribing a fictionalist view to Nietzsche would not be anachronistic. Indeed, given the historical context, it would hardly come as a surprise.

However, I presume that Leiter is interested in a more specific question, namely, whether fictionalism understood in a very specific, contemporary sense is plausibly ascribable to Nietzsche without anachronism. Such a fictionalism involves a denial of non-cognitivism. I will argue that the historical record shows that it would not be anachronistic to ascribe even this kind of fictionalism to nineteenth-century philosophers as long as we are willing to take talk of 'belief' or 'truth' and 'falsity' as signs of a commitment to cognitivism despite the lack of consideration of non-cognitivist alternatives. Furthermore, the historical evidence does suggest precisely what we need for fictionalism, in the sense that needs to be ascribed to Nietzsche, namely an attitude other than belief towards the same content—an attitude such that whether the content is false is no longer relevant.

One could argue, however, in the spirit of contemporary non-cognitivists like Allan Gibbard and Simon Blackburn, that just as talk of 'belief' or 'truth' and 'falsity' should not be taken as evidence that ordinary moral discourse is cognitivist, we should not take the use of such language by a philosopher as evidence that he or she is committed

---

[51] R. Lanier Anderson, 'Nietzsche on Truth, Illusion, and Redemption,' *European Journal of Philosophy* 13/2 (2005): 185–225, and John Richardson, *Nietzsche's New Darwinism* (Oxford and New York: Oxford University Press, 2004), 72, 127.

[52] Brian Leiter, 'Nietzsche's Moral and Political Philosophy', in Edward N. Zalta (ed.), *The Stanford Encyclopedia of Philosophy (Fall 2004 Edition)*, URL=<http://plato.stanford.edu/archives/fall2004/entries/nietzsche-moral-political/>.

to cognitivism.[53] Whatever plausibility the claim has for our ordinary moral practice, I think the plausibility decreases when we are talking about nineteenth-century philosophers many of whom do make what sound for all the world like semantic claims. Nonetheless, if this contemporary non-cognitivist point is insisted on, then there will still remain, I shall argue, a form of fictionalism that I would want to ascribe to Nietzsche and that is compatible with both cognitivism and non-cognitivism.

Before I proceed it will help the exposition below to remind ourselves of some relevant distinctions. First, there is a useful distinction to be drawn between 'hermeneutic' and 'revolutionary' fictionalism.[54] A hermeneutic fictionalist interprets the current discourse in fictionalist terms while the revolutionary fictionalist proposes fictionalism as a reform. Revolutionary fictionalism combines most naturally with an error theory about our existing discourse. I have basically argued for ascribing a form of revolutionary fictionalism to Nietzsche. As we will see, the nineteenth century gives us examples of both hermeneutic and revolutionary fictionalisms. Second, it is useful to remind ourselves of the distinction for certain kinds of language, such as fictionalist and metaphorical language, between the literal content and the content that is conveyed: David Hills usefully puts the point in terms of a distinction between the 'presented thought . . . entertained in a spirit of assertion' and the 'presenting thought . . . entertained in a spirit of *pretence*'.[55]

Now for the quick historical tour. We can begin with Jeremy Bentham who worked on fictionalism at the beginning of the nineteenth century mostly in the context of developing a theory that would provide resources for giving fictionalist accounts of legal and moral terms such as 'duty', 'obligation', 'property', 'right', though, as can be seen from the example used to introduce the theory below, fictionalism was not restricted to this domain of terms:

A fictitious entity is an entity to which, though by the grammatical form of the discourse employed in speaking of it, existence be ascribed, yet in truth and reality existence is not meant to be ascribed.

Ever noun-substantive which is not the name of a real entity, perceptible or inferential, is the name of a fictitious entity . . . .

To be spoken of at all, every fictitious entity must be spoken of as if it were real. . . .

---

[53] Allan Gibbard, *Thinking How to Live* (Cambridge, Mass.: Harvard University Press, 2003) and Simon Blackburn, *Ruling Passions: A Theory of Practical Reasoning* (Oxford and New York: Clarendon Press; Oxford University Press, 1998).

[54] John P. Burgess and Gideon A. Rosen, *A Subject with No Object: Strategies for Nominalistic Interpretation of Mathematics* (Oxford and New York: Oxford University Press, 1997), 6–7, and Jason Stanley, 'Hermeneutic Fictionalism', *Midwest Studies in Philosophy* 25 (2001): 36. See also John P. Burgess, 'Why I Am Not a Nominalist', *Notre Dame Journal of Formal Logic* 24 (1983): 93–105.

[55] David Hills, 'Aptness and Truth in Verbal Metaphor', *Philosophical Topics* 25/1 (1997): 147.

A body is said to be in motion. This, taken in the literal sense, is as much as to say—Here is a larger body, called a motion; in this larger body, the other body, namely, the really existing body, is contained.[56]

The similarity of the view to contemporary hermeneutic fictionalist strategies of philosophers like Mark Crimmins, Ken Walton, and Stephen Yablo is, I think, pretty clear.[57] Bentham's overall view is quite complicated and sophisticated. In some cases, he deploys an error theory to argue for rejection. In others he declares the practice to be pernicious as it stands because the participants believe in the relevant entities, but argues that the practice would be acceptable and useful if the entities were treated as fictions, thus advocating revolutionary fictionalism. Cases where fictionalism is acceptable are cases where the presented thought is worth presenting and where it is hard to see how it could be presented without a presenting thought that is literally false.

In the German nineteenth-century context, fictionalism plays a central role both in Hegelian critiques of traditional Christianity like those of David Friedrich Strauss and Ludwig Feuerbach, and also in the work of neo-Kantians like Friedrich Lange and Hans Vaihinger. German readings of the Christian religion as 'myth' came to prominence with David Friedrich Strauss's *The Life of Jesus Critically Examined* (1835–6). Strauss did not claim that readings of the biblical narratives as myth were original to him.[58] Strauss's

---

[56] Jeremy Bentham, *Bentham's Theory of Fictions*, ed. C. K. Ogden (London: Kegan Paul Trench Trubner & Co., 1932), 12–13.

[57] See Mark Crimmins, 'Hesperus and Phosphorus: Sense, Pretense, and Reference', *Philosophical Review* 107/1 (1998): 1–47; Kendall Walton, 'Existence as Metaphor?', in Anthony J. Everett and Thomas Hofweber (eds.), *Empty Names, Fiction, and the Puzzles of Non-Existence* (Stanford: CSLI Publications, 2000), 69–94; and Stephen Yablo, 'A Paradox of Existence', in Anthony J. Everett and Thomas Hofweber (eds.), *Empty Names, Fiction, and the Puzzles of Non-Existence* (Stanford: CSLI Publications, 2000), 275–312.

[58] David Friedrich Strauss, *The Life of Jesus Critically Examined*, trans. George Eliot, 6th edn. (London: George Allen, 1913), §8–9, §14:81–2. For a useful study of the use of myth in interpretations of the Bible, see Christian Hartlich and Walter Sachs, *Der Ursprung des Mythosbegriffes in der modernen Bibelwissenschaft* (Tübingen: J. C. B. Mohr, 1952). For more discussion of the degree of originality of Strauss's position, see Horton Harris, *David Friedrich Strauss and his Theology* (Cambridge: Cambridge University Press, 1973), 259–71. Strauss distinguishes his use of the notion of myth in biblical exegesis from his predecessors both in terms of the extensiveness of his application of this strategy and in terms of his distinction between mythical explanation and various forms of rationalist explanations (Strauss, *Life of Jesus*, §10–12, §14:80–2, §15–16). The Old Testament had often been treated as myth; however, rationalist readings tended to still treat some of the Gospels of the New Testament as having apostolic authorship and thus as eye-witness reports. Strauss treated all of the New Testament as myth. Rationalist readings, in the sense intended here, were interpretations that attempted to explain away references to, for example, miracles by providing naturalistic explanations for the events described as miracles. Both naturalists and rationalists deployed naturalistic explanations; however, naturalists, as used here, deployed explanations that were morally undermining of religious figures and their followers: their explanations involved claims of deceit and manipulation. Rationalists, on the other hand, attempted to provide naturalistic accounts that did not ascribe anything morally reprehensible to the historical figures involved (Strauss, *Life of*

phenomenal impact is best explained by the thoroughness of application of the notion of myth and the level of detailed support presented.[59] These myths were the result of an unconscious and unintentional poetizing as opposed to intentional deception. For Strauss, the claims of biblical texts literally interpreted were false. The common believer accepted the literal interpretation and thus his or her beliefs were also false.[60] A central reason for taking biblical texts as myths, and thus as literally false, was the impossibility of the truth of the literal claims being compatible with the current naturalistic picture of the world as a closed causal system.[61]

So far we have been given what looks like a straight error theory. However, for Strauss, the mythical language was a poetic or figurative representation of certain philosophical truths, for Strauss certain Hegelian claims. The sophisticated interpreter who realized that the literal interpretations were false could take these myths as fictions, but as fictions that figuratively expressed what Strauss considered to be true philosophical claims.[62] The theologian can still talk about the resurrection of Christ. Such talk still makes rational sense because, to use Hills's language, the presented thought—a Hegelian truth about the relation between humanity as a whole and Absolute Spirit—is something the theologian believes in, while the presenting thought—the claim that a historical individual was resurrected—is something the theologian does not actually believe in. Viewed this way the theologian is 'in himself no hypocrite' just as I am no hypocrite when, to use Yablo's favorite example, I say of an athlete who is playing very well, 'Jim is on fire'.[63] As Strauss realizes, though, the question of hypocrisy becomes more complicated when the speaker knows that his audience does not share his fictionalist attitude. If I know that my audience will come

---

Jesus, §6:47–§6:48, §8:52–4). According to Strauss, the rationalist is mistaken in taking the fundamental function of the text to be the reporting of historical events. Such rationalist accounts failed to explain the occurrence of supposedly similar notions of the relation between God and the world that recurred in different religious settings—that perhaps even defined the religious (Strauss, *Life of Jesus*, §1:39–§4:43, §6:47, §7:51, §8:52, 56, §14:75–8, 80–2; see also Edwina Lawler, *David Friedrich Strauss and his Critics: The Life of Jesus Debate in Early 19. Century German Journals* (New York: Peter Lang, 1986), 22–32, 37, 42).

[59] Strauss, *Life of Jesus*, xxix, §4–5; Otto Pfleiderer, 'Introduction to *The Life of Jesus Critically Examined*', in David Friedrich Strauss, *The Life of Jesus Critically Examined* (London: George Allen & Co., Ltd., 1913), pp. xi–xii; Lawler, *David Friedrich Strauss and his Critics*, 22–39, 44; Marilyn Chapin Massey, 'Introduction to *In Defense of My "Life of Jesus" Against the Hegelians*', in David Friedrich Strauss, *In Defense of My Life of Jesus against the Hegelians* (Hamden: Archon Books, 1983), p. xi; Richard Sidney Cromwell, *David Friedrich Strauss and his Place in Modern Thought* (Fair Lawn, NJ: R. E. Burdick: 1974), 68–9. For a useful, brief summary of Strauss's mythical interpretation of religion see Sidney Hook, *From Hegel to Marx: Studies in the Intellectual Development of Karl Marx* (New York: The Humanities Press, 1950), 82–4.

[60] Strauss, *Life of Jesus*, §13:69. See also Massey, 'Introduction to *In Defense of My 'Life of Jesus' Against the Hegelians*', p. iv.

[61] Strauss, *Life of Jesus*, §16:88. In earlier editions, Hegelian commitments play a greater role in driving the interpretation.

[62] Strauss, *Life of Jesus*, §151–2.   [63] Ibid. §152:782–3.

to believe that Jim is literally on fire, then it does not seem sufficient for me to defend such an utterance by insisting that I do not believe it. For Strauss this is a matter of tremendous importance for the theologians he is concerned about are also preachers whose audience 'can conceive no faith in the dogmatical truth of the resurrection of Christ, for example, apart from a conviction of its historical reality: and if it comes to discover that the theologian has not this conviction, and yet preaches on the resurrection, he must appear in the eyes of the church a hypocrite'.[64] Knowing this, the theologian must 'ultimately appear a hypocrite to himself'.[65] I interpret Strauss as in the end granting that there is no way to eliminate some kind of hypocrisy here; what can justify the theologian's continuing to preach is that though he uses 'the forms of the popular conception' he is trying slowly to get his audience to believe in the presented Hegelian truths rather than the presenting falsehoods.[66] Strauss's revolutionary fictionalism is thus revolutionary for the Hegelian theologian, but, so to speak, rather gradualist for the rest of the population. I emphasize these concerns with the situation of the theologian because these are precisely the concerns that should arise if one is proposing a revolutionary fictionalism—they thus are further evidence of the fictionalism.

Not surprisingly, Strauss's book was met with a fire-storm of controversy; the error theory was all that was discussed and the fictionalism was merely regarded as hypocrisy. Strauss was dismissed from his post as a tutor at the Tübingen seminary, never again to be appointed to a teaching post let alone a ministerial appointment, and it was no surprise to some that 'the Hebrew letters forming Strauss' name added up to 666'.[67] This level of controversy was if anything surpassed by the reaction to Ludwig Feuerbach's work. Feuerbach's *Essence of Christianity* (1841) went beyond Strauss by rejecting Strauss's Hegelianism and thus even the Hegelian replacement for the traditional Christian God, namely, Absolute Spirit. Famously, according to Feuerbach, religion and theology are really anthropology. God is a projection of idealized human qualities.[68] Similarly, other traditional parts of Christianity, the Trinity, Resurrection, and so on are all in various ways about humans and their relations to each other. For example, 'the true unfalsified import of the Incarnation' is 'absolute pure love'—love of humans for other humans 'which impels the sacrifice of self to another'.[69] Thus 'religion—consciousness of God—is . . . the self-consciousness of man'.[70] This

is not to be understood as affirming that the religious man is directly aware of this identity; for, on the contrary, ignorance of it is fundamental to the peculiar nature of religion . . . religion is

---

[64] Ibid. §152:783.   [65] Ibid.   [66] Ibid.   [67] Harris, *Strauss*, 67.

[68] Ludwig Feuerbach, *The Essence of Christianity*, trans. George Eliot (Amherst: Prometheus Books, 1989), 14.

[69] Ibid. 53.   [70] Ibid. 13.

man's earliest and also indirect form of self-knowledge. Hence, religion everywhere precedes philosophy. . . . Man first of all sees his nature as if *out of* himself, before he finds it in himself.[71]

What Feuerbach's view shares with hermeneutical fiction is the idea that there is both a presented thought and a presenting thought. As Feuerbach puts it:

Religion is the dream of the human mind. But even in dreams we do not find ourselves in emptiness or in heaven, but on earth, in the realm of reality; we only see real things in the entrancing splendour of imagination and caprice, instead of in the simple daylight of reality and necessity. Hence I do nothing more to religion . . . than to open its eyes . . . , *i.e.*, I change the object as it is in the imagination into the object as it is in reality.[72]

There is a sense then in which Eugene Kamenka is right that for Feuerbach

Religion has to be explained and analysed as a natural, human phenomenon—as a false belief, or, on the positive side, as a fiction. . . . Religion is to be treated on the analogy of dreams, fantasies, works of fiction or imaginative art. . . . We look at them and we ask, 'Where did their creator get the idea?' and 'What is it that he wants to express?'[73]

However, Kamenka plays down the disanalogies. Clearly for Feuerbach religion involves 'ignorance', it involves the mistake of believing the presenting thought. Feuerbach still has a role to play in our story of nineteenth-century fictionalism because his approach shares two features of contemporary fictionalisms, hermeneutical or revolutionary: first, the two levels of content; and, second, the strategy of giving an entire discourse an error-theoretic reading.

It was the above critique of Hegelianism and Christianity within the theological context of the writings of Strauss and Feuerbach that partly led to the demise of Hegelian idealism and the rise both of materialism and—partly in reaction to materialism—neo-Kantianism in the later half of the nineteenth century.[74] For obvious reasons, I will focus here on the neo-Kantian Friedrich Lange.[75] Lange thinks that the 'great mass of believers of all religions' are 'in a state of mind like that in which children listen to fairy-tales'; however, 'all poesy and revelation are simply false, as soon as we test their material contents by the standard of exact knowledge' and so 'the classification of religion with art and metaphysics, will at no very distant time be generally conceded'. The demise of religion does threaten to undermine

---

[71] Feuerbach, *Essence of Christianity*, 13.   [72] Ibid., p. xxxix.

[73] Eugene Kamenka, *The Philosophy of Ludwig Feuerbach* (London: Routledge & Kegan Paul, 1970), 59.

[74] Cf. Frederick Gregory, *Scientific Materialism in Nineteenth Century Germany* (Dordrecht: Reidel, 1977), p. xi; Kamenka, *Ludwig Feuerbach*, 92; and Hans D. Sluga, *Gottlob Frege* (London: Routledge & Kegan Paul, 1980), 9–14.

[75] Jorg Salaquarda, 'Nietzsche und Lange', *Nietzsche-Studien* 7 (1978): 236–53; Jörg Salaquarda, 'Der Standpunkt des Ideals bei Lange und Nietzsche', *Studi Tedeschi* 22/1 (1979): 133–60; and George J. Stack, *Lange and Nietzsche* (Berlin and New York: Walter de Gruyter, 1983).

moral commitment as a matter of contingent, sociological fact. However, the coming realization that religion, and other moral ideals, are fairy-tales does not mean that 'the sense for poesy' is not important even when we are, so to speak, adults: 'if we could entirely abolish this poesy, it is a question whether anything would be left to make life worth living'.[76] Rather than the unintentional poetry that lead to the myths of religion and metaphysics we need an intentional '*Begriffsdichtung*'—'concept poetry'—the imaginative creation of conceptual structures. If we are to overcome our narrow interests and encourage morality, 'then myth asserts its rights'.[77] Lange declares, 'One thing is certain, that man needs to supplement reality by an ideal world of his own creation'.[78] If we in fact had knowledge about how reality is in itself, then the construction of this ideal world, these myths, would be irresponsible since it is reality that should guide us rather than some imaginary construction of our own. Fortunately, 'No thought is so calculated to reconcile poesy and science as the thought that all our "reality"—without any prejudice to its strict connexion, undisturbed by any caprice—is only *appearance*.'[79] This he takes to be Kant's lesson. Nonetheless, if we were actually to believe in our imaginary constructions, then these constructions would be susceptible to destruction by a critique that pointed out that they had no connection to reality. Instead:

We have no doubt of another solution of the problem, especially in Germany, since we have in the philosophical poems of Schiller a performance which unites with the noblest vigour of thought the highest elevation above reality, and which lends to the ideal an overpowering force by removing it openly and unhesitatingly into the realm of fantasy.[80]

'Free poetry' can thus 'without doing violence to the facts . . . entirely leave the ground of reality and make use of myth.'[81] People cannot do without something that plays the 'core' role of religion. Myth by its 'conscious elevation above reality' can play this role. It can thus block what would be an otherwise inevitable return to 'superstition' and the 'falsification of reality' despite all the enlightenment brought by philosophy and science.[82]

For my purposes, his emphasis on how intentional 'concept poetry' can help us avoid falsification is particularly important because of what I take to be Nietzsche's similar interest in how illusions can be honest. And Lange is well aware, as I think Nietzsche is, that it is not easy to get these honest illusions to play the role they are supposed to. As Lange grants, 'This advice will indeed appear to many an old or even

---

[76] Friedrich Albert Lange, *The History of Materialism and Criticism of its Present Importance*, 3rd edn. (New York: Humanities Press, 1950), III:280–5. In this section I draw on Nadeem J. Z. Hussain, 'Friedrich Albert Lange', in Edward N. Zalta (ed.), *The Stanford Encyclopedia of Philosophy (Summer 2005 Edition)*, URL=<http://plato.stanford.edu/archives/sum2005/entries/friedrich-lange/>.

[77] Lange, *Materialism*, III:299.   [78] Ibid. III:342.   [79] Ibid. II:234. See also Ibid. III:342.
[80] Ibid. III:343.   [81] Ibid. III:343.   [82] Ibid. III:344–6.

new believer, as if we were to draw the ground from beneath his feet and ask him to remain standing as though nothing had happened.'[83] Nonetheless, Lange's is basically a case of revolutionary fictionalism.[84]

It is Lange's neo-Kantian argument for the freedom to create new conceptual schemes and his emphasis on the fortunate irrefutability of fictions that Nietzsche trumpets in his letter to Carl von Gersdorff. After stating Lange's neo-Kantian conclusions about appearance and reality, Nietzsche writes, 'Consequently, Lange thinks, one leaves the philosophers free, assuming that they continue to edify us. Art is free also in the domain of concepts. Who would refute a phrase by Beethoven, and who would find an error in Raphael's Madonna?'[85] The last line is essentially a quotation from the penultimate page of Lange's discussion of the 'Standpoint of the Ideal', though the Beethoven example replaces a Mass of Palestrina in the original.[86]

Finally, let me just conclude this historical survey with the reminder that Hans Vaihinger's famous defence of fictionalism, *The Philosophy of 'As If'*, was basically written by the end of the 1870s even though it was not published till 1911. The first part of the eventual book was submitted as his *Habilitationsschrift* in 1877.[87] Perhaps not surprisingly, Vaihinger had sent a brief, unsolicited description of his fictionalism to Lange in the hopes of encouragement. Despite the advanced state of Lange's cancer—he was to die that year—Lange replied: 'Although a difficult illness prevents me from almost any correspondence, I would like nonetheless to express with a few words my complete agreement with the thoughts you have taken up.'[88] Indeed, it was Vaihinger's reading of Nietzsche at the end of the 1890s, whom he regarded as drawing on the same sources of inspiration as himself—Schopenhauer and Lange—that was one of the things that convinced him that the world was ready for his *Philosophy of 'As If'*.[89] Given

---

[83] Lange, *Materialism*, III:346.

[84] His final view is more complicated. Among other things he suspects that 'the wise' even in past times did not really believe the dogmas of religion and that an awareness of the falsity of religion must have been present 'at least dimly in the consciousness of the people also'. Otherwise, how, he asks, could poets and philosophers, Greek, Roman and Catholic, have got away with taking such liberties with 'the material of religion'? (Lange, *Materialism*, III:346–7). For warnings against too much revolutionary fervor and arguments for gradualism, see ibid. III:355–6, 358.

[85] August 1866, *KGB* I/2:160; translation in Friedrich Wilhelm Nietzsche, *Selected Letters of Friedrich Nietzsche* (Chicago: University of Chicago Press, 1969), 18. The translation in the text is mine.

[86] Lange, *Materialism*, 360.

[87] Hans Vaihinger, *Die Philosophie des als ob: System der theoretischen, praktischen und religiösen Fiktionen der Menschheit auf Grund eines idealistischen Positivismus*, 5th and 6th edns. (Leipzig: Verlag von Felix Meiner, 1920), p. ii.

[88] Lange's letter of 16 May 1875 is quoted in Vaihinger, *Philosophie des als ob*, p. xiii. For Vaihinger's letter of 9 May 1875, see Friedrich Albert Lange, *Über Politik und Philosophie: Briefe und Leitartikel 1862 bis 1875*, ed. Georg Eckert (Duisburg: Walter Braun Verlag, 1968), 354–5.

[89] Vaihinger, *Philosophie des als ob*, pp. iii–iv, xiv–xv. The reasons for not publishing sooner are varied. In part Vaihinger put aside the manuscript to work on his massive commentary on Kant's *Critique of*

the very large gap of time between conception and publication, Vaihinger wrote an 'Editor's Foreword' to the first edition since he regarded his current self as in some ways merely the editor of a work produced by a much earlier self.

Thus it seems to me that fictionalism was very much part of the nineteenth-century philosophical landscape. No doubt there was much work that remained to be done. Consider, for example, the long list of different expressions that Vaihinger borrows and uses to point to whatever is supposed to be the alternative to believing something: as-if-acceptance (*Als-Ob-Annahmen*), conscious fictions, as-if-consideration (*Als-Ob-Betrachtung*), conscious self-deception (*bewussten Selbsttäuschung*), as-if-attitude (*Als Ob-Einstellung*), or, in English, 'the consciously-false judgments'. There is no standardization here, but there is some attempt to outline the alternative to believing something—one should remember that in fact there is not that much more standardization or articulation of what this attitude comes to today. Furthermore, what the attitude of belief, and this alternative attitude, is directed towards is something that can be true or false. The whole concern here is to ensure that by changing our attitude we avoid having a false belief.

It was, I suspect, the logical positivists' concerns with empiricism about content that led to the demise of nineteenth-century fictionalism. For the regions of discourse that fictionalism was most naturally applied to—for example, religious discourse—providing a reduction of the purported content to something that was verifiable seemed impossible and so the tendency was to take the purported claims of apparently ontologically problematic discourse as meaningless rather than false.[90] In turn, I would suggest, the easing of empiricist worries about content has led to the return of fictionalism. Gideon Rosen sums up the current situation well:

Fictionalism has undergone a revival lately in a variety of domains. Time was, when an indispensable region of discourse began to look ontologically problematic, the first philosophical response was reductionism: 'Sure, we seem to be saying that there are *F*s, but all we really mean is . . . ' But for various reasons of detail and principle the more ambitious reductionism programs tend not to work out. And at this point the best alternative to realism about the objects in question is fictionalism. The discourse is to be interpreted literally or 'at face value'; so our theories are true only if the problematic objects exist. We skirt a commitment to those objects simply by denying that the theories are true. They are good and we accept them. But goodness isn't truth, and acceptance is not belief. And that's why we

Pure Reason from 1879 to 1892. This project allowed him to support himself financially. The commentary was followed by the effort of setting up the journal *Kantstudien* (Vaihinger, *Philosophie des als ob*, pp. ii−v). Supposedly it was working out the section on Nietzsche's fictionalism that also took a large amount of time Hans Vaihinger, *The Philosophy of 'As If '*, trans. C. K. Ogden, 2nd edn. (London: Routledge & Kegan Paul, 1935), pp. xl−xli.

90 Cf. Arthur Fine, 'Fictionalism,' *Midwest Studies* 18 (1993): 3.

don't inherit the obnoxious commitments of the theories we use or the languages we speak.[91]

Contemporary fictionalism is a return, for better or for worse, to a standard approach to ontologically problematic domains that was widespread in the nineteenth century.

Now, as I have suggested already, one could argue that despite the apparently cognitivist language that these nineteenth-century thinkers were using we do not have sufficient grounds to ascribe to them a form of cognitivism let alone fictionalism. Perhaps because they lack the philosophical resources to articulate a non-cognitivist alternative we should not see them as even implicitly denying this alternative. Perhaps in the spirit of contemporary metaethicists' arguments for non-cognitivism, just as the apparent cognitivist language of ordinary moral discourse is not to be taken as settling the question of whether cognitivism is the correct account of ordinary moral discourse, we should not take the use of cognitivist language by nineteenth-century philosophers as settling whether they were cognitivists. I find both arguments unconvincing, but will not try to take them on here. Rather I want to point out that even if we accept them, as long as we countenance contemporary non-cognitivist theories, there would still be space for an interesting form of fictionalism to ascribe to Nietzsche. Recall that the kind of non-cognitivism that Blackburn or Gibbard defend, allows for talk of moral facts and beliefs. Such forms of non-cognitivism allow us to say, for example, that there are no moral facts and that all moral beliefs are false. Now it is true that non-cognitivists do not usually talk about pretence, but they will have to have some theory of pretence to account, for example, for what morally decent actors are doing when playing Caligula. Assuming they can provide such an account, we would then be able to ascribe revolutionary fictionalism—error theory plus replacement fictionalist practice—to Nietzsche without having to assign to him any view about the semantics of moral claims. The point here is just the standard one: if cognitivist language does not settle in favor of non-cognitivism for the reasons contemporary non-cognitivists give—namely that such language is compatible with non-cognitivism—then ascribing some view to a thinker using such language, for example, ascribing fictionalism to Nietzsche, does not have to involve ascribing a denial of non-cognitivism.[92]

References

ANDERSON, R. LANIER (2005). 'Nietzsche on Truth, Illusion, and Redemption'. *European Journal of Philosophy* 13/2: 185–225.

---

[91] Gideon Rosen, 'What is Constructive Empiricism?', *Philosophical Studies* 74/2 (1994): 168.

[92] For an extended discussion of these issues, see Nadeem J. Z. Hussain and Nishi Shah, 'Metaethics and its Discontents: A Case Study of Korsgaard' (MS, 2005).

AUSTIN, J. L. (1958). 'Pretending'. *Aristotelian Society: Supplementary Volume*: 261–78.

BENTHAM, JEREMY (1932). *Bentham's Theory of Fictions*, ed. C. K. Ogden (London: Kegan Paul Trench Trubner & Co.).

BERGMANN, FRITHJOF (1973). 'The Experience of Values'. *Inquiry* 16: 247–79.

BLACKBURN, SIMON (1984). *Spreading the Word: Groundings in the Philosophy of Language* (Oxford: Clarendon Press).

—— (1993). *Essays in Quasi-Realism* (New York and Oxford: Oxford University Press).

—— (1998). *Ruling Passions: A Theory of Practical Reasoning* (Oxford and New York: Clarendon Press; Oxford University Press).

BREAZEALE, DANIEL (ed.) (1979). *Philosophy and Truth: Selections from Nietzsche's Notebooks of the Early 1870's* (Atlantic Highlands, NJ: Humanities Press International).

BURGESS, JOHN P. (1983). 'Why I Am Not a Nominalist'. *Notre Dame Journal of Formal Logic* 24: 93–105.

BURGESS, JOHN P. and GIDEON A. ROSEN (1997). *A Subject with No Object: Strategies for Nominalistic Interpretation of Mathematics* (Oxford and New York: Oxford University Press).

CRIMMINS, MARK (1998). 'Hesperus and Phosphorus: Sense, Pretense, and Reference'. *Philosophical Review* 107/1: 1–47.

CROMWELL, RICHARD SIDNEY (1974). *David Friedrich Strauss and his Place in Modern Thought* (Fair Lawn, NJ: R. E. Burdick).

DANTO, ARTHUR C. (1965). *Nietzsche as Philosopher* (New York: Columbia University Press).

DARWALL, STEPHEN, ALLAN GIBBARD, and PETER RAILTON (1992). 'Toward *Fin de siècle* Ethics: Some Trends'. *The Philosophical Review* 101/1: 115–89.

DARWALL, STEPHEN L. (1992). 'Internalism and Agency', in James E. Tomberlin (ed.), *Philosophical Perspectives* (Ridgeview: Atascadero), 155–74.

ELSTER, JON (1983). *Sour Grapes: Studies in the Subversion of Rationality* (Cambridge: Cambridge University Press).

FEUERBACH, LUDWIG (1989). *The Essence of Christianity*, trans. George Eliot (Amherst: Prometheus Books).

FINE, ARTHUR (1993). 'Fictionalism'. *Midwest Studies* 18: 1–18.

FRANKFURT, HARRY (1971): 'Freedom of the Will and the Concept of a Person'. *Journal of Philosophy* 68/1: 5–20.

GIBBARD, ALLAN (2003). *Thinking How to Live* (Cambridge, Mass.: Harvard University Press).

GREGORY, FREDERICK (1977). *Scientific Materialism in Nineteenth Century Germany*, Studies in the History of Modern Science (Dordrecht: Reidel).

HARRIS, HORTON (1973). *David Friedrich Strauss and his Theology* (Cambridge University Press).

HARTLICH, CHRISTIAN, and WALTER SACHS (1952). *Der Ursprung des Mythosbegriffes in der modernen Bibelwissenschaft* (Tübingen: J. C. B. Mohr).

HILLS, DAVID (1997): 'Aptness and Truth in Verbal Metaphor'. *Philosophical Topics* 25/1: 117–53.

HOLLINGDALE, R. J. (1985). *Nietzsche: The Man and his Philosophy* (London: Routledge and Kegan Paul).

HOOK, SIDNEY (1950). *From Hegel to Marx: Studies in the Intellectual Development of Karl Marx* (New York: The Humanities Press).

HUNT, LESTER H. (1991). *Nietzsche and the Origin of Virtue*, Routledge Nietzsche Studies (London and New York: Routledge).

HUSSAIN, NADEEM J. Z. (2004). 'Nietzsche's Positivism'. *European Journal of Philosophy* 12/3: 326–68.

——— (2005). 'Friedrich Albert Lange', in Edward N. Zalta (ed.), *The Stanford Encyclopedia of Philosophy (Summer 2005 Edition)*. URL=<http://plato.stanford.edu/archives/sum2005/entries/friedrich-lange/>.

HUSSAIN, NADEEM J. Z., and NISHI SHAH (2005). 'Metaethics and its Discontents: A Case Study of Korsgaard' (MS).

KAMENKA, EUGENE (1970) *The Philosophy of Ludwig Feuerbach* (London: Routledge & Kegan Paul).

KAUFMANN, WALTER, (1974). *Nietzsche: Philosopher, Psychologist, Antichrist*, 4th edn. (Princeton, NJ: Princeton University Press).

KORSGAARD, CHRISTINE (1996). *The Sources of Normativity*, ed. Onora O'Neill (Cambridge: Cambridge University Press).

LANGE, FRIEDRICH ALBERT (1950). *The History of Materialism and Criticism of its Present Importance*, 3rd edn. (New York: Humanities Press).

——— (1968). *Über Politik und Philosophie: Briefe und Leitartikel 1862 bis 1875*, ed. Georg Eckert (Duisburg: Walter Braun Verlag).

LANGSAM, HAROLD (1997). 'How to Combat Nihilism: Reflections on Nietzsche's Critique of Morality', *History of Philosophy Quarterly* 14/2: 235–53.

LAWLER, EDWINA (1986). *David Friedrich Strauss and His Critics: The Life of Jesus Debate in Early 19. Century German Journals*, American University Studies: Series VII: Theology and Religion (New York: Peter Lang).

LEITER, BRIAN (2000). 'Nietzsche's Metaethics: Against the Privilege Readings'. *European Journal of Philosophy* 8/3: 277–97.

——— (2004). 'Nietzsche's Moral and Political Philosophy', in Edward N. Zalta (ed.), *The Stanford Encyclopedia of Philosophy (Fall 2004 Edition)*. EURL=<http://plato.stanford.edu/archives/fall2004/entries/nietzsche-moral-political/>.

MAGNUS, BERND (1988). 'The Use and Abuse of *The Will to Power*', in Robert C. Solomon and Kathleen M. Higgins (eds.), *Reading Nietzsche* (New York: Oxford University Press), 218–35.

MASSEY, MARILYN CHAPIN (1983). 'Introduction to *In Defense of My "Life of Jesus" Against the Hegelians*', in David Friedrich Strauss, *In Defense of My Life of Jesus against the Hegelians* (Hamden: Archon Books), pp. ix–xxxix.

MORGAN, GEORGE ALLEN (1965). *What Nietzsche Means* (New York: Harper).

NIETZSCHE, FRIEDRICH WILHELM (1969). *Selected Letters of Friedrich Nietzsche* (Chicago: University of Chicago Press).

PFLEIDERER, OTTO (1913). 'Introduction to *The Life of Jesus Critically Examined*', in David Friedrich Strauss (ed.), *The Life of Jesus Critically Examined* (London: George Allen & Co., Ltd.), pp. v–xxvi.

RICHARDSON, JOHN (1996). *Nietzsche's System* (New York and Oxford: Oxford University Press).

——— (2004). *Nietzsche's New Darwinism* (Oxford and New York: Oxford University Press).

ROSEN, GIDEON (1994). 'What is Constructive Empiricism?', *Philosophical Studies* 74/2: 143–78.

SALAQUARDA, JORG (1978). 'Nietzsche und Lange'. *Nietzsche-Studien* 7: 236–53.

——— (1979). 'Der Standpunkt des Ideals bei Lange und Nietzsche'. *Studi Tedeschi* 22/1: 133–60.

SAYRE-MCCORD, GEOFFREY (1988). 'Introduction: The Many Moral Realisms', in Geoffrey Sayre-McCord (ed.), *Essays on Moral Realism* (Ithaca and London: Cornell University Press), 1–21.

SCHACHT, RICHARD (1983). *Nietzsche*, The Arguments of the Philosophers (London: Routledge).

—— (1995). *Making Sense of Nietzsche: Reflections Timely and Untimely*, International Nietzsche Studies (Urbana and Chicago: University of Illinois Press).

SLUGA, HANS D. (1980). *Gottlob Frege*, The Arguments of the Philosophers (London: Routledge & Kegan Paul).

SMITH, MICHAEL (1994). *The Moral Problem: Philosophical Theory* (Oxford: Blackwell).

STACK, GEORGE J. (1983). *Lange and Nietzsche*, Monographien und Texte zur Nietzsche-Forschung (Berlin and New York: Walter de Gruyter).

STANLEY, JASON (2001). 'Hermeneutic Fictionalism'. *Midwest Studies in Philosophy* 25: 36–71.

STRAUSS, DAVID FRIEDRICH (1913). *The Life of Jesus Critically Examined*, trans. George Eliot, 6th edn. (London: George Allen).

VAIHINGER, HANS (1920). *Die Philosophie des als ob: System der theoretischen, praktischen und religiösen Fiktionen der Menschheit auf Grund eines idealistischen Positivismus*, 5th and 6th edns. (Leipzig: Verlag von Felix Meiner).

—— (1935). *The Philosophy of 'As If'*, trans. C. K. Ogden. 2nd edn., International Library of Psychology, Philosophy and Scientific Method (London: Routledge & Kegan Paul).

WALTON, KENDALL (1978). 'Fearing Fictions'. *The Journal of Philosophy* 75/1: 5–27.

—— (1990). *Mimesis as Make-Believe: On the Foundations of the Representational Arts* (Cambridge: Harvard University Press).

—— (1993). 'Metaphor and Prop Oriented Make-Believe'. *The European Journal of Philosophy* 1/1: 39–56.

—— (2000). 'Existence as Metaphor?', in Anthony J. Everett and Thomas Hofweber (eds.), *Empty Names, Fiction, and the Puzzles of Non-Existence* (Stanford: CSLI Publications), 69–94.

WATSON, GARY (1982). 'Free Agency', in Gary Watson (ed.), *Free Will* (Oxford: Oxford University Press), 81–95.

WILCOX, JOHN T. (1974). *Truth and Value in Nietzsche: A Study of His Metaethics and Epistemology* (Ann Arbor: The University of Michigan Press).

WILLIAMS, BERNARD (1993). 'Nietzsche's Minimalist Moral Psychology'. *European Journal of Philosophy* 1/1: 4–14.

YABLO, STEPHEN (2000). 'A Paradox of Existence', in Anthony J. Everett and Thomas Hofweber (eds.), *Empty Names, Fiction, and the Puzzles of Non-Existence* (Stanford: CSLI Publications), 275–312.

YACK, BERNARD (1986). *The Longing for Total Revolution: Philosophic Sources of Social Discontent from Rousseau to Marx and Nietzsche*, Studies in Moral, Political, and Legal Philosophy (Princeton: Princeton University Press).

8

Nietzsche and Moral Objectivity: The Development of Nietzsche's Metaethics

Maudemarie Clark and David Dudrick

This essay begins from the uncontroversial assumption that Nietzsche holds certain ethical or moral values and expresses them in his work. Its question is whether his philosophy allows him to claim objectivity for these values. Many have thought that his metaethical position prohibits him from doing so, that it entails, in Brian Leiter's words, a denial that "there is any objective vindication for his [or any other] evaluative position." As Leiter notes, this is "the most familiar reading *outside* the secondary literature on Nietzsche," shared by such thinkers as Max Weber and Alasdair MacIntyre (Leiter 2002: 146). We will reconstruct the development of Nietzsche's metaethical position in order to show that this widely shared view is mistaken. The upshot is that Nietzsche does and can consistently claim that his evaluative position is objective and that this is a central component of his understanding of himself as a philosopher. We agree with Leiter that the secondary literature has not provided an adequate defense of this interpretation of Nietzsche. But since Leiter himself has made the most recent and compelling case against the position we want to argue for here, we will take him as our main interlocutor in this essay and organize it as an argument against his interpretation.

The essay has five sections. It begins from Leiter's interpretation. Leiter claims (*a*) that Nietzsche's naturalism entails a rejection of realism about moral values and assumes (*b*) that such anti-realism entails or is equivalent to a denial of moral objectivity.

Section 1 argues that Leiter is right about (*a*), at least in the middle-period work, *Human, All-Too-Human* (1878; hereafter HA). In this work, Nietzsche's naturalism leads him to anti-realism with regard to moral properties, a denial that such properties have what we call *ontological objectivity*. In section 2 we argue that in the same work Nietzsche also denies that moral claims have *normative objectivity*, that they deserve acceptance by others. However, this does not confirm (*b*), for the denial does not follow directly from his anti-realism, but from the "error theory" of moral discourse at work in HA. As it is at work in HA, this theory implies not just that moral claims refer to a realm that is cognitively superfluous, but that all evaluations are "partial" and so "unjust." Section 3 then argues that by the time he wrote the first edition of *The Gay Science* (1882; hereafter GS), Nietzsche had overcome the error theory of HA by abandoning the cognitivism presupposed by it. Section 4 adds that GS's non-cognitivism is a more complicated position than the one attributed to Nietzsche in section 3. This section offers an interpretation of Nietzsche's claim that values are created, and argues that he actually understands *value* claims (attributions of normative properties) as claims about *reasons*. To show that value claims are objective, therefore, Nietzsche needs to show not that there are ontologically objective facts that correspond to value claims, but that claims about what one has reason to do can be objective. In section 5, we argue that in *On the Genealogy of Morality* (1887; hereafter GM) Nietzsche offers a conception of objectivity according to which such claims can be objective, and that Nietzsche's new conception of objectivity is connected to a new understanding of the nature of philosophy, and therefore of his own task.

1. Nietzsche's Value Anti-Realism

Leiter takes Nietzsche to object to a version of morality he labels "MPS" ("morality in the pejorative sense") on the grounds that MPS "is not conducive to the flourishing of human excellence" (Leiter 2002: 136). The question that motivates Leiter's discussion of Nietzsche's value anti-realism is what Nietzsche does or should say about the *value* of this flourishing: why it is more important than the values defended by MPS. Leiter explains that this question is a "metaethical" one concerning the metaphysical or epistemological status of the values Nietzsche uses to undertake his revaluation of moral values: whether they are "veridical" or "justified" in "some sense" in which the moral values he finds wanting are not. What "animates" these questions, Leiter claims, is "a worry about Nietzsche's critical project that might be summed up simply as follows: in offering a revaluation of morality is Nietzsche doing anything more than giving his idiosyncratic opinion from his idiosyncratic evaluative perspective? Is there, in short, anything about Nietzsche's evaluation of morality that ought to command *our* attention and assent?" (Leiter 2002: 137).

This is a question concerning the normative status of Nietzsche's position: is his critique of morality *worthy* of our attention and assent? Leiter suggests that the answer one can legitimately give to this normative question is dependent on one's metaethical position, in particular, on whether one is a realist or an anti-realist about moral values.[1] More specifically, Leiter holds that if Nietzsche were a realist about moral values, he could claim that his evaluative position deserves the attention and assent of others. Because he is an anti-realist, however, he must admit that he speaks merely from his own "idiosyncratic evaluative perspective."

To evaluate Leiter's contention, we need an account of what is it to be a realist about value. According to Leiter, it is to hold "that there are *objective* facts about value" (Leiter 2002: 137). The "intuitive idea" behind this idea of objectivity, Leiter tells us, "is simple enough": "facts are objective just in case their character and existence is *independent* of the states of mind of persons in some appropriate sense. *Epistemic* independence is most often what is at issue: a fact is objective if its character and existence does not depend on what people believe or would have reason to believe about it."

Leiter takes Nietzsche to be a realist about prudential value: the facts concerning what is good *for* an individual are objective; they do not depend on "what people believe or would have reason to believe about" them. However, he takes Nietzsche to be an anti-realist about moral or ethical values—we use "value anti-realism" to designate this position concerning moral value throughout the essay.

What Leiter here calls "*epistemic* independence" is perhaps better termed *ontological* independence. The independence in question is certainly independence *from* epistemic considerations ("what people believe or would have reason to believe"), but it is a fact's "character and existence" that possesses this independence. What makes a fact "objective" is that its ontological status does not depend on what anyone believes or has reason to believe about it. That the objectivity Leiter has in mind is of the ontological variety is confirmed by his discussion of what he takes to be "Nietzsche's central argument for anti-realism about value." This argument, he says, "is *explanatory*: moral facts don't figure in the 'best explanation' of experience, and so are not real constituents of the objective world. Moral values, in short, can be 'explained away.' Such a conclusion follows from Nietzsche's naturalism" (Leiter 2002: 148). Nietzsche's naturalism, according to Leiter, is of the methodological variety; it holds that philosophy should cohere with the results and follow the methods of the sciences. Leiter assumes above that following such methods will show that moral facts can be "explained away" (need not be referred to in explanations of experience,

---

[1] Although, as we have noted, Leiter claims that the question of objectivity concerns the metaphysical and epistemological status of Nietzsche's values, he does not introduce independent considerations concerning the epistemological status of these values, thereby writing as if the objectivity of these values follows directly from their metaphysical status, from their lack of what he calls "naturalistic objectivity" in the material quoted below.

including moral experience). That moral facts therefore do not belong to "the real constituents of the objective world" (the world that exists independently of what we believe or have reason to believe about it) is precisely the value anti-realism Leiter attributes to Nietzsche. It is the reasoning that establishes it that he calls "Nietzsche's central argument for anti-realism about value."

Before considering Leiter's claim that Nietzsche's anti-realism implies a denial of moral objectivity, we need a better picture of this anti-realism. Although Leiter cites a few specific passages as evidence for attributing value anti-realism to Nietzsche, his main evidence is a general feature of Nietzsche's work, his explanation of value judgments in terms of naturalistic factors. How else, Leiter asks, can we explain Nietzsche's "relentless pursuit of the psycho-physiological roots of our value judgments" if it is not an attempt to show that so-called moral facts—the goodness or badness of acts and characteristics judged to be good and bad—can be "explained away" and are therefore not part of the objective world? This rhetorical question may not be convincing if we are thinking of Nietzsche's major works (e.g., GM and *Beyond Good and Evil* (henceforth BGE)). There is little reason to think that the account of the origin of moral value judgments—the genealogy of morality—in these works is designed to show that moral properties aren't part of the objective world. However, that may be because Nietzsche takes that point for granted after HA. In the remainder of this section, we will therefore explain how HA exhibits anti-realism about moral value.

HA is widely acknowledged as marking a turning point in Nietzsche's career, the point at which he turns his back on the metaphysical or quasi-metaphysical commitments of his early works and embraces science as that which provides access to the "disclosed" or "real nature of the world" (HA 10; HA 29).[2] Nietzsche explicitly acknowledges that this has consequences for philosophy, specifically that the "historical philosophy" he takes himself to be practicing in HA is "no longer to be separated from natural science" (HA 1). HA thus shows that Nietzsche embraces the doctrine Leiter terms "methodological naturalism," that philosophy should cohere with the results of and follow the methods of the sciences, and that he embraces it precisely because he takes science to be, in Leiter's words, our guide to the "real constituents of the objective world."

Nietzsche does not merely "embrace" this doctrine in *Human, All Too Human*, he argues for it. The book's main project is to undermine metaphysics, which Nietzsche takes to involve commitment to the existence of a second world, a metaphysical or "true" world, in comparison with which the empirical world disclosed by science counts as "mere appearance." These two worlds are distinguished in terms of the

---

[2] We take responsibility for all translations and list the various published translations we have consulted in the References.

methods that give access to them. The empirical world is precisely the world to which the empirical methods of the sciences give access, whereas the metaphysical world is one that can be accessed only through non-empirical or *a priori* methods. Nietzsche argues that the postulation of this latter world is cognitively superfluous. Taking for granted the adequacy of empirical methods to explain what goes on in the nonhuman world (presumably, on the basis of the success of science), HA focuses its attack on the assumption that the postulation of a metaphysical world—Plato's Forms, Kant's thing-in-itself—is necessary to explain certain value-related aspects of the human world. Nietzsche employs two main strategies against this assumption.

In some cases he argues that the belief that has led thinkers to posit a non-empirical world is an error; the object of the belief does not exist. For instance, the beliefs in free will and in unchanging entities (which becomes the basis for belief in an immortal soul)—both of which he implausibly claims were originally shared with "everything organic"—are mistakes which arose "in the course of the overall evolution of organic being" because they contributed to our ancestors' survival and reproduction, and we therefore now inherit them as part of our cognitive equipment (HA 18). Nietzsche assumes that it is already clear to his readers that the objects of these beliefs do not exist, that the beliefs in these objects are contradicted by the "real nature of the world," the world as disclosed to us by modern science (HA 29; HA 10). His contribution is to remove any remaining tendency to think there must be some truth in them—for how else can one explain why they are so commonly believed?—by showing that we can fully understand how people have come to hold such beliefs without granting that they contain any truth.

HA is more centrally concerned with the justification for postulating a metaphysical world offered by the existence of things taken to be of the highest value in the human world. Nietzsche's strategy here gives the book its name: to show that these things are "human, all too human," mere sublimations and transformations of things of lower value. Once it is clear that we can explain disinterested contemplation, for instance, as a sublimation of lust and give comparable explanations for other things taken to be of higher value, we show that these things offer no basis for positing a metaphysical world because they can be adequately explained from a purely naturalistic viewpoint.

If these two lines of argument succeed, Nietzsche expects interest in metaphysical questions to die out (HA 10). There could be a metaphysical world, he admits. The possibility that truth is simply not accessible from the empirical perspective cannot be ruled out. "We behold all things through the human head and cannot cut this head off; while the question nevertheless remains what of the world would still be there if one had cut it off" (HA 9). But although the question about the "thing in itself" therefore remains, Nietzsche's suggestion is that no one would be driven by the thought of discovering its nature (i.e., driven to metaphysics) simply by the question of what things are like apart from our knowledge of them (what the world would be like if we could cut the human head off). That is a purely theoretical problem and is "not very well calculated to bother people overmuch; but all that has hitherto made metaphysical assumptions *valuable, terrible, delightful* to them, all that has begotten these assumptions, is passion, error, and self-deception."

Metaphysics is begotten by error, as we have seen, insofar as it seeks to explain the existence of things (1) that we only erroneously believe to exist, or (2) whose existence we erroneously believe cannot be explained by empirical methods. The role that passion and self-deception play in the acceptance of such errors is suggested by the following passage:

It is probable the objects of the religious, moral and aesthetic sentiments belong only to the surface of things, while man likes to believe that here at least he is in touch with the world's heart; the reason he deludes himself is that these things produce in him such profound happiness and unhappiness, and thus he here exhibits the same pride as in the case of astrology. For astrology believes that the starry firmament revolves around the fate of man; the moral man, however, supposes that what he has essentially at heart must also constitute the essence and heart of things.   (HA 4)

In other words, in religion, morality, and art, humans experience certain feelings, the objects of which are the objects of ordinary experience, which counts as the "surface of things" from the viewpoint of both science and metaphysics. But "metaphysical and artistic ages and human beings" (HA 3) delude themselves into believing that these feelings are directed towards objects that are closer to the "heart of things"—as when the object of awe or gratitude is taken to be God, or when moral feelings are taken to be bound up with the perception of Platonic forms. The point is that they do not want to think that these value-laden feelings are simply *their* feelings, their reactions to empirical objects. They want some kind of support or validation for these reactions, which they get by taking the feelings to put them in touch with deeper level of reality, the "heart of things." And they do this by inventing a metaphysical world inaccessible to empirical investigation to house the purported objects of the feelings. This is why the metaphysical world has seemed so important: not for purely theoretical or cognitive reasons, but because it seemed to provide external support for moral, religious, and aesthetic feelings.

This passage suggests that HA is committed to value anti-realism, to a denial that moral properties belong to the objective world. It implies that the true objects of moral feelings and of the statements to which they give rise are the naturalistic properties of empirical objects, and not specifically moral properties, such as rightness or wrongness. Indeed, it is hard to see in HA the resources for recognizing such moral properties as constituents of the objective world. The general point, as we have already indicated, is that Nietzsche takes the "constituents of the objective world" to be only those objects and properties accessible through perception or the empirical methods of the sciences, and he certainly has no resources (unlike some twentieth-century naturalists[3]) for seeing how moral properties could be among those. HA takes the positing of specifically moral or ethical properties to be cognitively superfluous; it thus endorses anti-realism about moral value.

Leiter is therefore correct to count Nietzsche as a value anti-realist, at least in HA. Anyone denying that later Nietzsche is a value anti-realist must assume the burden of showing that and why he changed his mind on this issue. In the next section, we turn to the question whether his anti-realism has any implications for the normative question of moral objectivity, i.e., any implications concerning whether his own values are deserving of acceptance by others.

2. The Cognitivism of *Human, All-Too-Human*

To answer our question concerning the relationship between anti-realism and moral objectivity, it seems important to consider Nietzsche's view of moral discourse. What does he think is going on when we say of particular actions, for instance, that they are right or wrong, and that particular persons are virtuous or vicious? Turning our attention from metaphysics to semantics seems necessary given that the issue of moral objectivity is a question of whether moral statements are objective and therefore worthy of our acceptance, a question it is difficult to answer without considering whether such statements make genuine claims attributing moral properties to things (actions and persons) or are instead to be understood simply as expressions of attitudes. We sympathize with Leiter's suggestion that we should not expect Nietzsche to offer us a semantics for moral discourse and that a number of different accounts seem compatible with Nietzsche's claims about morality. That said, there are reasons for interpreting *Human-All-Too-Human* as committed to an "error theory" of morality according to which moral discourse involves the making of genuine but false claims about moral properties.

As we have indicated, Nietzsche admits in HA that the empirical world *may* be only the appearance of the thing-in-itself (and therefore, in Schopenhauer's terms, "only representation"). He nevertheless counts it as the "real nature of the world" because it is the only world of any cognitive or theoretical interest once we recognize that any metaphysical world is cognitively superfluous (HA 10, 29; see Clark 1998: 47–9; 1990:

---

[3] See Miller (2004: 138–242) for an account of these options. Our suggestion is not that any of these would be congenial to Nietzsche, but only that he could have had little inkling of them, hence that we can rule them out as anything that would have kept his naturalism from leading him to anti-realism about moral values.

ch. 4). There is a second world that plays a major role in HA, namely, the value-laden world of our practical concerns. But instead of taking this world to point us towards a higher or "true" world, as Plato did, Nietzsche dubs it "the world as representation (as error)" (HA 29). Now to say that the value-laden world is the "world . . . as error" is to take it to be the object of erroneous beliefs. The error involved seems to be the postulation of normative properties, and Nietzsche's story about this postulation presupposes that moral claims make genuine claims, attributing to things normative properties that do not actually exist.

Nietzsche's view, as we saw in section 1, is that humans respond to the world with feelings and concerns for which they want external support and this leads them to posit objects of these concerns that could in fact exist only in a non-empirical world. So we are, for instance, appalled by violence and concerned to banish it from the world, whereas we respond positively to acts of charity and are concerned to promote them. Wanting external support for these feelings and concerns, we attribute normative properties such as goodness and evil to the empirical actions we classify as charitable or violent, properties for which there is no room in an empirical world. This is no problem for those belonging to metaphysical ages. In fact, it is an advantage because it makes it possible to suggest that the objects in question have properties that include them in the "heart of things." Moral claims are validated, therefore, as expressing knowledge of a "higher" or "deeper" world than the ordinary empirical world. But in an age of methodological naturalism, it becomes a disadvantage that moral properties have no place in the empirical world. It suggests that the moral person is in touch not with a higher world, but with a lower one, a world of illusion, one that has been invented in order to make moral claims appear to be validated. HA's view therefore seems to be that the real world, the world disclosed by science, does not contain value (normative properties), although the passions and errors of human beings make it appear to contain such properties. In doing so, they construct a second world alongside of the world revealed to us by science. This merely apparent value-laden world is the "world . . . as error."

So it is hardly surprising that Nietzsche ends Part I of HA (which contains all of the sections we have been considering) by asking whether "our philosophy [will] not thus become a tragedy?" The issue is whether "truth [does] not become inimical to life, to the better man," and "whether death would not be preferable" to being obliged to "consciously reside in untruth" (HA 34). Nietzsche's answer is that it is possible to love in full view of the truth exposed by his philosophy if one can achieve

a simpler and emotionally purer life [in which] the old motives of violent desire . . . would gradually grow weaker under the influence of purifying knowledge. In the end one would live among human beings and with oneself as in *nature*, without praising, blaming, contending, gazing contentedly, as though at a spectacle, upon many things for which one formerly felt only fear. (HA 34)[4]

Such an (admittedly rare) person is one "from whom the ordinary fetters of life have fallen to such an extent that he continues to live only to know better." He achieves what Nietzsche calls "practical world affirmation" in the face of his "logical world denial" (HA 29)—that is, he finds satisfaction and perhaps even joy in living even though he denies that anything is of value. The crucial point here is that what allows this person to avoid the need to "reside consciously in untruth" is his abstention from value claims. This conclusion of Part I of HA thus adds further support to our claim that Nietzsche is committed to something very much like Mackie's "error theory" of moral value and its presupposed cognitivist account of moral discourse. Nietzsche's position is that a commitment to truth requires one to abstain from moral claims, and this clearly presupposes that moral claims make genuine claims that are in fact false.

Leiter therefore appears to be correct in thinking that Nietzsche denies moral objectivity at the same time that he embraces anti-realism about moral properties. Since moral claims are all erroneous, how could anyone's be worthy of acceptance by others? In fact Nietzsche goes further. He denies that one's moral claims are worthy of acceptance by oneself. That is surely what he commits himself to when he portrays his "knower" and "better man" as living without making value judgments. But note that this doesn't follow directly from his anti-realism, his denial that moral properties belong to the objective world, but from the combination of such anti-realism with a cognitive account of moral discourse. Nietzsche might continue to hold to his anti-realism regarding moral properties and yet come to a quite different understanding concerning moral objectivity if he gave up his cognitivist assumptions concerning moral discourse. In section 3, we consider evidence that he did just that.

Before turning to this evidence, we need to add that there is another factor perhaps even more directly relevant to Nietzsche's view of moral objectivity in HA, namely, his claim that all evaluations are "unjust." Nietzsche stresses this point in the passages that immediately precede his presentation of the "better man" as one who abstains from evaluation. All belief in the value of life "rests on false thinking" and is therefore "unjust" (HA 32); all inclination and aversion at the root of value claims involve "unjust assessments" (HA 33). The basis for this claim appears to be that our judgments of value always focus on one aspect of things at the expense of

---

[4] The passage continues: "One would be free of emphasis, and no longer prodded by the thought that one is only nature or more than nature. . . . A man from whom the ordinary fetters of life have fallen to such an extent that he continues to live only to know better must rather, without envy or vexation, be able to forego much, indeed almost everything upon which other men place value. He is happy to communicate his joy in his condition, and he *has*, perhaps, nothing else to communicate" (HA 34).

other aspects which we forget or ignore; evaluation is based not on a pure knowing of the matter to be evaluated but on a very interested and thoroughly partisan view of it. Valuing is thus directed by the will, not the intellect; the "colored" world of our concerns is a projection not simply of our errors but also of our passions, where passions are understood as partial, as wearing "party colors," "taking sides," being "for and against" (HA 371). For Nietzsche, then, even if they did not refer to a cognitively superfluous world, value claims would still not be justified or worthy of acceptance by others, because they represent a partisan's view of things and are not objective. Leiter is right, therefore, about the Nietzsche of HA: he does regard moral discourse as a matter of giving one's "idiosyncratic opinion from [one's] idiosyncratic evaluative perspective," even though such discourse is presented so as to give the impression that it "ought to command *our* attention and assent."

3. The Non-cognitivism of *The Gay Science*

No one doubts that Nietzsche's later and greater works differ substantially from HA. In particular, no one would claim that Nietzsche continued to adhere to the ideal of the "knower" and "better man" that he presents in HA 34. Indeed, it is that ideal of knowing that he has Zarathustra mock as "immaculate perception" in *Thus Spoke Zarathustra* (Z II, "Immaculate Perception"). Because that ideal was bound up with his denial that moral judgments are objective, the question is whether the change in his view has implications for Nietzsche's position on the possibility of normative objectivity for value claims.

We begin our attempt to answer this question with Clark's view that *The Gay Science* represents a major shift in Nietzsche's thinking about values. Clark characterizes the shift from HA to GS as follows:

In *Human, All too Human*, Nietzsche divided Schopenhauer's "world as representation" into two parts, the disenchanted empirical world revealed by science and the enchanted or value-laden world of our practical concerns. He called the latter "world as representation (as error)." In *The Gay Science*, he still makes a distinction between the two worlds, but now he celebrates the second world as a human creation, rather than looking down on it as an error. (Clark 1998: 68)

Why this should be so? What changes in Nietzsche's thinking allowed him to celebrate in GS the world that HA dubs "the world as representation (as error)"? The answer is evidently not that he came to accept value realism in GS; Nietzsche's commitment to value anti-realism in that work seems evident. In a passage Leiter cites as endorsing value anti-realism, for instance, Nietzsche writes: "Whatever has value in our world now does not have value in itself, according to its nature—nature is always value-less, but it has been given value at some time, as a present—and it is *we* who gave and bestowed it. Only we have created the world *that concerns human beings*" (GS 301). If Nietzsche continues to endorse value anti-realism, how is the change to be explained? One possibility is that it might be explained by a shift in Nietzsche's understanding of the status of moral discourse. As stated above, we agree with Leiter that we can hardly expect Nietzsche to have a clearly worked out position on the semantics of moral discourse. Yet it is hardly unreasonable to suppose that Nietzsche might have had thoughts about the function of moral discourse, and that some such thoughts might have led to a change in his position. It therefore seems reasonable to look for suggestions of the view of moral discourse his work tends towards, one that he presumably would have developed if he had been working in the light of the distinctions and possibilities recognized within contemporary metaethics. Indeed, we have already done that insofar as we found an "error theory" at work in HA. Admittedly, Nietzsche never says that statements such as "murder is wrong" should be understood as the expression of a belief that a normative property attaches to all actions that count as instances of "murder," but that such a property does not in fact exist. Yet, that is an obvious reading of what he was assuming when he labeled the world of our moral concerns "the world as representation (as error)" (HA 29). And one possibility is that he came to rethink that assumption and recognize something akin to a non-cognitivist account of moral discourse. This would explain why the Nietzsche of GS no longer considers the world of our moral concerns erroneous as he did in HA: not because he now takes value claims to be capable of truth, but because he thinks they are neither true nor false. The point would be that they function to express not a cognitive state, a belief, but a non-cognitive state, such as emotion. This is pretty much the account Clark offers (Clark 1998).

Nietzsche's reflections on artists in GS provides support for a non-cognitivist reading. Consider GS 299, which begins with a question and a statement: "What means do we have for making things beautiful, attractive, and desirable when they are not? And in themselves I think they never are!" Nietzsche is clearly not talking about "things in themselves" here. The assumption behind his question is that if considered merely as they are in nature, in terms of their naturalistic properties, things are not "beautiful, attractive, and desirable." This obviously cannot mean that they do not provoke desire or attraction. So the question and the assumption behind it must concern normative properties rather than naturalistic ones. Nietzsche is asking how to make things *worthy* of aesthetic appreciation and desire. This interpretation of GS 299 fits well with the part of GS 301 quoted above, which claims that "nature is always value-less, but it has been given value at some time, as a present." Nietzsche's question in GS 299 concerns precisely how to confer the "present" of value on nature.

That GS continues to maintain the anti-realism we found in HA makes sense of the presupposition of this question, namely, that in themselves things are never "beautiful, attractive, and desirable." This means that from the viewpoint of science, which determines the "real nature of the world" (HA 29), things do not possess normative properties that would make them worthy of aesthetic appreciation or desire. But unless Nietzsche's metaethical view underwent some change between HA and GS, it is difficult to make sense of the question itself. In particular, if Nietzsche still accepts the error theory of HA, that question could only concern how to make things *appear* to be beautiful and desirable when in fact they are not. Yet the question clearly concerns how we can make things *be* beautiful and desirable, worthy of aesthetic appreciation and desire. This suggests that Nietzsche is backing away from the error theory of HA. As we interpreted that theory, it applies to statements attributing both aesthetic and ethical value to things. Interpreting this passage in the light of HA suggests—and our section 4 will confirm it—that, contrary to appearances, Nietzsche's question in GS 299 concerns how to create not only aesthetic but also ethical value, how to make things worthy of appreciation from the viewpoints of both aesthetics and ethics.

Our interpretation of Nietzsche's apparent answer takes off from the section's title: "What one should learn from artists." What one should learn evidently is how to confer on nature the "present" of value by changing people's perceptions of, and therefore reactions to, natural things. Nietzsche first suggests that "we have something to learn from physicians, when for example they dilute something bitter or add wine and sugar to the mixing bowl." The physician makes the medicine attractive—or at least more attractive—by changing how it affects our taste buds and thus how we react to it. From what Nietzsche goes on to say, the artist does something similar. The general point seems to be that the artist induces in us certain reactions to things by manipulating our perspectives on them, for instance, by getting us to look at things from a distance "until there is much in them that one no longer sees and much that one *must add in order to see them at all*," or "extracted from their context," or "through colored glass or in light of the sunset." GS 7 implies that the passions constitute "all that has given color to existence." Accordingly, looking at things "through colored glass" would be seeing them through the "lens" of one's passions. So artists can make things beautiful and desirable by portraying them in ways that evoke certain passions, which then color one's view of them. Clark has argued that "color" functions throughout HA and GS as a metaphor for value (Clark 1998: 68 ff.). In that case, the obvious conclusion to draw here is that artists show us something about how to create values by showing us how to evoke non-cognitive reactions, such as preferences and attitudes.

This gives us strong reason to conclude that Nietzsche's metaethical position in GS is the basically Humean one that values are projections of passions and feelings. That is, we take ourselves to be talking about what has value—what is beautiful and desirable and not merely desired—precisely when we mix our own reactions with the object, seeing it in terms that are borrowed from our own reactions to it. Nietzsche's use of color imagery in GS can easily remind one of the famous passage in which Hume distinguishes the offices of reason and taste:

The former conveys the knowledge of truth and falsehood; the latter gives the sentiment of beauty and deformity, vice and virtue. The one discovers objects as they really stand in nature, without addition or diminution; the other has a productive capacity; and gilding and staining all natural objects with the colors borrowed from internal sentiment raises, in a manner, a new creation.

Hume's metaphor of "gilding" even appears, more or less explicitly, in *Gay Science* 139. Entitled "The Color of the Passions," it contrasts those like St. Paul, who have "an evil eye for the passions" and therefore aim at their annihilation, with the Greeks, who "directed their ideal tendency precisely towards the passions and loved and elevated, gilded (*vergoldet*) and deified them." In the latter case, the passions "evidently made them feel happier, but also purer and more godlike," whereas those in the former group know of the passions only "what is dirty, disfiguring, and heartbreaking." The passions themselves thus come to be valued—as opposed to merely lived or perhaps sought—through the projection of feelings and passions. Seeing them from the perspective of love "gilds" them, bestowing on them attractive colors borrowed from our own positive feelings of love and happiness, whereas an "evil eye" stains the passions, projecting negative feelings onto them. Looking at the passions through the lens of unhappiness and disappointment, it finds in them only those qualities that produce these feelings.

We can thus explain why Nietzsche celebrates as a creation in GS what he decries as an error in HA, then, by supposing that he comes to think of ethical discourse as expressing not the cognitive state of belief, but such non-cognitive states as preferences, attitudes, emotions, and sentiments of approval and disapproval. This would allow Nietzsche to leave behind the error theory of HA by rejecting the cognitivism about value discourse that it presupposed. In itself, however, this would do nothing to show that ethical discourse isn't a subjective affair in which individuals express their own personal preferences. We turn now to arguing that the non-cognitivism of GS is more complicated than we have so far suggested, and that the expression of moral claims can be objective.

4. Value Creation and Reasons in *The Gay Science*

We begin by returning to Nietzsche's claim that value is something that *"we"* create and bestow on nature as a "present": "Whatever has value in our world now does not have value in itself, according to its nature—nature is always value-less, but it has been given value at some time, as a present—and it is *we* who gave and bestowed it.

Only we have created the world *that concerns human being*" (GS 301). This might be taken to suggest that Nietzsche's way of getting over the error theory of HA is to reiterate its implicit claim that nature itself lacks normative properties, but to insist that through the act of valuing, human beings bestow normative properties (goodness, rightness, etc.) on things, persons, or states of affairs hitherto lacking them. This is how Richardson evidently interprets the above passage: "there are values only in and by our valuing them" (Richardson 2004: 109). Since Richardson definitely does not take Nietzsche to be a non-cognitivist, the position he attributes to him amounts to the claim that things come to have normative properties they otherwise lack in and through our acts of valuing them. This is evidently the view Bernard Reginster calls "normative subjectivism," which is a denial of "normative objectivism," the view that the source of the normative authority of values is to be found outside "the particular inclinations that make up an individual's will" (Reginster 2006: 58).

If this is what value creation entails, however, Nietzsche's position seems implausible: the goodness and badness of things does not seem to be conferred on them by the valuings of human beings. Murder's wrongness, for example, is due to the fact that it is the intentional killing of an innocent, that it causes pain and suffering, etc. Murder's wrongness is not dependent on anyone considering it wrong. But this implies the falsity of normative subjectivism, as presented above. Unless it can accommodate intuitions like these and so avoid normative subjectivism, Nietzsche's view of value creation seems implausible.

Before considering alternatives to this reading of GS 301, we pause to consider an objection. It may seem that the need to accommodate such intuitions is a feature that distinguishes what Leiter calls "morality in the pejorative sense" (MPS), thus that the kind of morality Nietzsche rejects is precisely one in which the possession of normative properties (e.g., an action's being good) cannot be recognized as dependent on the valuings—beliefs or attitudes—of human beings. But this will not get around the problem. There is no doubt that Nietzsche recognizes certain virtues: e.g., loyalty, honesty, courage. But it is no more plausible that courage is good or admirable because people admire it than that murder is wrong because people disapprove of it. Recall that our project is to determine whether Nietzsche does and can consistently claim that his elevation of his own values over those of MPS reflects anything more than his "idiosyncratic opinion from his idiosyncratic evaluative perspective" (Leiter 2002: 137). Following Leiter, we have treated this as a question concerning Nietzsche's metaethical position, and we have traced that position from the error-theoretic claim of HA that all valuations, that is, all attributions of normative properties, are based on "false thinking" to the non-cognitivism of GS. But one factor that makes non-cognitivism implausible to many is its apparent implication that values are dependent on the contingent affective responses of human beings. Is there a way of interpreting Nietzsche's metaethical position without taking it to have this implication?

Nadeem Hussain (2007) and Bernard Reginster (2006) offer "fictionalism" as a response. The fictionalist reading avoids attributing to Nietzsche the normative subjectivism found problematic above by taking Nietzsche to accept that to be valuable, a thing must be so "objectively," i.e., "independent of contingent feelings and inclinations or contingent beliefs about value that agents have" (Reginster 2006: 89). It further holds, however, that nothing is objectively valuable. Fictionalism thus combines a "*cognitivist* semantics for value judgments"—it takes value judgments to express beliefs about the objective properties of things rather than affective states—and an "*anti-realist* metaphysics of value" (Reginster 2006: 85–6). In these respects it is fully in accord with Nietzsche's position in HA. How, then, does it differ from that book's error theory, which we claim GS overcomes? The answer is that it does not overcome the error theory; the fictionalist accepts that nothing *really* is valuable. The "gaiety" of GS is to be explained not by Nietzsche's overcoming of the error theory, as we claim, but by his discovery of a new strategy for dealing with what Reginster calls the "nihilistic disorientation" brought about by its acceptance. Instead of resorting to HA's fantasy of pure knowers who can live without valuing (HA 32–4), Nietzsche now advocates that we "avert [nihilism] by engaging in make-believe in objective values, or imagining that there are such values" (Reginster 2006: 85), even though he believes this is false. The fictionalist Nietzsche claims that we "create" values in the sense that he exhorts us to engage in such "*make-believe*."

Although some philosophers have recently defended fictionalism (Joyce 2001), we admit to not finding it a very plausible ethical position.[5] So although Hussain and Reginster offer subtle defenses of interpreting Nietzsche as a fictionalist, we consider it worthwhile to pursue our alternative view that Nietzsche was able to overcome the error theory of HA by accepting a non-cognitivist account of moral discourse.[6] To strengthen our account, it would be especially helpful to have an alternative account of GS 301's claim that "we" give and bestow value on nature, which Hussain

---

[5] See Blackburn (2005) and Hussain (2004) for arguments that support reservations about the fictionalist approach to ethics.

[6] One reason to consider the fictionalist account of Nietzsche's metaethics implausible is that it is difficult to see how it could cohere with the importance he accords to the will to truth. In HA 34 he asks, in relation to this very question about the erroneousness of values, whether death "would not be preferable" to being obliged to "consciously reside in untruth?" The burden of our account in this essay is to show that he came to recognize that valuing does not require one to "reside in untruth." The burden of the fictionalist account must be to show that he overcame his commitment to not residing in untruth. One strategy for defending the fictionalist account would be to argue that Nietzsche was able to overcame his commitment to truth enough to affirm values, even though they are fictions, because of his commitment to the value of art. One problem with such a strategy is that it would seem to have Nietzsche reverting too much to the stand on art present in his earlier works. Our forthcoming book on *Beyond Good and Evil* argues that Nietzsche's later philosophy is designed to give full satisfaction to the will to truth, and we do not see this as compatible with the fictionalist option.

and Reginster take as a central piece of evidence for the fictionalist interpretation. We seem to face a dilemma here: given that Nietzsche endorses talk of values and value creation in GS, either Nietzsche is a cognitivist and so a fictionalist or he is a non-cognitivist and a normative subjectivist. On our account, the dilemma posed here is false. The non-cognitivism Nietzsche endorses in GS has the resources to overcome normative subjectivism and to endorse normative objectivism: the view that things are objectively valuable, that their value does not depend on our attitudes toward them.

Although we will be able to make good on this claim only in the final section of this essay, we begin here to fill out this alternative non-cognitivism by challenging the widespread assumption that the "we" identified in GS 301 as creating values are human beings in general. Attention to the context provided by the rest of the passage shows beyond any serious doubt that "we" are instead the "contemplative ones" of its title who are characterized in its first line as "higher human beings." The point of the passage is to rebut the self-misunderstanding of "the higher human being," who "can never shake off a delusion. He fancies that he is a spectator and listener who has been placed before the great visual and acoustic spectacle that is life; he calls his own nature *contemplative* and overlooks that he himself is the poet who keeps creating this life" (GS 301). That he "calls his own nature *contemplative*" means that he takes his defining activity to be an essentially cognitive pursuit, a matter of *representing* or *describing* what is already there. Nietzsche's point is clearly that the "contemplative" has this wrong, that he actually creates the world he takes himself to be merely contemplating. Now what exactly is this world or life that the higher human being actually creates? It is "the whole eternally growing world of valuations, colors, accents, perspectives, scales, affirmations, and negations." So Nietzsche's point is that it is the higher human beings, not human beings in general, who create values or the world that can be said to contain normative properties (of both the aesthetic and ethical variety). The next line of the passage makes explicit the contrast between the higher human and other humans: "The poem that we have invented is continually studied by the so-called practical human beings (our actors) who learn their roles and translate everything into flesh and actuality, into the everyday." Given this contrast between "we" and "practical human beings," "we" clearly does not refer to humans in general, but to the higher humans with whom Nietzsche here identifies himself. In that case, the same must be true when Nietzsche continues:

Whatever has *value* in our world now does not have value in itself, according to its nature—nature is always value-less, but has been *given* value at some time, as a present—and it was we who gave and bestowed it. Only we have created the world *that concerns human beings!*—But precisely this knowledge we lack, and when we occasionally catch it for a fleeting moment we always forget it again almost immediately; we fail to recognize our best power and underestimate ourselves, the contemplatives, just a little. We are *neither as proud nor as happy* as we might be. (GS 301)

The "contemplatives" are not as proud as they might be because they fail to recognize that they themselves—and not the so called practical or active human beings—are really the creative ones. In considering their nature contemplative, they underestimate themselves by failing to recognize *not* that human beings in general create values, but that they themselves, *unlike other human beings*, do so. And they create "whatever has *value* in our world." So even though Nietzsche does not specifically mention ethical value in the passage, he is certainly claiming that it is created by these contemplatives. It is precisely because they create ethical value that "the poem that [they] have invented is continually studied" by other humans who learn from it "their roles and translate everything into actuality." This claim makes little sense unless he is taking the so-called contemplatives to be the creators of ethical value.

But now we are left with the question of *how* exactly higher human beings create ethical value. GS 301 is evidently not interested in telling us, but only in correcting the self-understanding of the creators. We think it offers us a small clue, however, insofar as it refers to them as "thinking-feeling [or: thinking-sensing] ones," and tells us that "what distinguishes the higher human being from the lower is that the former see and hear immeasurably more, and see and hear thoughtfully" (GS 301). So even though the point of the passage is that the creators of value mistake their defining activity as a merely cognitive pursuit, a matter of *representing* or *describing* what is already there, Nietzsche seems to think that there is at least a grain of truth in the creator's self-understanding. If he denies that value creation is purely cognitive activity, he also implies that thought or cognition plays an essential role in it.

What is this "thinking" component? The answer begins to come into focus when we recognize that the value creators of GS 301 are or include the "ethical teachers" who are also called "*teachers of the purpose of existence*" in the title of GS 1. On reflection, it should be obvious that these religious leaders and philosophers of GS 1 are included among the self-described "contemplatives" of GS 301. The connection doesn't strike one immediately because Nietzsche praises the latter as "higher human beings" whereas he seems highly critical of the former. For all his criticism of these "ethical teachers," however—and he does say, e.g., that their "ethical systems hitherto have been so foolish and contrary to nature that humanity would have perished from every one had it gained power over humanity"—he also calls them "heroes on this stage." And by the end of GS 1, it is clear that he identifies with them, saying "We, too, have our time!" What is it, then, that Nietzsche finds so important about these teachers? The answer, it seems, is what in fact results from their activity: "Life and I and you and all of us became *interesting* to ourselves once again for a while." We suggest that this is Nietzsche's way of saying that with the advent of these "ethical teachers," human life appears as bearing *value*. Nietzsche includes himself and his "brothers" among them precisely because these teachers are the original value creators of GS 301.

We can therefore hope to gain some insight into how Nietzsche thinks the "contemplatives" of GS 301 create values by considering how he characterizes the defining activity of the teachers of GS 1. He tells us that each of them "shouts" such things as "Life is worth living," and "There is something behind life, beneath it; beware!" But they do not simply shout or proclaim; they offer *reasons*, saying things like "Life *ought* to be loved, *because*—! Man *ought* to advance himself and his neighbor, *because*—" And they are arguably "teachers" only because they do so. So creating values seems to have something to do with giving reasons.

We therefore take reason-giving as central to Nietzsche's understanding of value creation and ethical discourse. Now, before we examine the implications of this fact, we must allow that there are several aspects of the passage that make it appear that Nietzsche does not hold the activity of giving reasons in high regard; in fact, these aspects make it seem as if his purpose here is precisely to *debunk* reason-giving. We shall discuss briefly three such aspects of GS 1 and then offer an alternative to interpreting them as debunking. First, after describing the teachers' activity of reason-giving, Nietzsche says "the ethical teacher makes his appearance as the teacher of the purpose of existence in order that what happens necessarily and always, by itself and without purpose, shall henceforth seem to be done for a purpose and strike man as reason and an ultimate commandment." The teachers' proclamation of purpose is intended to make all events in the natural world ("what happens necessarily and always") appear to be purposeful, done for a reason. The first reason to think that Nietzsche is debunking the activity of reason-giving is that the teachers who introduce it do so in order to advocate a teleological view of the natural world, one that we know Nietzsche clearly and rightly rejects, based on the achievements of modern science.

A second apparently debunking point is Nietzsche's claim that the teaching of reasons and purposes has altered human nature such that man has become a "fantastic animal": "Man has gradually become a fantastic animal that must fulfill one condition of existence more than any other animal: man *must* from time to time believe that he knows *why* he exists; his race cannot thrive without a periodic trust in life—without faith in the *reason in life!*" (GS 1). So evidently all the teachers' attempts to satisfy the need they have created in man lead to false beliefs (e.g., that man's purpose is to serve God). It may therefore seem that Nietzsche thinks reason-giving leads man to become a "fantastic animal" in the sense that he needs such metaphysical fantasies in order to exist.

Third, Nietzsche claims that in their effort to make "what happens" seem to be done for a reason, these teachers invent "a second, different existence and takes by means of his new mechanics the old, ordinary existence off its old, ordinary hinges" (GS 1). This "second . . . existence" would appear to be a metaphysical world, like that Plato's Forms, or some version of a supernatural world, which we know from HA that Nietzsche rejects as cognitively superfluous.

These suggestions of GS 1 to the contrary notwithstanding, it is evident that Nietzsche's attitude toward the activity of reason-giving introduced by the teachers of GS 1 cannot be wholly negative. Consider the very next section, GS 2: *Intellectual conscience.* There Nietzsche tells us that *"the great majority lacks an intellectual conscience."*

I mean: *to the great majority* it is not contemptible to believe this or that and to live accordingly *without* first becoming aware of the most certain reasons pro and con, and without even troubling themselves about such reasons afterwards: the most gifted men and noblest women still belong to this "great majority."

The passage makes clear that Nietzsche does consider it *"contemptible"* to lack an intellectual conscience; his fullest respect goes only to those who live in accord with beliefs that have been formed or confirmed through an examination of the reasons for and against. He cannot, therefore, regard reason-giving as having been debunked by the considerations of GS 1.

This opens the way for our contention that Nietzsche regards the teaching of reasons and purposes as making a contribution to which he and his kind (the "thinking-feeling ones" of GS 301) are heir. We take the key claims of GS 1 to be that the capacity to consider reasons for and against attitudes, beliefs, or actions—and particularly non-prudential reasons—and to act on these reason is essential to being human, and that it is the teachers of the value of existence that firmly established this capacity among human beings. To exercise this capacity is to partake in a "faith" introduced by these teachers: the faith that there are reasons to do things and that there are events that happen for such reasons. It is, however, a refined version of this faith, since it significantly narrows the range of such events: the teachers held that all events are like this, while Nietzsche holds this to be true only of a subset of events, namely, actions undertaken for non-prudential reasons.[7] So Nietzsche criticizes the teachers' practice of reason-giving when he presents it as the attempt to make all events in the natural world ("what happens necessarily and always") appear to be purposeful, done for a reason—the first "debunking" aspect discussed above. He, of course, denies the teleological view of nature, according to which *everything* happens for a reason, indeed is *done* for a reason. But that is perfectly consistent with recognizing that these teachers achieved something great by establishing the practice of ethical reason-giving among human beings, thereby making it possible for things to be done for non-prudential reasons.

---

[7] Nietzsche clearly doesn't think that it was religious teachers who introduced prudential reasons into human consciousness. For evidence of this, consider both the opening sections of GM II on punishment, and the related account of the beginning of reliance on consciousness and prudential reasons in GM II: 16. Thus, if it is the case, as we have been arguing, that Nietzsche thinks these teachers introduced a practice of reason-giving, it has to be the practice of offering and thinking in terms of non-prudential reasons.

It is the work of these teachers, then, that firmly establishes the capacity of human beings to think and act in terms of non-prudential reasons. This suggests an alternative to our debunking interpretation of Nietzsche's claim that these teachers have caused man to "become a fantastic animal": with the institution of reason-giving, human beings can engage in behavior that cannot be fully understood in non-teleological, purely causal terms.[8] Because Nietzsche holds that the natural world *can* be fully understood in such terms, this makes human beings "fantastic." It also makes human actions part of a world other than the natural world, "a second existence." This helps explain the third debunking aspect of the passage, the claim that the teacher of reasons and purposes invents "a second, different existence and takes by means of his new mechanics the old, ordinary existence off its old, ordinary hinges." This world is not a metaphysical world, as was supposed above, but a "space of reasons," in contrast with the natural world, which is a "space of causes."[9] Although human actions certainly exist in the latter space, they can also be located in relation to the space of reasons. When the teachers institute the practice of reason giving, the "old existence" (i.e., the space of causes) is "lifted off its old hinges" into the "second existence" (i.e., the space of reasons), where it now operates according to a "new mechanics," insofar as events in the natural world can now be accurately described and explained in reference to reasons.

Before we use this interpretation of GS 1 to draw conclusions about how Nietzsche thinks the "contemplative ones" of GS 301 create values, it will be helpful to make explicit two distinctions in the use of "value" or "values." First, we can use the terms in a descriptive or a normative sense. "Value" is used in a descriptive sense when one talks about values *without* endorsing them. When one refers to "John's values" or "the values of the Enlightenment," the term is being used in the descriptive sense; it does not commit one to endorsing the values in questions. But if John says that he considers justice a value, he would normally be understood as endorsing the value of justice, as claiming that justice is valuable or good, hence as using the term in the normative sense. Second, John Richardson helpfully brings out that there are two ways one can use "value" in the descriptive sense. Nietzsche wants to study but not to endorse, for instance, Christian values. But " 'Christian values' could refer either to such *goods* as relief from suffering, or to the attitudes [involved in] valuing such goods" (Richardson 2004: 71). So in studying values, Nietzsche studies both "the act or activity of **valuing** some content—positing it as good"—and "the **valued**, the content so

---

[8] See Clark and Dudrick (2005).

[9] The distinction between the space of causes and the space of reasons is made explicitly in the twentieth century by Wilfred Sellars. We think Nietzsche picked up the distinction, though not by these names, from African Spir (Spir 1877). See the essay cited in the previous note for information about Spir and evidence of his influence on Nietzsche regarding this and other issues.

posited."[10] The former could be more clearly termed a "valuing" or an "assessment," so that "a value" in the descriptive sense would be reserved, as we shall use it here, for the latter, thus for objects or contents posited as valuable, that is, posited as values in the normative sense. These distinctions help to make sense of Nietzsche's otherwise puzzling claim to be investigating "*the value of these values,*" "*der Werth dieser Werthe*" (GM P: 6). While the plural "Werthe" is used in a descriptive sense, and to refer to objects valued (not to the act of valuing), the singular "Werth" is used in a normative sense. These distinctions make clear that "the issue for [Nietzsche]" is whether things that have been *posited* as good *are* good (GM P: 5), thus that his concerns are both descriptive and normative.

We can now argue that Nietzsche holds that values are created in both the descriptive and the normative sense. We interpret Nietzsche's claim that "genuine philosophers" create values (BGE 211) in the descriptive sense. These philosophers create values, as Nietzsche himself does in his own writings, by inducing people to posit things as valuable. They do this in part by inducing in people new affective responses to things. This helps us to see why Nietzsche thinks that "we"—presumably the creators of values of GS 301—"should learn from artists" (GS 299). We saw in section 3 that Nietzsche takes artists to provide perspectives on things that lead us to react to them in particular ways. In doing so, artists influence our affects, our dispositions to feel in particular ways about those things. This means that artists are proficient in some of the skills involved in creating values (in the descriptive sense). To create new values in this sense, one has to lead others to have dispositions to feel towards things in certain ways and to act accordingly. Yet, this is not sufficient, as we have inferred from GS 1 and contrary to what we suggested in section 3. To create values in this descriptive sense one must induce people not only to develop dispositions to act and react to things in certain ways, but also to take these ways of acting and feeling to be justified, to be supported by reasons. Nietzsche does this in his own writings by offering new *interpretations* of the dispositions he induces in people (to which he seduces them), ones designed to induce people to regard these dispositions as justified.

But this descriptive sense of creating values does not seem to capture the sense of "creation" in the passage from which we have repeatedly quoted the following: "Whatever has *value* in the present world has it not in itself, according to its nature—nature is always value-less—but rather has been given, granted value at some time, and *we* were the givers and granters!" (GS 301). Here the claim seems to be not simply that the creators of values have induced others to take things to be valuable, but above all, that they have made things valuable, bestowed upon them their

---

[10] Richardson points out that Nietzsche normally uses words build on "schätzen" to refer to the former, whereas he uses "Werthe" to refer to the latter, "the thing that is valued, but as valued" (Richardson 2004: 72).

normative properties. We have already said that this would be highly problematic if it meant that they have, for instance, made murder wrong or friendship good. The link we have established between GS 301 and GS 1 and our reading of the latter allows us to formulate an alternative to both the subjectivist and the fictionalist interpretation of the passage: namely, that by instituting practices of non-prudential reason-giving, the "teachers of the purpose of existence" bring into existence the space of reasons, and that it is only this space that makes it possible for anything to be a bearer of normative properties, e.g., to be good or bad, right or wrong. The position we are thus attributing to Nietzsche is a plausible one, given the following (we think plausible) assumptions: first, that to value something—as opposed to merely desiring it—is to accept that there is *reason* to take certain actions and attitudes towards it (for instance, to approve or disapprove of it, and to do or refrain from doing it); second, that there are reasons (i.e., reasons exist) *only* for beings who can appreciate reasons—in the case under consideration, non-prudential reasons. So the teachers of the value of existence create values in the sense that, by instituting the practice of non-prudential reason-giving, they help create beings who can consider and appreciate reasons. And this makes it possible for there to *be* reasons and therefore values.

We can now say how our reading of "value creation" can allow Nietzsche to avoid the kind of subjectivism that would take the goodness of loyalty, for instance, to be conferred upon it by the valuing of human beings, without taking values to be fictions. The "present" that the "contemplatives" of GS 301 bestow on an otherwise value-less nature is simply that of covering it with—reconfiguring it as—a space of reasons. On this interpretation, Nietzsche's commitment to value creation in the normative sense is perfectly compatible with claiming that once this space of reasons comes into existence, the normative properties there discerned are determined not by the contemplatives or by anyone else, but rather by what reasons there are to act and feel in certain ways. If this is the correct interpretation of Nietzsche's claim, in making possible the space of reasons the contemplatives of GS 301 "create the world *that concerns human beings*," the world of value, even though they do not determine which things in that world bear which normative properties.

It may seem that we have now turned Nietzsche into a cognitivist and value realist along the lines of Thomas Nagel or John McDowell. If value claims are claims about what there is reason to do or feel, and what there is reason to do or feel depends on the constitution of the space of reasons, it sounds as if value claims should be understood as *expressing beliefs* about the space of reasons, beliefs made true or false by the facts concerning what we have reason to do or feel. But this would leave us with a highly implausible interpretation of Nietzsche's metaethics. Recall that our major reason for interpreting Nietzsche as a non-cognitivist in GS is that it explains how he overcome HA's ideal of abstaining from value judgments and arrived at the "gaiety" of *The Gay Science*. It is just not plausible that he did this instead by deciding that there really hadn't been any problem about values to begin with, that recognizing that value claims are claims about reasons solved all of the problems that led him to the error-theoretic view of HA. It was his naturalism that led Nietzsche to the error theory we found in HA, and it is not plausible that he concluded that naturalism posed no problems for moral objectivity once we recognize moral claims as claims about reasons. Consider Jerry Fodor's challenge to John McDowell, who endorses such a view: "Having situated . . . the ethical . . . outside the realm of law [in the space of reasons] McDowell needs to face the embarrassing question how, by any natural process, do we ever manage to get at it?" (Fodor 1995: 11, quoted in Miller 2004: 258). In other words, the cognitivist-Nietzsche (if he is not a fictionalist) would have to be able to explain what capacities we, as natural beings, have developed that allow us to have accurate beliefs about this space of reasons that floats free of the merely natural space of causes. It is difficult to see how he could answer this question short of espousing a full-blown Platonism, which we know he rejects. Fortunately, there is an obvious alternative to the realism endorsed by McDowell and Nagel that accords with the emphasis we have argued Nietzsche puts on the connection between value and reasons, namely, to suppose that Nietzsche would endorse a non-cognitivist account of taking something to be a reason. To take something to be of (non-prudential) value, on the view we are attributing to Nietzsche, is to take it that there are reasons (i.e., it is rational) to feel and act towards it in certain ways. On a non-cognitivist account of the type offered by Alan Gibbard, such claims about reasons are to be understood as expressing a non-cognitive mental state. "To say that X is rational is not to ascribe a property to X, to utter a truth-conditional statement about X; rather, it is to *express acceptance* of a system of norms which permits X" (Miller 2004: 96). So the emphasis we take Nietzsche to place on the connection between values and reasons is perfectly consistent with taking him to hold that when we make claims about reasons (and so about values) we are not expressing beliefs; rather, we are expressing a commitment to a system of norms that sanctions some set of reactions and actions.

We do find some evidence that points to a non-cognitivist account of reason-giving in GS 1. In particular, Nietzsche says about the activity of reason-giving that a drive "erupts from time to time as reason and passion of mind; it is then surrounded by a resplendent retinue of reasons and tries with all its might to make us forget that fundamentally it is drive, instinct, stupidity, lack of reasons" (GS 1). Initially this might appear to be just another aspect of the passage that debunks reason-giving. In advocating reason-giving, the "teachers of the value of existence" evidently teach human beings to offer what they take to be a reason or justification for seeking what is already the object of a drive they have. So drives do all the work; reasons seem epiphenomenal at best. However, as we have already argued, Nietzsche's view cannot involve a debunking of reasons, given the contempt he expresses in the very next section of GS towards those who do not "consider it contemptible to believe this or that and to live accordingly without first having given themselves an account of the most certain reasons pro and con, and without even troubling themselves about such reasons afterwards" (GS 2). Nietzsche is certainly claiming that in instituting practices of reason-giving, the "teachers of the value of existence" teach human beings to offer what they take to be a reason or justification for seeking what is already the object of a drive they have. Love of life is already there, as "drive, instinct, stupidity, lack of reasons." But if Nietzsche's emphasis on this point is not meant to debunk reasons, as we have argued, the obvious alternative is that it is meant to deny a cognitivist account of what it is to take something to be a reason. His claim is that when a person takes something to be a reason, a drive is erupting "as reason and passion of mind," thereby surrounding itself "with a resplendent retinue of reasons" and attempting to make us forget its affective nature (GS 1). It is difficult to see what this could mean if it is not that taking oneself to have a reason is not a matter of representing the world in a certain way, of claiming to be in touch with something beyond the natural world, even a space of reasons, but is instead, at least first and foremost, an expression of some aspect of the person's affective nature, in Nietzsche's language, of the drives or instincts. It is the manifestation in consciousness or language of the activity of such drives. Nietzsche's suggestion in GS 1 that drives underlie reason-giving can thus be read as debunking not the practice of reason-giving, but the cognitivist understanding of that practice as expressing, first and foremost, beliefs or representations of the world.

This non-cognitivist reading fits well with what we said above about Nietzsche's views concerning the role of the artist in value creation (GS 299, e.g.). If value claims are expressions of commitments, then value creation (in the descriptive sense) will require the ability to modify people's dispositions to feel and to act—an ability found in artists. Now, for a claim to express a commitment and not just a preference—i.e., for the claim to be about what is valuable—it must express a disposition the person regards as justified, as supported by reasons. The non-cognitivist reading helps make clear how philosophers might learn from artists not just how to change dispositions, but also how to induce people to take themselves to have reason to feel and act in accord with a disposition. The key here is to see that to be a valuer in a descriptive sense, one need only to regard oneself as justified, one need not have considered the "reasons pro and con" concerning the disposition in question. If the latter were a requirement, having an intellectual conscience would be a requirement for being a valuer *at all*. Nietzsche's claims about the rarity of intellectual conscience and his claim about the advent of values in religious and moral hucksterism shows that he must deny this. Intellectual conscience, Nietzsche thinks, is something that most valuers *lack*: he regards being *thoughtful* about the "thinking" component of values as a goal or ideal, not a necessary condition.

What, then, *is* involved in taking a disposition to be justified, supported by reasons? It involves the feeling of acting in accord with one's "conscience," as described in GS 335. The one who takes herself to act in accord with *values* and not just desires "listens" to her conscience when she judges "This is right." It is this (largely inchoate) feeling of being justified that is the key to having a value (in the descriptive sense)—as opposed to a mere set of desires or dispositions. Now, in GS 335, Nietzsche tells us that the judgment " 'This is right' has a prehistory in your drives." This fits nicely with what he says about the role of the drives in GS 1, which we used above as evidence for Nietzsche's non-cognitivism: i.e., that when a person takes herself to have a reason, a drive is surrounding itself "with a resplendent retinue of reasons." It is important that what the drive surrounds itself with allow the person to feel justified; thus, the *resplendence* of this finery is as important as its being composed of *reasons*.

5. Normative Objectivity

Nietzsche's new philosophers would no doubt suffer the same fate as the poets in Plato's republic. And one need not be a Platonist to wonder whether there is something underhanded about Nietzsche's proposal. If philosophers are to promote values, we expect them to offer arguments—we don't expect philosophy to have a direct effect on our affects, much less for a philosopher to *seek* this effect. This puts the issue with which this essay is concerned, that of the objectivity of values, in a new light. Recall that Leiter asks whether Nietzsche is "doing anything more than giving his idiosyncratic opinion from his idiosyncratic evaluative perspective. . . . Is there, in short, anything about Nietzsche's evaluation of morality that ought to command *our* attention and assent?" (Leiter 2002: 137). On the account we've given, Nietzsche does more than "offer" his evaluations—insofar as he seeks to create values, he attempts to *change* people's affects, *without necessarily letting them know what he is doing*. Who does Nietzsche think he is? What gives him to the right to promote his values by trying to change people's affects, while (at least sometimes) intentionally concealing this fact? How can he do this in good conscience? Moreover, does Nietzsche even see that there is an issue to be confronted here?

Nietzsche's description of this task in BGE 211 only sharpens the challenge; he tells us that *"True* [eigentlichen] *philosophers. . . are commanders and law givers:* they say "thus it *shall* be!," it is they who determine the Wherefore and Whither of mankind. . . they reach for the future with creative hand, and everything that is or has been becomes for them a means, an instrument, a hammer" (BGE 211). We take the value creation with which Nietzsche is concerned in this passage to be of the descriptive variety distinguished in our previous section; it is a matter of inducing people through various non-philosophical (and certainly non-argumentative) means to adopt certain values, thus to make certain commitments. In particular, it seems that the task of Nietzsche's new philosophers is the same as that of the old-style contemplatives. What he wants from these philosophers is what he himself starts to provide—an interpretation of ethical practices, practices of judging and acting, which reconceives their value[11]—and one that they hope will influence other people in a way that, at least sometimes, bypasses their rational faculties. But what gives philosophers the right to create values in this way?

If Nietzsche were a cognitivist and realist, he might have the makings of a response; the value creation he advocates could be seen as belonging to the Platonic tradition of noble lying, a matter of bringing people who lack the intellectual power to do it on their own to make the correct judgments regarding the ontologically objective value properties of things—even if they do not do so for the right reasons. But what can a non-cognitivist and anti-realist say in his defense? In this section, we will argue that Nietzsche has a plausible response to this challenge; in fact, we find in his later works a conception of objectivity that is meant precisely to show how philosophers can be justified in creating values. This begins to become apparent when we see that Nietzsche links objectivity to *justice*. In HA, Nietzsche denied the possibility of objectivity in ethics in part because he insists that making ethical evaluations is always unjust (HA 32–3). In his later works, he comes to endorse the possibility of objectivity in ethics precisely because he thinks value claims can express commitments taken up *justly*. It is, we'll argue, Nietzsche's commitment to justice that makes him a philosopher and not simply an artist: his intellectual conscience requires him to seek to become "aware of the most certain reasons pro and con" when he engages in value creation. His having done so makes him justified in thinking that what he values is valuable "objectively," i.e., "independent of contingent feelings and inclinations or contingent beliefs about value" that he happens to have (Reginster 2006: 89).

The link we suggest between objectivity and justice in Nietzsche's thought may seem implausible, given his well-known assertion that "objectivity and justice have nothing to do with each other" (*UO* "History": 6). But this appears in an early essay (1874) in which Nietzsche was still operating under the influence of Schopenhauer's idea of objectivity. Following Schopenhauer, Nietzsche took objectivity to be a matter of aesthetic contemplation, and therefore to have nothing to do with the active judging he associated with justice. But this Schopenhauerian conception of objectivity is precisely what Nietzsche rejects in his defense of perspectivism in GM III: 12.

---

[11] A major point here is that the old-style "contemplatives" offered ascetic interpretations of the value of such ethical practices, whereas Nietzschean philosophers will offer non-ascetic interpretations, ones that do not devalue the natural world. See the end of Clark (1998) for a brief account of what this amounts to.

Denouncing Schopenhauer's conception, Nietzsche claims that one should think of objectivity

> not as "disinterested contemplation" (which is a non-concept and an absurdity), but rather as the capacity to have one's pro and contra *in one's power* and to shift them in and out, so that one knows how to make precisely the difference in perspectives and affective interpretations useful for knowledge.... There is only a perspectival seeing, only a perspectival "knowing"; and the more affects we allow to speak about a matter, the more eyes, different eyes, we know how to bring to bear on the same matter, the more complete will our concept of this matter, our "objectivity" be. (GM III: 12)

Nietzsche was originally drawn to the contemplative or "mirror" conception of objectivity, presumably, because an "interested" perspective would seem to make one's view of an object reflect the peculiarities of one's own subjectivity rather than revealing the object's own features, its "objective" features. Some still take Nietzsche's defense of the perspectival character of knowledge as designed to deny that knowledge can ever be objective. But this is clearly what the passage rejects. Nietzsche denies that the affects that constitute perspectives keep us from grasping the objective features of things; instead they serve as our very access to these features (objective properties or facts). To try to free intellect from affect, Nietzsche goes on to suggest, is to "castrate the intellect." So it would seem that Reginster is correct that for Nietzsche perspectives are "conditions of possibility, rather than limitations" (Reginster 2006: 84). But this doesn't seem quite right either. In fact, while an interest or affect gives the intellect the only access it has to the objective features of things, by focusing the intellect's attention on them and pushing it to register them as important, the affect also limits the intellect to what can be known from the particular perspective that it constitutes. Affects light up certain features of the matter under consideration by hiding others from view. Nietzsche's new conception of objectivity is designed to address this problem. If the perspectives that give us our only access to the objective features of things also hide some of these features from view, the solution is not to try to avoid the influence of affect, but to bring different affective perspectives to bear on the matter. This is his recipe for increasing our "concept of the matter, our 'objectivity' "—our grasp of the objective features of the matter.

Nietzsche's focus in this passage is clearly on knowing rather than valuing. He exhorts us not to be ungrateful, "particularly as knowers," to traditional philosophy's penchant for reversing "familiar perspectives and valuations" because it constitutes training for the intellect's "future 'objectivity,' " which is a matter of being able to bring different perspectives to bear on a matter in the service of knowledge. But his use of the phrase "particularly as knowers" raises the question of what other role Nietzsche's philosophers are to assume in which they might need the training provided by traditional philosophy's reversal of familiar perspectives and valuations. What about in their role as creators of values? We will argue that Nietzsche does consider the conception of objectivity defended in the passage we have been interpreting to be relevant to this task.

We begin by noting that GM III: 12 is clearly meant as a response to HA's conception of objectivity, one that (as we saw above) does have implications for valuations. As we saw in section 2, HA advocated

a simpler and emotionally purer life [in which] the old motives of violent desire . . . would gradually grow weaker under the influence of purifying knowledge. In the end one would live among human beings and with oneself as in *nature*, without praising, blaming, contending, gazing contentedly, as though at a spectacle, upon many things for which one formerly felt only fear.   (HA 34)

And indeed, although he did not use the metaphor then, it was precisely the *perspectival* character of valuing (e.g., "praising, blaming," etc.) that led the Nietzsche of HA to insist that all valuation is unjust. That is, Nietzsche saw valuation as unjust because he took it to be rooted in affects—in inclinations and aversions—and so to be based on a partial view of things. Now, GM's perspectivism certainly affirms HA's understanding of valuation as rooted in affects and so as partial—why, then should we think that GM would not conclude that valuation cannot be objective and, so, is unjust? Doesn't affirming the "inescapability of contingent perspectives" deny Nietzsche (or anyone else) "a point of view from which he could establish the objective standing of any value" (Reginster 2006: 83)?

To see how GM modifies HA's position on the objectivity of values, it's helpful to consider the (1886) preface to HA. Echoing GM III: 12, Nietzsche here tells us how the affects can be harnessed and used so as to make one's perspective more comprehensive, and so, more objective. But this time he is writing of values rather than knowledge. The context for the passage we quote is Nietzsche's question why the "free spirit" must turn against his earlier values and virtues (as Nietzsche himself turned against the values and virtues of *The Birth of Tragedy* in *Human, All-Too-Human*). The answer he tells us the free spirit hears is the following:

You must become master of yourself and master of your own virtues as well. Previously, they were your masters; but they should simply be tools among your other tools. You must acquire power over your For and Against and learn how to take them out and hang them back up according to your higher aim. You must learn how to grasp the perspectival element in every valuation—the displacement, the distortion, and seeming teleology of horizons and everything else that pertains to perspectivism; and also how much stupidity there is in opposed values and the whole intellectual loss that must be paid for every For and Against. You must learn to grasp the *necessary* injustice in every For and Against; injustice as inseparable from life, life itself as conditioned by perspective and its injustice. Above all, you must see with your own eyes where injustice is always the greatest: namely, where life has developed in the smallest, narrowest, neediest, most preliminary ways and yet still cannot avoid taking *itself* as the purpose and measure of things, and, out of love for its own preservation, secretly and meanly and ceaselessly crumbling away and putting into question all that is higher, greater, richer—you must see with your own eyes the problem of establishing *rank ordering* and how power and right and comprehensiveness of perspective grow up into the heights together.   (HA P: 6)

This passage provides the link between Nietzsche's understanding of the possibility of ethical objectivity in HA and GM. In both books he holds that valuations are made from perspectives constituted by affects. Unlike HA and like the later (1886) preface to HA, however, GM holds that this fact does not imply the impossibility of objectivity; it holds, rather, that one is *more* just—and so more objective—to the extent that one's value judgments express commitments that are taken up when one has seen things from different perspectives.

We can see Nietzsche developing the connection between objectivity and justice in GM's discussion of Dühring's conception of justice. Nietzsche rejects Dühring's proposition that "the homeland of justice is to be sought on the ground of reactive feeling," in particular, of resentment at being injured, claiming that the reverse is actually the case, that

the *last ground* to be conquered by the spirit of justice is that of the reactive feelings! If it really happens that the just man remains just even towards those who injure him (and not merely cold, moderate, distant: being just is always a positive way of behaving), if the high, clear objectivity—that sees as deeply as it does generously—of the just eye, the *judging* eye, does not cloud even under the assault of personal injury, derision, accusation, well, that is a piece of perfection and highest mastery on earth.

On Nietzsche's view, then, justice is

in the long run the opposite of what all revenge wants, which sees only the viewpoint of the injured one, allows only it to count—from now on, the eye is trained for an ever *more impersonal* appraisal of deeds, even the eye of the injured one himself (although this last of all, as was mentioned at the start).   (GM II, 11)

In this context, the just person is one who no longer evaluates actions from the narrowly personal perspective to which we are all at least initially inclined, but appraises it from a general perspective, one that sounds like Hume's "common point of view." Training in "*impersonal* appraisal of deeds" is thus the beginning of objectivity.

Nietzsche regards the training in objectivity that begins in the sphere of social justice as something that is carried to a much higher level in philosophical training, and seeing this is crucial as a response to the challenge with which we began this section. BGE 211 tells us that as "preconditions" for the task of creating values, thus of being "*commanders and law givers*," the education of a philosopher requires that

he has had perhaps to be a critic and a skeptic and a dogmatist and a historian and, moreover, a poet and a collector and a traveler and guesser of riddles and moralist and seer and "free spirit" and practically everything, in order to run through the range of human values and value feelings and *be able* to gaze with many eyes and consciences from the heights into every distance, from the depths up to every height, from the corner onto every expanse.   (BGE 211)

The "preconditions" for creating values, then, are the different stages of the process whereby the philosopher actually inhabits quite opposed perspectives, e.g., those of the dogmatist, the skeptic, and the critical philosopher, because precisely this is necessary to "run through the range of human values and value feelings" and "consciences" that have stood the test of serious philosophical examination. Although it may not be clear which and how many different perspectives Nietzsche's ideal philosopher would have to inhabit or take seriously to engage in this process, it does seem clear that Nietzsche regards the process as essential for anyone to be worthy of the task of creating values. BGE 219 connects this process to justice; after describing what is in effect the same process described in the quotation above, it tells us that the "lofty spirituality" of the one who is "empowered to maintain the *order of rank* in the world" (i.e., the philosopher who has a right to create values) is the "spiritualization of justice." Such "spiritualization" is a matter of bringing to bear on the appraisal of value systems one's training in the "impersonal appraisal of deeds," which was gained in the sphere of social justice, even to the point of turning that training against one's own favored system.

Our interpretation has the surprising consequence that Nietzsche's understanding of objectivity is similar to the one that has been attributed to Thomas Nagel. Nagel's conception of the objective point of view has been described as the viewpoint at which one arrives—or at least that one successively approximates—as one detaches oneself from one's own personal perspective and takes up an impersonal one. Now if this impersonal perspective were a matter of contemplating the world "without interest," Nietzsche would certainly deny that anything would be recognized as valuable from it. Nagel seems to agree, for he claims that "when we take up the objective standpoint, the problem is not that values seem to disappear but that there seem to be too many of them, coming from every life and drowning out those that arise from our own" (Nagel 1989: 147).

This conception of "the objective standpoint" seems close to the conception of objectivity we found in GM. As Sigrún Svavarsdóttir (2001) explains it, to occupy Nagel's impersonal viewpoint, we have to be able to see our own viewpoint as just one perspective among others. However, the point is not merely to realize that we could value other things than we actually do, but to come to "appreciate this 'from the inside,'" to "appreciate *what it is like* to see value in all sorts of activities and qualities we would not count among our values." For Nietzsche, we can put slightly differently what it is to appreciate other value perspectives "from the inside": it is to bring into focus the features of objects that give rise to affective responses that involve or lead to a different appraisal of them than one's own. To the extent one does this, one is more objective in holding the values that one does. For both Nagel and Nietzsche, then, to appreciate other value perspectives "from the inside" is to understand what they take to be *reasons* for that judgment. To do so is not simply to take note of them; it is to think and feel what it is like to consider the reasons in question *as reasons*. Having done so, she will have become "aware of the most certain reasons pro and con" for her own values, and will thus be able to affirm them in good "intellectual conscience" (GS 2; GS 335).

This comparison with Nagel may seem once again to place us in danger of committing Nietzsche to a version of cognitivism. In fact, however, there may be reasons to think that it is Nagel's cognitivism that the comparison renders dubious. Svavarsdóttir tells us that

Nagel's claim that there are objective values should not be understood as the claim that we there are evaluative properties that are objectively understandable or whose instantiations will be recognized from the objective standpoint. Rather, it should be understood as the claim that we will continue to value certain things—that is, have values—after going though the process of detachment. These would be the attitudes of valuing that all rational evaluators could share and are approximately described as objective: "It is beliefs *and attitudes* that are objective in the primary sense" (*Nowhere*, 4; italics mine). It is only in a derivative sense that we speak of their objects as objective values. (Svavarsdóttir 2001: 167)

The sentence that Svavarsdóttir quotes from Nagel's *The View from Nowhere* nicely captures what is at issue for the non-cognitivist Nietzsche in discussions of objectivity: if value claims are to be understood as expressions of commitments—i.e., of dispositions to act and react which one regards as justified—then the question of the objectivity of values is ultimately a question about those commitments. Whether some values are objective, then, will have to do not with the relationship between claims and things in the world that they purport to represent, but with the relationship of the person to her commitments.

To put the point differently, to ask whether a person's values are objective is to ask about the norms according to which the person has decided what norms to commit herself to. Alan Gibbard's model of objectivity provides a plausible model on which to understand Nietzsche's view. According to Gibbard,

A person who treats his normative judgments as objective has an epistemic story, and the story cannot center on him; it cannot treat him specially, just as himself and for no other reason. Or, more likely, the person acts as if there were such a story, even if he cannot find it. An eligible story will say what constitutes good conditions for judgment, and anyone in those conditions will count as a good judge. (Gibbard 1990: 181–2)

The "epistemic story" in question here is, of course, a normative one: it expresses one's commitment to a set of higher-order norms for making normative judgments and attempts to show that the person's normative judgments meet them. To judge a person's normative judgments to be objective is to express one's commitment to the higher-order norms inherent in the story and to judge that that person's judgments met them.

This is how Nietzsche is able to avoid normative subjectivism, the view that the value of things depends on the particular feelings and inclinations persons happen to have toward them. On the view we attribute to him, to say that a judgment is objective—determined by the weight of reasons rather than by something idiosyncratic to the person—is to express one's commitment to certain norms for good judging and one's belief that the person making the judgment satisfies them. In his perspectivism, Nietzsche puts forward an "epistemic story" which offers such norms for good judging. On this view, objectivity is a matter of degree: a person's value judgments are more or less objective to the extent that they reflect a process in which she has taken up and inhabited evaluative perspectives other than her own.

But there is no guarantee that objectivity will lead inexorably to convergence of opinion—i.e., no reason to think that there is one set of values that even ideal judges will agree on. It's helpful to contrast ethics with science here, since objectivity in science *does* guarantee convergence in opinion, at least ideally. Nietzsche would, on our reading, agree with Bernard Williams' claim that "the best explanation of the [hoped for] convergence [in science] involves the idea that the answer represents how things are." It is less clear that he would agree with Williams that "in the area of the ethical, at least at a high level of generality, there is no such coherent hope" (Williams 1985: 136). Because it is not primarily a matter of saying how things are, but of expressing a commitment to norms, Nietzsche cannot appeal to the way things are to guarantee a convergence of opinion in ethics. Yet, it is possible that the virtues required to go through the process of inhabiting many different value perspectives would lead to a convergence of opinion among the best judges, and we see no reason for denying that it is at least coherent to *hope* that it would, even if there is no guarantee.

It might be objected that, on the view we've attributed to Nietzsche, there *is* reason to deny the coherence of such a hope for convergence. For even if I have taken up alternative evaluative perspectives, I must ultimately judge what I have seen from them from the perspective of *my own commitments*, and so, according to the standards of my own values. While seeing the matter from the viewpoint of different sets of interests and affects may give me a fuller conception of the matter, I'll still have to invoke *my* values in making my eventual judgment. But if everyone who undertakes such a process of occupying different perspectives ends by judging the matter from their original perspective, how is convergence even a possibility? And that seems to raise an even more basic problem: if the process *doesn't* offer the hope of convergence among all who have taken the process to its ideal limit, why think that it increases objectivity at all?

Nietzsche has resources to respond to both challenges. To the first, he can respond that to deem incoherent the hope that the best judges will come to agree is based on a shallow understanding of the exercise in perspectivism. For it assumes that the one who seeks objectivity by inhabiting different evaluative perspectives is unchanged by this process. When Nietzsche says that a person has become "aware of the most certain reasons pro and con" he is not saying that she has simply rehearsed the considerations that she counts for and against some claim; he is saying, rather, that she has seen the matter from the perspective of affects other than her own, allowing these affects to "light up" those aspects of the situation that the perspective leads its occupants to regard as relevant. Even if she does not ultimately share the assessment of the aspects brought to the fore in the other perspective, she is at least likely to come to see them as relevant in a way she hitherto had not. Further, there is certainly no reason to think that one who has gone through the whole process would simply revert to her original perspective at the end of it. Nietzsche undoubtedly thinks of the process as an alternative to the way of "purifying" affect of its partiality that he proposed in HA. There the idea was that affects would "grow weaker under the influence of purifying knowledge" (HA 34). Although later Nietzsche is no longer interested in affects becoming weaker, it makes sense that he would think that affects are "purified"—their partiality decreased—to the extent that they are the ones that survive a process in which one has truly seen and accepted the world from the perspective of different affects.

To the second challenge, Nietzsche can respond that having inhabited different perspectives increases objectivity, even if it doesn't guarantee convergence of opinion, because it increases fairness. At the very least, allowing different affects to light up different aspects of a situation helps to ensure that one's evaluations aren't based on irrelevant considerations but on those aspects of the situation that are pertinent to the matter at hand. This response may strike us as unsatisfying: aren't questions about what is "irrelevant" or "pertinent" themselves normative ones? And if so, doesn't citing them in an explanation of what makes for objectivity beg the question against the one who challenges Nietzsche's position? Certainly, such a response begs the question against one who criticizes Nietzsche for failing to offer a value-neutral standard or perspective from which to make judgments about values. But as we saw above, this is no problem for Nietzsche: it should be no surprise that no measure of objectivity can be had from a value-neutral perspective, since he holds that *no* values show up from such a perspective. Objectivity is, for Nietzsche, a normative concept—it is among the values that he endorses. Now if someone objects to Nietzsche's conception not on the grounds that it is normative, but on the grounds that there is a better way to achieve objectivity—one other than identification with others' evaluative perspectives—then Nietzsche can and quite possibly should take it seriously. He will try to understand the reasons in favor of this alternative; he'll try to see it as do those who endorse it; and he'll reconsider his own conception of objectivity in light of what he learns. And he'll do this precisely because it is what his understanding of and commitment to objectivity requires of him.[12]

Finally, we want to suggest that it is no objection to Nietzsche's position that it is very difficult, if not impossible, to take leave of one's own evaluative perspective and to inhabit others. Nietzsche can grant this claim; in fact, he can insist on it: it is precisely this difficulty that makes the objectivity required of those who would create values such a rare quality. For Nietzsche value creation involves seeking to change others' dispositions by means other than the rational and argumentative ones of traditional philosophy. Given this understanding of his task, Nietzsche is concerned about objectivity not because he thinks he must justify his position to others, but because he must satisfy his own intellectual conscience. He can create values in good intellectual conscience only because, having inhabited many different evaluative perspectives, he deems himself to have achieved a very serious degree of objectivity.

References

BLACKBURN, S. (1999). 'Is Objective Moral Justification Possible on a Quasi-realist Foundation?' in *Inquiry* 42/2: 213–28.

_____ (2005). 'Quasi-Realism No Fictionalism', in M. E. Kalderon (ed.), *Fictionalism in Metaphysics* (Oxford: Oxford University Press), 322–38.

CLARK, M. (1990). *Nietzsche on Truth and Philosophy* (Cambridge: Cambridge University Press).

_____ (1998). 'On Knowledge, Truth and Value: Nietzsche's Debt to Schopenhauer and the Development of Empiricism', in C. Janaway (ed.), *Willing and Nothingness: Schopenhauer as Nietzsche's Educator* (Oxford: Clarendon Press).

CLARK, M. and DUDRICK, D. (2005). "The Naturalisms of *Beyond Good and Evil*" in K. Ansell Pearson (ed.), *A Companion to Nietzsche* (Oxford: Blackwell Publishing).

_____ (forthcoming). *Nietzsche's Magnificent Tension of Spirit: An Introduction to Beyond Good and Evil.*

FODOR, J. (1995). "Encounters with trees", *London Review of Books* 17 (8), 10–11.

GIBBARD, A. (1990). *Wise Choices, Apt Feelings: A Theory of Normative Judgment* (Cambridge, MA: Harvard University Press).

HUSSAIN, N. (2004). "The Return of Moral Fictionalism", *Philosophical Perspectives* 18/1: 149–87.

_____ (2007). "Honest Illusion: Valuing for Nietzsche's Free Spirits" in B. Leiter and N. Sinhababu (eds.), *Nietzsche and Morality* (Oxford: Oxford University Press).

JOYCE, R. (2001). *The Myth of Morality* (New York: Cambridge University Press).

LEITER, B. (2002). *Routledge Philosophy Guidebook to Nietzsche on Morality* (London and New York: Routledge).

MILLER, A. (2004). *An Introduction to Contemporary Metaethics* (Cambridge: Polity Press).

[12] See Blackburn (1999).

NAGEL, T. (1989). *The View from Nowhere* (Oxford: Oxford University Press).

NIETZSCHE, F. W. ([1874] 1998). 'On the Utility and Liability of History for Life', in *Unfashionable Observations*, trans. R. T. Gray (Stanford: Stanford University Press). Cited as UO.

―― ([1878] 1996). *Human, All Too Human*, trans. R. J. Hollingdale (Cambridge: Cambridge University Press). Cited as HA.

―― ([1878] 1997). *Human, All Too Human (I)*, trans. Gary Handewerk (Stanford: Stanford University Press). Cited as HA.

―― ([1882/1887] 1974). *The Gay Science*, trans. Walter Kaufmann (New York: Vintage Books). Cited as GS.

―― ([1882/1887] 2001). *The Gay Science*, trans. Josefine Nauckoff (Cambridge: Cambridge University Press). Cited as GS.

―― ([1883―85] 1982). *Thus Spoke Zarathustra*, trans. W. Kaufmann, in W. Kaufmann (ed.), *The Portable Nietzsche* (New York: Viking Penguin). Cited as Z.

―― ([1886] 2003). *Beyond Good and Evil*, trans. R. J. Hollingdale (New York: Penguin Classics). Cited as BGE.

―― ([1886] 2001). *Beyond Good and Evil*, trans. Judith Norman (Cambridge: Cambridge University Press). Cited as BGE.

―― ([1886] 1989). *Beyond Good and Evil*, trans. Walter Kaufmann (New York: Vintage). Cited as BGE

―― ([1887] 1998). *On the Genealogy of Morality*, trans. Maudemarie Clark and Alan Swenson (Indianapolis, Indiana: Hackett Publishing Company). Cited as GM.

REGINSTER, B. (2006). *The Affirmation of Life: Nietzsche on Overcoming Nihilism* (Cambridge, MA: Harvard University Press).

RICHARDSON, J. (2004). *Nietzsche's New Darwinism* (Oxford: Oxford University Press).

SPIR, A. (1877). *Denken und Wirklichkeit: Versuch einer Erneuerung der kritischen Philosophie*, 2nd edn. (Leipzig). All translations are Clark's.

SVAVARSDÓTTIR, S. (2001). 'Objective Values: Does Metaethics Rest on a Mistake?' in B. Leiter (ed.), *Objectivity in Law and Morals* (Cambridge: Cambridge University Press), 144―93.

WILLIAMS, B. (1985). *Ethics and the Limits of Philosophy* (Cambridge, MA: Harvard University Press).

9

Affect, Value, and Objectivity

Peter Poellner

1. Introduction

In this essay I want to explore four propositions about the relation between values, affectivity, and objectivity, all of which can be found in Nietzsche's thinking about the nature of value. At least two of them—(2) and (3)—are sometimes thought to be incompatible with each other. The propositions are: (1) Our fundamental mode of acquaintance with many values is through certain kinds of complex affective states, namely emotions. (2) Many values with which we are acquainted in this way are in a qualified sense objective—labelled here 'phenomenally objective'. (3) Values are *essentially* dependent on emotions and other affective states, such as hedonic bodily sensations. A world without such states would also be a world without value. Affective states therefore do not discover a realm of values capable of existing independently of them. (4) The question whether values are not only phenomenally objective, but real in a metaphysical sense, is of practical relevance only if we are committed to what Nietzsche calls the 'will to truth'. For those not subject to this 'kernel' of the 'ascetic ideal' (GM III. 27), the metaphysical status of value can rationally be a matter of indifference.

Three of these thoughts can be discovered quite unproblematically in the published writings of the later Nietzsche. The one which is not stated by him explicitly and prominently and which therefore has not received much attention in Nietzsche scholarship is proposition (2). However, I shall argue that it is entailed by a number of his reflections, and that an adequate description of the affective states through which, according to him, we encounter values, lends strong independent support to this conclusion. The arguments I shall offer for (2) are therefore proposed as rational reconstructions, outlining the contours of the kind of theory implied by Nietzsche's remarks and by his own evaluative practice. I shall be concerned not only with moral or ethical values, but with values, or value-properties, quite generally. Many values we recognize clearly are not moral values, on whatever interpretation of morality (although they may be relevant to morality)—for example, the pleasant, the beautiful, or the erotically attractive. The arguments below are intended to apply quite generally to values in this more comprehensive sense. Nietzsche characteristically also adopts this more comprehensive stance, which is what allows him to ask his distinctive question concerning 'the *value* of morality' (GM, Preface, 5). The idiom of values or value-properties in this essay should of course not be understood as begging the question in favour of a realist metaphysical construal of these properties. This terminology is merely intended to reflect the fact that the surface structure of ordinary evaluative discourse attributes value features to worldly items, whether these should ultimately be interpreted realistically, or as projections of world-independent subjective states ('sentiments'), or whatever.

The structure of the essay is as follows. Section 2 deals with some preliminary conceptual issues about evaluative properties and their relations to certain kinds of psychological attitudes, and about the ways in which these attitudes might involve a commitment to the objectivity of their contents. Section 3 will be devoted to a discussion of propositions (1) and (2) mentioned above. I shall sketch in it a view which is implied by some of Nietzsche's remarks and needed to explain them, and indeed needed to render plausible the basic Nietzschean idea of values as constituted or 'created' by 'affects'. According to this view the relation between affect, value, and objectivity can only be adequately understood by grasping the *essential interdependence of the nature of value and the nature of certain kinds of affective states*—perceptual emotions—in which evaluative properties are presented as qualifying the everyday objects of our life-world. Sections 4 and 5 will be devoted to a discussion and defence of, respectively, propositions (3) and (4) above, both of which I interpret Nietzsche as being committed to. The complex Nietzschean view that will emerge from the essay is one which insists that we need to distinguish, when we ask whether 'there are values in the world', between three different questions that are gestured towards by this formulation. The originality and novelty of Nietzsche's position consists in the combination of answers he gives to these questions. Its considerable contemporary relevance lies in promising an attractive way of doing justice to what is right about the apparently conflicting claims of *both* projectivism and anti-projectivist, non-reductionist cognitivism about value.[1]

---

[1] The two apparently conflicting positions I have in mind are represented, for example, by Blackburn's 'quasi-realism' on the projectivist side (see Blackburn, 1984: ch. 6, and the essays in his 1993); and on the anti-projectivist side by authors like Wiggins (1987), McDowell (e.g. 1978, 1981, 1985), Dancy (1993), and recently Johnston (2001).

2. Values, Attitudes, Objectivity: Some Preliminaries

Nietzsche expresses the idea that our basic mode of acquaintance with value is through 'affects' (*Affekte*) in many places. In a minimal interpretation, this point is of course implied by his general perspectivism, according to which *any* conceptualization, including any classification of items in evaluative terms, essentially involves affectivity (GM III. 12). But his more substantial point in this particular context is, I suggest, that thinking of things in evaluative terms, unlike (say) conceptualizing them as being coloured, rationally requires thinking of them *as* having a bearing on an actual or possible affectivity:

Every ideal presupposes *love* and *hatred*, *admiration* and *contempt*. Either the positive emotion is the *primum mobile* or the negative emotion. For example, in all *ressentiment* ideals *hatred* and *contempt* are the *primum mobile*. (KGW VIII.2.10.9)[2]

Evaluation is creation: hear it, you creative men! . . . The fire of love and the fire of anger glow in all the virtues . . . no greater power did Zarathustra find on earth than the works of those who love: their names are 'good' and 'evil'. (Z, 'Of the Thousand and One Goals')

. . . moralities too are only a *sign-language of the affects*. (BGE 187)

One may feel that not much is gained by such assertions in the absence of a detailed account of what 'affects' are supposed to be. Unfortunately, Nietzsche himself does not supply such an account, although some of his remarks offer important pointers which will be developed below. But he does give us several lists of 'affects' from which it transpires that he uses the term mainly, but not exclusively, to refer to what we would normally call emotions. 'Affects' in his sense include hatred, envy, and greed (BGE 23), as well as courage, shame, and anger (KGW VII.1.7.87). In the discussion that follows, I shall focus primarily on emotions, but it will be convenient to retain Nietzsche's broad usage of 'affect' for any mental episode which constitutively involves a pro- or con-attitude (or as I shall say, a favouring or disfavouring) with a distinctive phenomenology—some experience of attraction or repulsion. 'Affects' in this sense may include, for example, a feeling of shame, an occurrent *desire* for something absent, as well as a *bodily sensation* experienced unqualifiedly as painful or pleasant.

If we interpret, as I suggest, Nietzsche's remark that 'every ideal presupposes' love or hatred, admiration or contempt (or other emotions and affects) as the point that our most basic acquaintance with values is through affective states, and in many cases through emotions, then this opens the way to a possible reconciliation of two claims about value judgements both of which have strong credentials, while yet appearing irreconcilable to many. The first of these claims emphasizes the *necessarily*

---

[2] Translations from Nietzsche's writings are my own.

commendatory or *commitment-involving* character of value judgements. Sincerely to make an assertoric utterance with the grammatical structure of a categorical value judgement about an object involves, minimally, a commitment to an attitude of favouring or disfavouring towards some features of the judgement's object. This is surely the central truth captured by traditional expressivism. '(Dis)favouring' here designates a determinable property of mental states, some of whose determinates are (dis)liking, being attracted to, being repelled by, loving, hating, (dis)approving, being motivated to act in promotion of, wanting to see more (less) of, and so forth. What these attitudes involve can be *explicated*— I shall attempt to explicate some of them below—but, analogously to semantic properties, they are 'autonomous' in the sense of not being susceptible to analysis or definition without the use of expressions for other attitudes from the same range.

The core expressivist claim needs to be distinguished from various more ambitious ideas associated with 'moral internalism'. It does not mean, for one thing, that to accept a moral judgement is *ipso facto* to be *motivated to act* in accordance with it. As externalists have persuasively argued, this is not necessarily so.[3] The expressivist, in response to these arguments, should first draw a distinction between different kinds of prima facie evaluative concepts. There are, to begin with, *prescriptive* concepts, often expressed by terms like 'ought', 'should', or 'must'. Then there are evaluative concepts proper or verdictive concepts.[4] These include highly general, 'thin', or determinable concepts like *good, bad, excellent, beautiful,* or indeed *valuable.* They also include substantial (or determinate) evaluative concepts which are often expressed by terms some of which may occasionally also be used without an evaluative sense-component, like 'brave', 'generous', or 'elegant'. The expressivist's general point is that, however we construe prescriptive concepts, the use of properly evaluative (verdictive) concepts in categorical value judgements commits the subject to a (dis)favourable attitude towards some feature of its object. Such an attitude may be both dispositional and compatible with the absence of a corresponding motivational (appetitive or conative) state. Nevertheless, sincerely to call something 'good' or 'beautiful' is to regard some feature of it as meriting favour, and to regard it in this way *is* to favour it to some degree and in some respect.

---

[3] See e.g. Brink (1989), 45 f.; Shafer-Landau (2003), 185 f.; also van Roojen (2002: 42–7).

[4] On this distinction, see Mulligan (1998: 164–6). Mulligan argues, and Nietzsche, like many others, concurs (see n. 49), that evaluative concepts are more fundamental than, and supply the necessary justificatory basis for, prescriptive concepts. A world in which nothing is considered valuable, good, or worthwhile is one in which prescriptive concepts like 'ought' lose their sense. But there may well be values the recognition of which does not entail the applicability of any corresponding prescriptive concepts to finite agents in their actual circumstances. As Scheler remarks, it is not remotely clear what prescriptions might apply, say, to a solitary finite agent in his actual world as a consequence of his sharing Kant's awe at the aesthetic sublimity of the starry heavens above him (Scheler 1973: ch. 4.2).

A second claim often made about evaluation, which is often thought incompatible with the one just discussed, is that many of the contents of ordinary evaluative judgements and experiences appear as *objective*. What fundamentally motivates this claim is the recognition that evaluative commitments, in order to be even minimally intelligible, must be guided or constrained in some way. If Nietzsche's talk about 'affects' as 'creating values' (e.g. Z, 'Of the Thousand and One Goals') were to be read as the idea that affectivity is an entirely unconstrained, 'decisionist' plumping for one thing rather than another, his position would not only be unfaithful to most actual evaluative experience, but would also render the very concept of choice inapplicable to evaluative commitments at the fundamental level, since the possibility of choice presupposes criteria guiding it.[5] The incontestable core of the idea that there must be *some* kind of objectivity in play in evaluative commitments is just this: something must guide commitment and thus, in a very broad sense, rationalize it or make it intelligible to the agent herself, and potentially to others.

Among the philosophical interpretations of this minimal objective component in evaluation, one that is unequivocally rejected by Nietzsche is the putatively Kantian thought that the justification of ethical considerations should be independent of any contingent inclinations that we or any other affective beings might have.[6] But what are the alternatives? Nietzsche says: 'I have a "taste"..., but no reasons, no logic, no imperative for this taste'.[7] If we interpret 'taste' here as meaning a pattern of conscious affectivity, then the implication clearly is that, once liberated from philosophical and religious errors, we find that the 'affects' themselves provide the normative basis of evaluative commitment. There are two ways in which they might be thought to be able to accomplish that. The first identifies the relevant normative control, in this respect rather like Kant, with the experience of *obligation*. The idea is that some 'sentiments', those which happen to be most deeply lodged in one's individual psychology, produce in certain circumstances a higher-order, reflective, constraint in the shape of a sense of obligation, pulling *against* and capable of overriding some of one's actual or possible lower-order affects, desires, or intentions (e.g. 'I just couldn't live with myself if I cheated on my wife').[8] But those most deeply entrenched sentiments ultimately grounding the discipline are envisaged as being in principle characterizable at the personal level without reference to their 'objects' (the wife, in

---

[5] On a classical criticism of decisionist or 'radical choice' construals of evaluation, see Taylor (1982). For a detailed textual defence of an anti-decisionist interpretation of Nietzsche's talk of creating value, see Guay (2002).

[6] For one version of this Kantian approach, see Nagel (1970). Nietzsche's view of Kantianism in morals can be gleaned especially from BGE 187 and GM II. 6.

[7] Letter to Heinrich Köselitz (Peter Gast), 19 November 1886 (KGB III.2, p. 284). Cf. GS 39 and Z, 'Of the Sublime Men'.

[8] For this approach, see Blackburn (1981: esp. 175–8), and (1985: esp. 8).

the above example). Since they are Humean, i.e. logically distinct, *effects* of the object or of one's relation to it, they are not, in their intrinsic character, object-involving—the very same sentiment could in principle be caused by and directed at objects that are not represented by the agent as having any relevant features in common (other than their contingently causing the same sentiment). While Nietzsche in his writings of the middle period is drawn to something like this view (see HAH 133), this is not, as we shall see, his mature position on the nature of affectivity. His later view therefore avoids the difficulties which this type of theory has never been able satisfactorily to address, most importantly, its misdescription of most evaluative experience and its correlative inability to give a satisfactory account of what distinguishes a normal, reflective, and reasonably self-transparent subject's affective experience from that of a self-alienated subject experiencing her *de facto* most deeply entrenched emotional responses as a system of rationally unintelligible but irrepressible conditioned quasi-reflexes, or as compulsive (see 3.iv below).[9]

In his later writings Nietzsche sometimes suggests a different way of understanding the normative component of affectivity. In a number of passages he implies that the most fundamental phenomenon in ordinary evaluative experience which motivates talk of the objectivity of (some) values is not the force of *obligation*, but is rather itself a feature of our first-order affects themselves. We often experience an object, person, or action that we value (or disvalue) as exerting a certain affective pull, an attraction (or repulsion), on us which seems non-contingently connected with the way the object (etc.) itself is. Our affective response in these cases is itself experienced as not merely contingently *caused*, but as *merited* by the object's intrinsic character. To say that it is experienced as merited and not merely as caused is to say that its specification constitutively requires reference to the object—it is experienced as the appropriate or right response to some feature of the object, *as* a registering of the object's nature. For example, people often experience their love for the character of a person, or their aesthetic admiration for a work of art, to be merited by—to be itself an appropriate recognition of—the nature of their object. The idea that what people take themselves to be responding to in such cases is an objective feature, a property

---

[9] To respond to this problem by insisting that the normal subject, unlike the compulsive or self-alienated subject, *identifies* with her strongest sentiments is not to solve it but merely to re-describe it. The question that needs to be answered is what resources for 'identification' a rational and normally self-transparent subject can have if she, on reflection, needs to regard her most deeply lodged sentiments as essentially not revealing anything about the world, but as analogous to non-representational and sociologically fortuitous conditioned reflexes. It is hard to see where such resources might come from, if she is a projectivist of this type, without requiring her simply *not to reflect* in her evaluative practice on the adventitious nature and aetiology of her sentiments, thereby instituting a habitual division between her self-qua-theoretician and her self-qua-agent. Whatever else one might say about the questionable desirability of such a self-division, it clearly amounts to a type of habitualized bad faith.

of the object, should be understood in an everyday, metaphysically undemanding sense. What is objective in this sense is what is standardly presented as pertaining to the (everyday, phenomenal) object, just as the visible, phenomenal colour of a table appears as a property of the table itself, and not, for example, as a property of an 'inner sensation'. An item is objective, rather than subjective, in this sense (which I shall label *phenomenal objectivity*) just in case its existence and nature is not exhausted by any particular experiential state which purports to represent it, and it is available for various numerically distinct experiences of it by oneself and others—ready to be experienced, as it were.[10] If an item is objective in this way, then it can intelligibly be said to be a possible object of perceptual representations that can be veridical or illusory, and of judgements based on these which can be true or false. However, the claim that an item is phenomenally objective neither prejudges nor replaces the metaphysical issue of whether it belongs to the ultimate furniture of the universe. Colours as we perceive them, unlike sensations, are features of the objects populating our life-world—the phenomenal world, if one can use this idiom in a sense somewhat different from Kant's[11]—but they may not be part of the world as it is in itself. I shall return to the *metaphysical* issue concerning values in the final two Sections of this essay.

But the view I have just outlined and attributed to the later Nietzsche leaves us with a familiar problem. If we say that the properties which are experienced as being such as to merit a particular sort of attitudinal or affective response belong to the phenomenal, everyday object (or person, or action), then this seems to commit us to a 'queer' kind of objective properties, namely irreducibly evaluative properties:[12]

---

[10] This concept of objectivity has in recent years been associated especially with the writings of John McDowell. See his (1985); also Dancy (1993: ch. 9).

[11] Do 'phenomenal objects' as understood in this essay correspond to Kant's 'phenomena' or 'appearances'? On a classical phenomenalist reading of Kant, he takes phenomena to consist of actual and possible sensory appearances (see e.g. Bennett 1966: 22). If this reading is tenable, his 'phenomena' are one possible interpretation of 'phenomenal objects' in my sense. But there is good reason to think that Kant regards what he calls phenomena as constituted exclusively by 'tertiary' properties in Locke's nomenclature, that is, by non-sensible relational properties (forces) ascribed to them by physical science (see Langton 1998: 142–57). By contrast, phenomenal objects in the sense relevant in this essay are simply objects as they appear in ordinary experience (according to the 'manifest image', in Sellars's expression). Objects are called 'phenomenal' in this sense in so far as they are considered as possessing at least some *phenomenal properties*, such as Lockean secondary properties. A phenomenal property is one that involves some qualitative what-it-is-likeness. The concept of phenomenal properties cuts across the subjective/objective distinction as employed above. A subjective state such as a pain or a tickle has certain phenomenal properties, but so has an object like a tomato (it is phenomenally red). On the widespread conflation in current talk about 'qualia' between phenomenal properties of *experiences* and phenomenal properties which *objects* appear as having, see M. G. F. Martin (1998: 157–80). See also Stroud (2000).

[12] The term is, of course, J. L. Mackie's. See his (1977: 38 f.).

F is an irreducibly *evaluative* or *value property* just in case *F* is such that, necessarily, if a subject S experiences or believes *F* to be exemplified by some *x*, this involves an attitude of favouring or disfavouring by S towards *x* in virtue of its being represented as *F*.

Objective value properties would certainly be unlike any other properties in that they would have to-be-favouredness, as it were, built into them.[13] Representing them would require a special kind of representation *intrinsically* involving a favourable or disfavourable attitude towards what it represents. Furthermore, at least some of these representations would have to be *perceptual*, since the values in question are after all supposed to be presented as objective in *experiencing* them, and the fundamental mode of experientially encountering an item as objective is through perception. It is difficult to overemphasize the importance of this point: only if there is a type of representation that intrinsically involves favour or disfavour towards what it represents can there be any plausibility at all in the idea that value properties are on occasion experienced as objective even in the qualified sense outlined above. Are there such representations? In the following Section I shall explore and defend the thesis that some *emotions* fit these requirements and can therefore be regarded as *perceptions of values*. As I noted earlier, there are some remarks in Nietzsche's later writings suggesting that he holds precisely such a view, according to which our most basic affective relation to values is analogous to 'seeing':

> Master morality *affirms* just as instinctively as Christian morality *denies* . . . These contrasting forms of the optics of value are *both* necessary: they are ways of seeing which are unaffected by reasons and refutations. One does not refute Christianity, just as one does not refute a defect of the eyes.   (CW, Epilogue)

This talk about our fundamental experiences of value being perceptual is not mere metaphor, as emerges from the following passage from *The Gay Science*:

> [The higher human being] is always haunted by a *delusion*: He fancies that he is a *spectator* and *listener*, confronted by the great visual and acoustic spectacle of life; he calls his own nature *contemplative* and overlooks that he is also the real poet who keeps creating life . . . We, the thinking-feeling beings [*die Denkend-Empfindenden*], are the ones who really continually *make* something that was not there before: the entire ever growing world of valuations, colours, accents, perspectives, scales, affirmations, and denials . . . But precisely this knowledge we lack . . .   (GS 301)

The consequences of the 'delusion' Nietzsche is diagnosing here will occupy us later (Section 4). For now, the central point is that he *explains why* the 'higher human being' prior to critical philosophical reflection tends to suffer from the 'delusion' that values reside in the world independently of appropriate subjects of experience by the fact that her relation to value pre-reflectively appears to her as perceptual.

---

[13] Cf. Mackie (1977: 40).

This explanation of the 'delusion' is conspicuously different from Nietzsche's more familiar debunking explanations of 'slave morality'. There is no indication in this passage that the illusory appearance of a strong metaphysical objectivity of values might have its *origins* in false metaphysical beliefs—for example in the belief that there is a divine lawgiver. Presumably, the 'higher human being' is not inclined towards such beliefs anyway. Nor is the source of the illusion in this case said to be a belief about oneself or one's personhood—for example that one's real or intelligible self requires subjecting oneself to certain obligations or duties whatever one's (other) desires may be. Indeed, the ultimate origin of the illusion of strong objectivity is not to be found in the essentially *reflective* idea of obligation or in some self-imposed constraint on some of one's first-order desires and action-dispositions at all. Rather, even the 'higher human being' is said to be liable to error on this issue because of the very nature of her non-reflective *world-directed* evaluative experience. This experience seems to her to be 'contemplative', and when undergoing it she seems to herself to be a 'spectator' and 'listener'—to be sensitive to features of the world. The question needing to be asked here is, clearly: what must evaluative experience be like in order to present this appearance and, as one consequence, to tempt us into ontological error?

3. Emotions as Perceptions of Values

Nietzsche's claims that (i) all evaluation at the ground level involves 'affects', including prominently emotions, and that (ii) evaluative experience strikes us pre-reflectively as perceptual, point towards a construal of (some) 'affects' as apparent perceptions of value. As I indicated earlier, one powerful independent consideration in favour of such an account is that it promises to supply what is needed to ground and to reconcile two widely held views about evaluation, both of which have strong intuitive appeal: the necessarily *commendatory* (pro-or-con attitude involving) character of sincere categorical value judgements and the element of *objectivity* involved in much evaluative thought and experience. In the present context, such a theory can of course not be developed and defended in detail. What does seem possible and necessary, however, is to suggest some conditions that a theory of the kind pointed to by Nietzsche's remarks would have to satisfy, and to give some indications of the prospects for satisfying them.[14] Bearing in mind Nietzsche's warnings about the metaphysical 'delusions' lying in wait

---

[14] Recent sympathetic sketches of the idea by Johnston (2001) and de Sousa (2002) do not specify these conditions. Nor do earlier versions of it in Husserl (1989, esp. §4) and Scheler (1973, esp. ch. 2.5). My 'perceptual emotion' (see below) corresponds to what Johnston calls 'affect' or 'affective desire'. On the terminological issue, I agree with Wedgwood (2001: 215 n.) that 'emotion' is the most appropriate label for the states in question.

here, we first need to be clear about the concept of perceptual experience in play. It can only be that which is operative in our ordinary thought about perception. According to this ordinary 'folk' concept we perceive, for example, the colour of a table, and we also perceive that a certain sound is dissonant within a particular harmonic context, or that two people are having an argument. The claim that we perceive these things, in this perfectly ordinary sense, involves no metaphysical commitments regarding the reality of secondary qualities or of meanings. Here is a list of features constitutive of this ordinary concept of perceptual experience:

(i) Perceptual experiences have representational objects; they are *about* something not identical with themselves. The term 'object' should here be understood in a broad sense, including in its extension also events and states of affairs involving particulars.

(ii) Perceptual experiences neither are nor essentially include judgements/beliefs or dispositions to judge, but their representational contents enable them rationally to motivate judgements and actions.[15]

(iii) Perceptual experiences are epistemically direct, non-inferential, representations of their objects.

(iv) Perceptual experiences involve exemplifications of phenomenal properties. There is 'something it is like' to have a perceptual experience, and most of the relevant phenomenal characteristics are representational, i.e. they are features the object appears as having.

(v) In the central cases, perceptual experiences appear caused by objects they represent. For us, at least, perception is a mode of gathering information about the world only because the world causally affects us, or at least consistently *appears* to affect us so as to produce perceptual experiences in us.[16]

(vi) Perceptual experiences are representational states whose conditions of success include veridicality (unlike, for example, fantasies or desires).

---

[15] On the first of these points, see Crane (1992); on the second, see Brewer (1999: esp. ch. 3).

[16] According to the occasionalist picture of perception, a cause other than the objects of outer sensory perception causes both these objects and our perceptions in such a way that the contents of the perceptions reliably correlate with those objects and the states of affairs they enter into. This does not seem to be a misuse of the concept of perception (cf. Dummett 1979: 35–6). Child (1994: 173) asks: if occasionalism were true, what could possibly give us reason to believe that our perceptions are ever veridical, and how could we therefore ever rationally think of ourselves as in cognitive contact with a world independent of us? Well, the most fundamental reason for this belief, whether we are occasionalists or not, is surely the fact that objects consistently and lawfully *appear* causally to affect us. There are strong reasons for thinking that this *experienced* or *apparent* causality is a necessary condition for the possibility of substantial self-consciousness, that is, for a subject's ability to distinguish between itself and a world external to it. For a reconstruction of Nietzsche's argument to this effect, see Poellner (2001: 100–6).

Are there any emotions ('affects') that can plausibly be argued to exhibit all of these features? As we shall see, Nietzsche's own evaluative practice and his treatment of *ressentiment* and slave morality in particular imply that he considers condition (vi) to be applicable to emotions. But with respect to some of the other conditions, including those presupposed by (vi)—such as (iv)—a defence of their applicability to emotions needs to go beyond what Nietzsche himself says. What is thus needed is a rational reconstruction of the essential features of the kind of perceptual theory of (some) emotions which underlies Nietzsche's practice.

(i) Many Emotions have Representational Objects

As Nietzsche recognizes throughout his writings, most of the psychological states normally classed as emotions, whether episodic or dispositional, have representational objects (e.g. HAH 57, D 279, GS 14, GM II. 16). They are essentially *about* something distinct from themselves. I can only hate or love, grieve or rejoice, admire or despise, feel proud or ashamed, if there is someone or something that these emotions are directed at. We may call these targets the *particular* objects of an emotion.[17] Particular objects may be either real or merely intentional objects; they can be fairly determinate and simple, but may also be highly complex or indeterminate. I can admire a civilization or be afraid of something indeterminate in the dark. Many so-called moods which are sometimes regarded as objectless are best construed as emotions with indeterminate, complex, or highly comprehensive objects.[18] Emotion necessarily presents its particular object under some description or, more generally, under some *aspect* (when the object is presented in sense perception, the subject of the experience may not have the descriptive resources fully to express that aspect linguistically).[19] There is broad agreement among intentionalist theorists of emotion that the relevant characteristics are *evaluative*.[20] The claim that emotions represent their objects under

[17] See Lyons (1980: ch. 6), for a classification of the objects of emotion which I shall be drawing on in what follows.

[18] Cf. Sartre (2002: 44). Also Crane (1998: 242 f.); and Marcel and Lambie (2002: 237–40).

[19] To concede that perceptual content often is richer than the descriptive resources available to the subject is not equivalent to accepting the claim that perceptual content is wholly or partly non-conceptual (*contra* Mulligan 1998: 166 f.). See e.g. Brewer (1999: ch. 5), and Poellner (2003) for a discussion of this issue.

[20] See Husserl (1989: §4); Scheler 1973: ch. 5.2); Lyons (1980: 99–104); Nussbaum (2001: ch. 1); de Sousa (2002: 251); Doering and Peacocke (2002: 92–5). This point needs to be qualified. It is only full-blown or paradigm cases of emotions that involve an explicit appraisal or evaluation of the emotion's particular object. In reflex emotions, no such evaluation may occur. Most of these are best analysed as action dispositions being triggered by perceptual stimuli in conjunction with structural traces left by *previous* evaluations of objects of the relevant type (cf. Lyons 1980: 85–9). In what follows I shall ignore such 'automatized' and truncated emotional responses.

evaluative aspects should not by itself be taken to imply that they ascribe evaluative properties to their objects (but see Section 3.iv below). By itself it means no more than that they constitutively involve considerations or appraisals of their particular objects in terms of values the subject holds or recognizes (cf. Nietzsche's observations in TI IX. 8–9). There is fairly widespread consent that most ordinary emotion concepts used in Western cultures are *individuated* in terms of the evaluative aspects under which they represent their objects.[21] Fear essentially represents some particular object (e.g. a large, barking Alsatian) as *disagreeably dangerous* to the subject. Aesthetic admiration represents its object as *beautiful* or perhaps *sublime*. Contrary to what Nietzsche sometimes seems to suggest (HAH 57 and 133, BGE 220, KGW VII.2.26.224), in giving a specification of such evaluative aspects constitutive of emotions, no reference to the self, the subject of the emotion, is required in all cases.[22] When I aesthetically admire an object, I do not figure in the intentional content of my emotion. Matters stand differently with other emotions. Fear necessarily represents an object as threatening *to oneself* or one's interests.[23]

Can emotions be construed intentionally, i.e. as having conditions of correctness or appropriateness, but without ineliminable reference to evaluative aspects under which they present their objects? According to Kevin Mulligan, emotions are appropriate, or fail to be so, to the 'purely natural [i.e. non-evaluative] properties' of an object.[24]

---

[21] Lyons (1980: 80–5); Nussbaum (2001: 64); Doering and Peacocke (2002: 93–4). The converse does not hold, however: value types are not individuated through possible emotions directed at them. There can be no question, therefore, of a one–one correspondence between values and emotions qua types. It should be stressed that I am not concerned with giving necessary and sufficient conditions for the correct use of 'the' concept of emotion. 'Emotion' is quite possibly an equivocal term for a family of distinct but partly overlapping concepts. What is important for the present argument is only that there is a widely used concept of emotion which has the essential features mentioned in the text.

[22] Among recent theorists of emotion, Martha Nussbaum is notable for her agreement with Nietzsche on this particular point (see her 2001: 30–1, 40–1, 52–3). In her case, this view is motivated by her mistaken construal of emotions as essentially *judgements* of value (see Section 3.ii below). This construal obliges her to find some distinguishing mark between emotional and 'cold' value judgements, a difference which she believes can be found in an 'ineliminable reference to the self' (p. 52) in the former. Like Nietzsche in HAH 57 and 133, Nussbaum tends to slide from the correct claim that emotions evaluate objects from the *perspective* of a self to the quite different one that their content therefore involves *reference* to the self (pp. 52–3). But while it is necessary, if I am to perceive an object, that I should look at it from some perspective taken up by myself, this does not entail that I figure in the *content* of my perception.

[23] Self-referential emotions raise special complications for a perceptual account, since the subject when in the grip of them does not normally represent herself in an objectifying manner which could plausibly be regarded as perceptual. (Cf. Sartre 2002: 42; Marcel and Lambie 2002: 223; Poellner 2003: 48–56.) A fully developed perceptual theory of (some) emotions will need to accommodate, in addition to their perceptual elements, also the non-perceptual phenomenal components of such emotion episodes.

[24] Mulligan (1998: esp. 175–7).

For example, a perceptual presentation as of a large, aggressive-looking dog moving rapidly towards me can serve as the representational basis, and thus the appropriate intentional object, of the emotion of fear.[25] But, *pace* Mulligan, no list of such non-evaluative properties involved in the content of a subject's perceptual experience, however detailed it may be, will suffice on its own to make intelligible a subject's *being afraid* of what that content represents. Someone may, for a variety of reasons, be entirely fearless and indeed emotionless in the face of large, aggressive dogs attacking him, and there is nothing irrational or unintelligible about this. It is only once we say that the subject represents the object of fear as endangering or threatening something *he values* that fear becomes intelligible or 'appropriate'. The use of value predicates is thus essential for capturing the intentional components of emotion.

(ii) Perceptual Emotions are Non-Doxastic

Occurrent emotions are mental states with representational contents capable of rationally motivating beliefs, but they are not necessarily themselves beliefs or judgements about their objects, nor are they necessarily based on such beliefs. To be sure, many emotional episodes *are* based on beliefs. A father may feel anguish owing to his belief that his son is suffering from a mortal illness. But in many other cases, the relevant state of affairs involving the particular object of the emotion is not only, or indeed not at all, an object of belief, but rather one that is being currently experienced. I shall refer to these emotions as *perceptual*.[26] Consider the character of Swann in Proust's *In Search of Lost Time*, listening with rapturous admiration to the Vinteuil sonata;[27] or any nature lover contemplating a landscape he is enthusiastic about. In all these instances, the particular object of the emotion is presented perceptually. It seems clear that perceptual emotions are, in general, more fundamental than belief-based emotions, just as sensory perceptions are more basic, in general, than beliefs about the sensory properties of objects. What crucially distinguishes perceptual emotions, just like sense perceptions, from beliefs (judgements) is that they can persist in the presence of beliefs simultaneously held by the subject and contradicting their contents.[28] Barring mental

---

[25] Mulligan (1998: 167).

[26] Perceptual emotions as defined above are emotions whose *particular* objects are presented in sense perception. It is a separate question, and the topic of the present discussion, whether such emotions may be said to be perceptual also in a second sense, that is, whether they involve perceptions of the *evaluative features* of their particular objects.

[27] Proust (2002: i. 250–2).

[28] See Goldie (2000: 74–6); Doering and Peacocke (2002: 94–5). It is this evidently passive or receptive, and thus potentially counter-rational, element of many emotions that theories such as Lyons's (1980) and Nussbaum's (2001), which construe emotions in terms of *judgements* of value, are incapable of accounting for.

division, the distraught father's *belief* about his son's fatal illness and his distress about this state of affairs cannot persist once he finds out and accepts that the belief was based on a false diagnosis and therefore groundless. But a subject's *perceptual emotions* may be impervious to beliefs she simultaneously and consciously holds, and whose contents contradict the content of the emotion. The person who fell onto a nest of bees as a boy may even as an adult tend to panic every time he sees a swarm of bees, or perhaps just sees something looking like a swarm of bees, while knowing quite well that bees are normally harmless, and perhaps even knowing that what he is seeing is actually just a swarm of flies.[29] The general point here is also made by Nietzsche when he remarks that the affective modes of experience underlying moralities are 'ways of seeing which are unaffected by reasons and refutations' (CW, Epilogue). It is true that emotional illusions are normally less immune to conflicting beliefs than ordinary perceptual illusions (such as the Müller–Lyer illusion), and this partial disanalogy is what makes something like an *education sentimentale* feasible. But the mere *possibility* of emotional illusions is sufficient to show the difference of perceptual emotions from beliefs/judgements.

Like other contents of perception, the representational contents of perceptual emotions can, when taken at face value, directly (non-inferentially) *justify* judgements and actions. —My feeling of being pleasantly attracted to a person on account of her likeable manner in conversation with me can justify my judgement that she *is* likeable (by my standards, at least), and also my seeking her company.

(iii) Perceptual Emotions are Epistemically Direct Representations

There is in ordinary, successful sense perception no intermediary between the perceiver and the object that is both experiential and epistemic (reason-giving). Sensory perception therefore constitutes in this sense a direct, non-inferential, relation between the subject and the object (if there is one). To say that there is no *epistemic* intermediary between the perceiver and the object is of course compatible with recognizing that there are *causal* intermediaries between them, such as impacts of refracted light on the retina, electrical impulses in the optical nerves, and so forth.

Do perceptual emotions relate us to their objects in a similarly direct fashion? With respect to their *particular* objects, this follows from having narrowed the class of emotional states we are considering to those whose particular objects are presented in ordinary sense perception. But what about the *evaluative* aspects under which those objects are represented in emotion? In many perceptual emotions, the relevant evaluative properties clearly are presented directly, irrespective of whether they are best interpreted as 'subjective' or as 'in the object'. In disgust, say, an object is often directly apprehended as disgusting without one's being aware of anything figuring

---

[29] The example is from Drummond (2004: 109–10).

as a sign, symptom, or likeness of that property, from which the presence of an instance of the property itself would have to be consciously inferred. The point is implied in Nietzsche's observation, cited above, that morality-generating affective 'ways of seeing' and what they reveal are *prior* to inferential 'reasons and refutations' concerning what is thus 'seen'. This claim encounters prima facie difficulties in the case of emotions where the relevant evaluative aspects of the object are associated with, or perhaps identical with, psychological properties. In contempt for a person's *ressentiment*, or in gratitude for someone's generosity, are we directly aware of the relevant exemplifications of value?

In order to meet the directness condition in these cases, a view of intersubjectivity, associated with both classical phenomenology and Wittgenstein, recommends itself which insists that we can be said, in favourable circumstances, to perceive others' psychological states through their expressive behaviour, although those states are not simply identical with the behaviour. According to this view, when I see someone stamping his feet, shouting at a colleague, etc., I do not need to *simulate* his anger in order to understand his psychological state, nor do I need to *infer* that he is angry from signs contingently associated with his psychological state; rather I can be said to *see his anger*.[30] This would entail that the relation between a conscious psychological state and its behavioural expression is closer than the contingent and extrinsic correlation between a 'Humean' cause and its effect. If some such theory of the basis of our 'knowledge of other minds' can be vindicated, then there is no reason why the evaluatively relevant properties of another person's psychological states should not also in principle be directly perceived in this way when we respond to those states emotionally.

(iv) Perceptual Emotions Represent Phenomenal Properties of Objects

When I perceive a sharp, pointed knife, the properties of being sharp, pointed, and chrome-coloured are represented as properties *of the knife*. Is something similar true for perceptual emotions? The question needs to be understood with care. What is being asked is, whether those *evaluative aspects*, in virtue of which a representation of an object is an *emotional* representation, are (*a*) phenomenal, and (*b*) representational, i.e. whether they appear as qualifying the object itself, or as non-contingently dependent on the object's properties. When Swann hears the Vinteuil sonata with enraptured admiration, are the evaluative properties entering into his appraisal of the music phenomenal properties, and if so, do they qualify the acoustic object, the

---

[30] See Stein (1980: 85–96). For an interpretation of Wittgenstein's claims along these lines, see McDowell (1982).

sonata—rather than some inner state of Swann's, in principle describable independently of it—as having a certain what-it-is-likeness?

The issue can perhaps best be approached by asking: what is different for someone in Swann's position between hearing the Vinteuil sonata as Swann hears it, being profoundly emotionally affected, and attentively hearing the same acoustic stimuli, but without any noticeable affective response to them, the piece 'leaving him cold'? The phenomenal differences experienced by the emotionally affected subject will be of two quite distinct kinds. First, the emotional subject often experiences various bodily sensations caused by physiological changes such as an increased pulse rate, respiratory rate or peripheral vascular changes including sweating or pallor. These changes are generally regarded, surely correctly, as *effects* of the subject's appraisal or evaluation of the object, or of the physical correlate of that appraisal.[31] The subjective registerings of these physiological changes are the various 'pangs', 'throbs', and 'twinges' that ordinary emotion talk tends to associate with the 'hot' emotions. While they may be intentional, presenting the subject's *own body* in a state of upheaval, there is no temptation to interpret them as being about the object of the emotion.[32] When your face is flushed with anger you may feel this, but the feeling of a flushed face has no tendency whatsoever to appear as a representation of the person you are angry about. So there must be another and more fundamental kind of phenomenal difference between hearing the sonata as Swann does, and hearing it unmoved. One suggestion would be that this difference simply consists in Swann's conscious *belief* that 'this piece of music is uniquely beautiful'. But this cannot be right either. For, as we saw in 3.ii above, it is perfectly possible to experience a perceptual emotion concerning an object while having no corresponding evaluative beliefs about the object.[33]

A second type of difference between the experience of the emotionally affected subject and the 'cold', unaffected listener is often referred to as the 'hedonic tone' or '(dis)pleasurable feeling' associated with the experience of the object for the former, but not the latter. The central question to ask here is whether this 'feeling' is supposed to be characterizable without reference to the *object* as presented. If it is, then it would have to be a non-intentional quasi-sensation, a subjective 'warm glow' as it were, whose connection with the object of the experience was merely contingent and causal.

---

[31] Lyons (1980: 118 f.); Marcel and Lambie (2002: 232).

[32] On the intentionality of bodily sensations, their presenting parts of the subject's own body as being a certain way, see Crane (1998: 232–8).

[33] Another proposal is that the emotionally affected subject experiences some hedonic tone, or feeling of pleasure, in the presence of, or caused by, hearing the melody, and accompanied by a positive evaluative judgement about the whole experience (Wedgwood 2001: 217–20). But we have already seen that perceptual emotions need not involve any judgement at all, let alone a *reflective* judgement about the subject's own experience. On the latter point, see also Sartre (2002: 34–7); Marcel and Lambie (2002: 223 and 235–6).

In order to experience it non-inferentially as associated with the object of the emotion at all, this non-intentional feeling of pleasure would have to be experienced *as caused* by the object, while the object itself would have to be presented in affectively neutral terms, exactly as it is to someone who remains unmoved by its presence. Since the relation between the pleasure and its cause would be contingent, it would in principle be possible for the same type of pleasure to be caused by quite diverse sorts of objects.

The fundamental objection to this picture is that it seriously misdescribes ordinary emotional experience. No doubt it does capture *some* affective phenomena, but we tend to think of these as unusual or in some cases even pathological.[34] For example, someone may not find her sexual partner aesthetically attractive at all, while yet enjoying her erotic relations with him on account of the 'feelings of pleasure' they cause her. This is an intelligible situation and one that no doubt does occur, but for all that it is probably not how most people experience their sexual relations, and almost certainly not how they would like to experience them. But while in the present example it is at least uncontroversial that non-object-directed 'feelings of pleasure' are actually present, with most other emotions it is not remotely clear what the relevant feelings are supposed to be. When I enjoy a painting, or admire a landscape or a person, what and where are the non-intentional, and in this sense purely 'subjective', feelings of pleasure? In the lover's affection at the sight of his beloved, or the *ressentiment* subject's hatred of his master's power, or the despair experienced by the person suffering from depression, where are the putative hedonic qualia or raw feels, on the one hand distinct from the subjective registerings of the physiological effects of one's appraisal of the situation (the dry throat, trembling, flushing, or whatever it may be) and on the other hand logically independent of any intentional, object-directed experiential contents? I submit that such 'pleasures' or 'pains' cannot be found at all. They are entirely mythological, in the pejorative sense of that word.[35]

The 'pleasure' that Swann experiences in Proust's Vinteuil episode therefore needs to be construed in an 'externalist' way.[36] It is an essentially environment-involving mental content, consisting in the experienced *attractiveness of the acoustic object* he hears, an important aspect of which happens to be its adumbratory, partly revelatory, yet

---

[34] Scheler (1973: ch. 5.1); also Johnston (2001: 201–4).

[35] I take it that this is also Wiggins's point when he insists that the 'sentiments' we have in relation to various objects are not adequately describable without predicates whose semantic values are properties of these very objects. See Wiggins (1987: esp. 106–7).

[36] The type of content externalism referred to here can be found in, e.g., McDowell (1994) and Brewer (1999). It needs to be distinguished from early Putnam-style theories of wide content and from the kind of externalism associated with causal theories of reference. A content is environment-involving in the sense relevant here just in case its adequate characterization at the personal level (i.e. from the subject's point of view) necessitates reference to spatiotemporal phenomenal objects, including objects outside the boundaries of the subject's phenomenal body.

also elusive structure. The *musical performance itself*, a particular worldly object (see Section 3.i), appears as promising 'delights' and 'vistas' without fully disclosing them.

(v) Perceptual Emotions Appear Caused by Value Features of their Objects

Ordinary sense perceptions, if successful, involve causal input from their intentional objects, or at least they systematically *appear to* be thus caused. Can something similar be said for perceptual emotions? Do the evaluative features on account of which a representation of an object is an *emotional* representation of it, cause or systematically appear as causing the emotional state? The answer to the question, I suggest, should be affirmative. When Swann is listening to the Vinteuil sonata, what appears to him as causing his emotional response is the particular configuration and texture of sounds which constitute the beauty or attractiveness of the piece. In just the same way a person who is startled by the sound of a gun being fired nearby is aware of his experience as being caused by a sudden violent noise, and this awareness of being-affected is in part what makes his experience a perceptual one. In none of these cases is it necessary, in order for the experience to count as perceptual, that the causal powers involved 'really', in a metaphysical sense, are powers of the phenomenal properties as experienced—the visible beauty or audible noise, respectively. Even if the causal powers in the auditory case metaphysically pertain not to the noise as heard, but to sound waves as described by physics, or to some other 'occasionalist' cause, this is in the present context irrelevant. The perception of the noise is ordinarily considered a perception of it because it appears caused by its phenomenal properties, and because there are reliable correlations of such apparent causality between sound events phenomenally like it and subjects' experiences. Leaving aside for the moment the issue of the reliability and possible veridicality of these experiences (see 3.vi below), as regards the issue of apparent causality in each individual case, there seems to be no relevant disanalogy between the experience of value properties of objects, and the experience of other phenomenal properties such as sounds or colours.[37]

A critic might object that what appears to cause Swann's aesthetic emotion is not a property whose adequate characterization needs to make use of evaluative predicates, but simply the arrangement of sounds describable by him non-evaluatively, for

[37] One disanalogy might be thought to be that, unlike for colours or sounds, we evidently do not have sense organs for picking up values. But if we think of value properties as higher-order phenomenal properties of objects or of lower-order sets of properties, this objection ceases to impress. There are many other higher-order phenomenal properties which we perceive without special sense organs dedicated to them: we can non-inferentially see that a smile is expressive of insincerity, and we can hear that a note is dissonant, or that a tune is in E-flat major. Yet we have no sense organs specifically for picking out sincerity, consonance, or musical keys.

example in terms of its secondary qualities. Against this, a consideration stressed by Jonathan Dancy is decisive:

[A] quality may be resultant but be perceivable without any awareness of the qualities from which, in this instance, it results. The quality of weakness is resultant. A chess position cannot be simply weak; it must be weak because of some other characteristic. But a chess expert can see weakness in a position without yet being able to see the particular failing in which its weakness consists.[38]

Analogously, Swann experiences and thinks of himself as emotionally affected by phenomenal properties of the sonata which strike him as determinately beautiful, without having any idea of what precise tonal and harmonic properties of the sound sequence he hears are the resultant or supervenience base of this beauty (Proust's narrator in fact stresses this point). But it is impossible to conceptualise one's experience as a being-affected by specific phenomenal properties F, G, H,. . ., if one cannot identify them. Therefore what appears to Swann as affecting him is the evaluative property perhaps resulting from, but not identical with, the sonata's secondary or other non-evaluative properties—in other words, the property of beauty or attractiveness. Perceptual emotions therefore resemble ordinary sense perceptions in appearing to the subject to be caused by phenomenal properties of their objects—in this case, their value features.[39]

(vi) The Conditions of Success of Some Perceptual Emotions Include their Veridicality

Can perceptual emotions, like sense perceptions, be veridical? It is a standard theme in current philosophy of emotion that emotions are assessable as appropriate or inappropriate.[40] The crucial question in our context is whether 'appropriateness' in the case of perceptual emotions can be construed in terms of the veridicality of their evaluative contents.

---

[38] Dancy (1981: 383–4).

[39] Can we consistently think of phenomenal property instances as causing or appearing to cause experiences such as perceptual emotions if we also hold that these emotions cannot be adequately characterized at the personal level without reference to the properties that appear to be their causes? The conjunction of these claims appears to violate the Humean injunction that cause and effect should be numerically and logically distinct. One solution to this problem would be to argue that the Humean requirement of logical distinctness—such that the presence of either the cause or the effect cannot be inferred deductively from the presence of the other—does not hold for all types of cause–effect relations (cf. Searle, 1983, 121). An alternative solution would be to say that in the case of perceptual emotions, and perhaps of conscious perceptions more generally, cause and effect are not 'distinct existences' at the phenomenal level of description, but are distinct at the level of the physical supervenience base only. For this and other possible responses to the objection, see Child (1994: 156–62).

[40] See e.g. Lyons (1980: 8, 78–80); de Sousa (1987: 121–3); Mulligan (1998).

We should not assume that the correct answer to this question must be uniform across all classes of perceptual emotions. I shall briefly sketch some considerations in favour of an affirmative answer for a type of case that figures centrally in Nietzsche's writings: emotions which take other conscious affective states as their objects. Much of Nietzsche's own mode and practice of evaluation consists of expressions of affective dispositions about *other* affective states, such as contempt and revulsion at *ressentiment* (GM I. 10–14), or enthusiasm for the 'noble' virtues of generosity and reverence (BGE 260, 263).[41] Nietzsche is explicit that these affective responses should be taken as primarily directed not at actions or behavioural dispositions, but at the—often conscious—affective states of mind motivating actions (BGE 268, 287). From a Nietzschean perspective, it is in a person's *affective structure* that much of his or her non-instrumental value ultimately resides (BGE 260). The question to ask in our context is whether Nietzsche's own extensively recorded affective responses to those affective structures he calls 'noble' and 'slavish'—his enthusiasm and contempt, his attraction and repulsion, respectively—can themselves plausibly be interpreted as potentially veridical representations of the value aspects of their objects. May, for example, his obvious revulsion at *ressentiment* be considered as a veridical representation of that emotion's value? Or can it be no more than an effect produced by a representation of *ressentiment* that might also be fully adequate without involving any affective response at all? If the latter were the case, Nietzsche's contempt for *ressentiment* might perhaps be caused by instances of it, but it would not be rationally constrained by anything intrinsically pertaining to *ressentiment*—someone who responded to it with admiration or respect would not necessarily have failed to detect, or misrepresented, any intrinsic features of it. Yet, when Nietzsche speaks of Christianity as involving a 'defect of the eyes', prior to any reflectively considered or inferential 'reasons' (CW, Epilogue), this implies a quite different view, according to which enthusiasm for *ressentiment* would indeed entail, at the most basic level, a *cognitive* deficiency.

But how *could* something like contempt for *ressentiment* represent that condition's value veridically? Arguably, one thing that Nietzsche wishes to retain from the 'noble' mode of evaluation is its 'aesthetic' grounding in 'taste', more specifically, in affective responses to the *phenomenally intrinsic value features* of things, including quite centrally other affective states, as illustrated by the noble's contempt for the *ressentiment* of the slave, or by his delight in manifestations of courage or trustful openness or reverence (GM I. 10; BGE 263). We may define the phenomenally intrinsic (dis)value of an occurrent conscious affective state as its first-personal experienced (un)attractiveness,

---

[41] The affective responses to *ressentiment* expressed by Nietzsche in the first essay of the *Genealogy* and elsewhere are clearly not perceptual emotions as defined in 3.ii, since their particular objects often lie in the remote past. But if their contents can be shown to be potentially veridical or truth-apt, then this will hold also for perceptual emotions, which are generally foundational for belief-based emotions.

if the state is considered purely by itself, and if it is adequately presented.[42] For example, the phenomenally intrinsic disvalue of *ressentiment* would be its experienced unattractiveness from the point of view of the *ressentiment* subject, if it were presented adequately to him. In the case of emotions, their being given adequately requires of course an adequate representation of the intentional objects which co-constitute them and of the relevant aspects under which those objects are represented. *Ressentiment* is essentially a purposeful distortion of the character of its objects in order to justify a negative affect—hatred—regarding them which is motivated by their possessing some power over the *ressentiment* subject, and which remains unacknowledged by the subject (see GM I. 10). An adequate presentation of the emotion of *ressentiment* therefore requires reference to, or explicit awareness of, all these features. Nietzsche's claim, on the present interpretation, would then amount to this: once the emotion of *ressentiment* is really adequately presented, and considered by itself, it *cannot fail* to be experienced with revulsion or in some other negative affective mode. Such revulsion is therefore *cognitive* in so far as it registers the necessary phenomenally intrinsic unattractiveness, the 'bad smell' (cf. GM I. 14), of a hatred that is transparently recognized by its subject as motivated merely by the power of another and as purposefully distorting both its own and its object's nature in order to legitimate itself. The reason why the *ressentiment* subject is not fully or explicitly aware of the intrinsic phenomenal disvalue of his condition, and therefore can unproblematically remain in it, is precisely that he avoids, through a strategy of self-deception (GM I. 10, 13; GM III. 14), recognizing it for what it is.[43]

If he were to become explicitly aware of it as what it is, he could not fail to recognize its disvalue and to experience it as, considered purely by itself, unattractive or indeed repulsive. It is in this sense that contempt may be said to be a veridical representation of the intrinsic phenomenal disvalue of an affective state such as *ressentiment*.

If we accept this interpretation, this not only supplies us with the materials for an answer to the question of how Nietzsche's theory of *ressentiment* can count as a *criticism* of it, it also enables us to see what this criticism actually is. It is not (or at least not primarily) that any kind of self-deception is *per se* objectionable because it militates against a certain notion of a unified self. Rather, the main point is that the particular type of self-deception Nietzsche calls *ressentiment* is, necessarily, an intrinsically unattractive state to be in, if seen in the open. Hence, no one who accepts Nietzsche's account of it can either desire to be in it or wish to remain in it, except for instrumental reasons (although it is surely doubtful whether *ressentiment* is

[42] For useful discussions of related concepts of intrinsic value, see esp. Goldstein (1989) and Zimmerman (1999).

[43] A detailed analysis of *ressentiment* as a form of purposeful self-deception about one's current mental state can be found in Poellner (2004). This essay also addresses the question of how Nietzsche's account can avoid the familiar problems ('paradoxes') associated with intentionalist theories of self-deception.

instrumentally useful for any projects whose aims do not involve it and which would not be more efficiently served without it).

For Nietzsche, not only *can* emotions on occasion be veridical as representations of their objects' intrinsic phenomenal value, their conditions of success qua representations include their veridicality in this respect. It is evident that what makes *ressentiment* an objectionable emotion for him is in part that it is co-constituted by *mis*representations of the relevant aspects of its objects (GM I. 10). This implies that if Nietzsche were persuaded that his own revulsion at *ressentiment* misrepresented that emotion's intrinsic phenomenal value, he would then be committed to regarding this affective response to *ressentiment* as inappropriate.

4. Affectivity as Constitutive of Value: Nietzsche's Rejection of Metaphysical Value-Objectivism

Nietzsche argues that our fundamental mode of access to values is through occurrent affective states. More specifically, we could not grasp the concept of value we actually have, or any relevantly similar concept, unless we can grasp what it is affectively to experience parts or aspects of the world or ourselves as worthwhile or pointless, attractive or repulsive, painful or pleasant. In the previous Section, I have defended the claim that evaluative content is often environment-involving: we often experience non-instrumental value as genuinely attaching to phenomenal objects, including our and other people's bodies, non-human animals, landscapes, cities, musical performances, and in favourable circumstances also others' actions and mental states. But are there any values that are objective in the stronger sense—call it *metaphysically objective*—of being existentially and/or conceptually independent not just of any particular affective experience, but of such experiences altogether? In other words, do affective experiences *discover* value properties exemplifiable without them, or do they *co-constitute* value? Nietzsche emphatically denies that values are metaphysically objective properties:

Whatever has *value* in our world now does not have value in itself, according to its nature—nature is always valueless—but has been given value at some time, as a gift; and *we* were the givers and bestowers! Only we have created the world *that concerns human beings*! (GS 301)

Truly, human beings have given themselves all their good and evil. Truly, they did not find it, it did not descend to them as a voice from heaven. Humans first placed values in things . . . Only through valuating is there value. (Z, 'Of the Thousand and One Goals')

Passages like these strongly support Brian Leiter's interpretation of Nietzsche as a (metaphysical) anti-realist about value, if this is understood as equivalent to the denial of metaphysical objectivism.[44] Nietzsche gives us no developed, explicit arguments for rejecting metaphysical objectivism about value. Usually he merely asserts the dependence of value on 'affect' or 'taste' (Z, 'Of the Sublime Men') as the only sane conclusion from a clear-headed reflection on the concept of value. And indeed, it is difficult to disagree with him in this assessment, once the question *whether there could be any values if there were no affective experiences at all* is clearly distinguished from several other superficially similar questions.[45] One of these is whether we can value things even though we have never been affectively acquainted with their value perceptually or imaginatively. This is obviously not only possible but happens quite frequently. I can believe on authority that traditional Japanese painting has a uniquely delicate beauty, and sincerely acknowledge its aesthetic value, without ever having become acquainted with it.[46] But the Nietzschean point is that I only have a grasp of what it is that I believe if I know what would verify my belief—and in the aesthetic case such verification would involve an appropriate affective response.

---

[44] Leiter (2002: esp. 146–55). In the light of my arguments in the text I would suggest a conceptual distinction, not usually drawn, between metaphysical anti-realism and metaphysical anti-objectivism about value. The latter is the view that values are properties not capable of actual existence in objects independently of experience. They are essentially phenomenal. The former is the stronger view that values are metaphysically unreal. If exemplifications of value properties, as I have argued, enter essentially into the identity conditions of certain affective states, such as perceptual emotions, then a metaphysical anti-realism about values entails an anti-realism about these psychological states. Yet we might want to be anti-objectivists about value without committing ourselves to a position about the metaphysical status of these psychological states.

[45] It might be objected that in the above passage I am sliding illegitimately from the claim that values necessarily involve affective *states* to the quite different one that they necessarily involve affective *experiences*. The substantive philosophical argument for the latter claim will be given in the main text. But as for the exegetical issue of whether this is an adequate interpretation of Nietzsche, he does indeed famously assert the existence of unconscious mental states, including affective states (e.g. GS 354, 357). However, as I have argued in Poellner (1995: ch. 5.2), in countenancing unconscious mental states Nietzsche is *not* necessarily denying that all occurrent mental states, qua mental, have phenomenal properties, i.e. some 'what-it-is-likeness'. Indeed, there are places where Nietzsche claims that *every* actual existent has phenomenal properties (GS 54). The most plausible reading of Nietzsche on unconscious mental states is that many occurrent mental states are inferentially unavailable to the mind's main-system, displaying no phenomenal properties *to it*, while nevertheless possessing such phenomenal properties. (See e.g. KGW VII.3.37.4.) For the distinction between mental main-systems and sub-systems, see esp. Pears (1985).

[46] A number of moral theorists have insisted on the absence of any distinctive phenomenology in *moral* judgement (Wright 1988: 11–13; Dancy 1993: 160–2). It is no doubt true that I can judge an action, for example a legal decision, to be 'right' without being affectively moved by it. But the important question in the present context is whether my grasp of the concept of moral rightness requires somewhere along the line reference to actual or possible affective experiences had by *someone* or other—for instance, the experiences of those to whom the legal ruling applies.

Second, the question is of course not whether one can only value what is or in fact could be presented in *one's own* affective experiences. The thesis that there would be no values in the world if there were no affective experiences is consonant with the idea that many values are realized in experiences that are not our own, or not had by—or even accessible to—human beings at all.

Once these potential misinterpretations of the question are ruled out, it seems difficult to see how an affirmative answer to it could be made plausible. If nothing ever showed up as mattering in actual affective experience (including perceptual emotions), where could the values possibly be? It seems clear that such a world would be a world without actual value, as we ordinarily understand it, just as a world in which there was no experience as of something coloured would contain no actual colours, as we ordinarily understand them.

I want briefly to consider some objections and putative counterexamples to this Nietzschean thesis. One worry is that some things we value are simply too complex or abstract ever to be perceivable or experiencable by any one subject. One can value the American way of life, or justice, but could one possibly *perceive* or *experience* either of them?[47] Now it is clear that such complex and/or abstract objects cannot be fully or completely perceived or experienced by any finite person—but this is true even for a table, which cannot in principle be perceived completely by anyone. All perception of particular objects or events is essentially horizonal or adumbrational, involving a full sensory or otherwise intuitive presentation of only some parts or aspects of the object, which function as bearers of unthematic anticipations regarding indefinitely many possible perceptual appearances of the remainder of the object, and it is only because of these anticipations that I can take myself to be perceiving the *object*, rather than merely one side or view or aspect of it.[48] There is therefore nothing incongruous in the idea of valuing, say, the American way of life on the basis of experiential (including imaginative) representations of activities, customs, social interactions, aesthetic preferences, modes of feeling and thought one takes *as typical* of that way of life.

A critic might concede that the actualization of value requires *mental states*, while denying that these states need to be or to include *affective experiences*. Can non-instrumental value perhaps actualize itself in non-affective mental states involving the entertaining of evaluative propositions, for example in *moral judgments* or in *intentions* to do something under a moral description? Now, the crux of Nietzsche's constitutive claim is precisely that we lose our grip on the point and the content of moral judgements or intentions—they become unintelligible to us—if all possible affective experience is abstracted from. If I judge that 'helping a friend in need is good', but do

---

[47] Cf. Johnston (1987: 142). [48] See Husserl (1983: §§41–2); Searle (1983: 53–5).

so neither from 'respect' or reverence for some moral (or perhaps divine) law,[49] nor because I believe and want my actions to have an effect on the experienced quality of life of my friend, or of myself, or of some third party, what *content* is left to my 'moral judgement'? If I even consider, as I must on the present proposal, my sympathy for a friend whom I imagine to be in need to be entirely irrelevant to my 'approval' of the relevant moral injunction, what is the substance of that approval? Perhaps 'approval' here can be cashed out in terms of action-dispositions to promote certain states of affairs over others, the dispositions being interpreted behaviouristically. But if this is what 'approval' amounts to, there is a clear sense in which my actions have become unintelligible to me, just as the behaviour of people with compulsive disorders is to them. This is not how ethical life and ethical concepts normally work. The proposal to abstract from affective experience, whatever other problems it generates, would amount to a fundamental *revision* of our evaluative concepts and evaluative practice, requiring us to view ourselves as analogous to individuals with compulsive syndromes. (See below for some further Nietzschean remarks on the prospects of such a revision.)

Granted that there could be no *actual* non-instrumental value in the world in the absence of actual affective experiences, might values not be *dispositions* to elicit such experiences in appropriate subjects and circumstances, analogous to secondary qualities according to dispositionalist construals of them? On this view, values would emerge as *conceptually* dependent on affective experiences, but as *existentially* independent of them—there could be values even if there were no actual affective experiences.[50] We might say, for example that

X is beautiful (short for: aesthetically valuable) just in case x is disposed to elicit emotions of contemplative admiration in appropriately receptive perceivers in suitable circumstances [with 'appropriate receptivity' and 'suitable circumstances' to be substantively specified].

Dispositionalist accounts face significant difficulties even when offered for secondary properties. As elucidations of the central features of evaluative concepts they are quite inadequate. In fact, the only feature of them that they do elucidate is their essential response-dependence; a dispositional account makes explicit that values cannot

---

[49] Nietzsche's remarks on Kant's ethics emphasize that the Kantian moral motive of respect for the moral law—a respect elicited by the mere idea of a categorical obligation that is independent of whatever my or other people's (other) inclinations may be—*also* involves affective experience, albeit misinterpreted by Kant (see BGE 187, GM II. 6). The affect-involving, but misinterpreted and non-veridical, experience of duty as apparently autonomously valuable or 'worthy' (BGE 187) is the necessary justificatory basis for any categorically action-guiding authority that the idea of duty may falsely be thought to have.

[50] For this distinction, see also Johnston (1987: 141). A dispositional account of *moral* value is proposed by Dancy (1993: ch. 9).

outrun the relevant responses (including, at the fundamental level, the affective experiences) of subjects. However, the right-hand side of the biconditional does not give an analysis of the concepts of the values in question, but presupposes a prior and independent grasp of these concepts, for at least two reasons. First, the specification of 'appropriate receptivity' needs to include a clause attributing to the perceivers an ability to pick out what is aesthetically valuable (thus making the 'elucidation' openly circular), not because a non-evaluative specification of this ability would be too complex, but because it would invite the 'so what?' objection—someone could fully *agree* that something is aesthetically very valuable, by the lights of the dispositional account, without himself approving of it at all aesthetically, thus failing to grasp that sincerely attributing value to x involves essentially favouring or commending x in the relevant respect.[51] Secondly, an understanding of the characterization of the relevant response in which the disposition is supposed to actualize itself requires a grasp of what aesthetic value is that is necessarily independent of any ability to conceptualize it as a disposition. In the same way, if I am to grasp the property *red* as a disposition to elicit experiences as of red, I must have a prior grasp of the phenomenal content of the relevant experiences.[52] Moreover, in the case of value (less clearly so in the case of the colours) the categorical sense of the concept is not just necessarily prior *epistemically,* but also in terms of the 'grammar' or use of the concept. A disposition to produce experiences of aesthetic value is itself a value only *derivatively,* because it tends to bring about experiences whose actual, non-dispositional contents include intrinsic phenomenal value properties. Analogously, an emotional disposition counts as an emotion only because and in so far as it tends to issue in occurrent emotions in the right circumstances.

I have argued that Nietzsche's view is that value existentially depends on the existence of affective experiences. This is what he means when he says that value is not 'found' but 'created' by 'evaluating' (GS 301), that morality is only a sign-language of the affects (BGE 187), and that '*every* ideal presupposes *love* and *hatred, admiration* and *contempt*' (KGW VIII.2.10.9). I have also suggested that Nietzsche very plausibly regards this affect-dependence of value to be evident from reflection on our concept of value or any relevantly similar concept.

One final route to escape Nietzsche's conclusion would be to propose a radical *revision* of the ordinary concept of value and construe 'value' in this revised sense as independent of affective phenomenal properties, just as one can revise our 'folk' concepts of the colours, say, as disjunctions of non-dispositional microphysical properties, or as light dispositions. But it is wildly implausible to believe that human beings might be persuaded to adopt such a revised concept as a functional replacement of the current concept of value or worth, with broadly the same pattern

---

[51] Cf. Johnston (1987: 157–8). Also Wright (1988: 22–5).   [52] See Stroud (2000: 127–44).

of action-guiding use. One might put this by saying that human beings are not only attached to various things they value or desire, but to valuing and desiring, as we currently understand these states or activities, *themselves*. This is the most important, albeit often neglected, part of Nietzsche's point when he has Zarathustra say that 'valuating is itself the value and jewel of all valued things' (Z, 'Of a Thousand and One Goals'), and when he himself says that what matters most fundamentally to us is not so much what is desired in any given instance, but the *desiring itself* (e.g. KGW VII.1.20.4; p. 661). It is because we have a non-negotiable interest in how things consciously matter to ourselves and others—because we profoundly *value* this form of intelligibility—that the affective phenomenal properties figuring in many ordinary psychological explanations have an irreplaceable role in our cognitive economy.

Is Nietzsche's position as interpreted here a version of 'quasi-realist' projectivism? It differs fundamentally from Blackburn's quasi-realism in neither giving a special or basic role to *obligation* in its account of evaluative objectivity, nor to a subject's *reflective* judgement (about her own ability to envisage an improvement of her attitudes) in producing the idea that some evaluations might be true.[53] But the Nietzschean position is compatible with the projectivist element in quasi-realism, provided projectivism is not committed to the view that the 'gilding and staining' of the world with value is in principle detectable at the personal level. Projectivism need not conflict with Nietzsche's position if the former is a purely metaphysical thesis, but it is incompatible with the latter if projectivism is also intended to be a phenomenological thesis.[54]

5. Value and Nietzsche's Metaphysical Indifferentism

What are the implications of the Nietzschean account suggested above, which conjoins a phenomenal objectivism about value (or at least about many values) with a metaphysical anti-objectivism? As GS 301 indicates, Nietzsche certainly regards the consequences of our realization that any values we can recognize are 'created' by us as momentous. For one thing, if the values we can acknowledge ultimately owe their binding and motivating character to their ability to engage us affectively, then there cannot be any obligations or duties for us that are radically external to our affective and motivational systems—to what we can in fact come to recognize as exercising an affective appeal on us. But what is perhaps just as important about Nietzsche's view is the way it conceptualizes the relation between the *phenomenology* of evaluative practice

---

[53] For these elements of Blackburn's quasi-realism, see e.g. his (1981: 173–6); (1984: 197–202); (1985: 8).

[54] Johnston (2001: 201–3) interprets projectivism as at least in part a phenomenological thesis, and therefore rejects it as fundamentally misconstruing most of the evaluative experiences and thoughts we are most deeply committed to.

and the level of *metaphysical theory*. Nietzsche has a highly distinctive and original view on how we should think about this relation, a view which applies not only to the relation between *evaluative* practice and the metaphysics of value, but between practice (the 'life-world') and metaphysics quite generally. I shall conclude with some remarks on this general thesis. It concerns the way we should think about the relation between the *phenomenal* properties the world appears to have—the way the world shows up for us in everyday 'life'—and our metaphysical beliefs, if we have any. Value properties are, according to the foregoing argument, a subclass of phenomenal properties; other phenomenal properties include the traditional secondary qualities, as well as various psychological properties. The crucial question here is whether there can be a conflict between what, according to Nietzsche, we are committed to at the level of practice, and what we are committed to at the metaphysical level. For Nietzsche, such a conflict is certainly possible—even for philosophically well-disposed agents ('free spirits')—as regards the *propositions* that their practice and their philosophical beliefs respectively commit them to.[55] For example, it is possible that some evaluative practices (certain kinds of art appreciation and criticism, say) may involve at least implicitly the belief that the aesthetic value properties of phenomenal objects have *causal powers*—that we can be causally affected by the beauty of a painting, for example. And it is not only possible, but often incontrovertibly the case, that we take ourselves to act because we believe that we or other people currently have various psychological phenomenal properties, for example feelings of pain. Now, let us assume that we also subscribe to a physicalist metaphysics according to which none of these phenomenal properties (beauty, feelings of pain, etc.) figure among the ultimate furniture of the universe. In this case, the contents of our various beliefs at the practical level would be incompatible with our metaphysical beliefs. One of the most characteristic and innovative features of Nietzsche's later philosophy is his view that such propositional incompatibilities need not necessarily, for a rational individual, involve a *practical* conflict, and that the practical beliefs in certain cases trump the metaphysical beliefs. This is the heart of his much-vaunted critique of the 'will to truth', the latter being for him the 'kernel' of the 'ascetic ideal' (GM III. 27): 'the falseness of a judgement is to us not necessarily an objection to a judgement: it is here that our new language perhaps sounds strangest' (BGE 4). Elsewhere he says, apparently continuous with such remarks: 'It is of cardinal importance that one should abolish the *real world*. It is the great inspirer of doubt and devaluator in respect of the world *we are*' (WP 583; cf. BGE 34).

But are such statements not tantamount to irrationalism? Do they not, for example, license the abandonment of the results of the scientific study of ourselves

---

[55] This view of Nietzsche's makes for a further difference from positions such as Blackburn's quasi-realism, according to which our evaluative practices are logically disengaged from any ontological commitments: 'The practice could be clipped on to either metaphysic' (Blackburn 1985: 3–4).

and of the world wherever these are, or seem to be, incompatible with our practical commitments and preferences? They do not. Nietzsche says that 'the falseness of a judgement is to us not *necessarily* an objection to [it]', and it is very important to be clear about the circumstances when it is not. These circumstances do not include the context of scientific inquiry. While the results of scientific research do not generally have overriding value for Nietzsche, he nowhere suggests that where they are pertinent, they should simply be ignored.[56] But, crucially, scientific explanations are *not* generally incompatible with everyday explanations that include reference to phenomenal properties, such as evaluative properties (phenomenological explanations, in short). To see this, consider the case of scientific psychology. It is arguably a foundational methodological principle of this science that the properties recognized by the physical sciences in a broad sense (physical properties, for short) are sufficient to account nomologically for all psychological phenomena, which can all be considered as elements of the physical world, and that phenomenal properties therefore have no autonomous causal powers potentially varying independently of, and affecting, physical states—the physical is in this sense a closed causal system. But this is quite compatible with both the *truth* and the *indispensability* of (some) phenomenological explanations just in case the following conditions are satisfied: (1) phenomenological explanations give us information, including rough generalizations sustaining true counterfactuals, about a person's abilities and powers to believe and act as she does, information that we value and that is not conveyed by other forms of explanation; and (2) the phenomenal properties adverted to in these explanations are strongly supervenient on (i.e. co-variant with) physical properties simultaneously exemplified.[57]

The scientific explanation of behaviour does not require a relation between phenomenal properties and physical properties that is any stronger than co-variance. And, importantly, such strong co-variance or supervenience is a weaker relation than *dependence*, and unlike the latter is not asymmetrical.[58] As regards clause (1), I earlier agreed with Nietzsche (in Section 4) that phenomenological explanations of our own and other people's behaviour—invariably making reference to what *matters* to us—that such explanations give us information that is itself valued highly by us

---

[56] On this point, see Gemes (2001: 47–9); and Leiter (2002: 264–6 and 279–81).

[57] The version of strong supervenience I have in mind is Kim's (Kim 1993: 65): If A and B are families of properties, then A strongly supervenes on B just in case, necessarily, for each x and each property F in A, if x has F, then there is a property G in B such that x has G and, necessarily, if any y has G, then it has F. The most plausible interpretation of the necessity operators in this context is nomological, although the laws in question may be disjunctive. Note that the supervenience adverted to here is not the more familiar supervenience of mental on physical properties, but of *phenomenal* properties more generally on physical properties.

[58] See Kim (1993: 143–8). Also Charles (1992: 272–5).

and that is not provided by other forms of explanation: they tell us how the world and our own and others' actions *make sense* to people.[59]

So, if strong supervenience holds, there is no systematic conflict between the explanations of scientific psychology and everyday psychological explanations adverting to phenomenal properties, including the values people hold or recognize. But it is often said that relations of co-variance or supervenience between properties themselves call out for explanation.[60] *Why* do phenomenal properties strongly supervene on physical properties, assuming that they do? Importantly, any such explanations of supervenience are not internal to the practice of science, but are rather *metaphysical* explanations. Physical science, for example, takes no view on the nature of the dependency relation (if any) between physical and secondary properties—the latter simply do not figure in its theories and experimental laws. It is only once certain metaphysical explanations of the co-variance between phenomenal and physical properties are offered that a logical incompatibility may emerge between the beliefs implicit in our everyday evaluative practice and these metaphysical beliefs.

Among metaphysical beliefs themselves we may distinguish between those that have an autonomously practical relevance or bearing, and others that do not. According to the argument in the preceding Section, it is only in so far as experience—of humans or other beings—is affected in one way or another that anything can matter, can actually exemplify some value, at all. But experience may be affected by metaphysical beliefs in two quite different ways. The psychological entertaining of the content by itself may affect a person's conscious relation and attitude to the world. For example, a believer in a Dionysian metaphysics may feel consoled by the thought that 'underneath the flux of appearances, eternal life flows on indestructibly' (*Birth of Tragedy* 18), although the truth of this metaphysics *per se* may imply nothing about the future course of his or anyone else's experience—it has no *predictive* consequences, unless it is fleshed out in various more specific ways. By contrast, the content of certain other metaphysical beliefs has necessary implications concerning the actual course our experience can take, whatever our attitudes towards these predicted experiential consequences may be. For example, if Christian metaphysical beliefs are true, we all will have a conscious personal life after this earthly life, and there will be a conscious continuity between this present life and that afterlife. Metaphysical beliefs of this latter kind clearly can have relevance for us even if we do not value knowing the truth for its own sake—if we have no purely cognitive

---

[59] For a similar argument, see Child (1994: ch. 6). In Poellner (2006) I argue that the above points are compatible with Nietzsche's revisionist and pragmatist advocacy of 'physiological' explanations for *some* phenomenal mental states which are standardly thought to call for intentional (phenomenological) explanations (cf. GM III. 17 and TI VI. 6).

[60] See Kim (1993: 144–8); Shafer-Landau (2003: 77–8).

or theoretical interests. It is in this sense that they have an *autonomously practical* relevance. Beliefs of the first kind, by contrast, will only be of evaluative significance for us if we have purely theoretical interests—if we value knowing the truth for its own sake. Here are some examples of such purely theoretical metaphysical beliefs: the intrinsic qualitative nature of real objects is mind-like or representation-like (Berkeley, Leibniz); consciousness does not figure among the fundamental intrinsic properties of the spatio-temporal world (reductive physicalism); the real spatio-temporal world includes objects with absolute (non-perspectival) qualitative properties (Locke, physicalism); being is at the fundamental level non-objectifiable (Schopenhauer, Heidegger). Among the purely theoretical propositions we also find the putative metaphysical 'explanations' of why certain scientific theories or experimental laws are predictively successful. Returning to the earlier example of scientific psychology, one might metaphysically explain the predicted nomological co-variance of phenomenal with physical properties by holding a form of physicalism, arguing that phenomenal items are token-identical with sets of physical items, and that phenomenal properties are higher-order properties of sets of physical properties. Or one might instead opt, more exotically, for some form of parallelist metaphysical explanation of the co-variance. Another example of purely theoretical metaphysical explanations, which is discussed in some detail by Nietzsche, would be metaphysical theories concerning the intrinsic qualitative nature of the forces which figure in the laws of physical science.[61]

Because none of these purely theoretical metaphysical explanations make any predictions, except accidentally, an experiential adjudication between them is in principle impossible and any arguments for them are necessarily a priori. (I include among a priori arguments also 'inferences to the best explanation', where the criteria for what is best do not include predictive superiority.)

Passages like the much-quoted TI IV, and perhaps even more clearly HAH 9, suggest very strongly that it is only purely theoretical metaphysical beliefs Nietzsche has in mind when he says that 'it is of cardinal importance that one should abolish the *real world*' (WP 583). Hypotheses concerning the 'real world' are 'refuted' by their 'useless[ness]'—the absence of autonomously practical relevance—not by any putative incoherence or meaninglessness of such claims (TI IV). To 'abolish' the 'real world' means to cease granting it importance in one's cognitive and evaluative

---

[61] Nietzsche argues that modern (Newtonian and post-Newtonian) science bypasses this question about the qualities that make physical forces efficacious when actualized—in Newton's words, physics does not need to 'feign hypotheses' about this. Such hypotheses, which are strictly irrelevant to the task of explanation as conceived by modern science, are therefore extra-scientific. They are instances of purely theoretical metaphysical propositions. For an account of Nietzsche's reflections on this important issue, see Poellner (1995: 46–57), and (2006).

economy, and to persuade others to do so as well. This is what the rejection of the 'will to truth' envisaged by Nietzsche centrally amounts to.

So, when Nietzsche says that 'the falseness of a judgement is to us not necessarily an objection to the judgement' (BGE 4), his point is this. Let us assume that we could prove the truth of certain purely theoretical metaphysical propositions entirely by a priori means.[62] Let us also assume that these propositions were incompatible with beliefs implied by ethical or aesthetic practices that we otherwise value. In this case, Nietzsche would urge indifference to the metaphysical truth. Rejecting the will to truth implies, therefore, a refusal to permit a practical conflict to arise where it might conventionally be thought to be inevitable: namely, where the truth of a proposition whose only really possible warrant is a priori contradicts theoretical commitments implicated in practices we otherwise regard ourselves as justified in valuing. Nothing in the course of causally possible experience could disconfirm the judgement that phenomenal properties—such as the experienced beauty of a piece of music or a friend's pain—in certain circumstances, including an appropriate physical supervenience base, affect a subject's conscious thoughts and actions, in so far as these are intelligible at all to the subject herself. Nietzsche's thought is that if one could know by a priori methods and only by these that the conscious what-it-is-likeness of phenomenal properties is not in any way causally efficacious, this knowledge should leave one's self- and world-conception entirely unaffected, *even if* this conception were to involve a commitment to the efficacy of phenomenal properties upon conscious subjects. The individual who is not beholden to the will to truth has no significant purely theoretical interests and is consequently indifferent as to whether the life-world which engages her practical concerns is illusory by the lights of a purely theoretical metaphysical inquiry.

To conclude: according to the later Nietzsche, we need to distinguish three questions when we ask 'whether values are part of the world'. First, the question whether (some) values are phenomenally objective, whether they characterize the *objects* of our life-world. Nietzsche implies an affirmative answer to this question. This is important if we are not seriously to misconstrue evaluative experience in the way even sophisticated forms of projectivism are often rightly accused of doing. Secondly, there is the question of whether values are *metaphysically objective*, which is answered negatively by Nietzsche. Thirdly, the question of whether values are metaphysically *unreal* emerges, in the light of his critique of the will to truth, as a matter of indifference to the individual not subject to the ascetic ideal.

---

[62] Nietzsche himself does not believe that any such proofs are actually available or likely to be forthcoming. For detailed discussions of various aspects of his metaphysical scepticism, see Poellner (1995: 57–78, 150–61, 173–86).

References

BENNETT, J. (1966). *Kant's Analytic* (Cambridge: Cambridge University Press).

BLACKBURN, S. (1981). 'Rule-Following and Moral Realism', in S. Holtzmann and C. Leich (eds.), *Wittgenstein: To Follow a Rule* (London: Routledge).

—— (1984). *Spreading the Word* (Oxford: Oxford University Press).

—— (1985). 'Errors and the Phenomenology of Value', in T. Honderich (ed.), *Morality and Objectivity* (London: Routledge).

—— (1993). *Essays in Quasi-Realism* (Oxford: Oxford University Press).

BREWER, B. (1999). *Perception and Reason* (Oxford: Oxford University Press).

BRINK, D (1989). *Moral Realism and the Foundations of Ethics* (Cambridge: Cambridge University Press).

CHARLES, D. (1992). 'Supervenience, Composition, and Physicalism', in D. Charles and K. Lennon (eds.), *Reduction, Explanation, and Realism* (Oxford: Clarendon Press).

CHILD, W. (1994). *Causality, Interpretation and the Mind* (Oxford: Clarendon Press).

CRANE, T. (1992). 'The Nonconceptual Content of Experience', in T. Crane (ed.), *The Contents of Experience* (Cambridge: Cambridge University Press).

—— (1998). 'Intentionality as the Mark of the Mental', in A. O'Hear (ed.), *Current Issues in Philosophy of Mind* (Cambridge: Cambridge University Press).

DANCY, J. (1981). 'On Moral Properties', *Mind* 90: 367–85.

—— (1993). *Moral Reasons* (Oxford: Blackwell).

DE SOUSA, R. (1987). *The Rationality of Emotion* (Cambridge, MA: The MIT Press).

—— (2002). 'Emotional Truth', *Proceedings of the Aristotelian Society*, supp. vol. 76:247–75.

DOERING, S., and PEACOCKE, C. (2002). 'Handlungen, Gründe und Emotionen', in S. Doering and V. Mayer (eds.), *Die Moralität der Gefühle* (Berlin: Akademie Verlag).

DRUMMOND, J. J. (2004). '"Cognitive Impenetrability" and the Complex Intentionality of Emotions', *Journal of Consciousness Studies* 11/10–11: 109–26.

DUMMETT, M. (1979). 'Common Sense and Physics', in G. MacDonald (ed.), *Perception and Physics* (London: Macmillan).

GEMES, K. (2001). 'Nietzsche's Critique of Truth', in B. Leiter and J. Richardson (eds.), *Nietzsche* (Oxford: Oxford University Press).

GOLDIE, P. (2000). *The Emotions* (Oxford: Clarendon Press).

GOLDSTEIN, I. (1989). 'Pleasure and Pain: Unconditional Intrinsic Values', *Philosophy and Phenomenological Research* 50: 255–76.

GUAY, R. (2002). 'Nietzsche on Freedom', *European Journal of Philosophy* 10: 302–27.

HUSSERL, E. (1983). *Ideas Pertaining to a Pure Phenomenology and to a Phenomenological Philosophy*, First Book (Dordrecht: Kluwer).

—— (1989). *Ideas Pertaining to a Pure Phenomenology and to a Phenomenological Philosophy*, Second Book (Dordrecht: Kluwer).

JOHNSTON, M. (1987). 'Dispositional Theories of Value', *Proceedings of the Aristotelian Society*, supp. vol. 63: 139–74.

—— (2001). 'The Authority of Affect', *Philosophy and Phenomenological Research* 63: 181–214.

KIM, J. (1993). *Supervenience and Mind* (Cambridge: Cambridge University Press).

LANGTON, R. (1998). *Kantian Humility: Our Ignorance of Things in Themselves* (Oxford: Oxford University Press).

LEITER, B. (2002). *Nietzsche on Morality* (London: Routledge).

LYONS, W. (1980). *Emotion* (Cambridge: Cambridge University Press).

MACKIE, J. L. (1977). *Ethics: Inventing Right and Wrong* (Harmondsworth: Penguin).

MARCEL, A. J., and LAMBIE, J. A. (2002). 'Consciousness and the Varieties of Emotion Experience: A Theoretical Framework', *Psychological Review* 109/2: 219–59.

McDOWELL, J. (1978). 'Are Moral Requirements Hypothetical Imperatives?', *Proceedings of the Aristotelian Society*, supp. vol. 52: 13–29.

———— (1981). 'Non-cognitivism and Rule-Following', in S. Holtzmann and C. Leich (eds.), *Wittgenstein: To Follow a Rule* (London: Routledge).

———— (1982). 'Criteria, Defeasibility and Knowledge', *Proceedings of the British Academy* 68.

———— (1985). 'Values and Secondary Qualities', in T. Honderich (ed.), *Morality and Objectivity* (London: Routledge).

———— (1994). *Mind and World* (Cambridge, MA: Harvard University Press).

MARTIN, M. G. F. (1998). 'Setting things before the Mind', in A. O'Hear (ed.), *Current Issues in Philosophy of Mind* (Cambridge: Cambridge University Press).

MULLIGAN, K. (1998). 'From Appropriate Emotions to Values', *Monist* 81: 161–88.

NAGEL, T. (1970). *The Possibility of Altruism* (Oxford: Oxford University Press).

NIETZSCHE, F. (1967–). *Werke: Kritische Gesamtausgabe*, ed. G. Colli, M. Montinari, et al. (Berlin: de Gruyter).

NIETZSCHE, F. (1975–2004). *Briefwechsel: Kritische Gesamtausgabe*, ed. G. Colli, M. Montinari, et al. (Berlin: de Gruyter).

NUSSBAUM, M. C. (2001). *Upheavals of Thought: The Intelligence of Emotions* (Cambridge: Cambridge University Press).

PEARS, D. (1985). *Motivated Irrationality* (Oxford: Oxford University Press).

POELLNER, P. (1995). *Nietzsche and Metaphysics* (Oxford: Clarendon Press).

———— (2001). 'Perspectival Truth', in B. Leiter and J. Richardson (eds.), *Nietzsche* (Oxford: Oxford University Press).

———— (2003). 'Non-conceptual Content, Experience and the Self', *Journal of Consciousness Studies* 10/2: 32–57.

———— (2004). 'Self-Deception, Consciousness and Value: The Nietzschean Contribution', *Journal of Consciousness Studies* 11/10–11: 44–65.

———— (2006). 'Phenomenology and Science in Nietzsche', in K. J. Ansell-Pearson (ed.), *A Companion to Nietzsche* (Oxford: Blackwell).

PROUST, M. (2002). *In Search of Lost Time*, vol. i: *Swann's Way* (London: Vintage).

SARTRE, J.-P. (2002). *Sketch for a Theory of the Emotions* (London: Routledge).

SCHELER, M. (1973). *Formalism in Ethics and Non-formal Ethics of Value* (Evanston: Northwestern University Press).

SEARLE, J. (1983). *Intentionality* (Cambridge: Cambridge University Press).

SHAFER-LANDAU, R. (2003). *Moral Realism* (Oxford: Oxford University Press).

STEIN, E. (1980). *Zum Problem der Einfühlung* (Munich: Kaffke).

STROUD, B. (2000). *The Quest for Reality: Subjectivism and the Metaphysics of Colour* (Oxford: Oxford University Press).

TAYLOR, C. (1982). 'Responsibility for Self', in G. Watson (ed.), *Free Will* (Oxford: Oxford University Press).

VAN ROOJEN M. (2002). 'Humean and Anti-Humean Internalism About Moral Judgements', *Philosophy and Phenomenological Research* 65: 26–49.

WEDGWOOD, R. (2001). 'Sensing Values?', *Philosophy and Phenomenological Research* 63: 215–23.

WIGGINS, D. (1987). *Needs, Values, Truth* (Oxford: Blackwell).

WRIGHT, C. (1988). 'Moral Values, Projection and Secondary Qualities', *Proceedings of the Aristotelian Society*, supp. vol. 62: 1–26.

ZIMMERMAN, M. (1999). 'Virtual Intrinsic Value and the Principle of Organic Unities', *Philosophy and Phenomenological Research* 59: 653–66.

10

Vengeful Thinking and Moral Epistemology

Neil Sinhababu

Daybreak, the book in which Nietzsche's "campaign against *morality* begins" (*Ecce Homo*, D:1), itself begins with the following aphorism:

Supplemental rationality—All things that live long are gradually so saturated with reason that their origin in unreason thereby becomes improbable. Does not almost every precise history of an origination impress our feelings as paradoxical and wantonly offensive? Does the good historian not, at bottom, constantly *contradict*? (1)

Six years later, in *On the Genealogy of Morality*, Nietzsche traces the historical development of contemporary moral beliefs from their "origin in unreason." While the *Genealogy* may have impressed the feelings of many readers as "wantonly offensive," its import for moral theory has not been fully understood, and the focus of this essay will be to make clear the significance of histories like Nietzsche's for contemporary debates about whether belief in moral properties is justified. One might worry that arguments against believing something whose premises involve the ways that the belief originated will commit the Genetic Fallacy, mistakenly claiming direct logical connections between the circumstances of the belief's origin and its truth. There are, however, good arguments connecting the origins of beliefs to their justificatory status, and I will present two such arguments in this essay.

The first essay of the *Genealogy* describes the way that the vengeful fury of oppressed classes in ancient Rome caused them to invert the value system of their rulers and embrace slave morality. Nietzsche's account does not rely on moral properties to do any explanatory work, and it presents the slaves' mechanisms of belief-formation as ones that are unreliable in generating true belief. If this account (or an account that is like it in the relevant respects) is correct, it will support a pair of arguments that moral anti-realists could use against non-reductive naturalistic moral realism. According to the Explanatory Argument, we should reject moral properties because the best explanation of our observations makes no reference to them. Gilbert Harman makes this argument in *The Nature of Morality*, and Brian Leiter deals with realist counterarguments to it in "Moral Facts and Best Explanations". According to the Unreliability Argument, processes of belief-formation that are unreliable in getting us to the truth are responsible for our beliefs in moral properties. As many plausible theories of epistemic justification claim, we have little reason to hang on to beliefs that we know were caused by unreliable processes. Therefore, we should give up the beliefs about moral properties that we know to be caused by these unreliable processes. This argument for anti-realism has not attracted as much attention, and it will be a major focus of this essay to develop it.

First I will go over Nietzsche's account of the origins of our moral practices in the first essay of the *Genealogy*. Then I will address the disputes about moral realism that the Explanatory Argument and the Unreliability Argument will enter into, and spell out these two arguments. I will show how Nietzsche's account advances the arguments by giving us reason to accept their premises.

According to Nietzsche's account in the *Genealogy*, the contemporary Western system of moral values was born thousands of years ago in ancient Rome when oppressed slaves embraced a moral system that was the reverse of their noble oppressors' values. Both systems of moral values were formed under conditions of intense emotion, not out of cold calculations of prudence or after sober reflection on what is valuable. The former set of values arose from the pride of the nobles, who first "ranked themselves and their doings as good" (GM I:2). Proud of themselves and their deeds, nobles' evaluations of other people reflected the degree of similarity between these people and themselves. Actions that expressed a powerful, brave, truthful, honorable character similar to that of the nobles themselves were admired, while weak, cowardly, dishonest, and base actions that expressed an ignoble character met with disapprobation. In *Beyond Good and Evil*, Nietzsche describes this kind of valuing and the emotional state that drives it: "Everything it knows as part of itself it honors: such a morality is self-glorification. In the foreground there is the feeling of fullness, of power that seeks to overflow" (260). The nobles' beliefs about what is valuable arise out of emotion rather than clearheaded reflection on what would serve them best: "The viewpoint of utility is as foreign and inappropriate as possible, especially in relation to so hot an outpouring of the highest rank-ordering, rank-distinguishing value judgments: for here feeling has arrived at an opposite of that low degree of warmth presupposed by every calculating prudence, every assessment of utility" (GM I:2). Nietzsche describes the mental states that give rise to all systems of values in *Thus Spoke Zarathustra*: "Good and evil have always been created by lovers and creators. The fire of love glows in the names of all the virtues, and the fire of wrath" (Z I: "On the Thousand and One Goals").

It is the fire of wrath that glows brighter in slave morality. The historical preconditions for the formation of slave morality involve the oppression of slaves at the hands of their masters. The slaves are infuriated at their mistreatment and at the miserable conditions of their lives, and since they are powerless to avenge their sufferings, their fury builds inside them. Their treatment by the nobles brings about the emotional state that Nietzsche calls *ressentiment*—a vengeful hatred of those whom they blame for their sufferings. While nobles are not immune to *ressentiment*, their power enables them to act on their hatreds and discharge their *ressentiment* quickly (GM I:10). But the slaves' powerlessness and inability to act causes their *ressentiment* to build up inside them until it begins to reshape their beliefs and values. The psychological effects of *ressentiment* play a major role in explaining how the slave morality arises—"the slave revolt in morality begins when *ressentiment* becomes creative and gives birth to values" (GM I:10).

How does *ressentiment* give birth to values and bring the slave morality into being? To understand this process, it is important to imagine how people full of *ressentiment* would see their oppressors—that their attitudes towards the oppressors would arise "out of the brewing cauldron of unsatiated hate" (GM I:11). Unsatiated hate, like other intense emotional states that include unsatisfied desire, can affect belief-formation.[1] This is nothing strange—in fact, it happens quite often in ordinary cases of wishful thinking. In cases of wishful thinking, an agent's desiring that *p* causes her to believe that *p*. Wishful thinking seems to play a key role in determining the slaves' beliefs about a number of topics. Since the wish that drives the slaves' belief-formation is a wish for revenge against their masters, driven by their unsatiated hate, "vengeful thinking" would be a more specific name for this phenomenon.

As is the case with all varieties of wishful thinking, vengeful thinking disposes the slaves to believe that the states of affairs which they desire will come to pass. The more satisfying a kind of revenge against the nobles would be, the more powerfully vengeful thinking will dispose them to believe in it. As is generally the case in wishful thinking,

---

[1] There is debate about what kind of anti-realist Nietzsche is. I read him as an error theorist about existing moral discourse. This would justify the attribution of a view to him where moral dispositions are beliefs rather than, say, desires or norm-acceptances. Consider *Daybreak* 103: "it is errors which, as the basis of all moral judgments, impel men to their moral actions. This is my point of view . . . Thus I deny morality as I deny alchemy, that is, I deny their premises: but I do not deny that there have been alchemists who believed in these premises and acted in accordance with them." While it's possible that non-cognitivism would have appealed to Nietzsche, it is anachronistic to ascribe such an innovative view about semantics to him. Error theory, by contrast, has been around at least since Parmenides' claim that all talk of change was systematically mistaken.

the slaves acquire the belief that their revenge fantasies will come true, even when they lack sufficient evidence to justify this belief. The belief that they have the property of moral goodness while the nobles have the property of moral badness arises because of their desire for revenge. This set of beliefs about moral properties is satisfying to them in several ways. For one thing, it allows the slaves to regard themselves as fully justified in hating the nobles, as one is justified in hating evil people. For another thing, it plays a key role in explaining why the afterlife will be pleasant for them and terrible for the nobles. Since they are good and the nobles are evil, God will reward them while punishing the nobles.

The beliefs about the afterlife that result from vengeful thinking are presented in the long quotation from the early church father Tertullian, who vividly describes the torments that the enemies of Christianity will endure in hell when Judgment Day arrives. He describes the provincial governor and other "persecutors of the name of the Lord, being liquefied by flames fiercer than those with which they themselves raged against the Christians!" (GM I:15). Great tragedians, athletes, and philosophers who teach doctrines contrary to Christianity are all described roasting in hell. An important part of Tertullian's vision is that Christians will be able to watch from heaven and enjoy the suffering of their enemies. In fact, part of Tertullian's purpose in describing these torments is to convince other early Christians that pleasures far exceeding those of the public spectacles await them on the Day of Judgment. He exults in the thought of the pagans' torment: "What variety of sights then! What should I admire! What should I laugh at! In which should I exult, seeing so many and great kings . . . now groaning in deepest darkness!" (GM I:15).

There can be no denying the significance of vengeful thinking in causing someone to accept such a conception of the afterlife. Tertullian's intense desire for the nobles to suffer causes him to believe that they will have an afterlife of fiery torment. And his desire to have the fullest possible appreciation of their suffering causes him to believe that he will get a chance to see this suffering when he is in heaven and they are burning. Nietzsche highlights the role of vengeful thinking in proposing an inscription for the gate to heaven. Parodying the words on the gate to Dante's hell, Nietzsche remarks that "I, too, was created by eternal *hate*" would be an apt inscription on the gate to a heaven where Christians rejoice in the torment of their oppressors, "assuming that a truth may stand above the gate to a lie!" (I:15).

In this case, it is clear that the beliefs of the slaves are wildly in error. Even most theists who believe in an afterlife will regard Tertullian's beliefs about the nature of heaven and hell as false. Contemporary theistic accounts generally do not portray the inhabitants of heaven exulting in the miseries of the damned. I take this to be a powerful illustration of how vengeful thinking can lead one into error. Certainly, not all instances of vengeful or wishful thinking involve such absurd beliefs. Sometimes, these forms of belief-formation even give rise to true beliefs. But

I take it as uncontroversial that wishful thinking is an unreliable process of belief formation, as is the special case of vengeful thinking, and that the slaves' beliefs about the afterlife are an illustration of how badly awry vengeful belief-formation can go.

One of the most significant effects of *ressentiment* on the slaves—and the effect that the first essay describes in greatest detail—concerns the particular system of values that they adopt. In their hatred of the nobles and their "opposition to the aristocratic value equation (good = noble = powerful = beautiful = happy = beloved of God)" the slaves invert the noble system of values (GM I:7). Nietzsche presents the view about values that they come to hold:

> the miserable alone are good, the suffering, deprived, sick, ugly, are also the only pious, the only blessed in God, for them alone is there blessedness—whereas you, you noble and powerful ones, you are in all eternity the evil, the cruel, the lustful, the insatiable, the godless, you will eternally be the wretched, accursed, and damned!   (GM I:7)

All the features of the nobles—especially the ones that were involved in the infliction of harm on the slaves—are regarded as evil. Nietzsche claims that the slaves' belief in the evil of the nobles arises first, and that the slaves' belief in their own goodness arises as a response. He invites us to "imagine 'the enemy' as the human being of *ressentiment* conceives of him—and precisely here is his deed, his creation: he has conceived of 'the evil enemy,' 'the evil one,' and this indeed as the basic concept, starting from which he now thinks up, as reaction and counterpart, a good one—himself!" (GM I:7). This is the process by which the values of slave morality—both the negative values associated with the nobles and the positive values opposite the nobles—are formed. Furthermore, it is the process by which the slaves come to make the distinctive set of moral observations associated with slave morality. In regarding the nobles as evil, they observe that the property of being evil exists in the world (specifically, in the part of the world that is the nobles). In regarding themselves as good, they observe that the property of being good exists in the world (namely, in the part of the world that is themselves). In addition to supporting a picture of the afterlife where their vengeance is carried out, this set of moral beliefs allows the slaves to see themselves as blessed creatures loved by God, while the nobles are hated by God as well as damned.

Here one might wonder about the justificatory status of the nobles' own moral beliefs. Their process of moral belief-formation is similarly driven by powerful emotions. Does Nietzsche think their beliefs are subject to the same criticisms? And if so, why does Nietzsche express more positive attitudes towards the noble morality than towards the slave morality? On my interpretation, Nietzsche regards the nobles' moral beliefs as unjustified and false as well. He describes how the noble mode of valuation sometimes "lays a hand on reality and sins against it" and "forms a wrong idea of the sphere it holds in contempt" (GM I:10). But Nietzsche allows that one can rise to a fairly high level of human excellence without much epistemic virtue, and epistemic virtue is not the justification for his positive attitude towards the nobles. Nietzsche approves of the noble morality not because it is true or because the nobles are epistemically justified in accepting it, but because it promotes the active, proud, strong-willed lifestyle that the nobles enjoy.[2]

I should deal with an interpretative issue here. Nietzsche occasionally uses language that suggests intentional, conscious action in describing how the slaves form their new set of values. He says that the slaves perform "an act of spiritual revenge" (GM I:7) that comes out of "vengeful cunning" and exhibits a "prudence of the lowest order" (GM I:13) when they "*fabricate ideals* on earth" (GM I:14). On this reading, one is almost tempted to add to the beginning of section 14 a scene where one of the priests in the dark underground workplace says, "Hey guys! Let's just get everyone to reverse all the nobles' values, and we'll have our revenge!" I have resisted this interpretation[3] and treated the slaves' inversion of values as the outcome of a passive and mostly subconscious process—vengeful thinking—and not as the intended outcome of an action. (Not much will hang on this regarding the larger argument which I will present later about the justificatory status of our moral beliefs—one need not invoke moral properties to explain a conscious and intentional inversion of values, and it would be quite surprising if the beliefs formed by this process were reliably caused.) One reason I have interpreted the inversion of values as passive and subconscious is that Nietzsche's account makes much less sense to me if the inversion of values is achieved by a conscious intentional action. One cannot change one's beliefs merely by desiring some state of affairs, believing that a belief-change will bring about the desired state, and performing the necessary belief-change through an act of will. Unfortunately for anyone who wants to make Pascal's Wager, beliefs do not change in this way. Even those who reject the assumption that moral values are beliefs will probably agree that values (whatever kinds of mental states they may be) do not change that way either. One can act because one believes that an action will bring about the desired vengeance, but one cannot simply swap the values one holds for another set of values as a means of inflicting vengeance. Powerful emotions like *ressentiment* can reshape one's values or cause one to regard new things as valuable, but intentional action is not the process by which a change in values occurs.

---

[2] I cannot properly argue for this claim here. But let me point to BGE 4, where Nietzsche says that "the falseness of a judgment is not necessarily an objection to a judgment . . . The question is to what extent it is life-promoting, life-preserving, species-preserving, perhaps even species-cultivating." I contend that when Nietzsche speaks approvingly of noble morality, it is on these grounds.

[3] In Chapter 5 of this volume, Jay Wallace also criticizes this interpretation of the Genealogy, which he calls the "strategic interpretation." I am sympathetic to his criticisms, which differ in some respects from mine.

In section 13, Nietzsche twice describes as "self-deception" the process by which the slaves come to see merit in their weakness. Self-deception is not a process in which one forms a conscious intention to believe something and carries that intention out by an act of will. It is a subconscious process in which discomfort with the belief best supported by the evidence causes one to avoid accepting it or seriously considering the evidence for it. I consider wishful thinking to be a kind of self-deception, but even if this is wrong, wishful thinking is a lot closer to the "self-deception" that Nietzsche attributes to the slaves than intentional action is.

The comment about the prudence displayed in the slaves' inversion of values actually works against the interpretation on which the slaves invert values by means of an intentional action. This "prudence of the lowest order" is something Nietzsche attributes to insects when they play dead in times of danger (GM I:13). Unless we are willing to say that Nietzsche sees insects as having the deliberative complexity that would make an attribution of prudence appropriate, we should regard this suggestion of intentional action as merely figurative. Indeed, Nietzsche often describes the non-intentional behaviors of organisms in ways that seem to attribute an inappropriately robust intentional background to them. The following aphorism, from *Twilight of the Idols*, is a nice example: "When stepped on, a worm doubles up. That is clever. In that way he lessens the probability of being stepped on again. In the language of morality: *humility*" ("Maxims and Arrows" 31). The talk of action and cunning in reversing values should, I think, be read as figuratively as talk of the clever humility of worms.

Rudiger Bittner (in his "Ressentiment") has offered an interpretation according to which the slaves' creation of values is part of a phenomenon of "sour grapes". Like the fox in Aesop's fable, who avoided being frustrated by his inability to get some ripe grapes by believing that they were actually sour, the slaves avoid being frustrated about their inability to enjoy the nobles' pleasures by believing that the nobles are mired in immorality for enjoying those pleasures. In this way, they reduce the frustration involved in believing that they are missing out on something good. Even more clearly than the account where the slaves invert values through conscious intentional action, this account will be congenial to my broader argument. It does not invoke moral properties to do any explanatory work, and it is clear that the "sour grapes" way is not a reliable process of belief-formation. I disagree with it as an interpretation of the first essay, however, because it does not put enough emphasis on the vengefulness of the slaves. It seems that Nietzsche wants to emphasize how the slaves make their moral values out of "revenge and hate" and out of the "hope for revenge" (GM I:14). While Bittner can adequately explain why Tertullian would predict a bad afterlife for the nobles, Tertullian's vehement hatred of the nobles and the way he exults in their suffering when he expresses his vision of the afterlife is better accounted for by a "vengeful thinking" interpretation than a "sour grapes" one. Bittner's interpretation is better suited to accounts of irrational belief formation about the afterlife that appear elsewhere in Nietzsche's work, where vengefulness seems to play a less significant role.[4]

Why does vengeful thinking bring the slaves to these particular beliefs about the afterlife and morality, but not to beliefs about other issues more directly related to the happiness of the nobles? One reason for the special potency of vengeful thinking in the cases I have described has to do with the difficulty of disconfirming the kinds of beliefs that the slaves do form. The slaves cannot easily form the belief that the nobles are starving to death, even though vengeful thinking might dispose them to embrace such a belief. That belief would be empirically disconfirmed when the slaves saw the nobles feasting and enjoying themselves, and when they saw that the nobles were not gaunt and emaciated. The situation is different with beliefs about the afterlife and beliefs about general principles of morality. These beliefs, if not totally isolated from empirical confirmation and disconfirmation, are at least difficult to confirm or disconfirm empirically. Evidence does not get in the way of vengeful thinking on these topics, while evidence can impede the belief-formation that arises from vengeful thinking about other issues.

All Nietzsche offers in the First Essay is an account of the historical origins of contemporary Western moral values. He does not present an explicit account of how this moral system was transmitted from one generation to the next, so that it could become the dominant moral system of our time. It is clear, though, that he thinks such transmission took place, and that his account needs to be supplemented by some story about how moral norms are handed down through the centuries so that we can inherit slave morality. An interpretation according to which *ressentiment* has generated new moral systems so frequently as to eliminate the need for mechanisms transmitting the slave morality from Roman times to us would not need such supplementation, but the text does not support it. Nietzsche does not present his account in the First Essay as one instance of a process that occurs again every time people come to believe in slave morality. Certainly, Nietzsche does hold that *ressentiment* has affected people's values at other points in history—the French Revolution (GM I:16), anarchism, and anti-Semitism (GM II:11) provide examples. But he does not give an account of a contemporary slave revolt that generated our entire system of values, and he does not suggest that our entire system of values is the result of one. Instead, he claims that the victorious values of today arose in the revaluation of two millennia ago, which he spends the majority of the First Essay describing—"Israel, with its revenge and revaluation of values, has thus far again and again triumphed over all other ideals, all more *noble ideals*" (GM I:8). When Nietzsche's opponent, the modern democrat, says that the slave revolt "happened

---

[4] Examples include the formation of beliefs about heaven discussed in *Zarathustra* I: "On the Afterworldly" and in the third essay of the *Genealogy*.

through the Jews . . . never has a people had a more world-historic mission," Nietzsche seems to regard this as a correct characterization of his view (GM I:9). The Jewish revaluation would not have been so world-historic if it were just one among many revaluations.

How was the slave morality passed down through the generations so that we moderns could inherit it? While Nietzsche does not provide an account of this process, one can be developed for him. One just needs to deploy whatever account one has of the processes by which parents transmit their moral values to their children, and by which societies cause their members to internalize prevailing moral values. The institutional power of the Church to perpetuate Christian morality is also a significant factor. And given the difficulties involved in finding genuine disconfirming evidence for one's beliefs about morality, one can see why the passage of time did not result in the accumulation of sufficient counterevidence to overturn the moral system that arose when the slaves completed their revaluation. Even if counterevidence had been available, it might not have been given sufficient attention under the intellectual stagnation that dominated most of the centuries between Tertullian and ourselves. It took well over a thousand years before Galileo discovered the simple physical fact that falling objects of different weights accelerate at a uniform rate, and moral-theory-disconfirming observable facts would probably have had a similarly difficult time attracting notice.

Now that I have presented Nietzsche's account of the origins of morality, I will turn my focus to the arguments against non-reductive naturalistic moral realism that it supports. Nietzsche's account supports the Explanatory Argument by furthering explanations of our moral observations that do not invoke any moral properties. His account supports the Unreliability Argument by making us aware that moral beliefs arise through a process that does not reliably generate true belief. After giving some background on the debates that these arguments will enter into, I will describe the arguments themselves in detail.

One way to defend moral realism is to argue that moral properties have a place in the best explanatory picture of the world. The explanatory power of moral properties is attacked by anti-realists like Harman and Leiter, and defended by naturalistic moral realists like Nicholas Sturgeon and Geoffrey Sayre-McCord. When these naturalistic moral realists discuss the existence of moral properties, they are talking about irreducible moral properties.[5] In "Moral Explanations," Sturgeon argues that it is

---

[5] The reality of reducible moral properties is a less complicated issue—one just has to establish the reality of the reduction base, and reductive moral realists usually offer reduction bases whose existence is uncontroversial. The challenge for reductive moral realists is finding a plausible reduction base. In writing about "moral properties" here, I will generally be referring to irreducible moral properties.

"plausible to cite moral facts as part of an explanation of non-moral facts, and in particular of people's forming the moral opinions that they do" (243). In saying this, he responds to Harman's view (in "Ethics and Observation") that in cases where we make the observation that some act was morally wrong, "neither the moral principle nor the wrongness of the act can help explain why you observe what you observe" (123). If what justifies us in believing in some property is that the property figures in the best explanatory picture of the world, Sturgeon's view will have us being justified in believing in moral properties while Harman's view will not.

In "Moral Theory and Explanatory Impotence," Sayre-McCord lays out several versions of the "Explanatory Criterion" which is being used in determining whether or not we are justified in believing that moral properties exist. The version of the Explanatory Criterion that he eventually relies on in his discussion of the issue is the following: "A hypothesis should not be believed if the hypothesis plays no role in the best explanation we have of our making the observations we do" (267).

Sayre-McCord attacks the anti-realists' Explanatory Argument, which can be expressed as follows:

(P1) The hypothesis that moral properties exist is not part of the best explanation of our observations.

(P2) If a hypothesis is not part of the best explanation of our observations, we are not justified in believing it.

(C) We are not justified in believing that moral properties exist.

P2 is a rephrasing of Sayre-McCord's Explanatory Criterion, accepted by both the realists and the anti-realists in this part of the debate. The disagreement between realists and anti-realists is about P1. Harman and Leiter believe that the hypothesis that moral properties exist does not figure in the best explanations of our observations; Sturgeon and Sayre-McCord believe that the hypothesis has an important role to play.

Consider a set of observations which moral realists might claim their hypothesis usefully explains—observations about the moral rightness and wrongness of various actions. If moral observations are construed in a parallel way to our observations about color, the case for moral realism might begin to look as strong as the case for realism about colors.[6] To many, it seems plausible to give a realist explanation for our color experiences on which my experience of red is explained by the property of redness being instantiated in a strawberry that is in front of me. Similarly, it can seem plausible to give a realist explanation for our moral observations. If I were asked what

---

[6] While realism about objective color properties is a popular position, it is far from uncontroversial. Furthermore, many realist positions—for example, the reductive physicalist position of Frank Jackson—won't supply the non-reductive moral realist with a comfortable analogy to the position he wants for moral properties.

I thought of Churchill's decision to block food imports into 1940s Bengal and allow millions of Indians to starve, I would respond that it was viciously wrong. In giving a realist explanation, one would assert that Churchill's actions had the property of being viciously wrong, and that this explained the belief I formed in thinking about the situation. (Here I do not fill out the realist explanation—most likely, there would be steps between Churchill's action and my judgment. I am just presenting the essential features of a realist explanation.)

Harman defends P1 of the Explanatory Argument, saying that moral properties are not necessary to explain moral observations. All we need for a good explanation are the non-moral facts—namely, that Churchill caused millions to starve, that I have learned the history of India, and that I have been acculturated to think that causing mass starvation is wrong. These factors are sufficient to explain my making the observations I do. As Harman writes, "an assumption about moral facts would seem to be totally irrelevant to the explanation of your making the judgment you make" (122).

Moral judgments are not the only things that moral properties are said to explain.[7] Sayre-McCord writes that

Many very useful, and frequently offered, explanations of events in the world (and so of our observations of those events) make reference to moral facts. Mother Teresa's goodness won her a Nobel Prize; Solidarity is popular because of Poland's oppressive political institutions; millions died in Russia as a result of Stalin's inhumanity; people are starving unnecessarily because of the selfishness of others; unrest in Soweto is a response to the injustice of apartheid. (275)

However, explanations of these events that appeal only to psychological, social, and physical properties seem to have satisfied scholars who study them. As Brian Leiter points out, "moral facts appear to play no role in any developed explanatory theory . . . there is no school of 'Moral Historians' using moral facts to do any interesting or complex explanatory work" (94). Here Leiter draws on existing explanatory accounts of historical and social phenomena to argue for the first premise of the Explanatory Argument.

---

[7] Even if it turned out that properties like honesty played a role in the best explanatory theories, that would not spell victory for the non-reductive moral realist. A reductive moral realist who wanted to reduce moral goodness to honesty would be able to declare victory, because the reduction base for morality had earned its explanatory credentials. (As few philosophers since Diogenes have been eliminativists about honesty, defending its reality by pointing out its role in best explanations might be unnecessary in contemporary debates.) But a non-reductive moral realist would have to show something further—that the moral value supervening on honesty played an important explanatory role. If aspects of honesty other than its moral value did all of the explanatory work, the existence of the moral value would not be successfully vindicated. I thank Geoffrey Sayre-McCord for helping me see this.

Nietzsche endorses the Explanatory Argument in an early passage of *Daybreak*. He claims that giving non-moral causal explanations of moral phenomena will eliminate the need to posit moral properties:

Sense for morality and sense for causality in counteraction—In the same measure as the sense for causality increases, the extent of the domain of morality decreases: for each time one has understood the necessary effects and has learned how to segregate them from all the accidental effects and incidental consequences (*post hoc*), one has destroyed a countless number of *imaginary causalities* hitherto believed in as the foundations of customs—the real world is much smaller than the imaginary . . . (10)

In this passage, "sense for causality" refers to the ability to identify correctly the causal processes explaining events. When Harman gives non-moral explanations of moral observations and Leiter cites non-moral explanations of historical phenomena, they work to destroy the "imaginary causalities" that Sturgeon and Sayre-McCord defend. With the moral properties eliminated, our overall explanatory picture of the world comes out to be "smaller." In a later work, Nietzsche describes our lack of justification for holding moral beliefs once the explanatory irrelevance of moral properties has been demonstrated as "the moral problem: *Why have morality at all* when life, nature, and history are 'not moral'?" (*Gay Science* 344).[8]

Nietzsche's explanation of how the slaves arrived at their moral beliefs in the *Genealogy* is one that moral anti-realists who accept the Explanatory Criterion could be happy with. It provides the support needed for the first premise of the Explanatory Argument. At no point does one need to invoke a moral property to explain anything. In order to explain how the slaves got their beliefs in the immorality of aggressive and violent actions like the ones the nobles often performed, we do not need to assume that an irreducible property of being immoral supervenes on the nobles' aggressive and violent behavior. (Nietzsche's unwillingness to attribute the property of immorality to the nobles' violent and aggressive behavior is one reason why the First Essay can be so unsettling to read.) All we need to assume is that the nobles did things that caused the slaves to desire vengeance, and that vengeful thinking caused the creation of slave morality in the way that I have described. To generate an explanation of present-day moral beliefs, we likewise need no reference to irreducible moral properties. We just need to discover the psychological properties that are involved in the acquisition of moral beliefs from other members of society.

This account of how moral beliefs originated will help the anti-realist explain moral observations by explaining how we acquired the "auxiliary hypotheses" that give these observations their moral content. Consider the way scientific observations

---

[8] In this section, Nietzsche suggests a parallel between the metaphysical status of epistemic and moral norms that is very similar to the parallel Sayre-McCord suggests later in his essay.

go—scientists encounter situations where some real entity (say, a proton) causes observable phenomena and apply their beliefs about the kind of entity that would be causally responsible for the observed phenomena, resulting in the formation of beliefs about the real entity. If the scientist's auxiliary hypotheses connecting the observed phenomena to the real entity are good, entities of the same kind as the real entity will probably have played a role in the construction of the auxiliary hypotheses. Harman's original example involves a scientist who sees activity in a cloud chamber and infers that a proton must have moved through the chamber. If the scientist is correct in holding the auxiliary hypothesis that such activity in a cloud chamber is caused by protons, the activity of protons probably plays some role in explaining why he accepts this hypothesis. Most likely, previous experiments establishing a link between protons and similar motions in cloud chambers played a role in causing his acceptance of the auxiliary hypothesis. So protons play a key role in explaining why the scientist holds the physical theory he does, in addition to explaining the events in the cloud chamber.

Now consider the way that a Harman-style explanation of moral observations would go—observers encounter situations constituted entirely by non-moral facts and apply their beliefs that certain moral properties supervene on the non-moral facts, resulting in moral observations. A realist might ask for an explanation of how the beliefs connecting moral properties to non-moral facts—the analogs of auxiliary hypotheses in the scientific case—arose. Nietzsche offers an explanation that establishes a disanalogy between the moral case and the scientific case. While protons need to be invoked to explain the existence of auxiliary hypotheses according to which protons are connected to events in cloud chambers, no moral properties need to be invoked in explaining why we hold auxiliary hypotheses according to which moral properties are connected to natural properties. To do the explanatory work, we just need violent aggression directed by nobles towards slaves, some vengeful thinking by the slaves, and the means to transmit the results of vengeful thinking down through the ages.

Evaluating the correctness of Nietzsche's historical account is beyond the scope of this essay. Of course, his particular account need not be correct for the Explanatory Argument to go forward. Nietzsche's account supports the Explanatory Argument by helping to explain our moral observations—in particular, accounting for the existence of the auxiliary hypotheses that they depend on—without invoking moral properties. Nietzsche's story is by no means the only one that could do this work. For example, if some Marxist account is correct in describing how economic relations give rise to the prevalent moral systems from which our auxiliary hypotheses are drawn, it might underwrite the first premise of the Explanatory Argument just as well.

Now I will move towards a discussion of the Unreliability Argument. The Unreliability argument comes into play if P1 of the Explanatory Argument is accepted, but P2—the Explanatory Criterion—is rejected. We might reject P2 if realists could show that we were justified in believing hypotheses according to which some properties existed, but did not play a role in our best explanations. In that case, anti-realists would have to offer a new argument which would rule out moral properties but not the properties cited in the realist argument that forced us to reject P2. This is what the Unreliability Argument will do.

While Sayre-McCord wants to contest the anti-realists' claims by arguing that moral facts cannot be dropped from the best explanations, he suggests a fallback position to defend if satisfactory non-moral explanations are available. Immediately after the passage where he claims that geopolitical events can be explained with reference to moral properties, he continues, "Even if such explanations could be replaced by others that appeal only to psychological, social, and physical properties, without mention of moral facts, the moral explanations would still be useful in just the way talk of colors remains useful in light of theories of light" (275). Even if reductions of color properties fail, it is not clear that non-reductive realism will triumph over anti-realism with regard to color. One might hold fast to the Explanatory Criterion and argue that we really are unjustified in positing color properties. Perhaps we should be error theorists about color, and give a similarly anti-realist account of moral talk.[9]

At the end of his essay, Sayre-McCord presents another set of candidate irreducible properties that can be analogized to moral properties, just as color properties can. These are the properties we appeal to in evaluating explanations. As Sayre-McCord argues, one cannot use the Explanatory Criterion against moral properties unless one has already accepted epistemic value properties in virtue of which explanations excluding moral properties are better than explanations including them: "If one explanation is to be better than another in virtue of being simpler, more general, more elegant, and so on, then simplicity, generality, and elegance cannot themselves be evaluatively neutral. Were these properties evaluatively neutral, they could not account for one explanation being better than another" (277). An error theorist about epistemic value who still wants to use the Explanatory Argument will not be able to explain why we are justified in accepting anti-realist explanations over realist ones. At least on this count, epistemic value is a better "partner in crime" for moral properties than color is.[10]

Depending on how the explanations go, there may be grounds for an objection to Sayre-McCord's fallback position. Suppose we discover, as we trace the genealogy of our moral beliefs, that they arose through an unreliable process of belief formation—a process that resulted in the formation of a number of other false beliefs. Then we would

[9] It is hard to see how the color–morality analogy would provide a powerful argument for non-reductive realism, since neither reductive realism nor anti-realism about color can be dismissed out of hand.

[10] That is, assuming that reductive realism does not work. Also, while error theory is not an available option here, one might still try to defend a non-cognitivist theory of epistemic value against Sayre-McCord, and argue for epistemic norms without the ontological commitments of realism.

have an additional reason to withhold belief in moral properties. Beliefs resulting from reliable processes are likely to be true, while beliefs resulting from unreliable processes are not. If we did not have unjustifying explanations of how we attained our color-beliefs and our epistemic value-beliefs, casting the reliability of these processes of belief-formation into doubt, belief in color properties and epistemic value properties would be justified.

This brings us to the Unreliability Argument against moral properties:

(P1) Our beliefs in moral properties were caused by a historical process that is unreliable in generating true belief.

(P2) We know whether an unreliable historical process caused our beliefs in moral properties.

(P3) Beliefs that we know to be caused by unreliable historical processes are unjustified.

(C) We are not justified in believing that moral properties exist.

If we get an independent source of justification for our moral beliefs—as we might if we discovered that moral properties played a role in the best explanations, defeating the Explanatory Argument—the Unreliability Argument will not obtain its conclusion. If the Explanatory Argument is false because moral properties actually do have explanatory power, and if our moral beliefs were caused by our seeing that moral properties have explanatory power, P1 of the Unreliability Argument will be false. (I intend 'cause' in P1 to be read so that beliefs that were initially caused by an unreliable process but which were then reinforced by a reliable process will count as reliably caused. In cases where one's doxastic state is causally overdetermined, one reliable cause will make the belief reliably caused.) Believing hypotheses because they are part of the best explanation of our observations is a reliable way of forming beliefs, and if we discover that moral properties figure in the best explanations, the causal influence that this discovery exerts by backing up our belief in moral properties will be sufficient to justify us in believing that they exist.

Even for a reliabilist, the mere existence of an unreliable step way back in the causal history of the belief may not be enough to make the belief unjustified, if we're unaware of the step and it's sufficiently disconnected from our acquisition of the belief. If we learned our moral beliefs from our parents, and most of the things our parents tell us are true, accepting our parents' beliefs may count as a reliable process. In this case, moral beliefs may be reliably formed regardless of the irrationality of their historical origin. (While it's unclear what the best way to individuate kinds of belief-forming processes is, reliabilists will generally put more emphasis on proximal factors than distal ones.) The view that the majority of contemporary people are currently justified in holding moral beliefs, because of the reliability of proximal belief-forming processes and despite the unreliability of the historical processes, is compatible with the soundness of the Unreliability Argument if the argument is applied only to the beliefs of a historically knowledgeable minority. If a reliable source actually makes everyone aware that their moral beliefs were formed in an unreliable way, even because of a step way back in history, this will eliminate the justification for continuing to hold them. One only loses one's justification for believing in irreducible moral properties when one becomes justified in believing an account on which belief in these properties is unreliably caused. A Nietzschean story about the origins of morality may not point out a pre-existing lack of justification for believing in moral properties—it can actually take one's justification away. This is why P2 is necessary to the Unreliability Argument.[11]

The appeal of P3 should not be limited to those who accept a version of reliabilist epistemology. Coherentists will accept P3 because maintaining belief in moral properties will cohere badly with the belief that the process that generated them is unreliable. Foundationalists will accept P3 because unreliable processes are unlikely to provide either foundational or inferential justification for beliefs. Those who accept a Nozick-style tracking account of justification will accept P3 as long as the process of belief-formation is unreliable enough that our beliefs would not track the existence of moral properties in counterfactual situations. Since the process that generated the slaves' moral beliefs would have brought about such beliefs even without the existence of the moral properties that would have made them true, these beliefs will be unjustified according to Nozick's theory.

Probably the best general way to understand P3 is as an instance of defeasible reasoning—specifically, as a case in which we have found an undercutting defeater for one of our beliefs. Undercutting defeaters give us reason to reject the conditionals tying putative evidence to the propositions that they are putative evidence for:

If P is a *prima facie* reason for S to believe Q, then R is an undercutting defeater for P iff R is a reason for S to believe that it is not true that P would not be true unless Q were true.[12]

We might take the fact that we make moral observations as *prima facie* evidence for the existence of moral properties. But if we see that the historical process that generated our moral observations does not reliably indicate that these properties exist, we will have an undercutting defeater for the existence of the moral properties. When we discover the absence of a reliable connection between the observations and the properties, we will be justified in rejecting the belief that the observations would not be made unless the properties existed.

If we come to know that Nietzsche's account from the First Essay of the *Genealogy* is correct, P1 and P2 of the Unreliability Argument will be true. P1 will be true because

---

[11] I thank Anthony Gillies for assistance on this point.

[12] Scott Sturgeon 102, adapting the terminology from John Pollack's *Contemporary Theories of Knowledge*.

the process by which we came to our beliefs—inheriting the outcome of past vengeful thinking—is clearly unreliable. Wishful thinking is generally unreliable, and we have an example of the unreliability of the slaves' particular brand of wishful thinking, in their absurd beliefs about the nature of the afterlife. Inheriting beliefs formed in this way is not a reliable way of getting at the truth. The fact of our knowing this account will make P2 true. Then if the epistemic norms we accept lead us to P3—as most contemporary theories of epistemic justification do—the Unreliability Argument will obtain its conclusion. We will be unjustified in believing in moral properties.

Now I will examine the implications of the Unreliability Argument for color and epistemic value properties. If the reduction of color properties fails, will colors be ruled out of our ontology along with morality because of the Unreliability Argument? There is no reason to think that they will. If we replace "moral properties" with "color properties," P1 becomes false. Beliefs caused by sense-perception under normal conditions are, in general, true. Most of our color perceptions fall into this category, and therefore it makes sense to believe in colors. That is something that cannot be said of beliefs caused by vengeful thinking, or wishful thinking in general. Vengeful thinking is not a reliable cause of true belief. So any concern that the rigorous requirements of the Explanatory Argument will force us to anti-realist conclusions about color properties is satisfactorily dealt with by the softer requirements of the Unreliability Argument.

Epistemic value properties will most likely pass the tests offered by the Unreliability Argument. Even if reductive accounts of epistemic value fail, many approaches to epistemology come with plausible stories about how the theories of justification that they issue are reliably caused. Consider, for example, naturalistic epistemologists who develop their views about epistemic value by studying sciences that yield correct predictions. They would be able to point to their study of science in defending the processes by which they arrived at their theories of epistemic value. At the very least, the Unreliability Argument will not support a global attack on any theory of epistemic justification.[13] If the skeptic thinks we are justified in accepting the conclusions of the Unreliability Argument with respect to epistemic value properties, this positive claim about justification—which presupposes epistemic value properties that can underwrite our justification for accepting the skeptical view—will contradict the global anti-realism, much as Sayre-McCord suggested.

It is possible—though unlikely—for all the premises of both the Unreliability Argument and the Explanatory Argument to hold in a world where moral properties

---

[13] While the Unreliability Argument doesn't support global error theory about epistemic value, it might be locally effective against some views, given an appropriate historical account. Suppose we discover that Alvin Goldman has been using subliminal messages to make us unthinkingly profess reliabilist intuitions when presented with his examples. Then we might be justified in reducing our credence in reliabilism, at least until new examples could be generated.

actually exist. (While the truth ratio of wishful thinking would rise in such a world, it might not rise far enough to falsify P1 of the Unreliability Argument and make wishful thinking count as a reliable process.) In this case, we would have unjustified true belief in the existence of moral properties, and so fall short of moral knowledge. This should not be counterintuitive. If wishful thinking causes me to believe that I will make a fortune on my trip to Las Vegas, and amazing luck at the craps table brings me great wealth, my prior belief will still be unjustified, even though it is true. To put the issue in terms of Nozick's tracking account of epistemic justification, vengeful thinking would still have us believing in moral properties, even in the worlds where the moral properties did not exist. So despite the truth of our beliefs, we are not justified in believing in moral properties.

As with the Explanatory Argument, Nietzsche's particular account need not be true in order for the Unreliability Argument to go forward. All that is needed is some story according to which moral beliefs arise as the result of an unreliable historical process. If our moral beliefs are the result of attempts by powerful individuals to encourage the beliefs that would help them consolidate their power, and if these attempts are generally unreliable sources of true belief, P1 of the Unreliability Argument will be vindicated.

If the two arguments of this essay are successful, and if Nietzsche's account advances them in the way I have suggested it can, we can see how a genealogy of morality bears on the justificatory status of our moral beliefs. To assert that the causal origins of our moral beliefs are relevant to their justificatory status is not necessarily to commit the Genetic Fallacy. If the things that make a belief true play a role in the best explanation of its genesis, we are justified in continuing to hold the belief. If they play no role in the best explanation of its genesis, a potential source of justification is eliminated. And if we find that the causal processes that historically gave rise to the formation of the belief are unreliable, this may destroy our justification for continuing to believe.

The combination of the Explanatory Argument and the Unreliability Argument set out in this essay is not necessarily doom to the non-reductive moral realist. For one thing, maybe Nietzsche's account of the origin of morality is wrong, and vengeful thinking did not play such an important role in the formation of moral belief. That would allow realists to set aside the Unreliability Argument and eliminate one possible explanation for how our moral beliefs were formed. It might also turn out that unreliable processes are implicated in the formation of some of our moral beliefs, while reliable processes are implicated in others. This would have interesting ramifications for the methodology of normative ethics. Rather than just building theories to fit the intuitions generated by various cases, moral theorists would have to ask whether the intuitions arose from reliable causes or unreliable ones. If a theory failed to fit prevalent moral intuitions that arose from unreliable causal processes, this would not be a flaw. But if there is a plausible explanation of all our moral beliefs in terms of vengeful thinking or some other unreliable process that does not involve moral properties, non-reductive moral realists have reason to worry. If such an explanation is in fact the best one, and if it is presented to them, they face the full force of both anti-realist arguments covered in this essay.

References

BITTNER, RUDIGER(1994). "Ressentiment", in Richard Schacht (ed.), *Nietzsche, Genealogy, Morality* (Berkeley: University of California Press).

HARMAN, GILBERT(1988). "Ethics and Observation", in Geoffrey Sayre-McCord (ed.), *Essays on Moral Realism* (Ithaca: Cornell University Press).

LEITER, BRIAN(2001). "Moral Facts and Best Explanations" in E.F. Paul et al. (eds.), *Moral Epistemology* (Cambridge: Cambridge University Press).

NIETZSCHE, FRIEDRICH(1966). *Beyond Good and Evil*, trans. Walter Kaufmann (New York: Random House).

_____ (1997). *Daybreak*, trans. R. J. Hollingdale (Cambridge: Cambridge University Press).

_____ (1974). *The Gay Science*, trans. Walter Kaufmann (New York: Vintage).

_____ (1998). *On the Genealogy of Morality*, trans. Maudemarie Clark and Alan Swensen (Indianapolis: Hackett).

_____ (1982). *Thus Spoke Zarathustra*, trans. Walter Kaufmann (New York: Penguin).

SAYRE-McCORD, GEOFFREY(1988). "Moral Theory and Explanatory Impotence", in Geoffrey Sayre-McCord (ed.), *Essays on Moral Realism* (Ithaca: Cornell University Press).

STURGEON, NICHOLAS(1988). "Moral Explanations", in Geoffrey Sayre-McCord (ed.), *Essays on Moral Realism* (Ithaca: Cornell University Press).

STURGEON, SCOTT(1991). "Truth in Epistemology", *Philosophy and Phenomenological Research* 51/1 : 99–108.

11

Perspectives, Fictions, Errors, Play

Simon Blackburn

In a climate in which the idea of 'fictionalism' as a philosophy of this or that is flourishing, it is natural to salute Nietzsche as an honourable ancestor. For Nietzsche's work is shot through with references to the fictions which in his view make up at least a part of the machinery with which the mind copes with its world. The notion of fiction stands alongside the three other words in my title, in apparent amity—at least, it often seems to be a lottery whether Nietzsche will announce any particular one of them as the key to some diagnosis of our situation, or some recommendation for the men of the future. And fictionalists may feel comforted by another strand in Nietzsche, which is that calling something a fiction is not a put-down, or prelude to elimination. Or at least, if it is then whatever is so put down is in excellent company, since normal predication, logic, cause and effect, and indeed the very idea of the identity of things through time are equally passengers in the one boat.[1] Nor is this diagnosis an arbitrary caprice. Nietzsche was the first philosopher to try to take the measure of Darwinism, and to recognize that throughout nature adaptation trumps truth. If creatures such as us live by imitation, faking, deceiving and self-deceiving, so be it. In summary, for Nietzsche (some) fictions *increase health*, and that is enough for us to cast off any sense of shame, and indeed to congratulate ourselves on our immersion in them. Perhaps our imaginations make up for the limitations of our cognitions or our reason. Of course,

I owe thanks to the discussants at Richard Schacht and Michael Moore's outstanding Nietzsche colloquium at the University of Illinois in 2003. I particularly recall contributions by Maudemarie Clark, Nadeem Hussein, John Richardson, and R. Lanier Anderson. Brian Leiter carefully steered me away from pitfalls in the interpretations of Nietzsche, and I am solely responsible for any tumbles I have nevertheless taken.

[1] See, for instance, *The Gay Science*, §111, *The Genealogy of Morals*, III, §24.

not all fictions will get this protection. Morality may depend upon fictions about human nature which are sufficiently fanciful, sufficiently at variance with the facts of life, to vitiate it. So the right response to finding fiction somewhere may vary from case to case. Indeed, there may be variation even within the case of morality, where we have to balance the possibility of a healthy function of ethics in general, against the pallid and unhealthy tone it has taken in the Christian world. It is not a task that Nietzsche shows any signs of relishing, and the question of whether he himself ever got that balance right is surely moot.

In this essay I argue that the apparent amity between my four title words is camouflage. We have to make distinctions, and any idea that Nietzsche somehow enables us to overcome them or get beyond them is unsustainable. If so, we then need to ask whether Nietzsche at some point took a wrong turning, and whether a different, and perhaps more sober, diagnosis of our situation is possible. I shall argue that this is indeed so. The upshot is philosophical, rather than exegetical. My concern is not so much with what Nietzsche did say, but with how we ourselves should think about the things that exercised him. In doing this I shall have little to say about scientific truth, or cause and effect, or logic or identity through time. I shall concentrate on the central issue of values. It would have been nice to salute Nietzsche as an ancestor of my own position, an expressivism tolerant of many of the forms of thought that people wrongly take to be characteristic of realism. But I think that would stretch the evidence, and it is more likely that Nietzsche's own tools are different, but in unfortunate ways. This leaves it that although we may sympathize with his goals, there are better ways of achieving them.

To identify the kind of unsustainability I have in mind, we must investigate the relationship between perspectives, fiction, error, and play. They consort together in a scattershot kind of way: adopting a perspective may result in our telling a story; if the story is fictional it may be an error to present it as fact, and one upshot may be to lighten up, substituting some more playful attitude for the sober concern with the truth. Or, we might argue that some of the things we say, taken as sober fact, are erroneous, but that the right rectification is not to stop saying them, but to preface them with an 'in the fiction' disclaimer, joyfully scattering myth about us as we go. This is one route to fictionalism.[2] But I shall argue that in the area of ethics, these scattershot associations soon dissipate, and with them the attractions of fictionalism. Other kinds of 'non-factualism' provide a much surer handle on the issues. The first relationship I shall consider is that between perspective and error.

---

[2] It is that of David Lewis, in his exploration of the idea of moral fictionalism. See Lewis, 'Quasi-Realism is Fictionalism', and my reply 'Quasi-Realism No Fictionalism', in Mark Kalderon (ed.), *Moral Fictionalism* (Oxford: Oxford University Press, 2005).

I

As has often been noticed, in its origin, the metaphor of perspective does not consort with any notion of error. A view of St Paul's cathedral may be from front or back, near or far, pavement level or roof level, through a wide-angle lens or a telephoto. But no such view is erroneous *per se*, or erroneous just because of the possibility of shifting our point of view. We might, perhaps, concede that any single view is *partial*, although in context even that could be a tendentious thing to say. After all, we may read that from some belvedere you get a *complete* or full view of a city or a church, and if I subsequently try to beat the hotel tariff down on the grounds that the panorama gives me only a partial view of them, since from it I cannot see the back of the church or the back alleys of the city, I will gain little sympathy. If we do say it, and use it to belittle whatever is given to us by such a view, then the remedy is clear: walk on, change the perspective, conjoin and synthesize it with other views or other ways of looking at the object. Sometimes we will know of the particular defects of a particular view: some things are best seen from afar, others from quite close. A mere glimpse may indeed mislead us, or more often, fail to reveal something that more sustained or careful attention would bring to light, in which case, again, the remedy is to look harder, and from different points of view. If we worry that reading one chapter of a book does not give us a fair picture of the whole, we read on and put together what we read. We know perfectly well in general how to supplement glimpses, glimmers, peeks, whiffs, echoes and snatches, by more sustained and extended attention.

To this it might be said that the metaphor of visual perspective is, indeed, only partially indicative of what Nietzsche wants. It is an analogy, and although it breaks down if pressed, it can nevertheless point us in the right direction. We can separate two different elements which may be disanalogies with the intended application of the metaphor. One is that which I have just mentioned, that we *can* shift visual perspective, and can typically do so easily and at will. And the other is that typically we *can* synthesize the different views we get as a result. There is no inconsistency between what we see from the front and the back, or near and far (when there is, we are of course nonplussed, and do search for a diagnosis of error). Perhaps neither possibility exists when we turn to intended applications. Suppose we said, for instance, that our colour vision gives us a particular perspective on the world. We cannot change our visual system, just like that. And we cannot well 'synthesize' what we get as things are, and anything we might imagine ourselves getting were we to see differently. In the case of valuations, we cannot well step outside our own skins, and shift our perspective so that we value what we presently do not. And if we think we can, perhaps by an exercise of imagination or empathy with a different culture, then we cannot conjoin the results, giving us any synthesis parallel to that which we effortlessly achieve in the visual case. If from our actual perspective, women deserve equal political rights to men, and from an imagined perspective they do not, this gives us no possibility of a synthesis from which they both do and do not. Nor, if the conflict were less blatant so that some sort of synthesis did exist, would that by itself give us any motive for moving towards it.

Do either of these disanalogies justify the transition from 'perspective', in this application, to error? They might do so, in some peoples' minds. What we have is a version of John Mackie's 'argument from relativism'. It would be the idea that since there is 'nothing to' the world being coloured or people having rights, beyond the fact that variously minded people will or might be appeared to in different ways and give various verdicts on such matters, then all such verdicts are erroneous, and all corresponding appearances falsify reality. But there is at least one missing premise in this line of thought—a premise that might be true in the case of colour, but which cannot be supposed true in the case of value. I certainly do not want to claim that supplying the missing premise makes the argument from relativism sound. But it does seem a necessary condition of its soundness, for without it the transition seems completely unmotivated.

The premise, of course, has to be that the verdicts or appearances that would make up the different views are all equally good, or equally 'no fault'. They are none of them better than another. But that only has to be stated to seem wrong in general. Perhaps in the case of colour we can imagine a defence: if we really think we can imagine a different kind of colour perception, and if we can also imagine that it stands its possessors in as good a position to discriminate surfaces and changes as we are, then indeed they might tie for first place with our own, and there would be no fault in implementing either (I abstract away from the question of why we would suppose them to be different in the first place). With colour, we do not have to quarrel with any imagined creatures who implement a different scheme. But with ethics we do. If I think that women deserve political equality with men, then I am not at all minded to admit that the perspective from which they do not ties with mine for first place, nor do I admit that there is no fault or flaw instanced by those who adopt it. It follows from my position that any such perspective is distorted or blind or deficient, and that there is at least one fault in people who adopt it, namely that they are wrong about the political equality deserved by women.

It might be replied to this that it does not get to the heart of the metaphysical issue, for in saying what I just did I am, inevitably, standing within my value system, and doling out verdicts of fault and deficiency to competing ones. Metaphysically, it might be said, there remains a symmetry between me doing this, and a competitor saying the same about me, from his standpoint of denying women's political rights. The vocabulary of fault and deficiency can be used by either of us of the other. Indeed, someone might continue, to get past the idea of 'no fault' disagreement by using this response begs the question. It seeks to shore up the status of one value judgment by pointing out that people making it also typically make another related judgment of the same kind. But since the original doubt applied equally to the status of all such judgments, the response has no traction, and is illegitimate in this context.

To which the counter is that the so-called 'metaphysical' symmetry is itself beside the point. The question was whether there is no fault in holding that women have different political rights, and the answer remains that there is. The question was not whether there was a *metaphysical* fault in holding it. Why should there be? The issue is a moral and political one, not a metaphysical one.[3] Supposing overall symmetry because of alleged metaphysical symmetry is like saying that since metaphysics is silent about whether Switzerland has a coastline, the view that it does is neither better nor worse than the view that it does not, and neither implies a fault in their proponents.

Nobody, of course, is going to make that mistake. So why is the corresponding move so common and so tempting in ethics? The answer, surely, is because the notions of real truth, or fact or objectivity, get in the way. We would like our opinion to be not just true—a compliment we can always pay it without extra cost in the same breath as that in which we voice it—but objectively true, and that, we imagine vaguely, implies the metaphysical asymmetry—the backing from real fact—that we have not got. Perhaps, then, it is the loss of that backing that Nietzsche is lamenting, and which is to leave him talking of fiction, perspective, errors and play? That would be very disappointing. Such a thought has an ancestry sure enough, but hardly one to recommend it to Nietzsche, for it is exactly that which leads Plato to buttress the ethical abilities of the elect with knowledge of the Form of the Good. Here metaphysics is called in to underpin ethics, and if it cannot do so, then the alternatives will seem to be either the wholesale loss of ethics which is nihilism, or a piece of necessary self-deception, whereby we slightly desperately maintain the fiction that it can. A Nietzsche who follows that line would be betraying almost everything for which he is usually supposed to stand. It would be more than a little disappointing to find Nietzsche, the great freethinker, the supposed patron saint of postmodernism, the iconoclast and hawk-eyed critic of metaphysics, blown about in the same vortex of 'piffle and hot air' as Plato.[4] It would mean that he is far from emancipated from the late nineteenth-century view that 'if God is dead, everything is permitted'—culturally explicable perhaps, but philosophically naïve and boring.

A clearer view of everything that objectivity can be in ethics should prevent us wanting to knock at the door of visionaries and spirit-seers, or feeling that if we cannot

---

[3] Someone might come to the wrong conclusion about the issue because of further, weird, metaphysics but that is an optional extra.

[4] Especially, of course, given the dismissive association of Plato with Christianity, in *Twilight of the Idols*, §4. For the idea that Platonic Forms introduce piffle and hot air, see Aristotle, *Metaphysics*, 991^{a}21–2. A passage showing that Nietzsche was emancipated from these imaginings about objectivity is *The Genealogy of Morals*, III, §12.

do this, then as a substitute we have to concoct the fiction that we have done so. The right response is to recognize that objectivity comes from within. Looking at St. Paul's objectively just means being careful of slant or distortion, taking account of tricks of light or other influences, bringing to bear such knowledge of Baroque architecture or Wren's career as we can muster. It does not mean averting our gaze from St. Paul's, and looking at something else (except, perhaps, en route to making comparisons). Similarly looking at the political situation of women objectively requires thinking of it as it is, adopting a common point of view, avoiding prejudice and bias, subjecting our own cultural prejudices to the best light we can. It does not mean panting for a Platonic or Gnostic illumination, to be got by looking at something other than the political situation of women. By making a fuss about the loss of metaphysical underpinning Nietzsche would in fact be collaborating with Plato's misunderstanding of our situation, even if his eventual resolution would be different.[5] Each of them would be imagining a need where there is in fact no need.

All that is required to say this is a certain confidence in the way things appear or the verdicts we incline to give. But we have not yet been given an argument for abandoning such confidence, so all is well. The dialectic, incidentally, shows not only that John Mackie's argument from relativism ultimately depends on the argument from 'metaphysical queerness'—for that alone justifies the sense that it would be queer if there were anything other than metaphysical symmetry between the rival perspectives—but also depends on subtly displacing the nature of the judgements with which we are concerned, by making them beholden to some imagined metaphysics, piffle and hot air, rather than to the ethics and politics, where they actually belong.

II

Does Nietzsche do better if we turn to the other two notions on our list, fiction and play? To focus our thoughts, let us concentrate on one famous passage, paragraph 107 of *The Gay Science*:

If we had not welcomed the arts and invented this kind of cult of the untrue, then the realization of general untruth and mendaciousness that now comes to us through science—the realization

---

[5] Aristotle was the first to charge that Plato invents the need for the Forms, and that nothing of their kind could be of any use (see also *Nicomachean Ethics*, 1097ᵃ8—11). I am not here taking sides on whether Plato himself might have meant something more innocent by talk of the Forms. On this, see Julia Annas, *Platonic Ethics Old and New* (Ithaca: Cornell University Press, 1999), ch. 5. The point is that the other-worldly interpretation was common, and is clearly that of Nietzsche himself.

that delusion and error are conditions of human knowledge and sensation—would be utterly unbearable. *Honesty* would lead to nausea and suicide . . . precisely because we are at bottom grave and serious human beings—really more weights than human beings—nothing does us as much good as a *fool's cap*: we need it in relation to ourselves—we need all exuberant, floating, dancing, mocking, childish, and blissful art lest we lose the *freedom above things* that our ideal demands of us. It would mean a *relapse* for us, with our irritable honesty, to get involved entirely in morality and, for the sake of the over-severe demands we make on ourselves in these matters, to become virtuous monsters and scarecrows. We should be *able* also to stand *above* morality—and not only to *stand* with the anxious stiffness of a man who is afraid of slipping and falling at any moment, but also to *float* above it and *play.* How then could we possibly dispense with art—and with the fool?—And as long as you are in any way *ashamed* before yourselves, you do not yet belong with us.[6]

In the first part of this passage it is we ourselves who have 'welcomed the arts and invented this kind of cult of the untrue'. The implication is that this diagnoses our actual situation. But in the second part of the passage the focus seems to switch. Now Nietzsche is talking of an ideal, and the 'exuberant, floating, dancing, mocking, childish and blissful' attitude that it demands of us. The implication in this case is that it is just the men of the future, Zarathustra and his followers, who manage to float above morality and instead play. Art will enable them to do so unashamed of themselves.

I do not want to offer any view about which emphasis accords better with the bulk of Nietzsche's views, but only to warn that they are different. The former purports to describe our situation as we are, fenced against nausea and suicide only by the arts, and by our cult of the untrue. The latter talks of a special kind of person, a playful, joyous, healthy soul for whom it would be a 'relapse' to get involved entirely with morality, thereby becoming a 'virtuous monster' or a 'scarecrow'. There is no implication that we are like this joyous soul, nor even that we could improve to become like it without a massive transformation and rebirth.

We shall come to this view in a moment, but meanwhile it is the former view that puts Nietzsche in contact with contemporary appeals to the notion of a fiction. Fictionalism comes in different forms, but let us take it first as a *practically conservative* doctrine. That is, we suppose that it is presented as a piece of theory that leaves everyday practice untouched. It only gives us a better picture of how to think about it. This better picture in turn can be presented either as an explanation of how we *do* actually think about the area, an interpretation of where we are, or perhaps more realistically, as a revisionary claim about how we *should* think about the area, but one

---

[6] The importance of this passage, and the possibility of divergent interpretations of it, was impressed upon me by Jonathan Ichikawa and Bronwyn Singleton, in a session at the University of Toronto graduate colloquium in 2005.

which nevertheless leaves our actual practice in the area just as it found it. In practice, these may not be as far apart as they sound, since the motivation for revision would presumably have to lie somewhere in things we actually think, and conversely the argument for saying that we do actually think about the area in this surprising way would almost certainly have to be that this is the right, reasonable, way to think about it.

For an example of a practically conservative fictionalism, consider one attitude to the institution of money. The attitude would be one of insisting that money is a social construction, a normative practice that we make up for ourselves. And it might express this insight in terms of fiction (although for reasons we shall explore, this ought actually to sound off-key). If it did, we need not anticipate the theorist campaigning for the abolition of money, or taking less seriously his or her debts and dues. The normative practice will sail on whatever the theorist says, and the theorist may not mind that at all. He might think that the fiction is just what was needed—what Leibniz would have called a *phenomenon bene fundatum*. The theory is only conceived as placing the practice, not as undermining it.

For another example, we might consider idealizations in science: point masses, perfect conductors, or frictionless planes. Suppose a theory is couched in such terms, but also used to generate predictions and explanations. A novice might be alarmed. But he might then be reassured if, for instance, the effect of the idealization is well understood, and any discrepancy with empirical reality outweighed by the convenience of calculation or modelling. After the reassurance, it may be that he can go on using the theory just as he did before the fictional character of the idealizations dawned on him. Nietzsche sometimes talks of fictions when idealization is on his mind. For example, the 'fiction' of identity through time with its alleged implication of changelessness seems to be an idealization abstracting from the fact that things change slowly enough for us to cope with them.[7] Faced with slowly changing things, perhaps we idealize and imagine ourselves surrounded by things in stasis (notice that this would not be a metaphysical fantasy, but a physical one). Understanding the role of such fictions may also leave practice untouched.

The contrast is with fictionalism as a *practically revisionary* doctrine: one whose appreciation penetrates the everyday practice, altering it in one direction or another. Nietzsche clearly thought that some of the things he wanted to say about morality were practically revisionary, and the emphasis on fiction seems to have been part of this campaign, so if he is a fictionalist at least sometimes it seems better to interpret him as a practically revisionist member of the species. And he would not be alone, for the idea that morality involves fiction clearly often consorts with practical revision. If someone like Bentham asserts that rights are a fiction, we expect practical consequences. We

---

[7] For instance, *Twilight of the Idols*, §3, 5.

expect Bentham to argue for particular practical policies in different terms, as indeed he did. If someone asserts that free will and responsibility are fictions, we expect her subsequent ethics to take on a certain hue, and we might expect her penal code to be rather different from that of someone who insists on the reality of the notion.

Closer to more lurid interpretations of Nietzsche than that is the tradition of Thrasymachus and Callicles. This gives us the kind of dismissive fictionalism espoused by Richard III:

> Conscience is but a word that cowards use,
> Devis'd at first to keep the strong in awe:
>
> (*Richard III*, V.3. 336–7)

Some writers seem to thrill most to an imagined Nietzsche as the heroic amoralist, dismissing the timid voice of conscience with triumphant will and force. They forget, as it were, that Richard III is a treacherous murderer at bay, and I believe they forget Nietzsche's fundamental seriousness.

It may not always be clear whether fictionalism ought to be taken as practically conservative, as practically revisionary, or as out and out dismissive. For example, some people are fond of saying that personal identity is a fiction. Well and good, but is the idea supposed to change the way I think about my future or how I relate to the people I care about, and if so, how?[8] Or does it leave my expectations and concerns untouched? Some theologians are cheerful about the continuation of religious practice in spite of the admission that God is a fiction. Others are not, but think the admission undermines the whole point and purpose of their religious activities. These theologians think of their states of mind as *beliefs* and these beliefs are straightforwardly inconsistent with the discovery that what we apparently believe in is actually a fiction. The former kind think only of other supposed benefits of immersion in ritual practice, and the fictional status of their gods is no problem.

When fictions are revisionary or dismissive of practice, I think we can suppose it is simply because some things have been shown to be a fiction, while by contrast others remain true. A worried defendant may be relieved to find that it is a fiction that she owes a plaintiff money, but this is because things would have been very different if it had been discovered to be true. She is not likely to be relieved if some constructivist or ontologically parsimonious philosopher comes as a witness, declaring that all money is a fiction. This does not win her the suit. But fiction here works by contrast: it is equivalent to falsity. It is much harder to interpret the idea that 'everything' is a fiction, or that all our practical reasoning depends on fiction. Why should such a

---

[8] Derek Parfit notoriously argued in *Reasons and Persons* (Oxford, Oxford University Press 1984) that it should loosen our attachment to ourselves, but observation of the world suggests that few if any have found it doing so.

thought, if it makes sense at all, nudge us towards one reaction rather than another? If we were attached to the Platonic fantasy, perhaps the discovery that we are, as it were, treading water rather than set on solid ground might disturb us. But it doesn't by itself instruct us in which direction to move. It doesn't say either that now women's political equality does matter, or that now it does not. In so far as Nietzsche was campaigning for us to ditch specifically Christian ethics we need such a steer—a way of satisfying ourselves that compassion is a corrupt motive compared to egoism, for example. After all, Richard III retains a code of how kings are to behave: decisively, nobly, and courageously. But if all we were given were a generalized interpretation of ethics as fiction, no such practical partiality could follow (nor do I believe that Nietzsche thought it would). We might just as well conclude that pagan self-assertion is corrupt and Christianity is by comparison the way to go. In other words, perhaps as a moralist Nietzsche can persuade us that Christian ethics is indeed slavish, or that pagan ethics is preferable. But if so, it will not be by deploying any generalized notion of a fiction. It will be by persuading us to set ourselves against some specific attitudes and stances and postures of the mind: compassion, humility, general benevolence, and the like. And this is a move within ethics, not a move out of it altogether.

Bernard Williams sympathized with what he takes to be Nietzsche's move out of 'morality'—the bit of ethics that comes with concepts of obligation and duty and thoughts about what I ought to do. But we need to specify the target more closely, because these do not depend especially upon any illusion or any fiction. Consider Hume's artificial virtues, of respect for promises and property. I said above that we should not automatically pass from the language of construction to that of fiction, and these provide a central example. They remind us that constructions of our own matter, and they may matter centrally by way of rules and obligations. That is why we create them. Money, for instance, is well described in terms of social construction, but badly described in terms of a fiction, as badly as are other constructions such as Buckingham palace or the game of cricket. If together we go through certain actions, it is then not a fiction that I have borrowed ten dollars from you, or that I owe you ten dollars. And this gives the notion of obligation a perfectly satisfactory foothold, just as it gives you the right to pursue me or my estate for the sum. The debt would be a fiction only if the contract were bogus or you fraudulently made up the story of the transaction, but not all contracts are bogus, and not all transactions are made up. My thought that I ought to pay you back is not a groundless thought; on the contrary, it is perfectly grounded in the monetary doings that have got us where we are.

More accurately specified, Williams's target was slightly different, and it was also a target of Nietzsche's. Both thought that the attitudes associated with specifically Christian practical reasoning, notably guilt, depend on fictions about ourselves, and in particular the false idea that we are responsible 'all the way down' for what we do and who we are. This is 'incompatibilism' or the view that 'real' free will is incompatible with things we know about ourselves, but is itself integrally involved with 'moral' practice, and this view is certainly found in Nietzsche.[9] I myself believe that in detail it turns out to be less than convincing. The free will we can have, namely responsiveness to reasons, is the only free will we need. But in any event, incompatibilism certainly does not infect obligation, duty, debt, and associated attitudes of rejection and resentment across the board. Our institutions of money and promises do not hinge on some fanciful and demanding metaphysics of freedom, any more than the rules of cricket or chess do, yet as I have argued they give us a perfectly satisfactory grounding for these notions. One idea might be that these are merely conditional sources of obligation, or sources only of 'hypothetical' obligations: ones that we can escape, rather as we can escape any obligations that the rules of cricket place upon us by refusing to play. But in that case the difference is not in the metaphysics of freedom, but in the fact that others may for good reason demand that we involve ourselves with money and promising, whether or not we would like to do so. Except in fantasy or emergency, belonging to a social world is not something we can opt out of with impunity. I explore this further in the following section.

III

In this section I consider the notion of play, as it appears to be an object of admiration in the quotation from *The Gay Science*, given above. However, I certainly do not want to imply that it is a serious or central part of Nietzsche's overall message, or that the apparent implications of that passage are ones that are intended in full generality, or as a general recipe for living. Nevertheless, like the Calliclean Nietzsche, they may excite some readers. So they need confronting.

It sounds rather gorgeous to be a man of the future, a free spirit 'exuberant, floating, dancing, mocking, childish, and blissful'. But just like the notion of a fiction the notion of *play* seldom seems perfectly in place when we consider our practical lives. Children can indeed play at buying and selling and borrowing money from one another, but only by imitating some part of what adults do when they actually *do* buy and sell and borrow money from each other, and the same applies to morality. I can play at admonishing you for some deficiency, but only by imitating some part of what I would do were I actually to admonish you. If I am a good enough actor I can simulate the emotion of white-hot indignation, but only because real white-hot indignation exists as a model for me to draw upon. So in the second part of the quotation, what

---

[9] See *Twilight of the Idols*, 'The Four Great Errors'. I owe thanks to Brian Leiter for discussion on this passage.

exactly is Nietzsche recommending to the disciples of Zarathustra, and does it make sense?

If he is recommending a generalized ludic attitude to life, I suspect that it makes sense only at first glance, when we might see something enviable in the Stoics' capacity to treat all life as a game, or in the casual laugh of the Rortian ironist. We may be familiar with the sociological perspective that 'everything is a game', just as we are familiar with Wittgenstein's constant invocation of games, together with his suggestion that the notion of a game is itself indefinable. Each idea may help us believe that we understand Nietzsche's recommendation. I deny that we do—or rather, if we do we ought to recognize not a noble aristocrat or brave Zarathustra, a free spirit of the future, but a perfect pest, an annoying idiot along the lines of Charles Dickens's character Harold Skimpole in *Bleak House*. Here is the flavour, with the moral touchstone Esther Summerson speaking:

I was reluctant to enter minutely into that question; but as he begged I would, for he was really curious to know, I gave him to understand, in the gentlest words I could use, that his conduct seemed to involve a disregard of several moral obligations. He was much amused and interested when he heard this, and said, 'No, really?' with ingenuous simplicity.

'You know I don't intend to be responsible. I never could do it. Responsibility is a thing that has always been above me—or below me,' said Mr Skimpole. 'I don't even know which; but, as I understand the way in which my dear Miss Summerson (always remarkable for her practical good sense and clearness) puts this case, I should imagine it was chiefly a question of money, do you know?' (*Bleak House*, ch. 61)

This by way of defence against Esther's contempt at him for betraying little Jo after being bribed by the police. Skimpole's character is real enough: it is an exasperated satire on the improvident and sponging Leigh Hunt. But his professions of childishness, his pose of being a mere spectator of life, his whimsical, mock innocent stance towards the business of living, is far from an ideal and Dickens has a great deal of fun with him, before finally dismissing him as a mere nothing. In so far as Skimpole is blissful, and not just pretending to be, it has to be at the expense of any adult life, and in particular any normal humanity.[10] Red-blooded (or adolescent) admirers of Nietzsche may initially seize upon Skimpole as a fictional model of the manly, pagan, expulsion of compassion, but Dickens's own attitude is very different. In one episode among many, when Skimpole puts forward his gospel of merely pretending to pay the butcher, but expecting real meat in return, he is exposed as a thorough nuisance, not a hero. Nietzsche may not think much of English moralists in general, but here at least, one of them is on solid ground.

---

[10] His rather horrible indifference to the plight of others, including children, is portrayed throughout.

Perhaps in taking Skimpole as a model, I am taking the notion of play too literally, whereas Nietzsche is more commonly associated with the tradition already mentioned, of Thrasymachus or Callicles or Richard III, for whom life is a nasty, bitter, dog-eat-dog business, not play at all. No doubt this is right, but it is still important to follow through what happens if we take the reference to play and bliss seriously. For they are not, I think, accidentally connected in many people's minds, and perhaps on and off in Nietzsche's, with the omnipresence of fiction and the recommended emancipation from conscience.

In a remarkable study, Bernard Suits ruminates on the life of the grasshopper, contrasted with that of the ant as a model of the life of play.[11] Notwithstanding Wittgenstein he gives a highly illuminating analysis of the notion of a game. To play a game, Suits argues, is 'to engage in activity directed towards bringing about a specific state of affairs, using only means permitted by rules, where the rules prohibit more efficient in favour of less efficient means, and where such rules are accepted just because they make possible such activity'. (p. 34) The four elements involved are ends, means, rules, and the attitude of the players, the acceptance of the rules just because they make possible the activity (which then becomes a further end in itself). Suits defends his analysis against worries derived from many sources: games taken dead seriously, games whose ends are themselves defined in terms of rules, pure make-believe play, games played professionally or for the sake of psychological rewards, solitary games, and so on. A striking consequence of the account is that the 'lusory attitude' of the game player is bound to be one of only conditional commitment: among human beings a game is an activity whose pursuit is set as an option within the background matrix of a life with needs and commitments that may at any time trump it.

In Suits's tale, the grasshopper has a dream in which he goes about persuading everyone that the activities of life are all really games. And in his dream, the moment people become persuaded of this, they vanish. His fable is an extended meditation on the meaning of this dream, which is that a life of pure play is not for human beings. This is not to suggest that a life of pure play is unimaginable. Indeed, Suits argues that game playing is the only thing left to do in Utopia, where there are no unfulfilled needs, and where no instrumental activities remain. A Utopian might decide, for instance, to build himself a house, but the 'difference in quality' between his activity and ours is that his activity has no external instrumental value (in Utopia you can come to possess houses by snapping your fingers) and meets no unfulfilled need. Hence, it could exist only for the sake of the activity itself, and then becomes a pure option, like the solving of a puzzle, and is to be categorized as an instance of game-playing:

[11] Bernard Suits, *The Grasshopper: Games, Life and Utopia* (Toronto: University of Toronto Press, 1978). I would like to thank Tom Hurka for drawing this neglected tour de force to my attention.

Thus all the things we now regard as trades, indeed all instances of organized endeavour whatever, would, if they continued to exist in Utopia, be sports. So that in addition to hockey, baseball, gold, tennis and so on, there would also be the sports of business administration, jurisprudence, philosophy, production management, motor mechanics *ad* for all practical purposes, *infinitum.* (p. 175)

But human beings are not grasshoppers, and in our actual lives these activities are not games. And in spite of the charm of utopias, it is doubtful if things would be better if we could jump free of our needs, so that they became only games. Setting ourselves games to play does not even stave off *ennui* for very long (let alone eternity).

This is not the place to explore all the ramifications of this account. Nor do I want to defend it to the last detail. However, it is plausible enough and offers enough insight into the notion of a game and of play for us to test the recommendation that we treat life as play against it. And, as we might expect, the recommendation does not seem to stand up very well. Essentially, a life of play has to be a life without *needs* and without *unconditional commitments*. But this is unrecognizable as a human life, and only even works as an ideal so long as it is not thought through.

So we are forced to conclude that the vocabulary of floating and mocking and putting on a fool's cap needs to be taken with a pinch of salt. You can mock needs and unconditional commitments only so long as you have neither, and while people can occupy such a state for a short period, and while as Stoics or ironists or even artists (of a certain kind) they may pretend to it for longer, it does not take much to puncture the balloon.

I do not actually believe that Nietzsche is recommending a generalized ludic attitude to life. It may be salutary to compare the passage from *The Gay Science* with *Beyond Good and Evil*, especially paragraphs 225 to 227. Here he is talking of a concern with what mankind could be, favourably contrasted with mere sympathy with rotten old humanity as it is:

OUR sympathy is a loftier and further-sighted sympathy:—we see how MAN dwarfs himself, how YOU dwarf him! and there are moments when we view YOUR sympathy with an indescribable anguish, when we resist it,—when we regard your seriousness as more dangerous than any kind of levity . . .

Honesty, granting that it is the virtue of which we cannot rid ourselves, we free spirits—well, we will labour at it with all our perversity and love, and not tire of 'perfecting' ourselves in OUR virtue, which alone remains: may its glance some day overspread like a gilded, blue, mocking twilight this aging civilization with its dull gloomy seriousness!

Here the 'levity' and the mockery are those which come from unflinching awareness of life as it is, more like those of Swift or Pope than Harold Skimpole, and this is surely the tone and the moral complexion of Nietzsche himself. As he tells us, it is only 'fools and appearances' that say of such characters that these are men without duty.

IV

I have not had much good to say about errors, fiction, and play. They are notions needed only by philosophers who misunderstand what ethics is and why we have it, and who find it convenient to read that misunderstanding in Nietzsche. But we can extract the seeds of a much better philosophy of value from the notion of a point of view, or a perspective, provided this is used with care. So first a warning. It is not that we should take perceptual vocabulary very seriously, when we look for a philosophy of value. Indeed, when we hear philosophers talking of sensitivities, perceptual capacities, recognition of demands, and generally assimilating the state of the *phronimos* to that of a well-tuned observer, we need to ask how literally the visual analogies are intended. And we need to give the warning that they should not be intended literally at all. Moral facts, or interpretations, are not objects of sight, any more than they are objects of hearing or touch or taste. The senses are involved only in that it is the world we cope with and care about, and it is also the things of the world that we see, hear, or touch. Duties and obligations are not among them. It is right, of course, to talk sometimes of seeing or hearing facts as well as things. But while you can see or hear that something is near or far, hidden or in the open, you cannot literally see that ingratitude is a vice, any more than you can hear it or taste it. Rather, the judgement is the upshot of a stance, attitude, or posture of the mind: the dispositions of a practical engagement with the world, not a mere responsiveness to the way of the world. Indeed, if we were talking of mere responsiveness, the 'argument from relativism' would be more of a threat, encouraging the worry that since most responses are illusory, perhaps they all are. The argument from queerness would be more of a threat, encouraging the worry that we have no business to convince ourselves of the importance of 'things' that cannot be seen and touched. But no such worries attend the forthright understanding that what we voice are our own attitudes, and what we stand on as we do so is our own feet.

However, our practical dispositions give us something analogous to a point of view or a perspective. They give us a practical centre from which things dominate or subside, loom or fade in practical importance. The perspective of someone to whom something looms as important is indeed different from that of someone to whom it is trivial, and if something must be done, then they will be in disagreement as to what it is. As these practical concerns matter, we express our values and our ethics, our admirations and detestations, and the boundaries to behaviour that we insist upon and the spaces for it that we permit. There is no error in that, and as we have seen, we are not usually playing either. Requiring conduct of others, sanctioning them for failures, worrying about our own projects and plans, is typically about as far from play as can be imagined—as far as the consequences of going wrong, such as prison

306 / Simon Blackburn

or war. Nor are we always imagining things, or making them up, or telling stories, any more than we are always imagining debts, or making up fictions about our needs or telling fantasies about past gifts or slights. But my practical centre is in a slightly different place from yours, meaning that our different perspectives have to be engaged and negotiated as we look for a shared or general point of view. It is not easy to know how to think and feel, or what to do.

Nietzsche is of course right to be alert to signs of unhealth, and no doubt in the late nineteenth century he was right to smell it as even more pervasive than at present. There are indeed virtuous monsters and scarecrows, and the self-righteousness of the moralist can obviously cloak all kinds of human flaw. An over-inflated superego is not a lovable thing, while simple stupidity leads people to mount 'crusades against evil', and we need not look far to find cruelties and hatreds, self-loathing, boredom, disgust and contempt, the desire for revenge or power, the hypocrisy and cunning of the slave. Perhaps the world would be better if we fenced ourselves round with fewer boundaries, and policed them with less enthusiasm. But if this is the problem, the solution is not an end to morality, but a better morality. Discount some of the rhetoric and the false starts, and we can perhaps find that this is what Nietzsche thought as well.

BIBLIOGRAPHY

I. Works by Nietzsche

Individual contributors have sometimes utilized other editions; if so, that is specified in the essay. The standard German edition of Nietzsche's works is *Sämtliche Werke: Kritische Studienausgabe in 15 Bänden*, ed. G. Colli and M. Montinari (Berlin: de Gruyter, 1980, 1999); this is cited as KSA, followed by the volume number, a colon, and the fragment number(s).

Some standard English editions of Nietzsche's works (followed by the standard English-language acronym) are as follows:

The Antichrist, in *The Portable Nietzsche* (below). Cited as A.

Beyond Good and Evil, trans. W. Kaufmann (New York: Vintage, 1966). Cited as BGE.

The Birth of Tragedy, trans. W. Kaufmann (New York: Vintage, 1966). Cited as BT.

The Case of Wagner, trans. W. Kaufmann (New York: Vintage, 1966). Cited as CW.

Daybreak: Thoughts on the Prejudices of Morality, ed. M. Clark and B. Leiter, trans. R. J. Hollingdale (Cambridge: Cambridge University Press, 1997). Cited as D.

Ecce Homo, trans. W. Kaufmann (New York: Vintage, 1967). Cited as EH.

The Gay Science, trans. W. Kaufmann (New York: Vintage, 1974). Cited as GS.

Human, All-too-Human, trans. R. J. Hollingdale (Cambridge: Cambridge University Press, 1986). Cited as HAH.

Nietzsche contra Wagner, in *The Portable Nietzsche* (below). Cited as NCW.

On the Genealogy of Morality, trans. Maudemarie Clark and Alan Swensen (Indianapolis: Hackett, 1998). Cited as GM.

Philosophy in the Tragic Age of the Greeks, trans. M. Cowan (Washington, D.C.: Regnery Gateway, 1962).

Philosophy and Truth: Selections from Nietzsche's Notebooks of the Early 1870's, ed. and trans. D. Breazeale (Atlantic Highlands, NJ: Humanities Press, 1979).

The Portable Nietzsche, ed. and trans. W. Kaufmann (New York: Viking, 1954).

Thus Spoke Zarathustra, in *The Portable Nietzsche* (above). Cited as Z.

Twilight of the Idols, in *The Portable Nietzsche* (above). Cited as TI.

Untimely Meditations, trans. R. J. Hollingdale (Cambridge: Cambridge University Press, 1983). Cited as U.

The Will to Power, trans. W. Kaufmann and R. J. Hollingdale (New York: Vintage, 1968). Cited as WP.

In general, in citing Nietzsche's works, roman numerals refer to major parts or chapters in Nietzsche's works; Arabic numerals refer to sections, not pages.

II. Works about Nietzsche

This section lists all the Nietzsche literature discussed or cited by contributors to this volume.

ANDERSON, R. LANIER, 'Nietzsche on Truth, Illusion, and Redemption', *European Journal of Philosophy* 13 (2005): 185–225.

BITTNER, RÜDIGER, 'Ressentiment', in Richard Schacht (ed.), *Nietzsche, Genealogy, Morality* (Berkeley: University of California Press, 1994).

CLARK, MAUDMARIE, *Nietzsche on Truth and Philosophy* (Cambridge: Cambridge University Press, 1990).

——— 'Nietzsche's Immoralism and the Concept of Morality', in Richard Schacht (ed.), *Nietzsche. Genealogy, Morality* (Berkeley: University of California Press, 1994).

——— 'Nietzsche, Friedrich', in E. Craig (ed.), *Routledge Encyclopedia of Philosophy* (London: Routledge, 1998).

——— 'On Knowledge, Truth and Value: Nietzsche's Debt to Schopenhauer and the Development of His Empiricism', in C. Janaway (ed.), *Willing and Nothingness: Schopenhauer as Nietzsche's Educator* (Oxford: Clarendon Press, 1998).

CLARK, MAUDEMARIE and DAVID DUDRICK, 'The Naturalisms of *Beyond Good and Evil*' in K. Ansell Pearson (ed.), *A Companion to Nietzsche* (Oxford: Blackwell Publishing, 2006).

——— *Nietzsche's Magnificent Tension of the Spirit: An Introduction to* Beyond Good and Evil (Cambridge: Cambridge University Press, forthcoming).

CONANT, JAMES, 'Nietzsche's Perfectionism: A Reading of *Schopenhauer as Educator*', in Richard Schacht (ed.), *Nietzsche's Postmoralism: Essays on Nietzsche's Prelude to Philosophy's Future* (Cambridge: Cambridge University Press, 2001).

GEMES, KEN, 'Nietzsche's Critique of Truth', in John Richardson and Brian Leiter (eds.), *Nietzsche* (Oxford: Oxford University Press, 2001).

GEUSS, RAYMOND, 'Nietzsche and Morality', *European Journal of Philosophy* 5 (1997): 1–20.

GREEN, MICHAEL S., *Nietzsche and the Transcendental Tradition* (Urbana: University of Illinois Press, 2002).

GUAY, ROBERT, 'Nietzsche on Freedom', *European Journal of Philosophy* 10 (2002): 302–27.

HAVAS, RANDALL, *Nietzsche's Genealogy: Nihilism and the Will to Knowledge* (Ithaca: Cornell University Press, 1995).

HILL, R. KEVIN, *Nietzsche's Critiques: The Kantian Foundations of His Thought* (Oxford: Oxford University Press, 2003).

HOLLINGDALE, R. J., *Nietzsche: The Man and His Philosophy* (London: Routledge and Kegan Paul, 1985).

HUNT, LESTER H., *Nietzsche and the Origin of Virtue* (London: Routledge, 1991).

HUSSAIN, NADEEM J. Z., 'Nietzsche's Positivism', *European Journal of Philosophy* 12 (2004): 326–68.

JANAWAY, CHRISTOPHER, 'Nietzsche's Artistic Revaluation', in Sebastian Gardner and Jose L. Bermúdez (eds.), *Art and Morality* (London: Routledge, 2003).

KAUFMANN, WALTER, *Nietzsche: Philosopher, Psychologist, Antichrist*, 4th edn. (Princeton, NJ: Princeton University Press, 1974).

LANGSAM, HAROLD, 'How to Combat Nihilism: Reflections on Nietzsche's Critique of Morality', *History of Philosophy Quarterly* 14 (1997): 235–53.

LEITER, BRIAN, 'Nietzsche and the Morality Critics', *Ethics* 107 (1997): 250–85.

—— 'The Paradox of Fatalism and Self-Creation', in Christopher Janaway (ed.), *Willing and Nothingness: Schopenhauer as Nietzsche's Educator* (Oxford: Oxford University Press, 1998).

—— 'Nietzsche's Metaethics: Against the Privilege Readings', *European Journal of Philosophy* 8 (2000): 277–97.

—— *Nietzsche on Morality* (London: Routledge, 2002).

—— 'Nietzsche's Moral and Political Philosophy', in Edward N. Zalta (ed.), *The Stanford Encyclopedia of Philosophy*, 2004. http://plato.stanford.edu/archives/fall2004/entries/nietzsche-moral-political/

MAGNUS, BERND, 'The Use and Abuse of the Will to Power', in Robert C. Solomon and Kathleen M. Higgins (eds.), *Reading Nietzsche* (New York: Oxford University Press, 1988).

MAY, SIMON, *Nietzsche's Ethics and his War on 'Morality'* (Oxford: Clarendon Press, 1999).

MIGOTTI, MARK, 'Slave Morality, Socrates, and the Bushmen: A Reading of the First Essay of the Genealogy of Morals', *Philosophy and Phenomenological Research* 58 (1998): 745–79.

MOORE, GREGORY, *Nietzsche, Biology, and Metaphor* (Cambridge: Cambridge University Press, 2002).

MORGAN, GEORGE A, *What Nietzsche Means* (New York: Harper, 1965).

NEHAMAS, ALEXANDER, *Nietzsche: Life as Literature* (Cambridge, MA: Harvard University Press, 1985).

PARKES, GRAHAM, *Composing the Soul: Reaches of Nietzsche's Psychology* (Chicago: University of Chicago Press, 1994).

POELLNER, PETER, *Nietzsche and Metaphysics* (Oxford: Clarendon Press, 1995).

—— 'Perspectival Truth', in Brian Leiter and John Richardson (eds.), *Nietzsche* (Oxford: Oxford University Press, 2001).

—— 'Self-Deception, Consciousness and Value: The Nietzschean Contribution', *Journal of Consciousness Studies* 11 (2004): 44–65.

—— 'Phenomenology and Science in Nietzsche', in Keith Ansell-Pearson (ed.), *A Companion to Nietzsche* (Oxford: Blackwell, 2006).

REGINSTER, BERNARD, 'Nietzsche on *Ressentiment* and Valuation', *Philosophy and Phenomenological Research* 57 (1997): 281–305.

—— *The Affirmation of Life: Nietzsche on Overcoming Nihilism* (Cambridge, MA: Harvard University Press, 2006).

RICHARDSON, JOHN, *Nietzsche's System* (Oxford: Oxford University Press, 1996).

—— *Nietzsche's New Darwinism* (Oxford: Oxford University Press, 2004).

RICHARDSON, J. and LEITER, B. (eds.), *Nietzsche* (Oxford: Oxford University Press, 2001).

RIDLEY, AARON, *Nietzsche's Conscience* (Ithaca: Cornell University Press, 1998).

RISSE, MATHIAS, 'The Second Treatise in *On the Genealogy of Morality*: Nietzsche on the Origin of the Bad Conscience', *European Journal of Philosophy* 9 (2001): 55–81.

—— 'Nietzsche's "Joyous and Trusting Fatalism"', *International Studies in Philosophy* 35 (2003): 147–63

—— 'Origins of *Ressentiment* and Sources of Normativity', *Nietzsche-Studien* 32 (2003): 142–70.

SALAQUARDA, JÖRG, 'Nietzsche und Lange', *Nietzsche-Studien* 7 (1978): 236–53.

—— 'Der Standpunkt des Ideals bei Lange und Nietzsche', *Studi Tedeschi* 22 (1979): 133–60.

SCHACHT, RICHARD, *Nietzsche* (London: Routledge, 1983).

—— (ed.), *Nietzsche, Genealogy, Morality* (Berkeley: University of California Press, 1994).

SCHACHT, RICHARD, *Making Sense of Nietzsche: Reflections Timely and Untimely* (Urbana: University of Illinois Press, 1995).

SCHELER, MAX, *Das Ressentiment im Aufbau der Moralen* (Frankfurt am Main: Vittorio Klostermann, 1978).

SOLL, IVAN, 'Nietzsche on Cruelty, Asceticism, and the Failure of Hedonism', in Richard Schacht (ed.), *Nietzsche, Genealogy, Morality* (Berkeley: University of California Press, 1994).

SOLOMON, ROBERT C., 'One Hundred Years of Ressentiment: Nietzsche's Genealogy of Morals', in Richard Schacht (ed.), *Nietzsche, Genealogy, Morality* (Berkeley: University of California Press, 1994).

STACK, GEORGE J., *Lange and Nietzsche* (Berlin and New York: Walter de Gruyter, 1983).

STERN, JOSEPH P., *A Study of Nietzsche* (Cambridge: Cambridge University Press, 1979).

THIELE, LESLIE P., *Friedrich Nietzsche and the Politics of the Soul: A Study of Heroic Individualism* (Princeton: Princeton University Press, 1990).

VAIHINGER, HANS, *Die Philosophie des als ob: System der theoretischen, praktischen und religiösen Fiktionen der Menschheit auf Grund eines idealistischen Positivismus*, 5th and 6th edns. (Leipzig: Verlag von Felix Meiner, 1920).

WILCOX, JOHN T., *Truth and Value in Nietzsche: A Study of His Metaethics and Epistemology* (Ann Arbor: The University of Michigan Press, 1974).

WILLIAMS, BERNARD, 'Nietzsche's Minimalist Moral Psychology', *European Journal of Philosophy* 1 (1993): 4–14. Reprinted in Bernard Williams, *Making Sense of Humanity and Other Philosophical Papers 1982–1993* (Cambridge: Cambridge University Press, 1995), 65–76.

—— *Shame and Necessity* (Berkeley: University of California Press, 1994).

YACK, BERNARD, *The Longing for Total Revolution: Philosophic Sources of Social Discontent from Rousseau to Marx and Nietzsche* (Princeton: Princeton University Press, 1986).

INDEX